LIVING
IN NATURE

LIVING IN NATURE

CONTEMPORARY HOUSES IN THE NATURAL WORLD

[1] AIR 7
[2] EARTH 77
[3] FIRE 137
[4] WATER 189

More than half of the world's population lives in urban areas, and that figure is set only to increase. The human race has become a species of town and city dwellers, existing in a landscape of paved streets and structures that keep the natural world at bay rather than belong to it. The urban home creates a contained environment: inserted into a bounded space, it must have a relationship to other buildings nearby, form an enclosure, and give some kind of privacy. The relationship to nature is often an afterthought rather than an integral part of the design.

It is little wonder, then, that many of us long to live in nature, even if just for a short while. We desire an Arcadia where we can immerse ourselves in waterways, mountain ranges, woodlands, or deserts and escape from noise, pollution, traffic, and crowds. Undoubtedly, being in nature is essential for both physical and psychological well-being.

This book celebrates houses in which nature is the architects' primary consideration, informing decisions about everything from the plot size to the materials, views, carbon footprint, and geometry within the landscape. In all aspects the architecture is intended to foster a deep connection with the outdoors. These projects often have to take challenging terrain and climate into account, but they do not aim to tame or colonize nature. Instead, these houses exist harmoniously within it. Footprints are kept small and respond flexibly to the topography through the use of modular elements. By employing natural and locally sourced materials and vernacular building techniques, the architects further ensure that the homes blend in and express a respect for nature.

Each house has been selected for its affinity to or expression of one of the four elements: air, earth, fire, and water. The first chapter, Air, is all about elevation—treehouses, mountain huts, and houses on stilts all embody the lightness of this most rarefied of elements. Earth looks at houses that are buried, hidden, and hunkered down, as much a part of the land as the mud or clay from which some of them are built. Fire explores houses that both embrace and endure the heat-scorched landscapes of volcanoes, deserts, and jungles. The final chapter examines houses overlooking lakes, rivers, or the sea, and that typify the calming properties of water.

    The designers of these houses have considered what it truly means to live within nature, rather than merely on or alongside it. And that question is becoming ever more urgent: climate change and population growth present enormous challenges, and as technology evolves and impacts working patterns, we may find that cities are no longer an essential part of life. As the importance of the natural world grows within our consciousness, ultimately the houses in this book demonstrate that nature is not something separate from us—as human beings, we are part of nature. Living more fully within it helps us to understand that more profoundly.

[1] AIR

10 YH2
DANS L'ESCARPEMENT

14 IA Arquitectos
MOUNTAINEER'S REFUGE

20 Olson Kundig
COSTA RICA TREEHOUSE

24 Intuitive Architects
ALPINE VISTAS

28 Olson Kundig
RIO HOUSE

34 Roberto Dini and Stefano Girodo
BIVOUAC LUCA PASQUALETTI

38 Malan Vorster Architecture
TREE HOUSE CONSTANTIA

42 SAA Arquitectura + Territorio
DOCK HOUSE

48 Felipe Assadi Arquitectos
CASA LA ROJA

52 Artistree
YOKI TREEHOUSE

56 Johan Sundberg Arkitektur
SUMMERHOUSE SOLVIKEN

60 Espen Surnevik
PAN TREETOP CABINS

66 Claudio Beltrame
PIGNA

70 CO-LAB Design Office
TULUM TREEHOUSE

Air is perhaps the most important element for humans. In literal terms it is crucial for our survival, and at its most abstract, air represents life force, creation, and the human spirit. Unsurprisingly, the desire to dwell in high places and to embrace air's transformative qualities gives rise to flights of imagination in architectural design.

Many of the most inventive designs are treehouses—a burgeoning genre in sustainable building and ecotourism. The experience of clambering up into a cocooning space deep in the forest or jungle evokes feelings of delight and wonder. With the lightest of footprints, treehouses can be built from freely available local materials. Their proximity to nature encourages a simpler lifestyle to which travelers are increasingly drawn. And in tropical climates, treehouses escape the worst heat and insects, and enjoy efficient ventilation. Other dwellings in this chapter were built in spectacular mountain locations: one a staggering 10,794 feet (3,290 meters) up—an extraordinary feat of planning, engineering, and teamwork. Simply getting materials to sites like this might seem impossible, but prefabrication, with sections helicoptered in, provides an elegant solution.

Beyond a building's location, other architectural concerns can also be used to imbue homes with the lightness of air. Ventilation is a major focus of several houses: they use windy conditions to the building's advantage, or they find ingenious ways of improving airflow with imaginative spatial design, screens, slats, and strategic window positioning. Lightweight materials are also used to conjure up the elemental feeling of air and many projects have considerable transparency, boosting illumination, views, and a sense of weightlessness. What unites all of these houses is their ability to transcend the everyday, bringing to their inhabitants a sense of liberation, adventure, and well-being.

YH2
DANS L'ESCARPEMENT
2018 | Saint-Faustin-Lac-Carré, QC, Canada

Viewed from the air, Dans l'Escarpement appears to hang from a steep hillside. To create the smallest-possible footprint on the landscape, architecture firm YH2 conceived the retreat as two separate concrete volumes—one a tall tower, the other a low horizontal block—connected by a glazed timber pavilion that floats above the ground. The three overlapping elements stretch across the hillside on the shores of Lac Carré, northwest of Montreal. A slender steel-and-wood footbridge leads to the entrance on the top floor of the tower, where there is a bedroom with panoramic glazing to maximize lake and forest views. One level down, the tower connects with the wood-and-glass pavilion that stretches through the trees. This section houses the kitchen, living area, and dining room, and a secluded office to the rear. The pavilion then connects with the lowest floor, a *béton brut* bedroom block. The thoughtful configuration of the house's elements creates outdoor spaces to keep inhabitants close to nature: the bedroom block's roof serves as a large terrace for the intermediate living level, while the space below the pavilion is a sheltered nook for a spa pool. Mahogany flooring, ceilings, beams, window frames, and kitchen units connect the interior with the forest beyond, while Corten steel sheathing echoes the trees' stunning autumn colors. Raw concrete exteriors reference the huge boulders strewn about the nearby slopes.

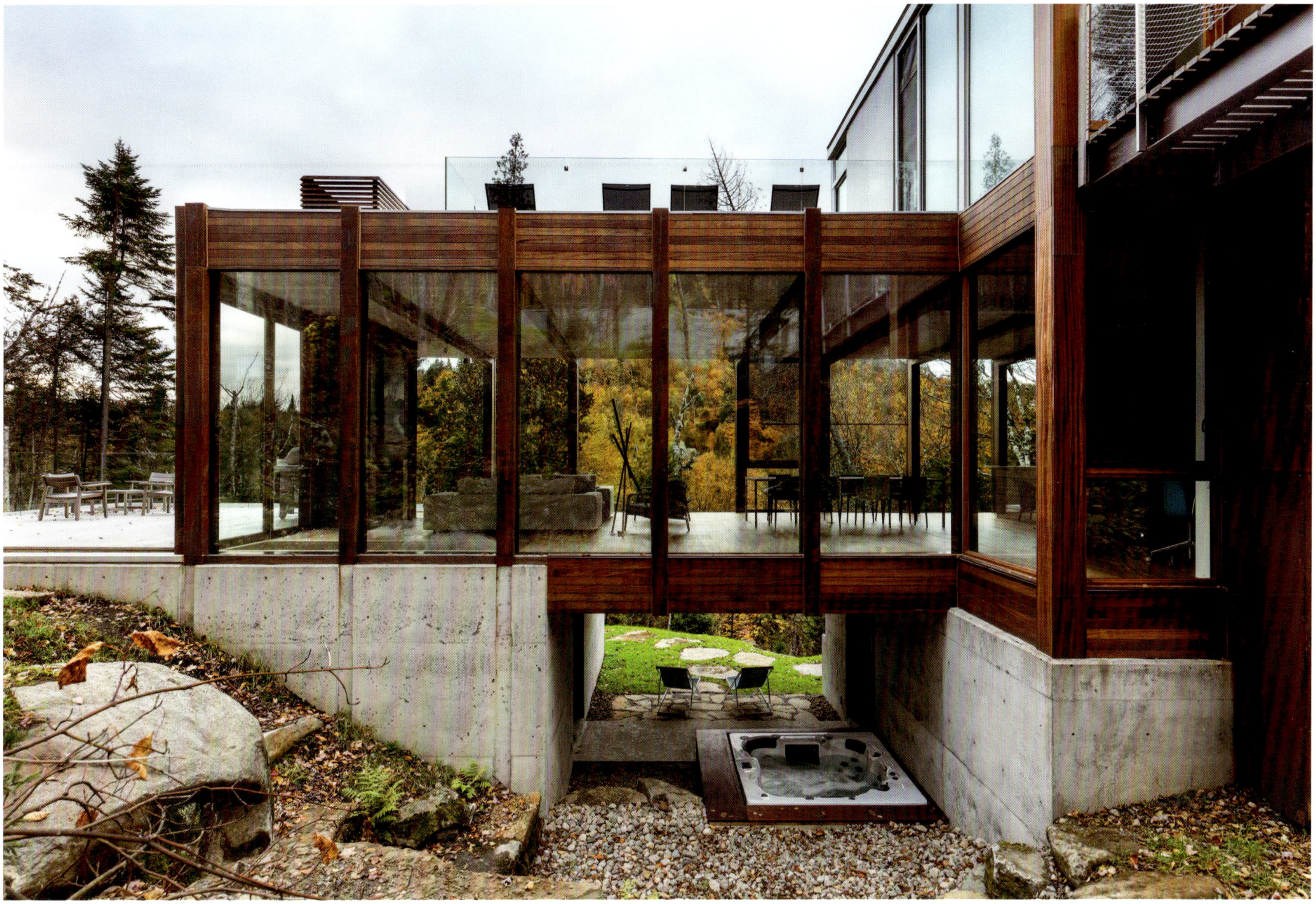

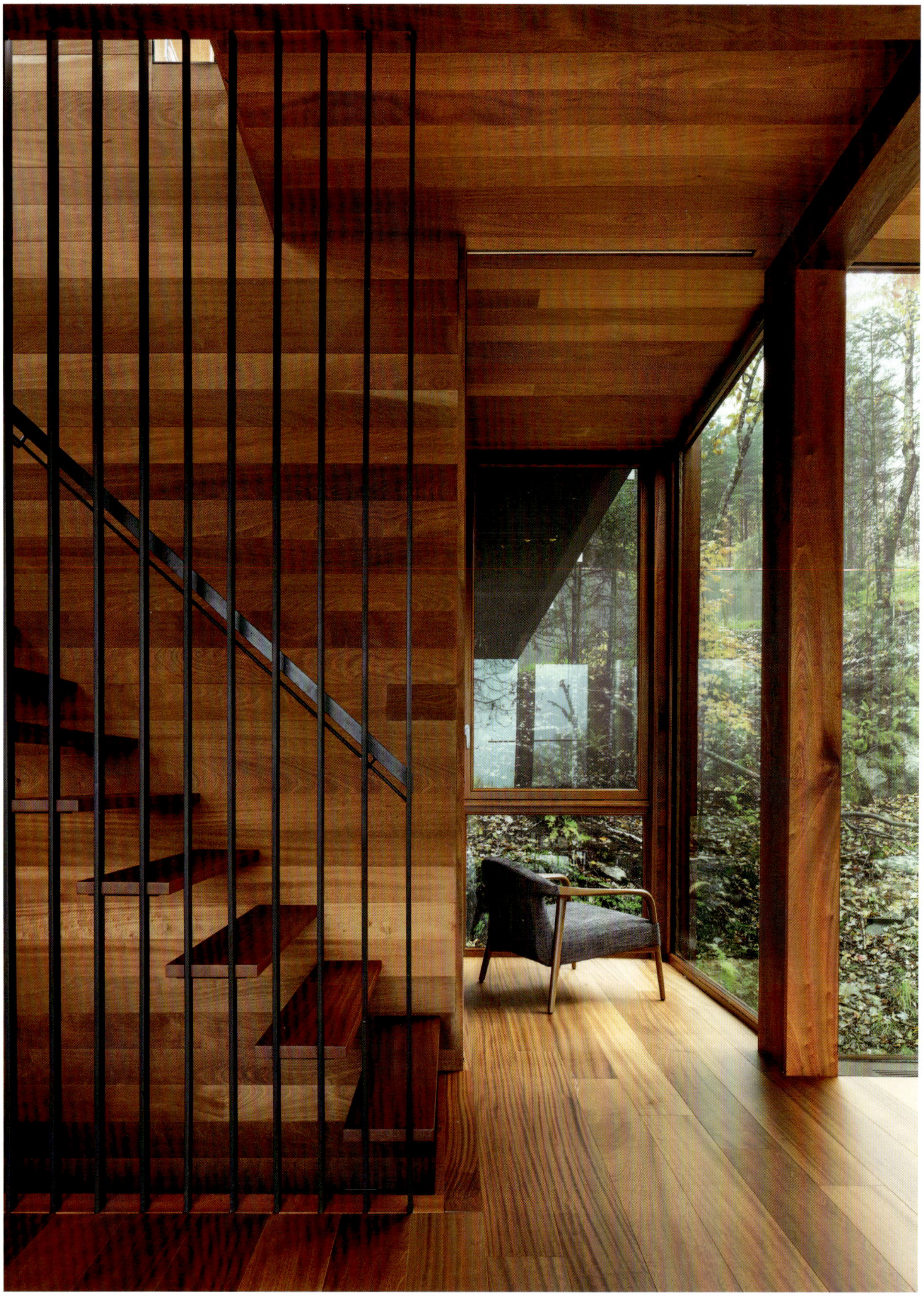

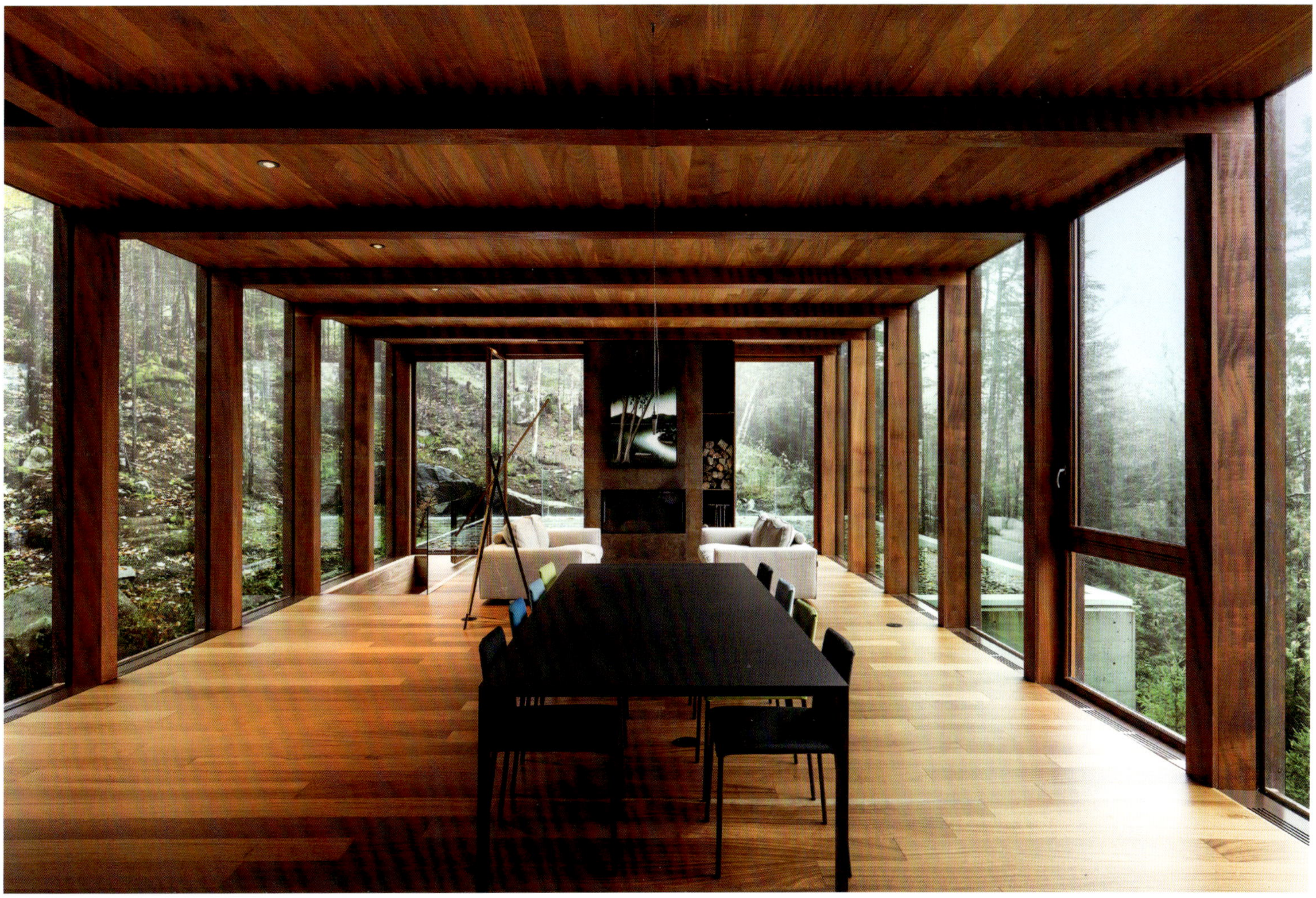

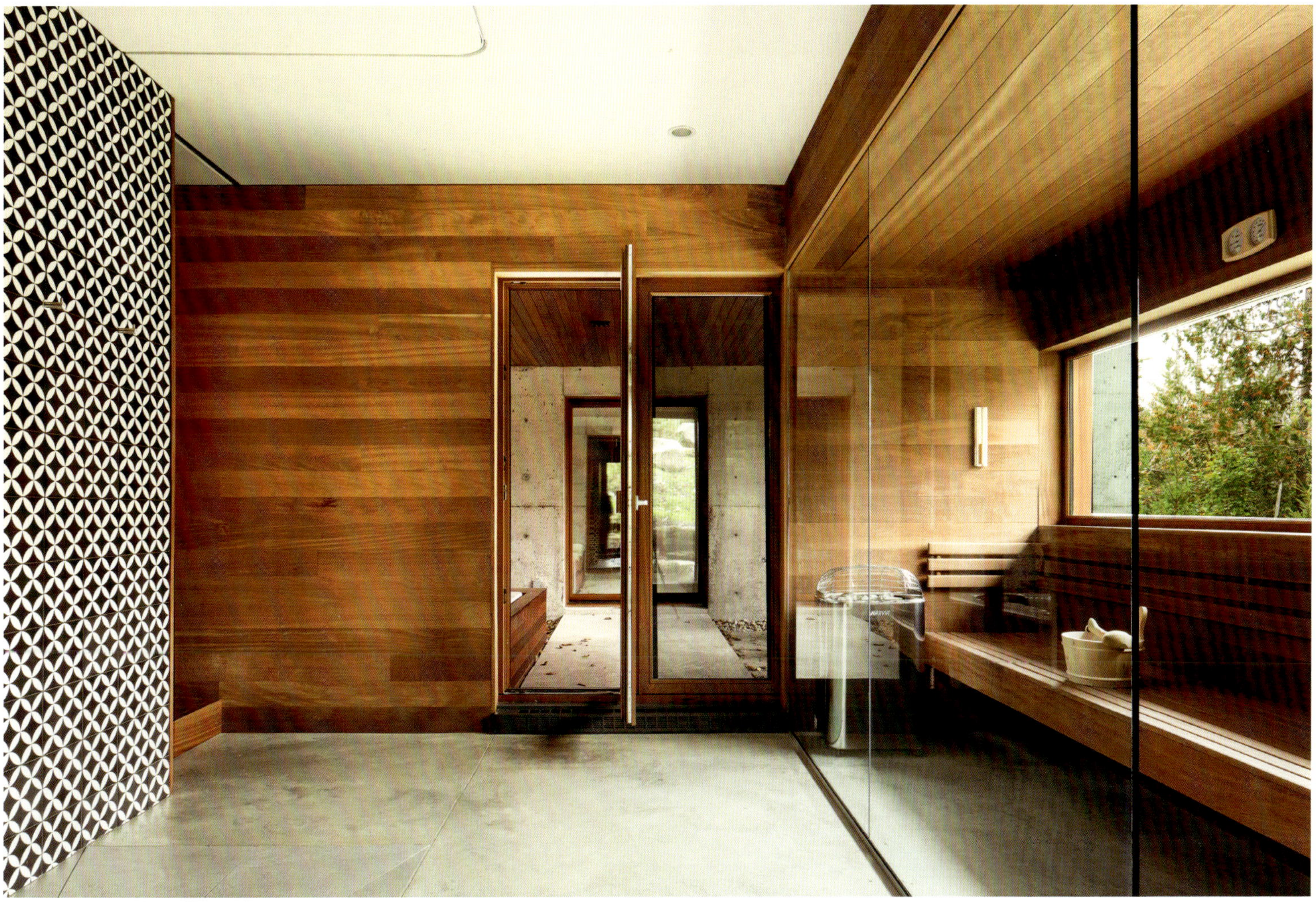

IA Arquitectos
MOUNTAINEER'S REFUGE
2016 | San Esteban, Chile

This compact refuge in the Chilean Andes near San Esteban has a ventilated facade on all sides that takes advantage of the mountains' rising air currents. Nestled on a ledge close to a summit, the folding planes of blackened pine reflect the form of nearby peaks and the morphology of boulders. It also resembles a black tent, with a "flap" stretching down from the roof, sheltering the entrance and grounding the structure. The one-story cabin, which rests on a series of piles driven into the rock, contains a kitchen and dining area, a bathroom, a storage room, and two bedrooms. Windows on each side of the house, in a variety of angular shapes, allow cross-breezes to penetrate. The eastern elevation is almost completely glazed, with an adjacent small deck, while the opening on the south elevation is akin to a camera's viewfinder, fixed on the mountainscape. The black exterior and the interior's black window frames, wood-burning stove, fixtures, and fittings contrast starkly with luminously pale floors and walls clad in untreated pine. A somewhat spartan indoor space is enhanced by handmade furniture, in the same wood, built into the walls. Mountaineer's Refuge has an undeniably strong visual presence, yet it blends in with the dark shadows cast by the rocky range it inhabits. Inclined ceilings and angled window frames create a slightly giddy dynamic, suggesting the exhilaration of living at such high altitude.

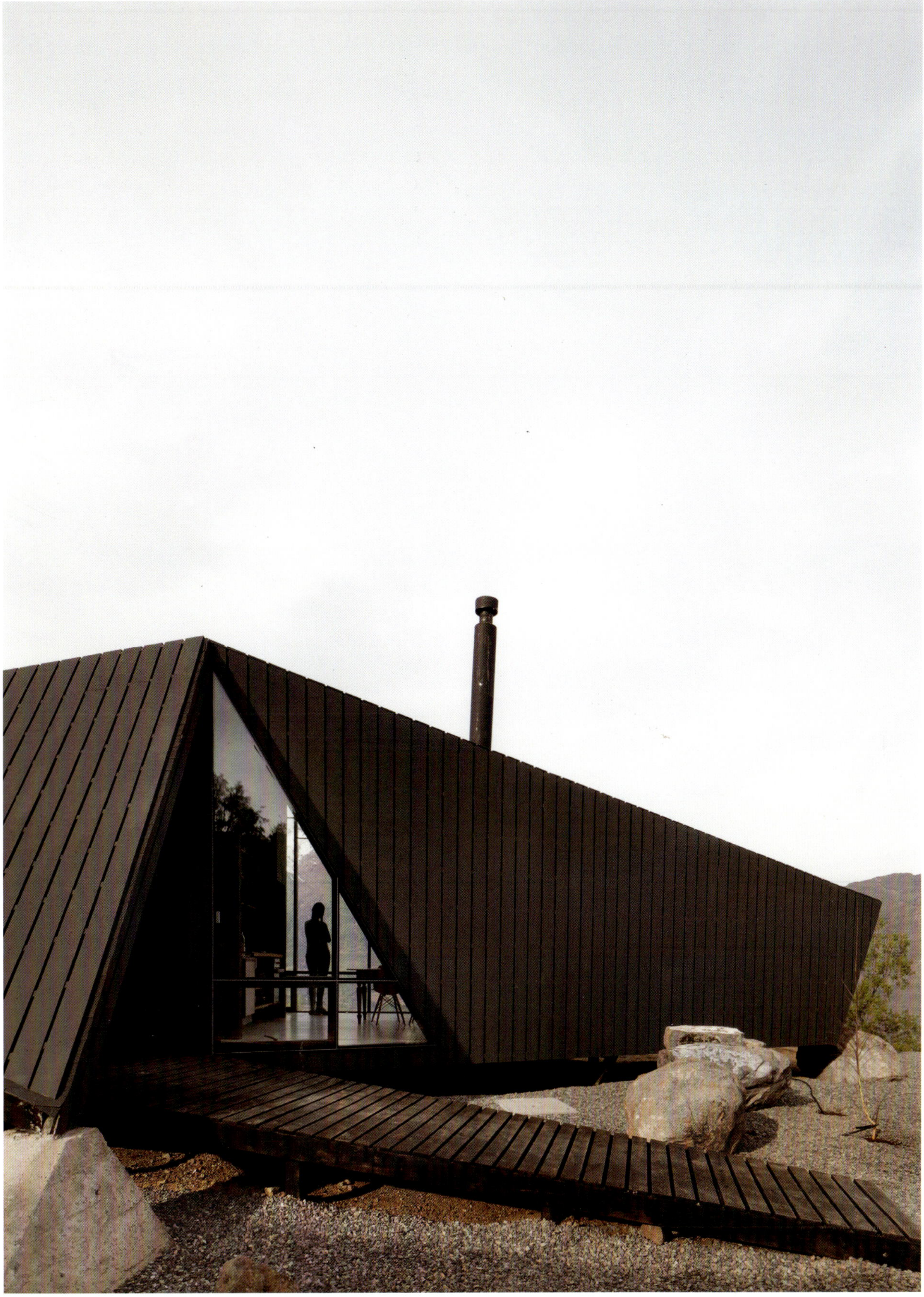

MOUNTAINEER'S REFUGE

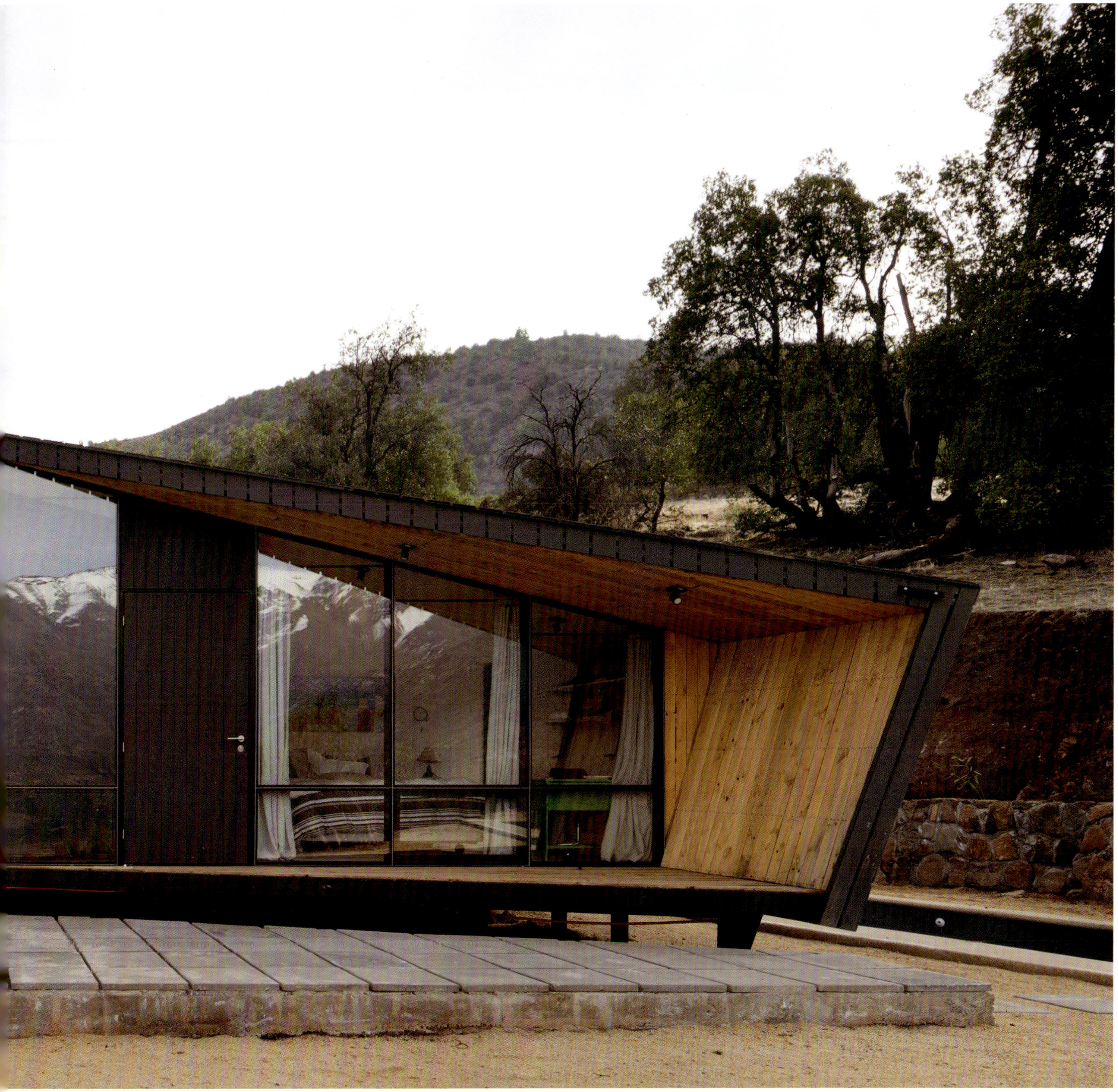

MOUNTAINEER'S REFUGE

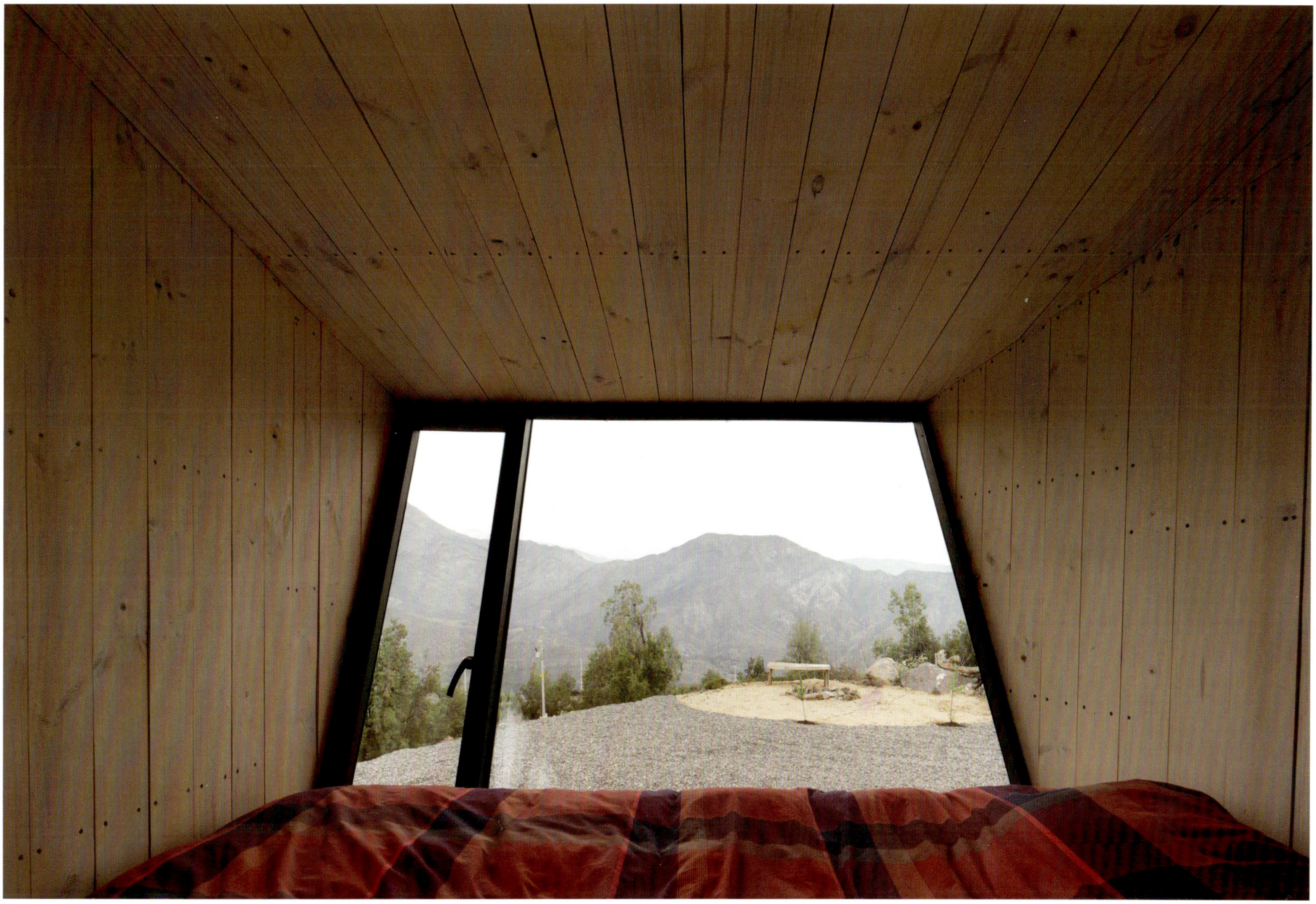

Olson Kundig
COSTA RICA TREEHOUSE
2017 | Santa Teresa, Costa Rica

An elegant jungle tower, Costa Rica Treehouse takes the concept of a beach hut to an entirely new level. A stone's throw from Playa Hermosa—a beautiful sweeping bay edged with tropical forest—the house is designed to make as little impact on the jungle as possible. Square on plan, the home has a minimal footprint, soaring upward like the magnificent trees circling it. It is constructed almost entirely from locally sourced teak and *cenízaro* (rain tree) wood, and sections of tree trunks serve as supporting columns inside. Each of the building's three stories provides a different and fully immersive experience of the jungle. The living, kitchen, and dining areas are housed on the ground level, which is exposed to the forest floor. The middle story, for sleeping, is precisely positioned to be right within the tree canopy. On the third level, another social space, inhabitants can drink in views of the jungle and the Pacific. Most of the house's walls are slatted, allowing cooling breezes to permeate and casting striated patterns of shadow inside. Depending on temperatures, ventilation panels can be pushed open or closed, and they can be fully secured when the owners are away. A photovoltaic array and rainwater collection system further add to the green credentials of the project, which is an outstanding example of Costa Rica's burgeoning genre of sustainable treehouses.

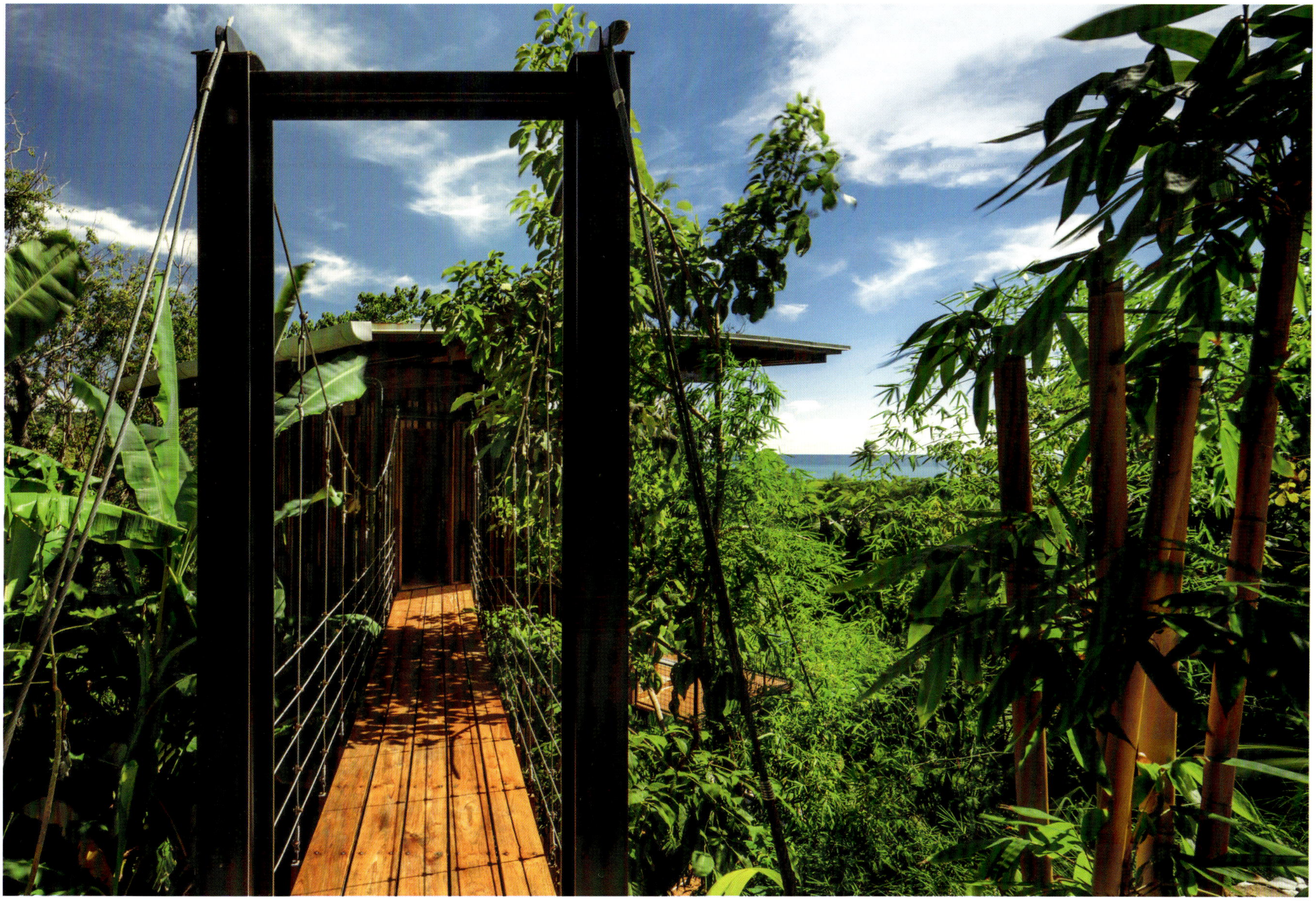

COSTA RICA TREEHOUSE

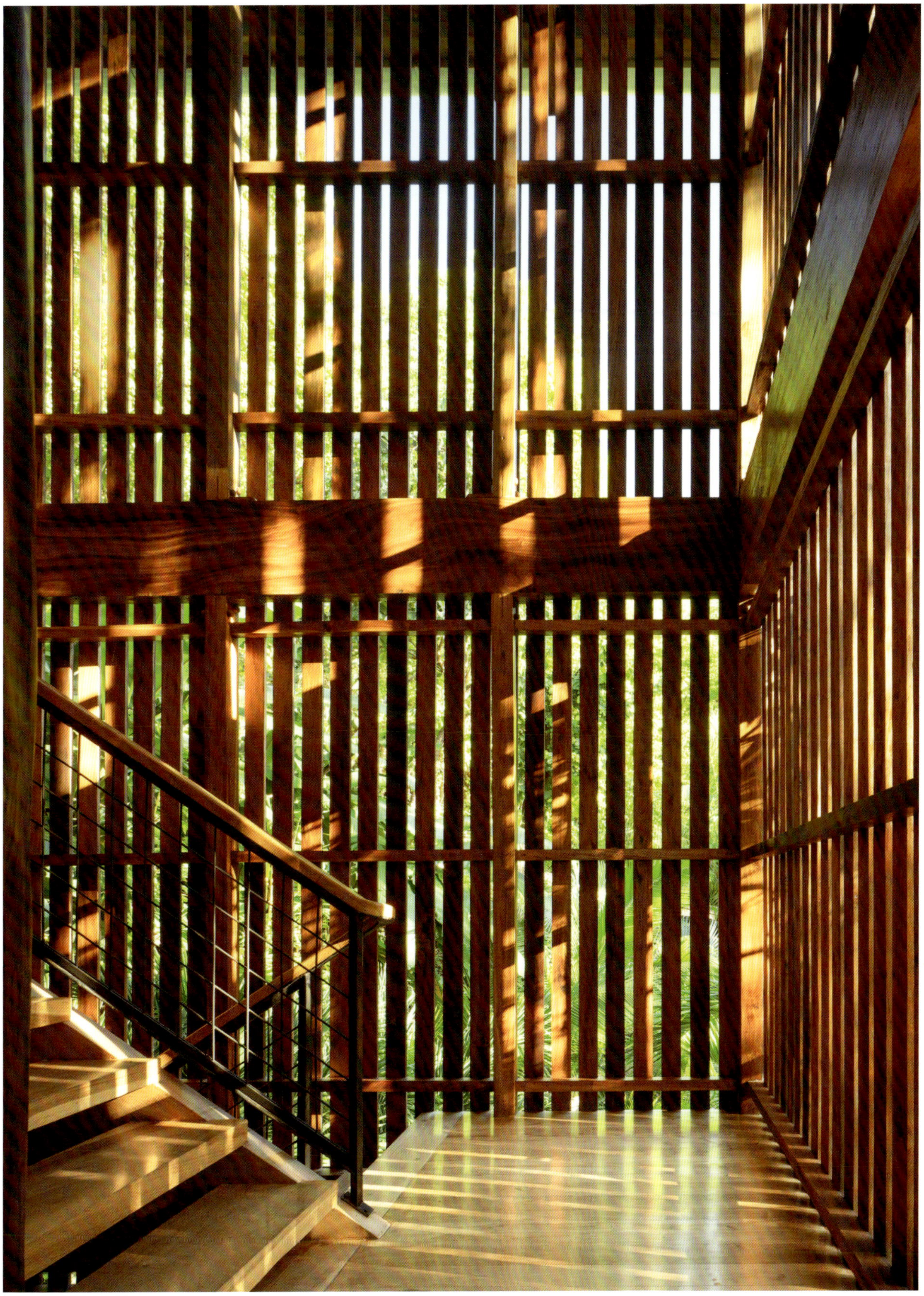

Intuitive Architects
ALPINE VISTAS
2018 | Wanaka, New Zealand

Inspired by local cribs—the New Zealand term for tiny, modest vacation homes—this simple family retreat has covetable lake and mountain views, but the site can be buffeted by strong winds. Intuitive Architects' solution was to design a house consisting of two pitched-roof volumes—one for three bedrooms, the other for living space—placed at right angles to one another. Connected via a glazed corridor, the volumes form a sheltered courtyard that, thanks to the north-south orientation of the living block, is protected from prevailing winds. Ventilation, however, was also important. Ample glazing on both sides of the living room affords views of the mountains, and when slid back, cross-breezes; strategically placed openings enable airflow from the courtyard to the sleeping volume. Cathedral ceilings in the open-plan kitchen, living, and dining area form an airy yet nurturing space, while a seating area with a wood-burning stove is set down a few steps to create a more intimate nook. Beautifully honed vertical timber cladding in western red cedar is used on the exterior: a pleasing counterpoint to the building's horizontality and a nod to the crib aesthetic. Inside, concrete for the flooring, plywood on the walls, and aluminum for the window frames contribute to a robust, stripped-back look that remains sleek without sacrificing comfort.

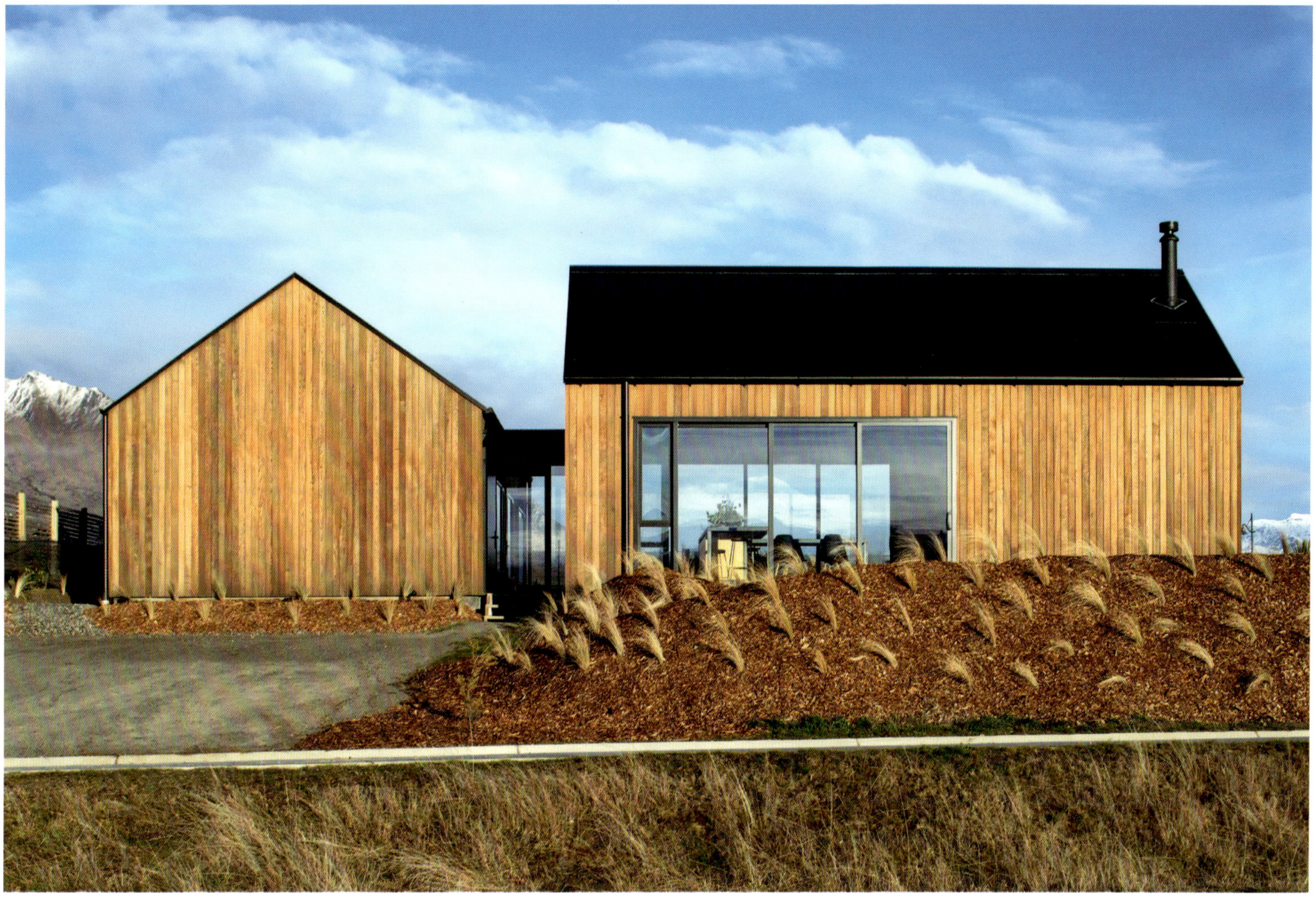
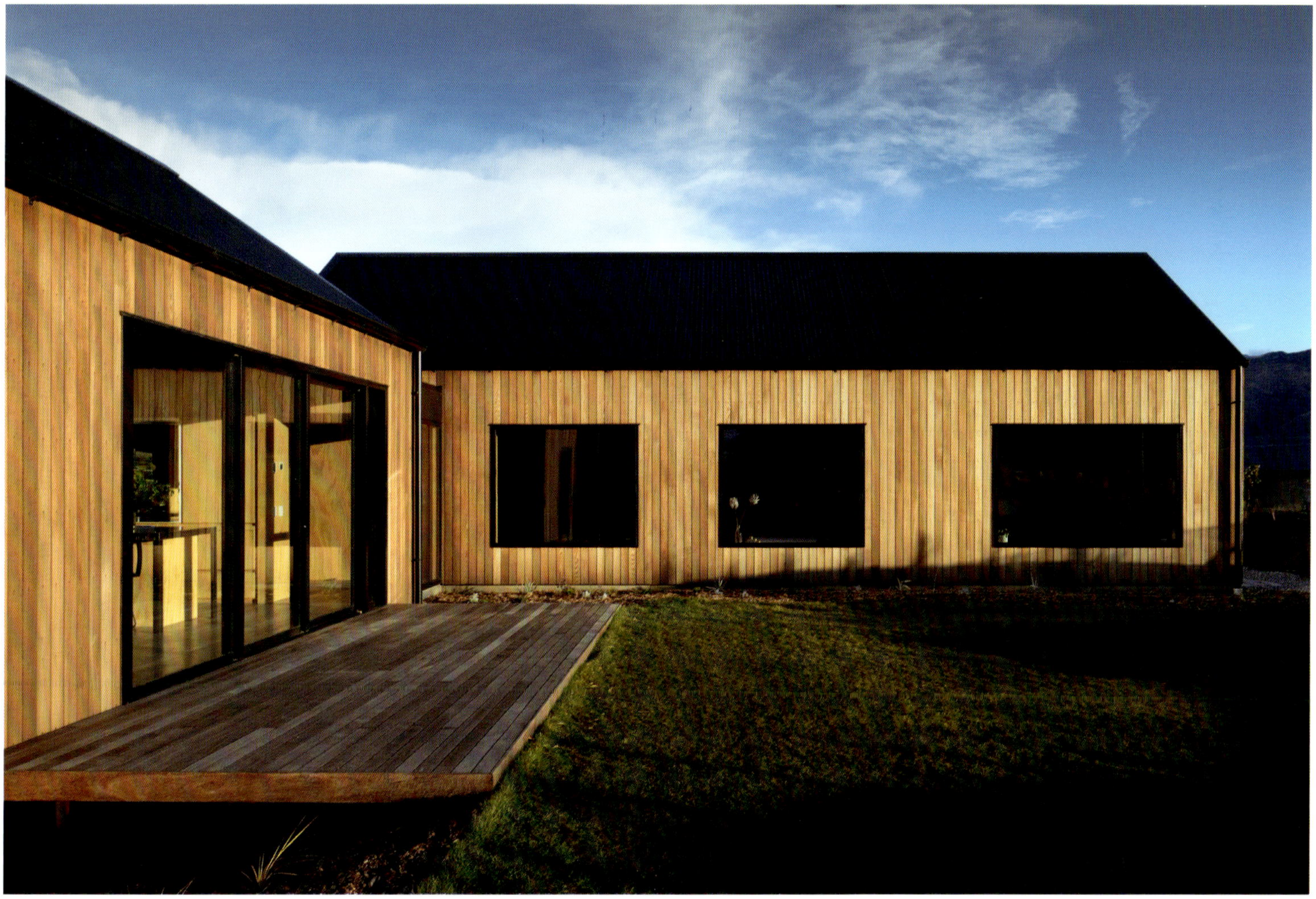

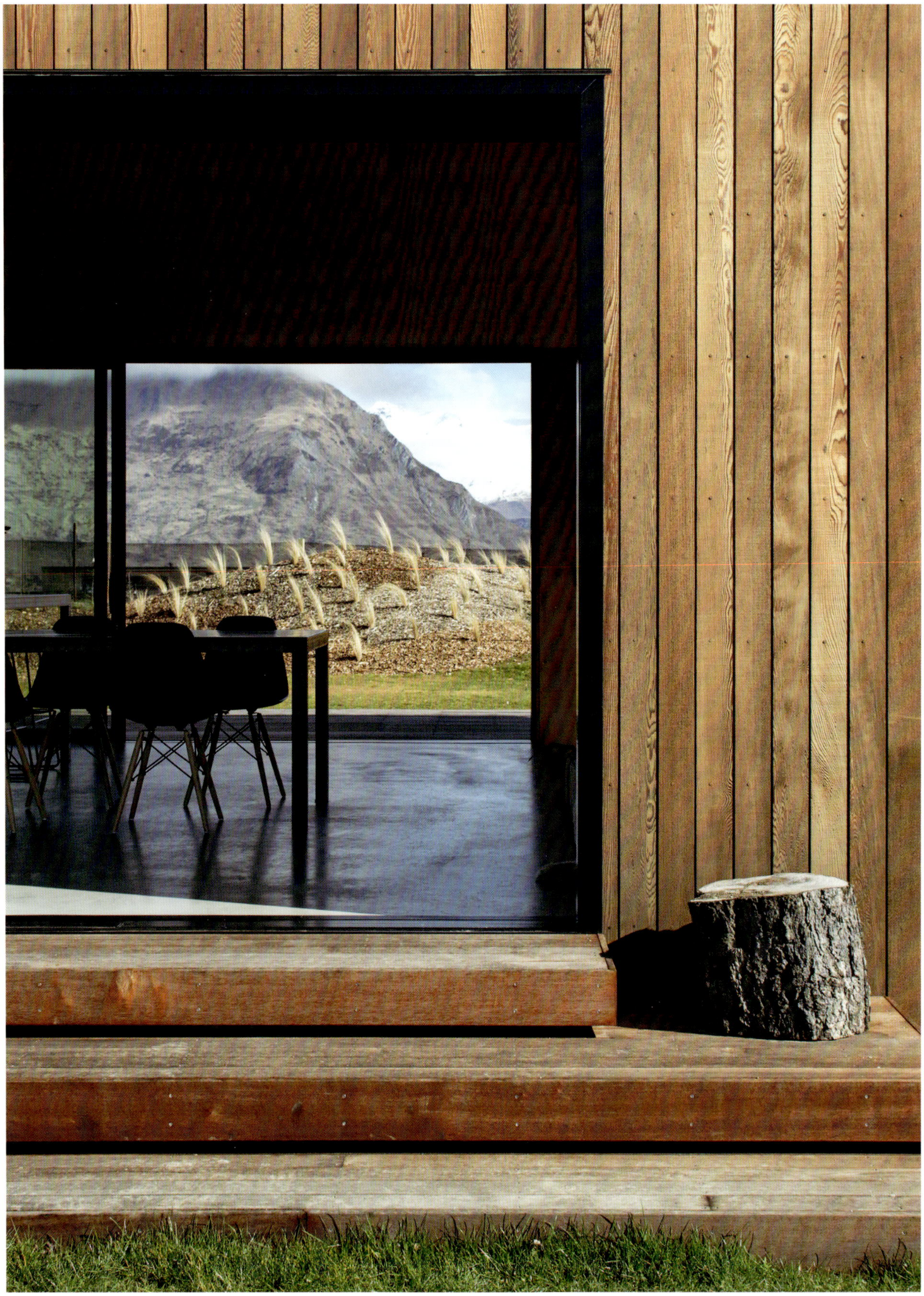

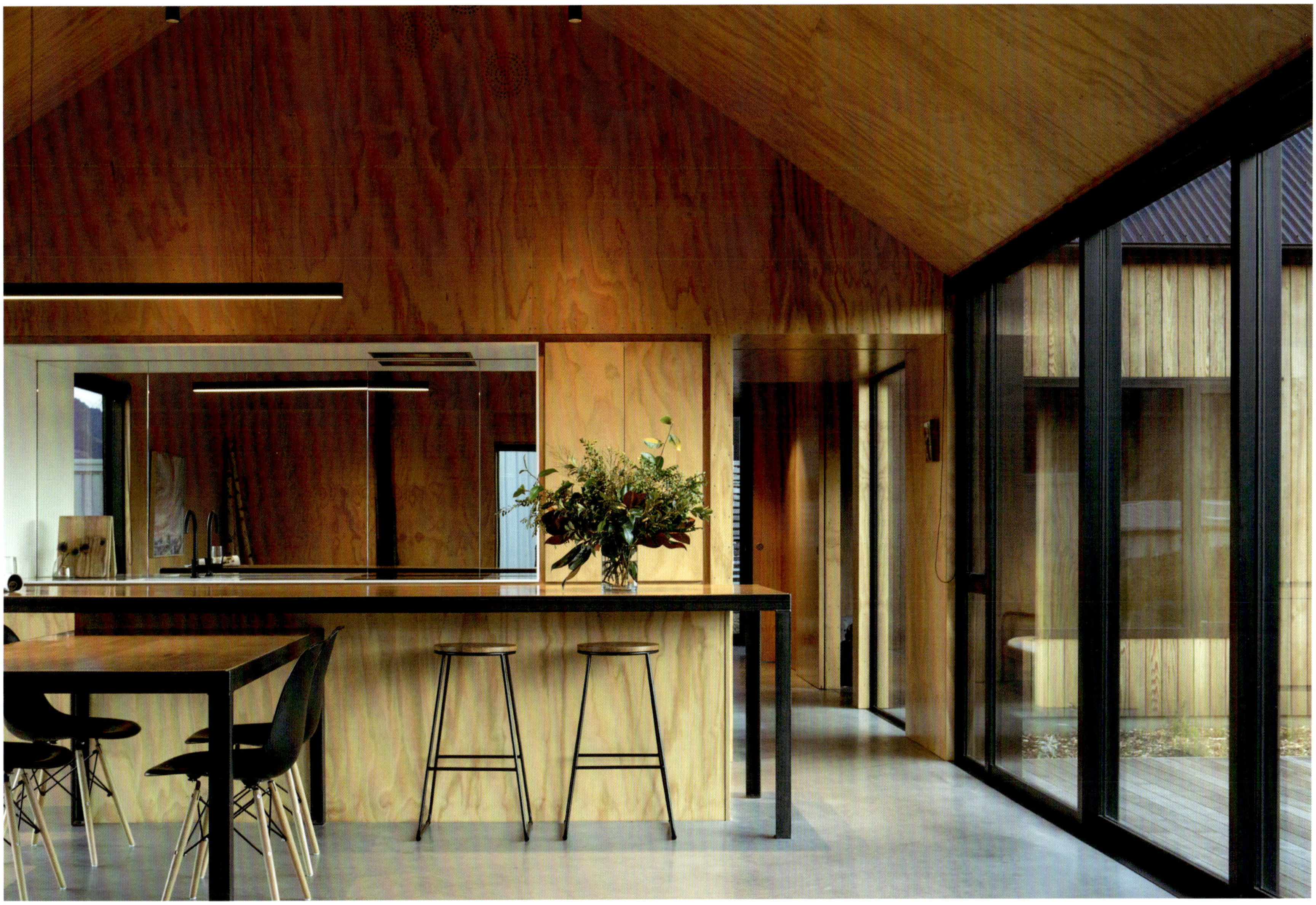

Olson Kundig
RIO HOUSE
2018 | Rio de Janeiro, Brazil

Located in a tropical forest adjacent to Tijuca National Park—one of the world's largest urban forests—this glass-sided one-bedroom retreat has the smallest of footprints. The striking rectangular steel-and-glass volume rests on just two cast-in-situ concrete pillars, which mimic the trunks of the juçara palm and *Cariniana* trees nearby. The pillars elevate the house to the level of the flora and fauna of the rain forest canopy. This raised position avoids the heat and insects at ground level and opens up views of the Atlantic Ocean, as well as the city of Rio and its famous Christ the Redeemer statue. The project sensitively employs an array of vernacular techniques and materials. These include brazilwood for the ceilings, walls, and shelving, and interior walls made of terra-cotta blockwork finished with colored plaster. The vermilion-stained concrete floor of the open-sided ground-level living and dining area recalls the local iron-oxide-rich soil and the exterior's board-formed concrete is a Brazilian architectural staple. Ventilation is natural, avoiding the need for air-conditioning; floor-to-ceiling fenestration pivots on a pulley system, creating airflows, while other parts are fully retractable, and a roof opening siphons off hot air. The architects used marine-grade black steel for the house's structure to protect it from the humid rain-forest climate. The impressive glazing of bird-safe glass further demonstrates the sensitivity of the design to its environment and is key to the sense of lightness that this house evokes.

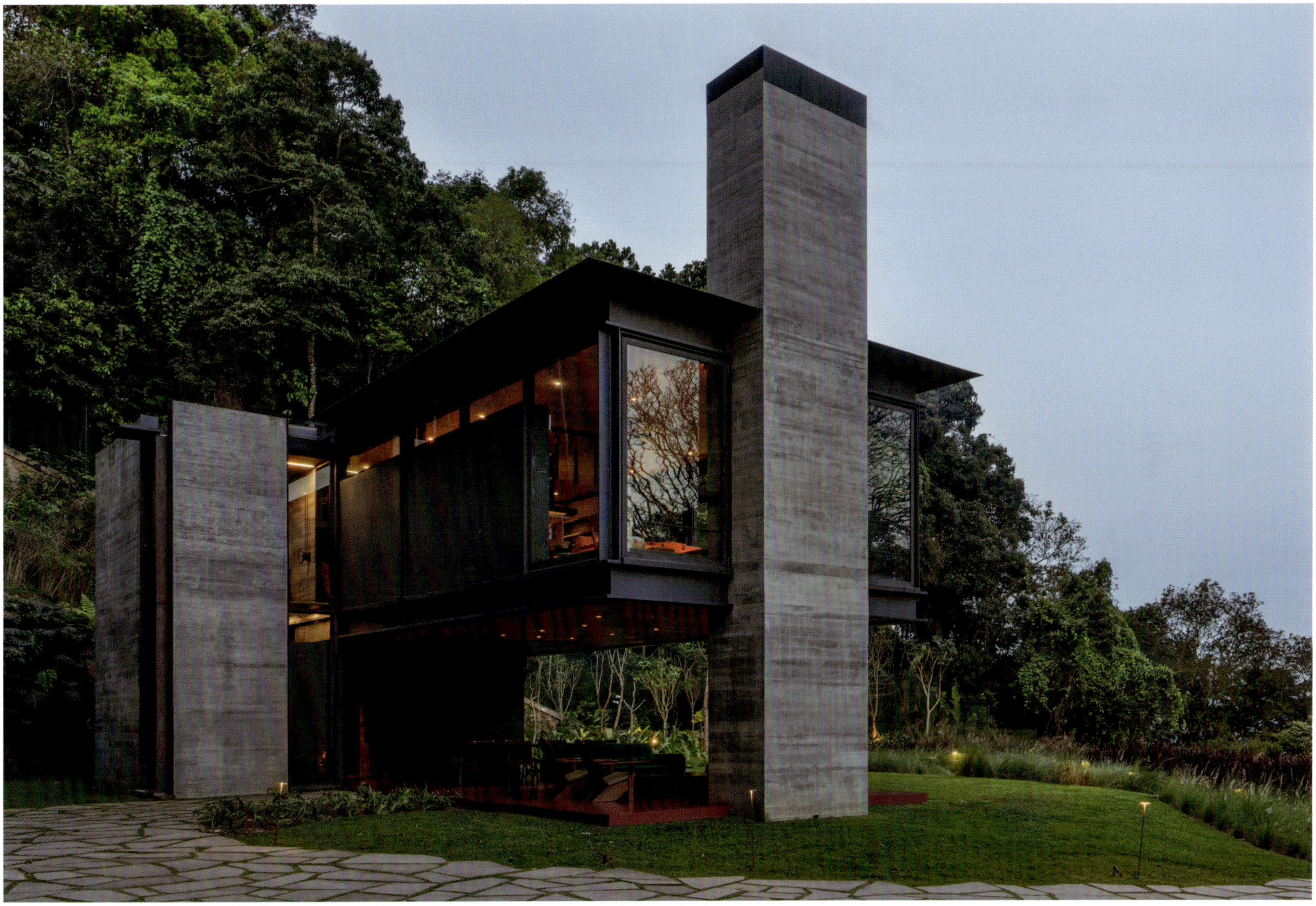

RIO HOUSE

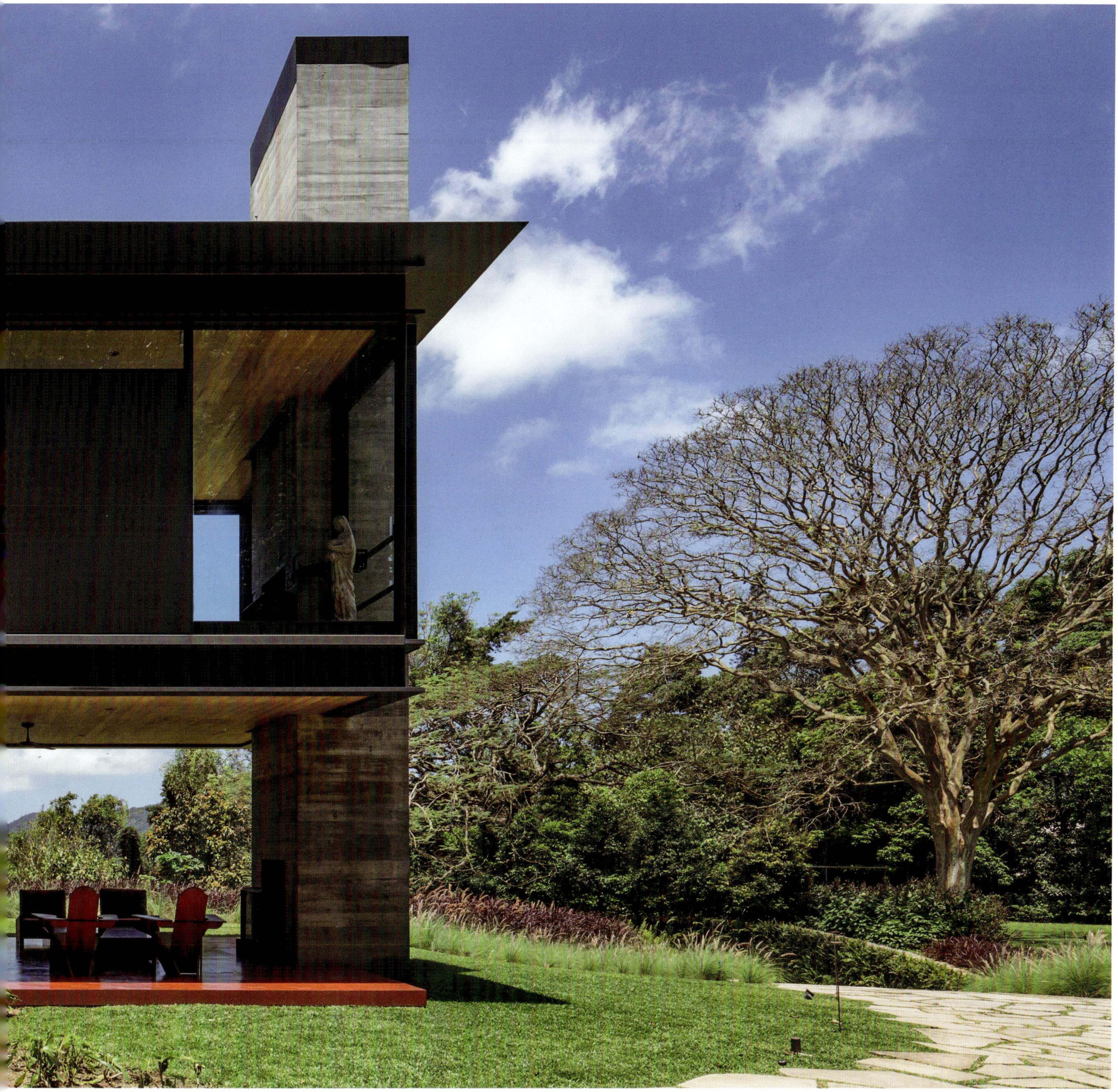

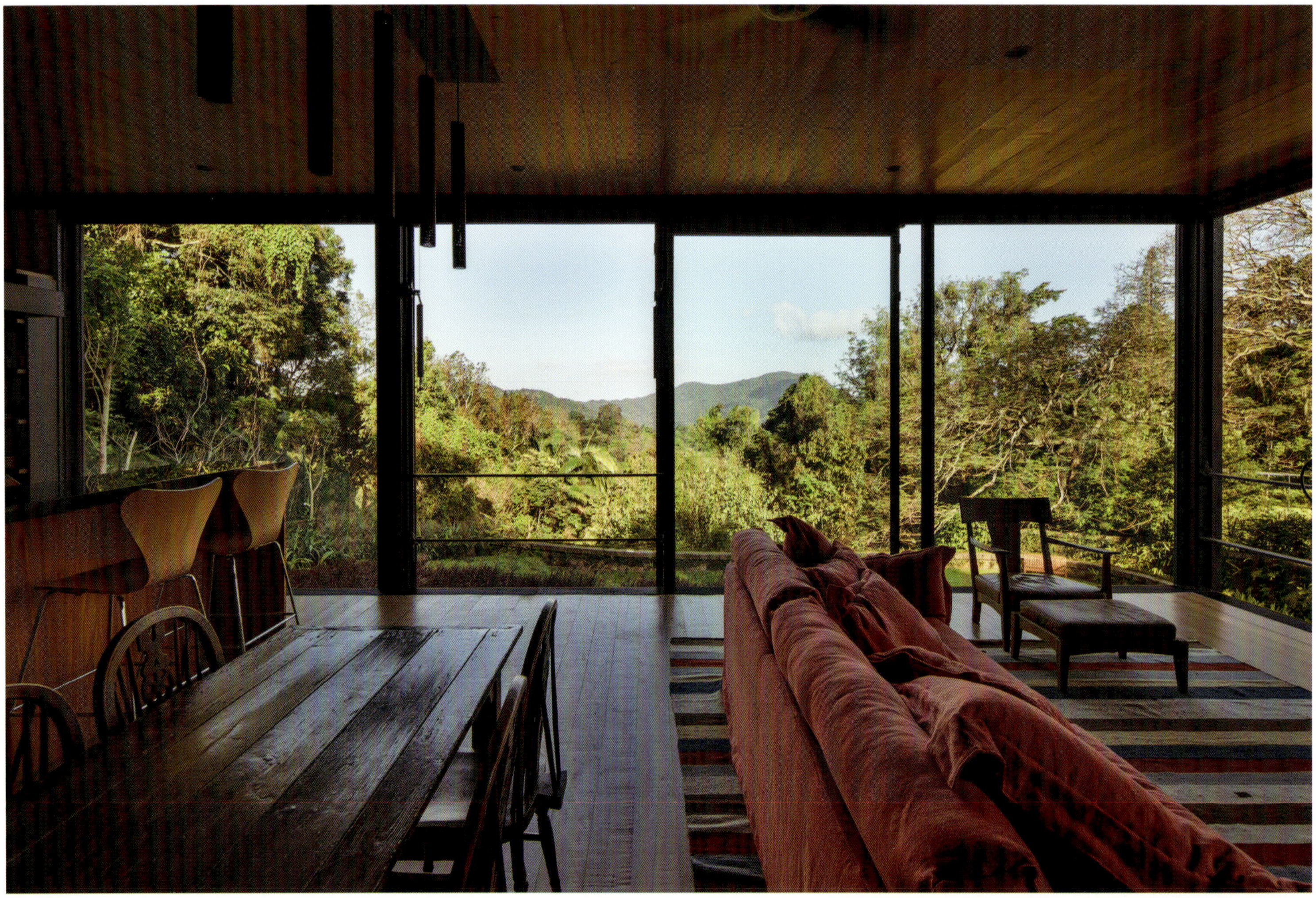

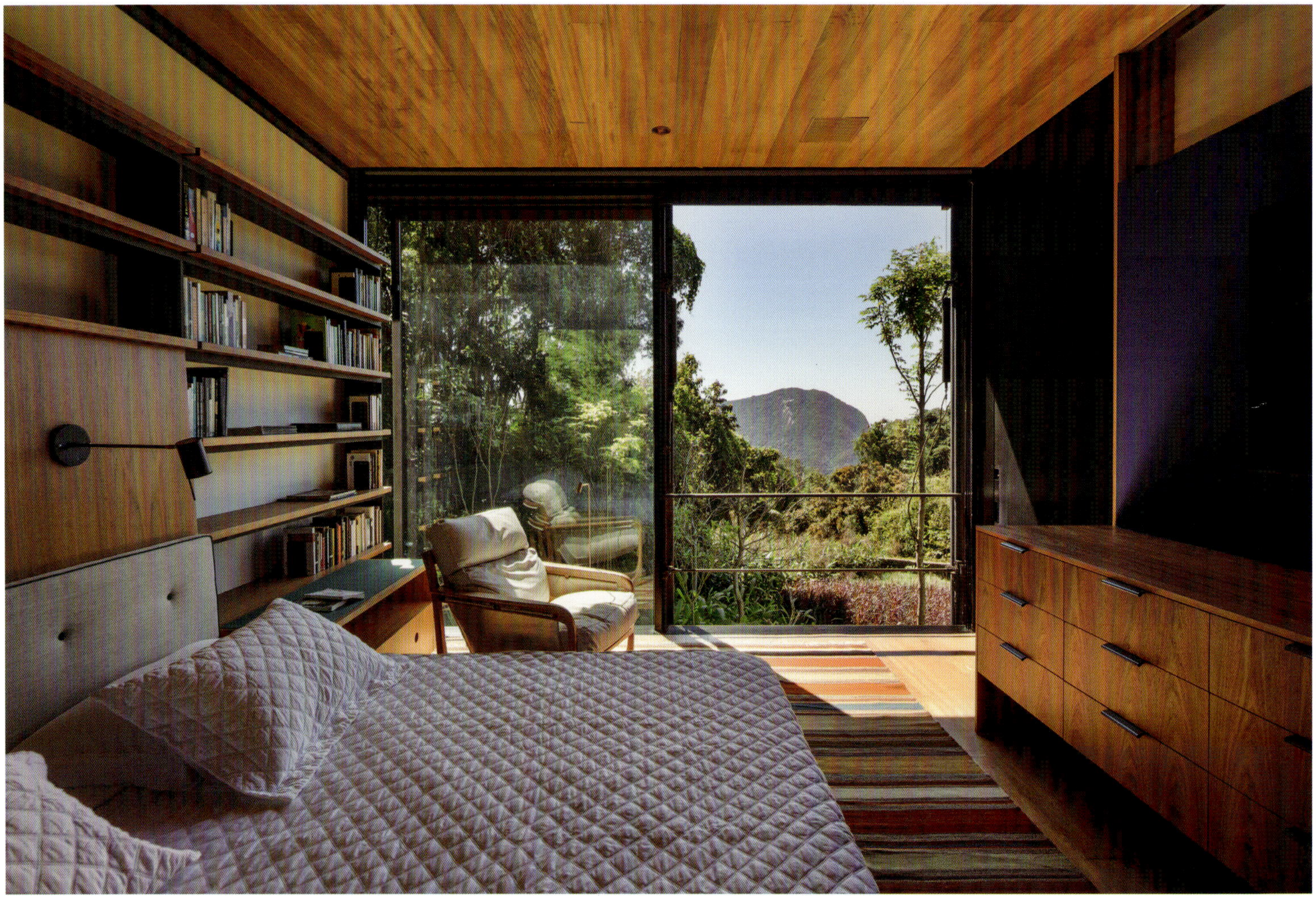

RIO HOUSE

Roberto Dini and Stefano Girodo
BIVOUAC LUCA PASQUALETTI
2018 | Morion Ridge, Aosta Valley, Italy

Teetering on a mountain ledge more than 10,000 feet (3,000 meters) above sea level, this shelter was commissioned by a group of local Alpine guides to encourage exploration of forgotten climbing routes and to commemorate a mountaineer, Luca Pasqualetti, who died in 2014. In a location with such extreme weather, the cabin had to be tough enough to withstand temperatures that plummet to -4 degrees Fahrenheit (-20 degrees Celsius), wind that blasts up to 124 miles (200 kilometers) per hour, driving rain, hail, and deep snowfall. It is held firmly in place by guy ropes and a metal "basement" that can be removed without impacting the mountain when the cabin's life cycle is over. The main structure, made of steel ribs and composite panels of pine and recycled polystyrene coated in aluminum the same gray as the mountain, was prefabricated in four sections and lowered into place by helicopter. A full-height window on the east facade, set back from a protective overhang, opens up views stretching as far as the Matterhorn and Monte Rosa massif, and welcomes in the sun's heat and light. The cabin's modest interior is lined with plywood; the living space has a table and benches, a built-in cupboard, and a food-preparation surface. At the rear are two wooden platforms with mattresses for eight people. Though comforts may be basic, the bivouac's magnificent views make it a truly breathtaking place to stay the night.

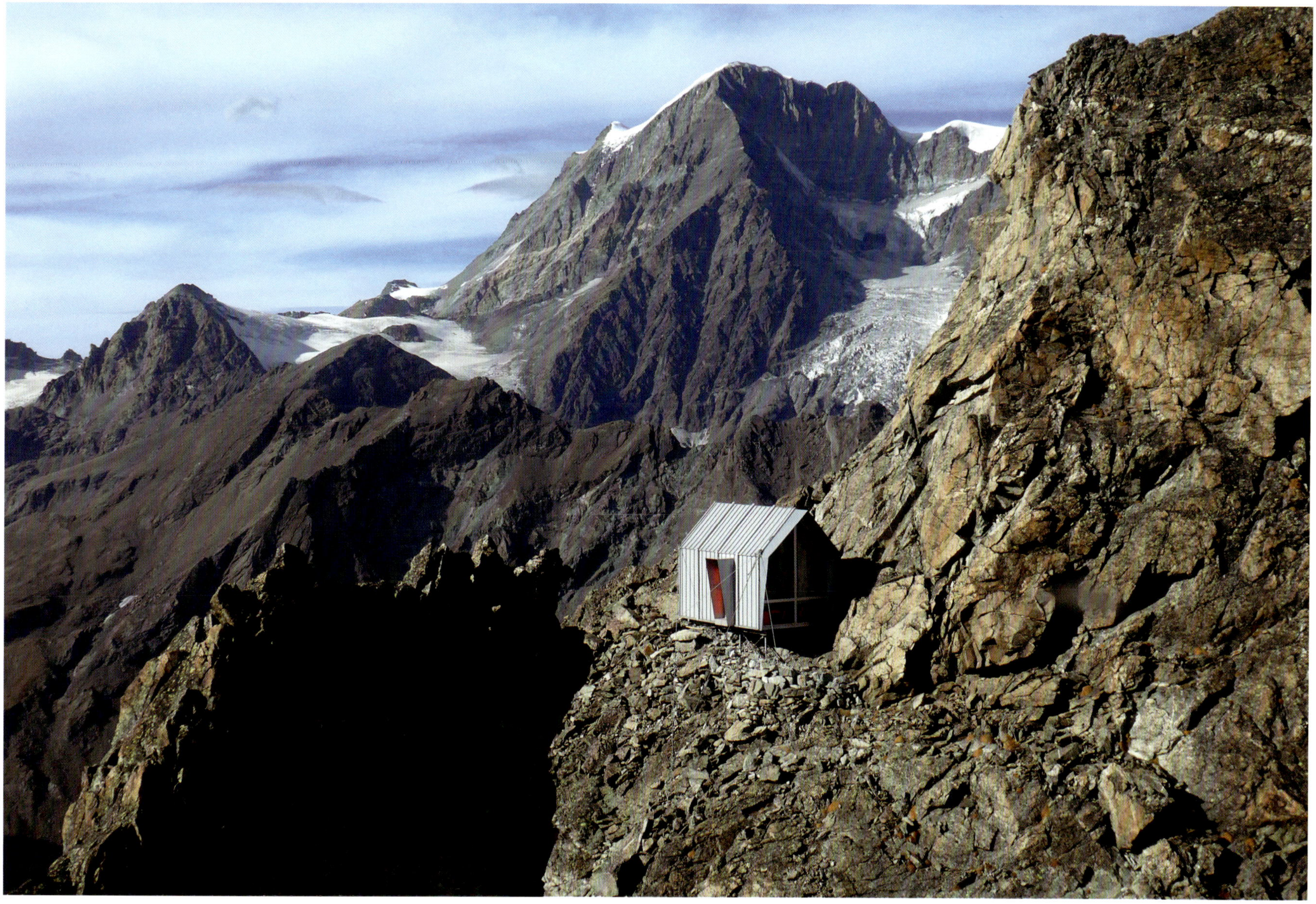

BIVOUAC LUCA PASQUALETTI

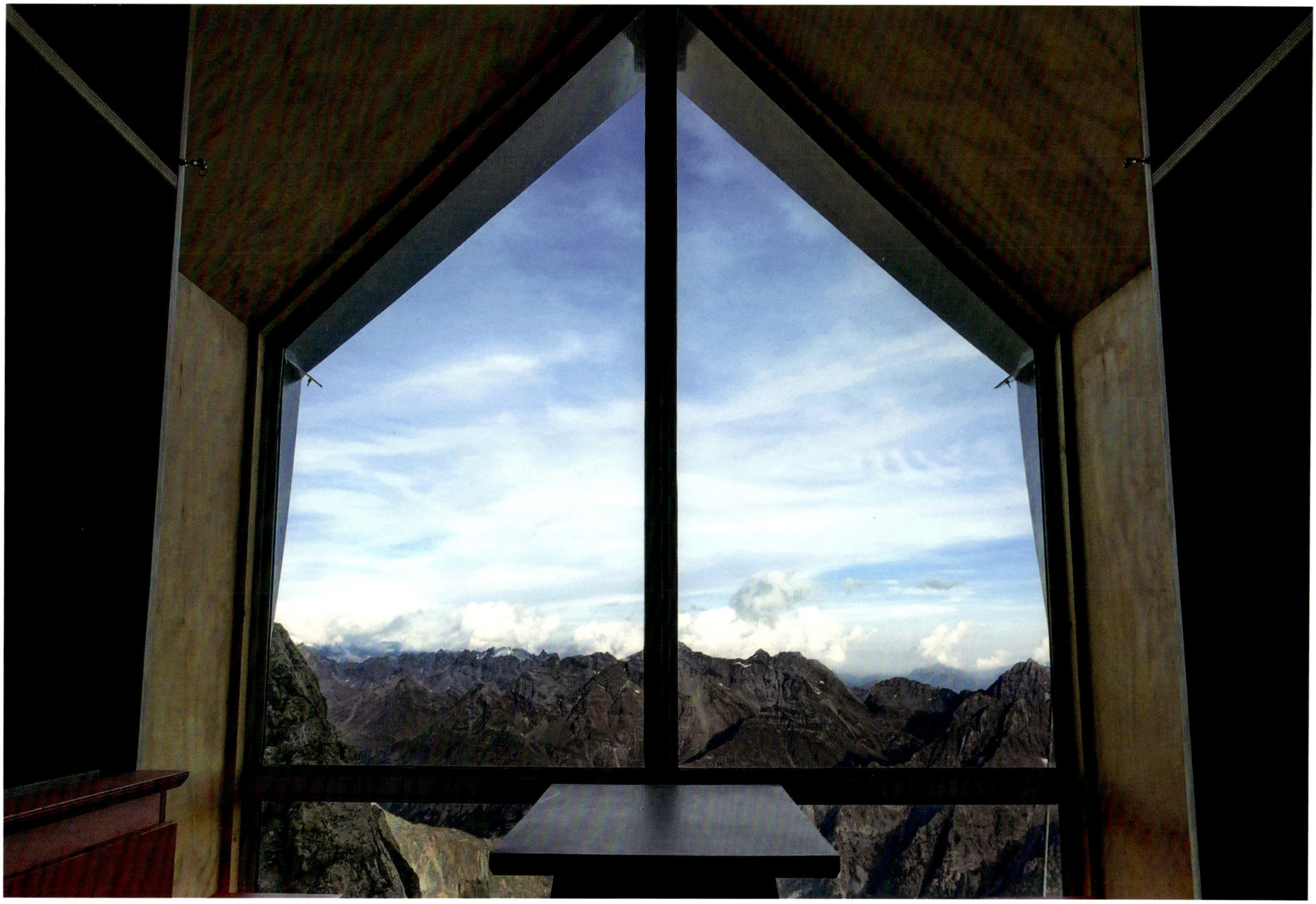

Malan Vorster Architecture
TREE HOUSE CONSTANTIA
2016 | Cape Town, South Africa

Tree House Constantia is a remarkable and somewhat fantastical escape. It appears to be four connecting wood-and-glass cylinders on stilts, but it is actually square on plan, with curving volumes wrapping each corner of the square to form bays. The three-story structure is elevated on four sets of columns, set back from the building's envelope, which emulate tree trunks. From these, "branches" stretch out to meet circular "tree rings" that support each floor plate. Columns, branches, and rings are all made of laser-cut and rolled Corten steel. A plant room occupies the ground level, and a ramp leads to the next floor up, which accommodates a kitchen and double-height living space. One bay hosts a dining area, while another stretches out to create a spacious balcony. The main bedroom, another level up, extends into the upper reaches of the living room; surrounded by a frameless glass balustrade, with glazing beyond, inhabitants can easily imagine they are floating above the landscape. The top floor is an open roof deck with built-in seating tucked into one of the alcoves. To provide privacy and shading, the facade is clad with western red cedar battens, which are left untreated to weather to a soft patina that will blend in with the trees.

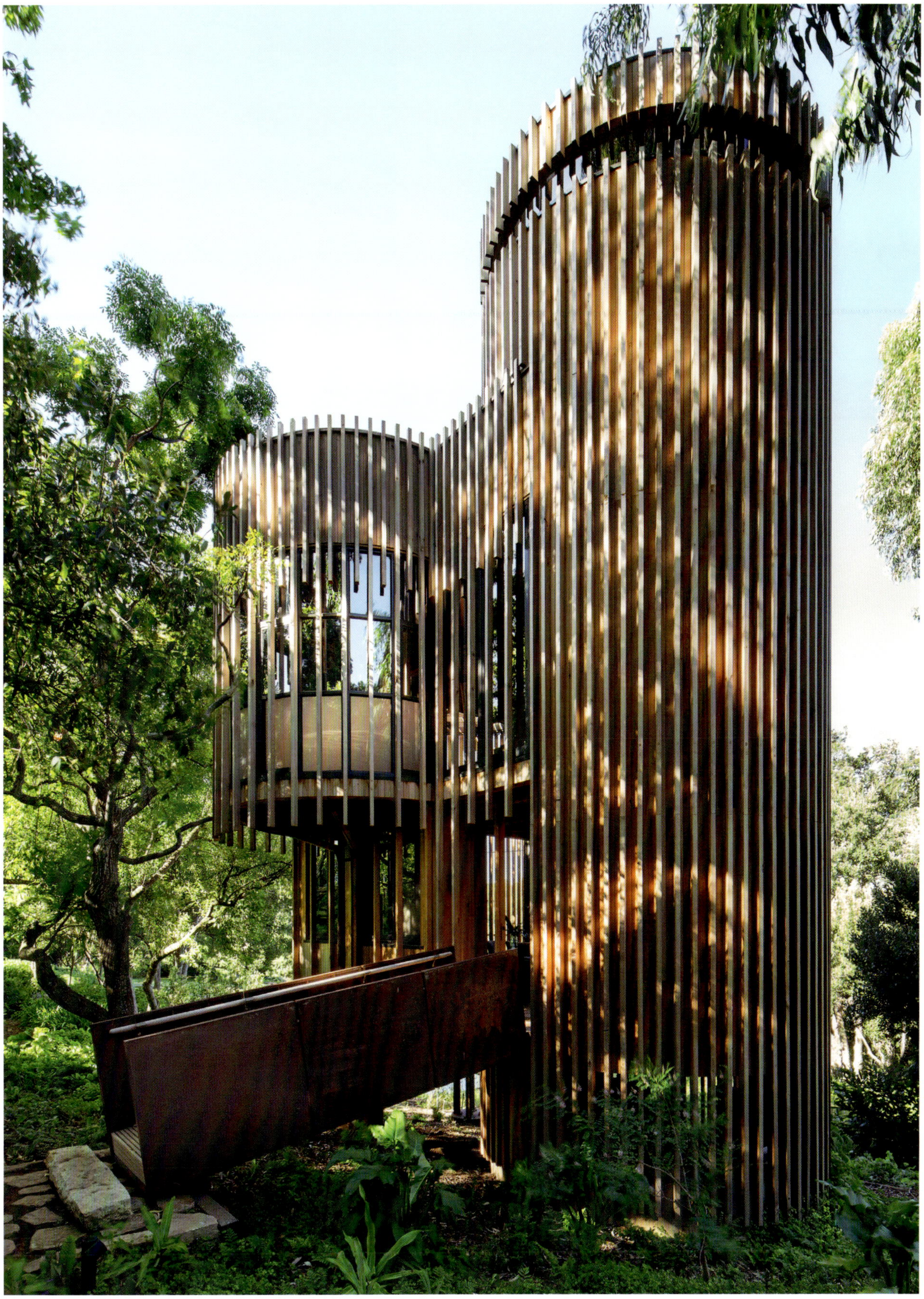

TREE HOUSE CONSTANTIA

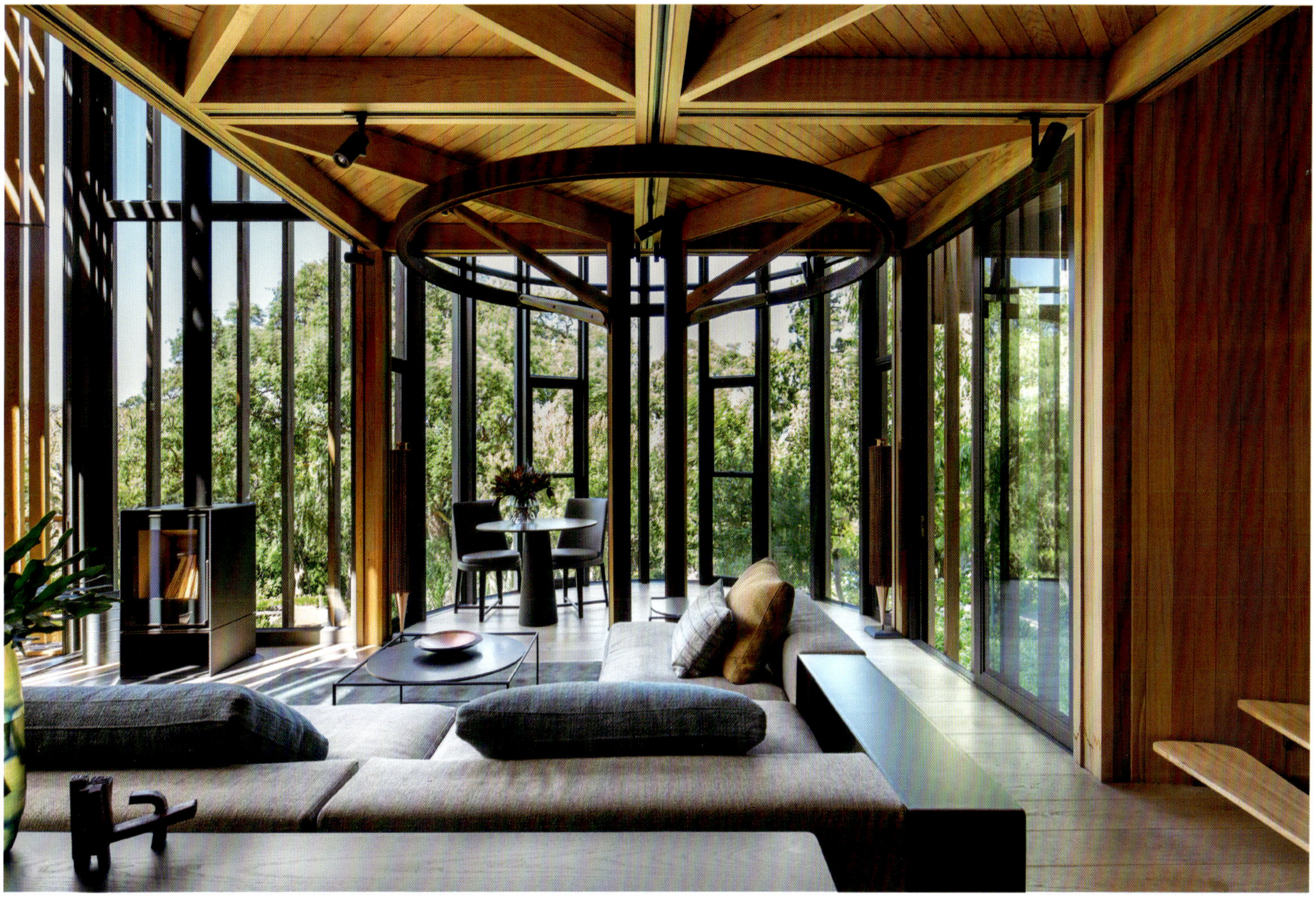

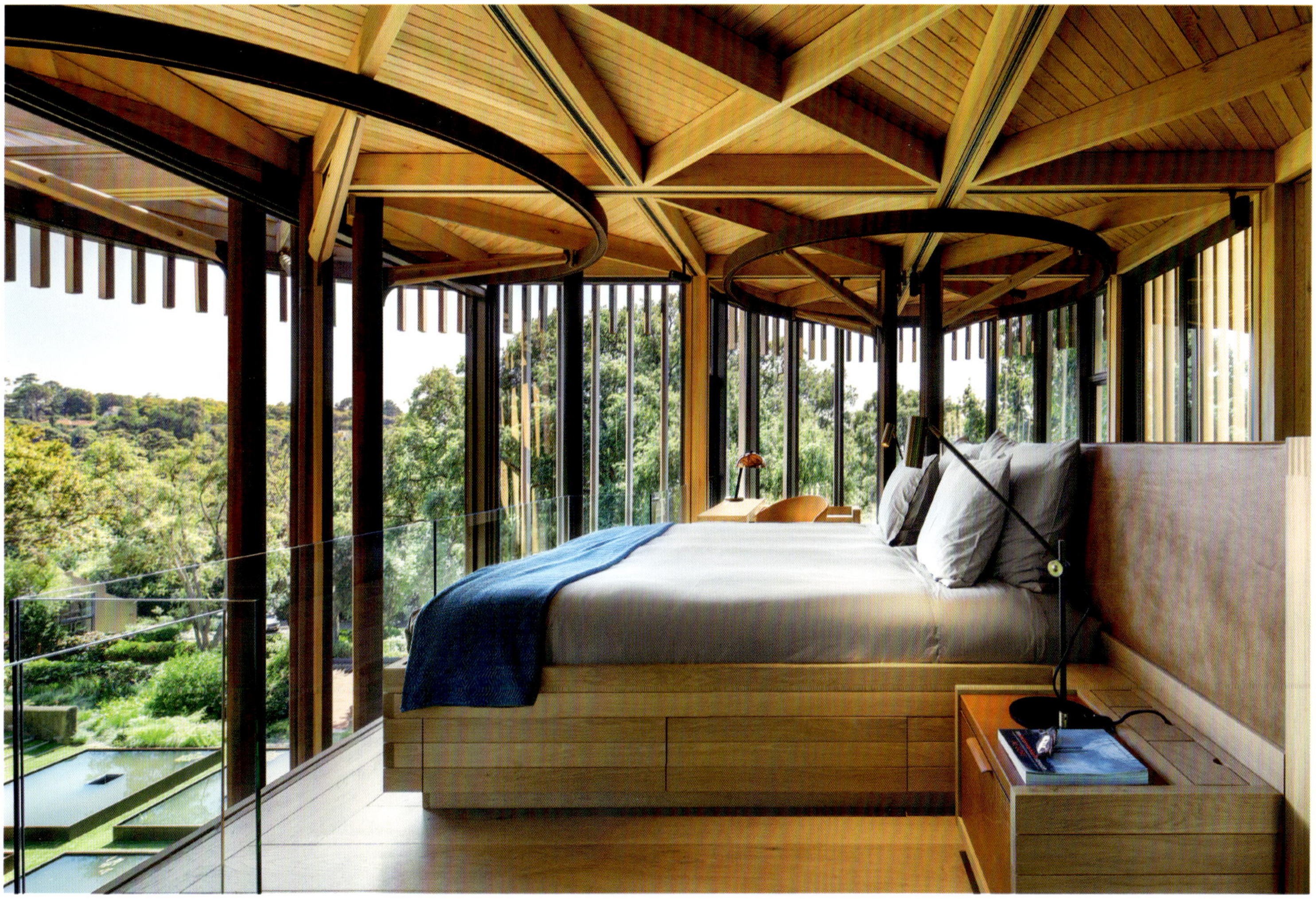

SAA Arquitectura + Territorio
DOCK HOUSE
2018 | Pichicuy, Chile

Dock House juts out from a hillside, like a seaside pier that only just falls short of the ocean. Resting on zigzagging wooden stilts that negotiate the site's sloping topography, the slender single-story volume is angled side-on to overlook the Valparaiso coast, forming an emphatic visual connection with the horizon. Stilts also give the whole construction a sense of levity and openness, and a playful, retro-modern twist. Their V-shaped forms remain the same width along the length of the house, but as the ground rises they lose height, creating a dynamic irregular rhythm that counterpoints the static horizontal structure they support. Expansive glazing on the southwest facade drenches the interior in coastal light and maximizes views of the Pacific below, while the private, hill-facing side remains introspective, with latticework screening the entrance and a bunk-bed sleeping area. The open-plan living and dining area is separated from the sleeping quarters by a glazed central space leading to an outdoor terrace on both sides, creating further visual permeability and a unity with the outdoors. More light penetrates the house through a long clerestory. Finely crafted honey-colored pine is used inside and out, creating a bright, boatlike space, and as the sun slowly sets, the wood turns an exquisite rose gold.

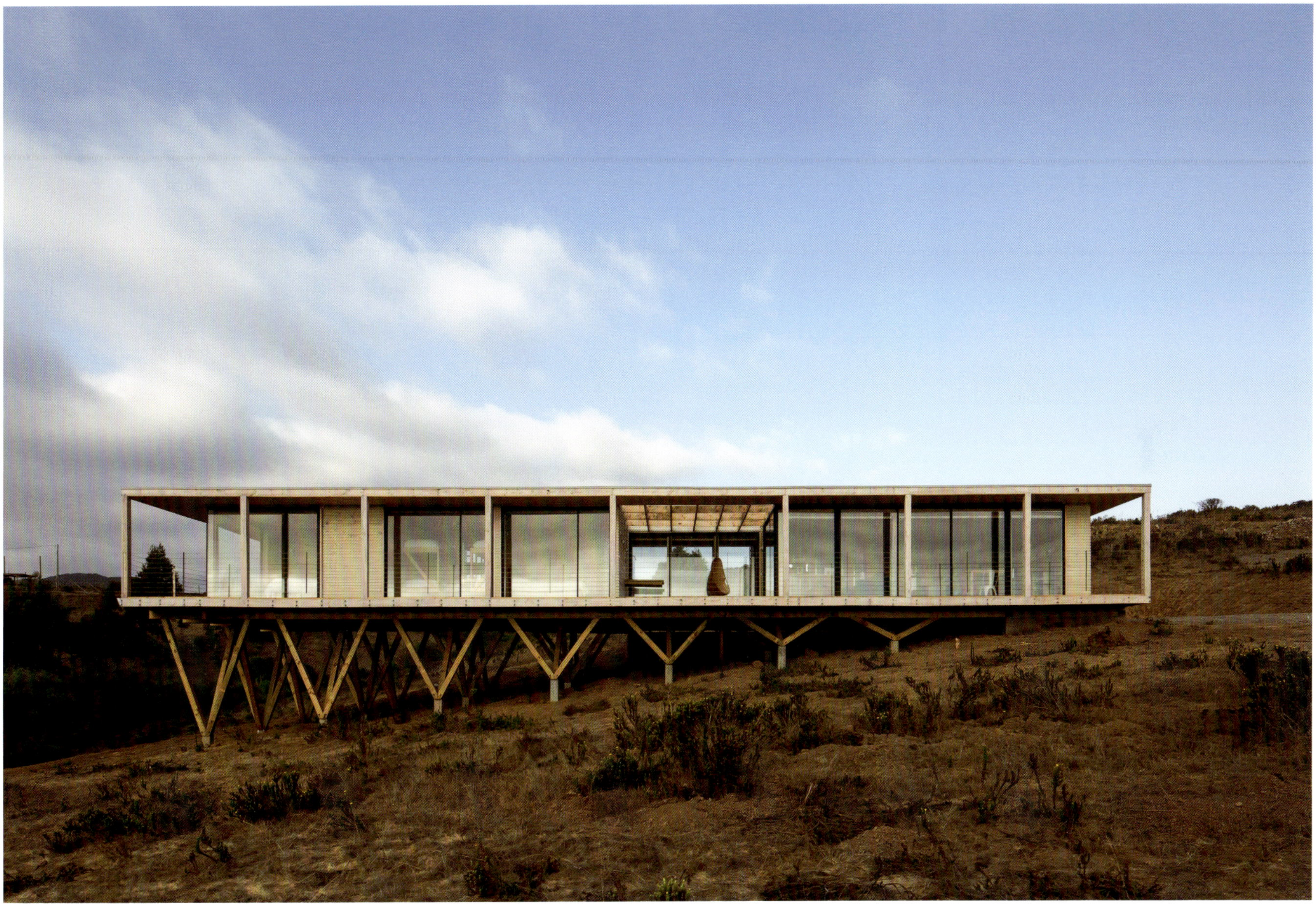

DOCK HOUSE 44

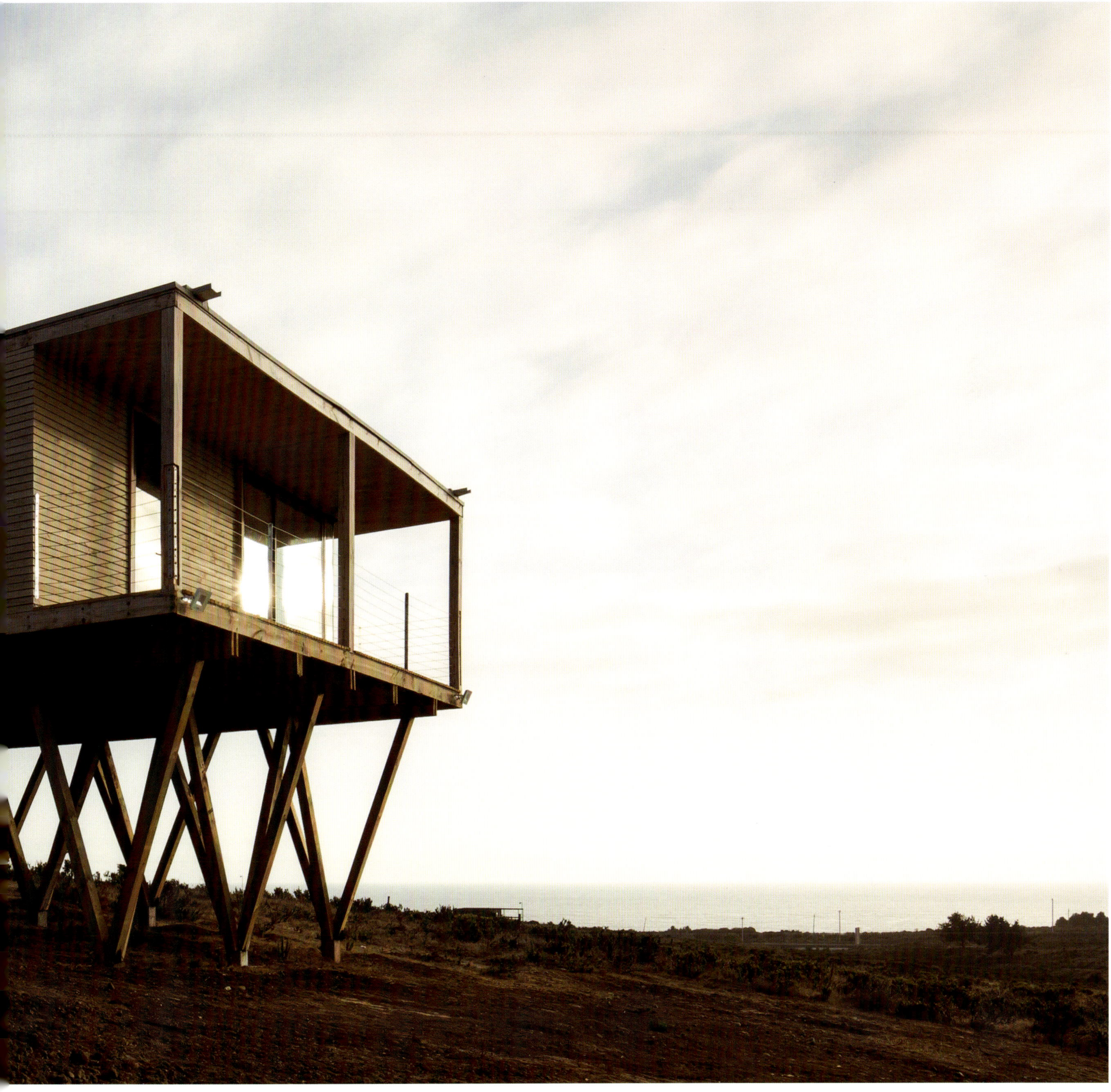

DOCK HOUSE 46

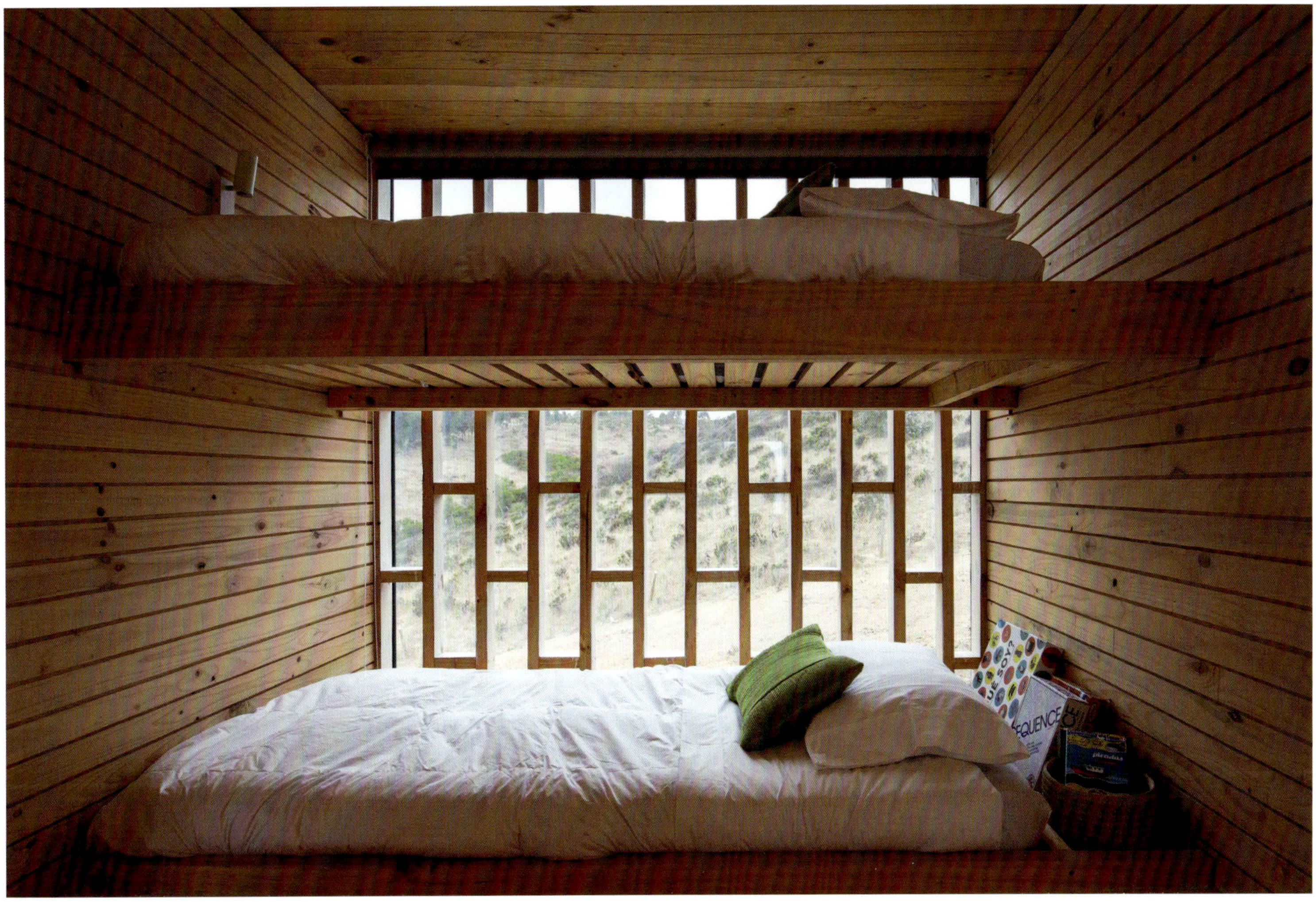

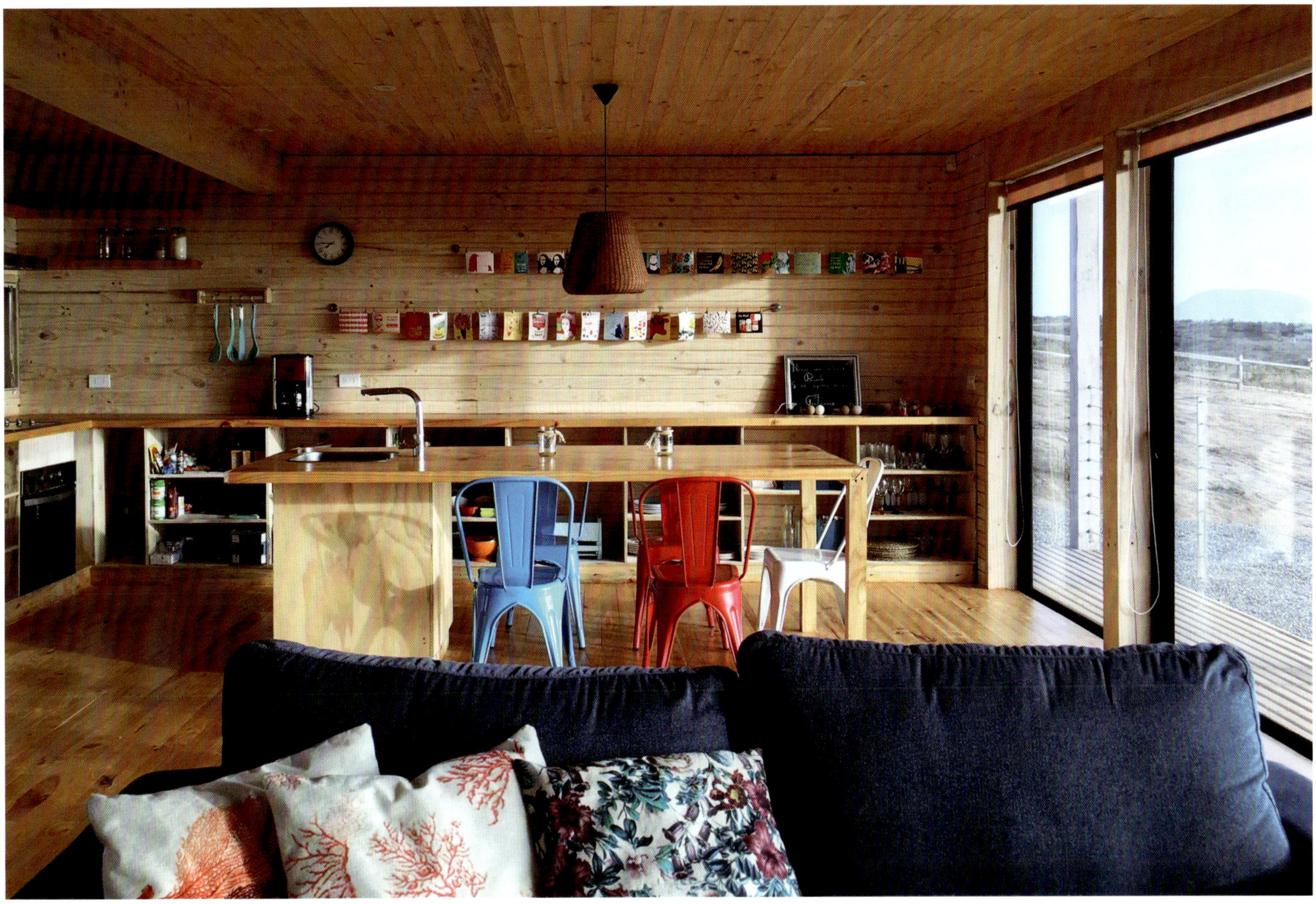

Felipe Assadi Arquitectos
CASA LA ROJA
2018 | San José de Maipo, Chile

High up in the mountains, Casa La Roja's scarlet exterior contrasts strikingly with its lush green surroundings. Red is often used to decorate the houses of local towns, but the bold color choice was further justified in this rural setting because the dwelling occupies a remote, expansive plot with no immediate neighbors. Casa La Roja's design began with a cubic form; portions were then cut away to bring in light and give it a more sculptural appearance. The angles of the gabled roof cleverly mimic the forms of nearby mountains, and while from a distance the house looks solid and barnlike, voids are used to create permeability and illumination. On the east elevation, a covered double-height porch has a section of its roof cut away, chanelling natural light down into the house. The slatted wooden screening of the porch, level with the upper floor's glazing, creates further transparency in the facade while maintaining privacy and shading. Upstairs, there are two bedrooms, and downstairs, an open-plan living, kitchen, and dining area. Each floor is made of two interlocking modules that were prefabricated and fitted together on-site. Further modules can be added with ease, making Casa La Roja as flexible as it is eye-catching.

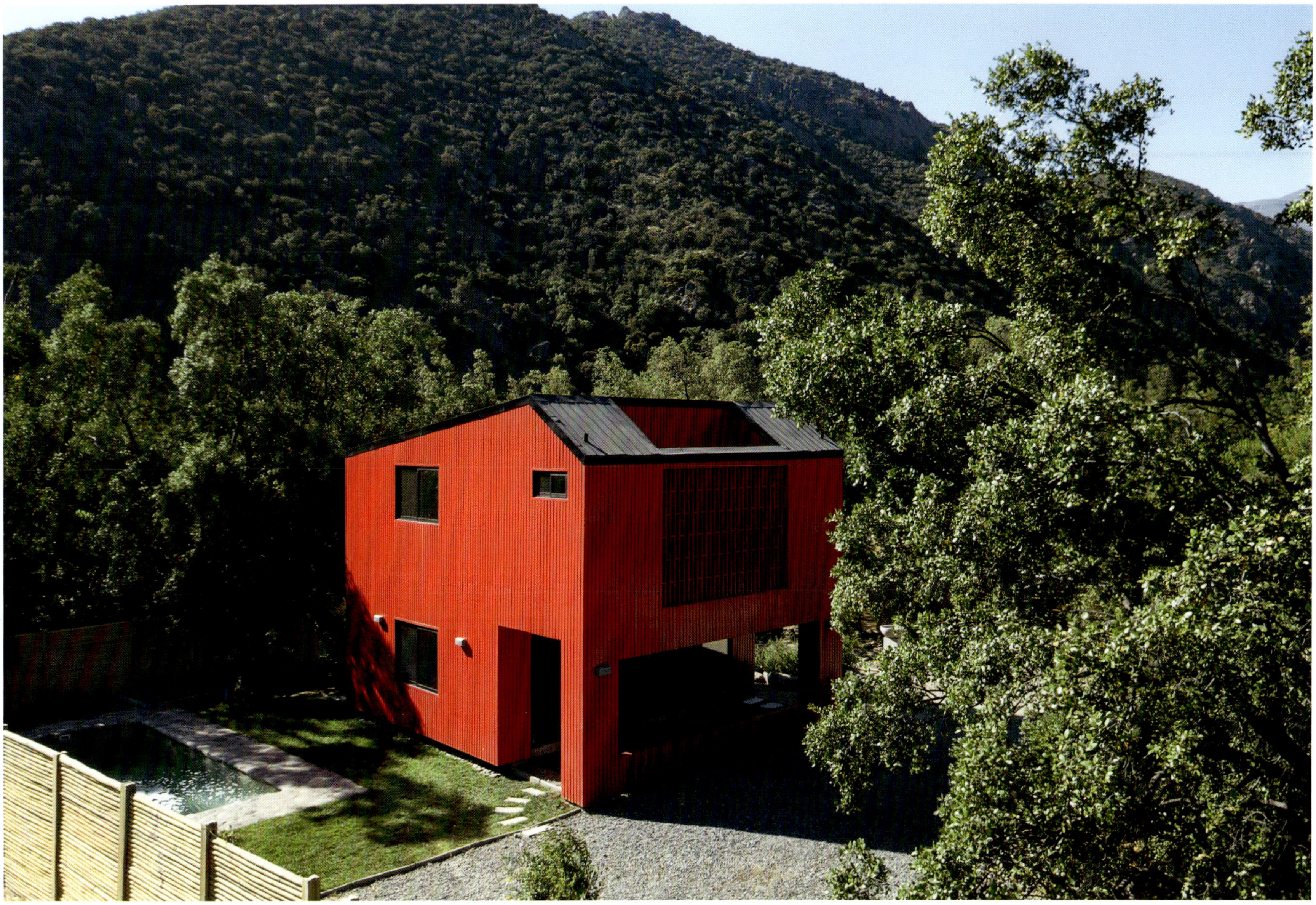

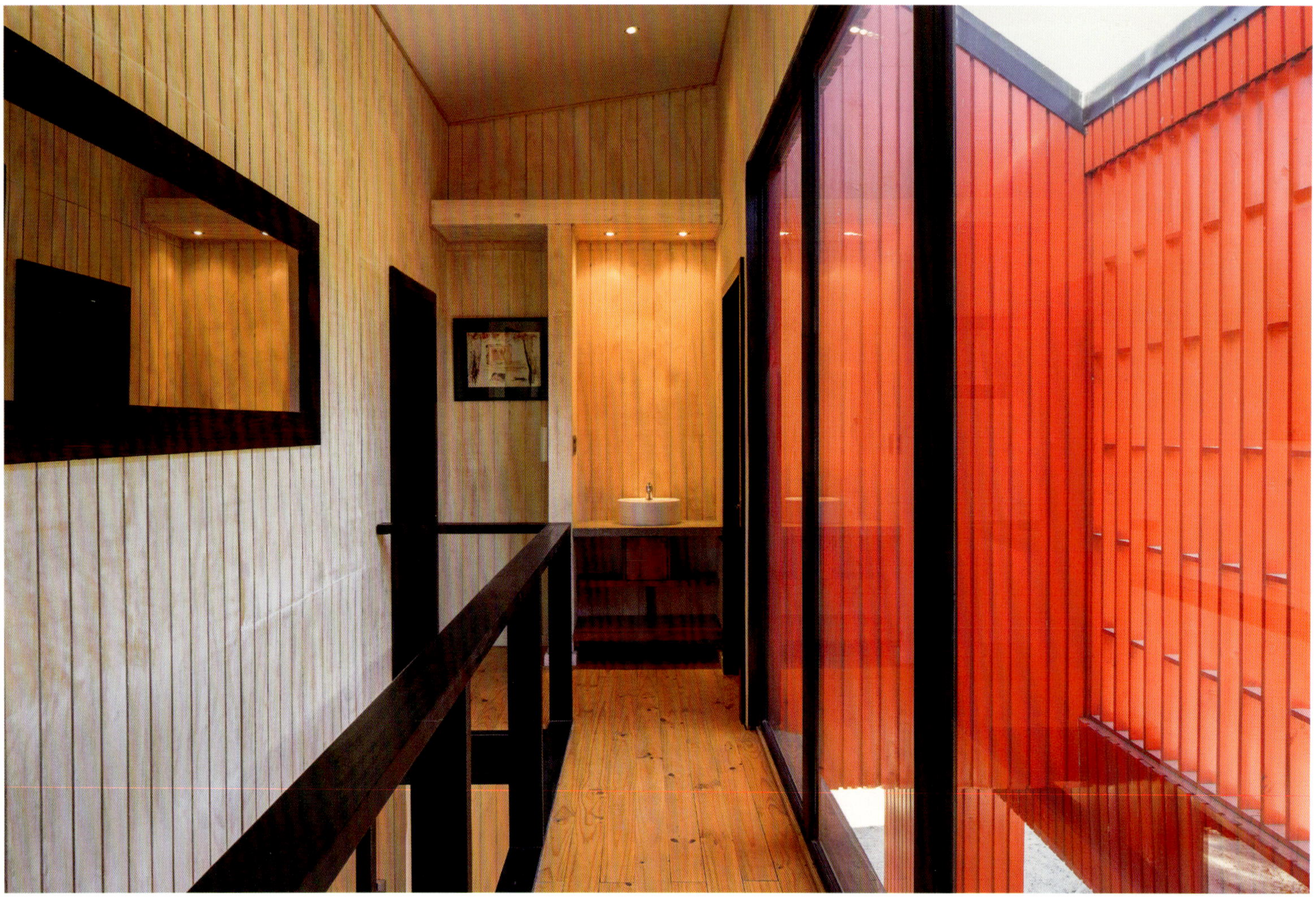

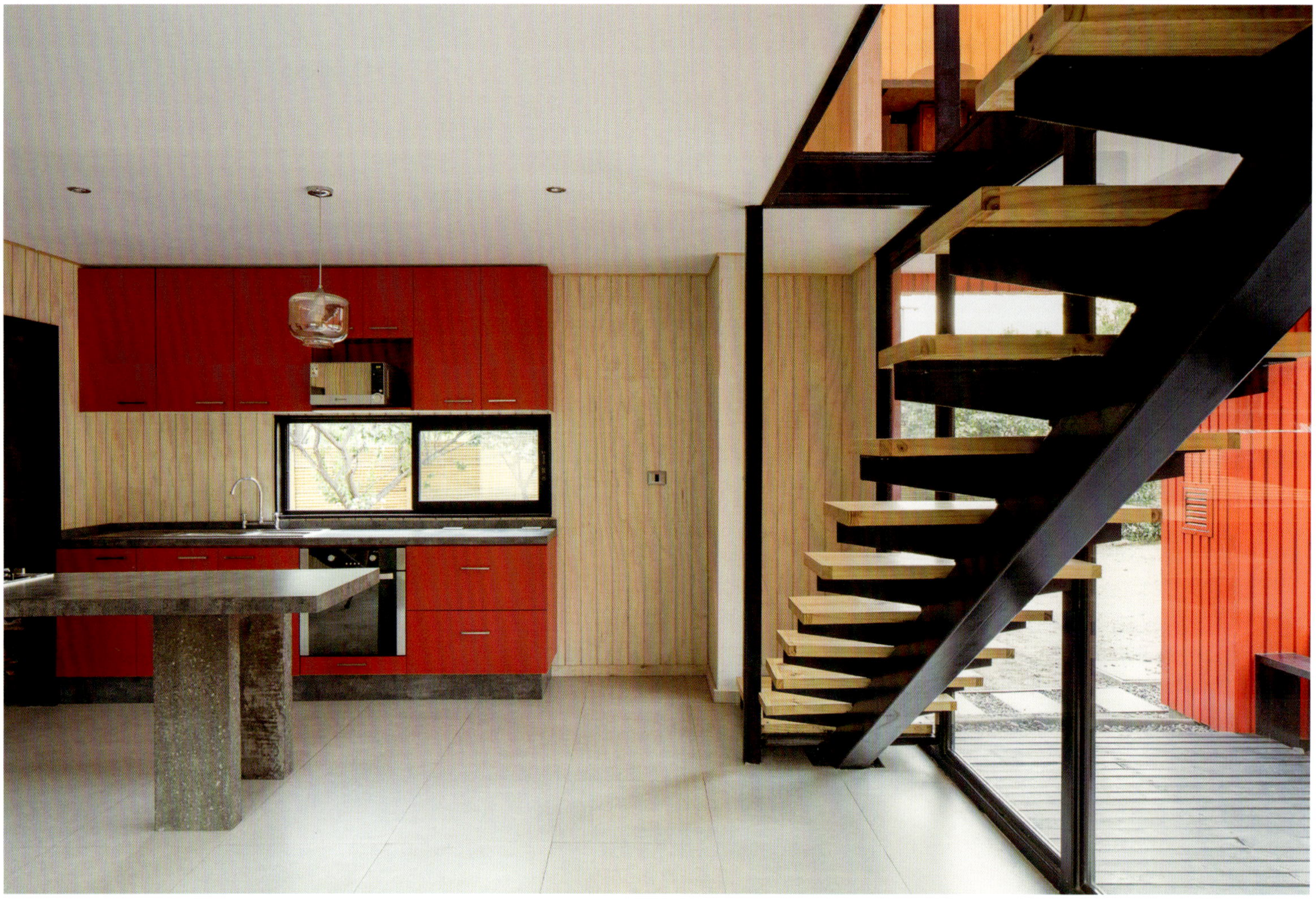

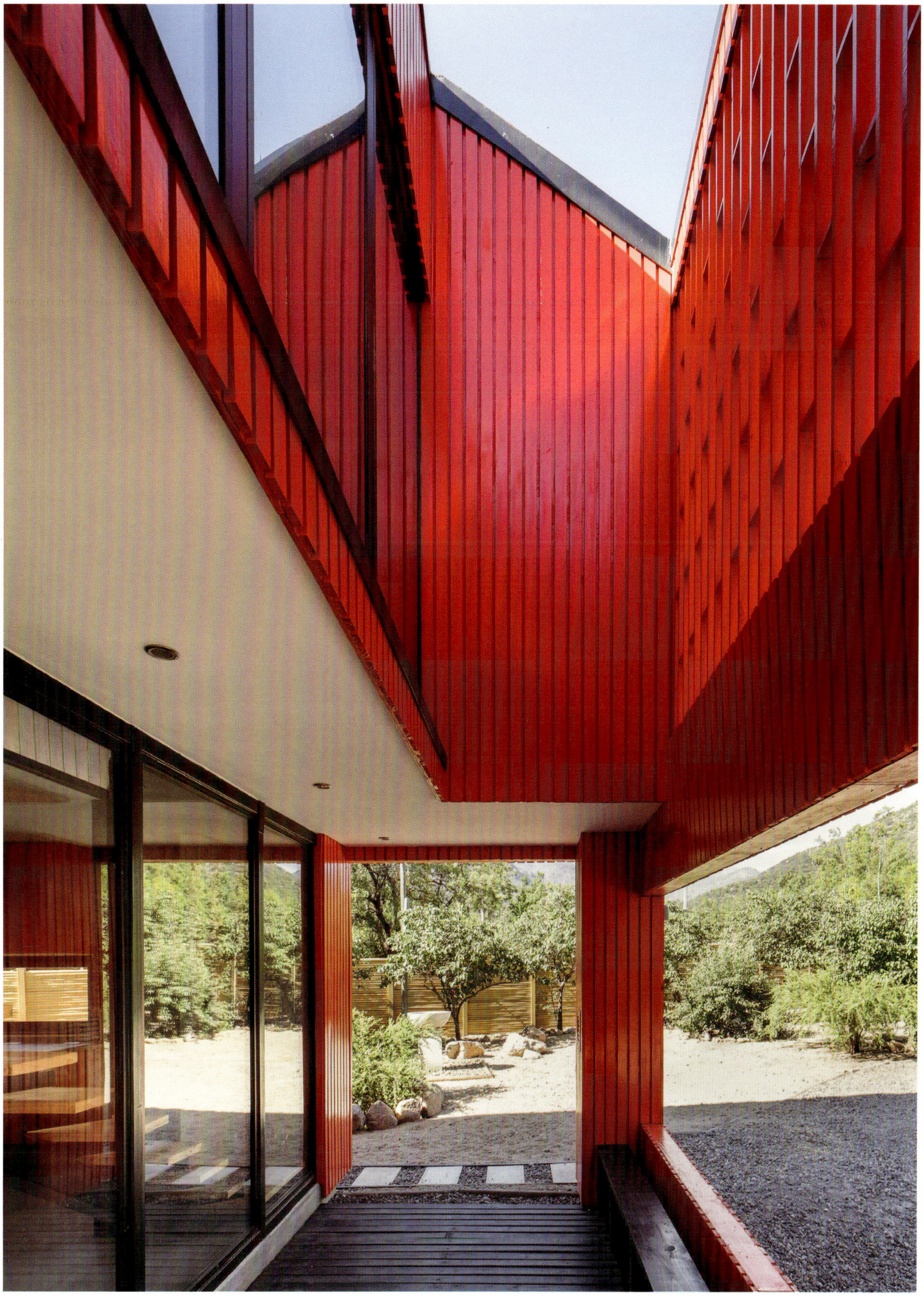

Artistree
YOKI TREEHOUSE
2018 | Austin, TX, USA

In an area punctuated by springs and aquifers, this whimsical treehouse near Austin, Texas, takes its name from the Hopi word for rain. In a truly idyllic woodland setting, the house hovers 25 feet (8 meters) above a small creek, well camouflaged by its gray cypress cladding. The wedge-shaped cabin is supported by metal struts driven into the tree trunks of two cypresses at its wider end, and another tree where it narrows. It presents a pleasing jumble of boxlike and curving forms: strategically placed cantilevering elements that maximize views, a rounded deck pierced by the cypresses, and a spiral staircase that connects the roof observation deck and living area. This volume, which features a compact lounge, dining area, and kitchen, is constructed from local and sustainably sourced materials, including elm, spruce, and cypress. Birch plywood cladding keeps the interior walls light and bright. One sleeping area is on a mezzanine, and there is an additional separate bedroom. The challenge of providing full-scale plumbing to treehouses is here made into a positive feature. After crossing a rope footbridge from the roof, lit by a string of dainty lights at night, one arrives at an enticing bathhouse set on an elevated mound. It features a concrete-and-pine onsen-style tub and expansive glass windows that give far-reaching views out over the treetops as one soaks. Both structures work together to create an unforgettable experience of the woods and the water.

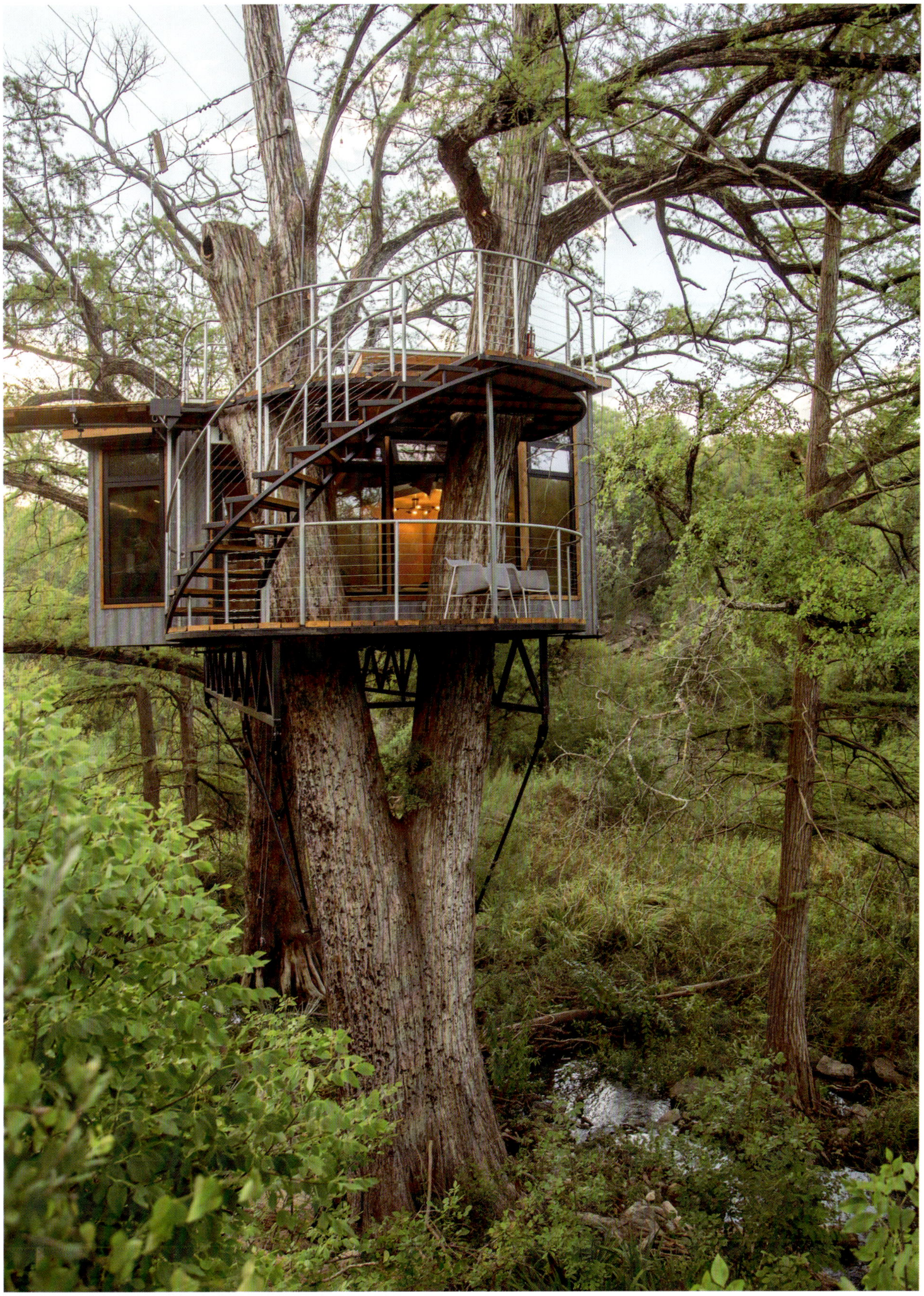

YOKI TREEHOUSE

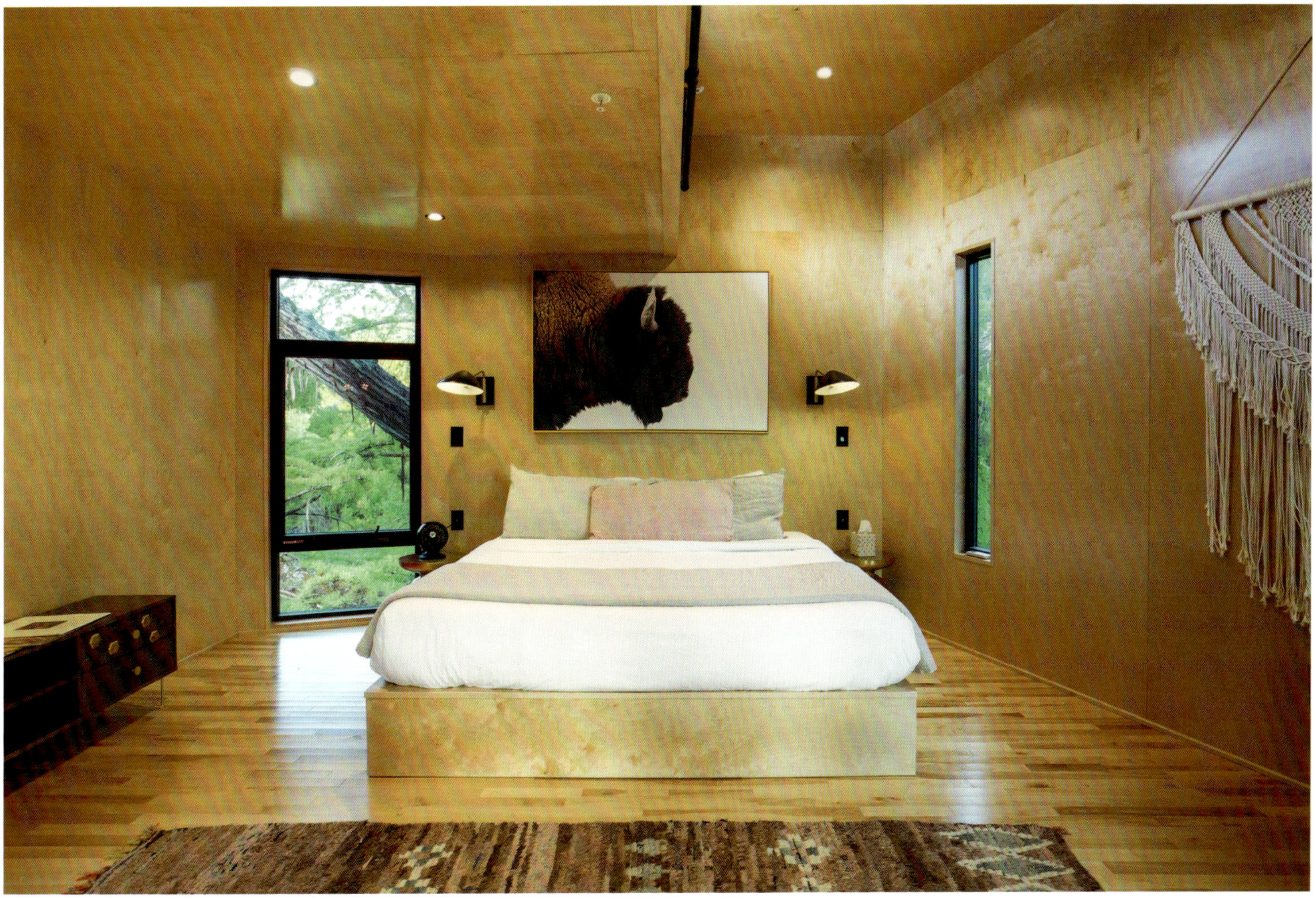
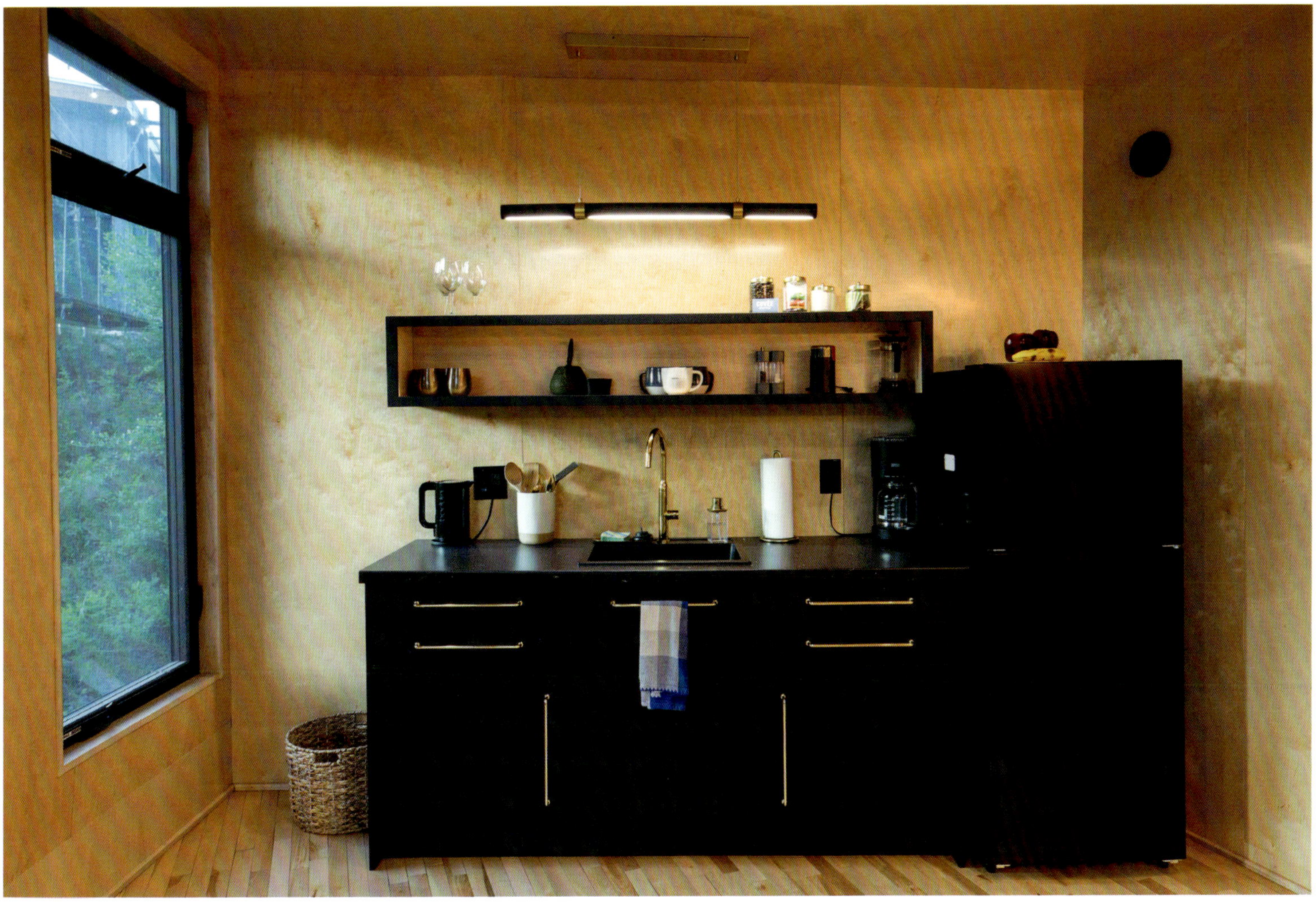

Johan Sundberg Arkitektur
SUMMERHOUSE SOLVIKEN
2018 | Mölle, Sweden

This modern summerhouse in the Swedish seaside town of Mölle is only just visible on the densely wooded hillside to which it clings. Twelve steel pillars elevate the structure to the level of the treetops, distancing it from neighboring residences and maximizing sea views. Entry to the simple rectangular volume is at the rear, via steps climbing the hill to a balcony that wraps generously around two sides of the house. The main bedroom also has a deck area with views to the front and its own connecting dressing room at the rear. Bedrooms, a bathroom, and a laundry room are grouped facing the hillside, while the kitchen, dining, and living room enjoy views to the front. Floor-to-ceiling glazing slides back to connect to the spacious balcony, where the adjacent oak tree canopy has been made a living feature of the home. The facade boards, balcony railings, and visible parts of the load-bearing structure are painted a subdued gray-green, camouflaging the house amid the trees and hillside rock formations. By contrast, the vertical facade cladding and eaves of the roof overhangs are made of pale-colored timber, which gives the whole ensemble a lightness and brightness. The minimalist interior features a muted palette to accent the vibrant, fresh foliage filling the views outside. There is a sense of harmony that stems from the house's simplicity, modesty, and wholehearted empathy with its surroundings.

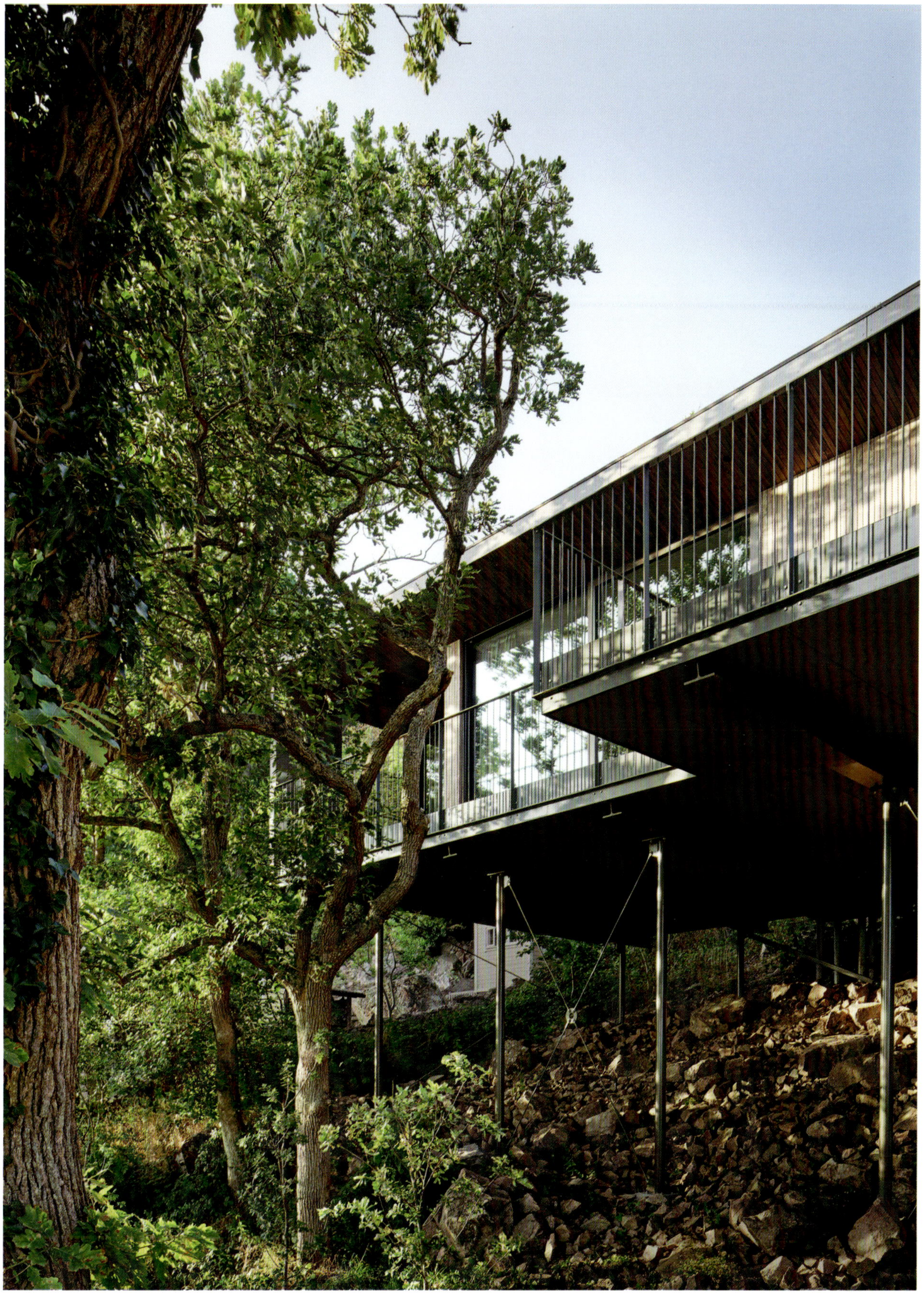

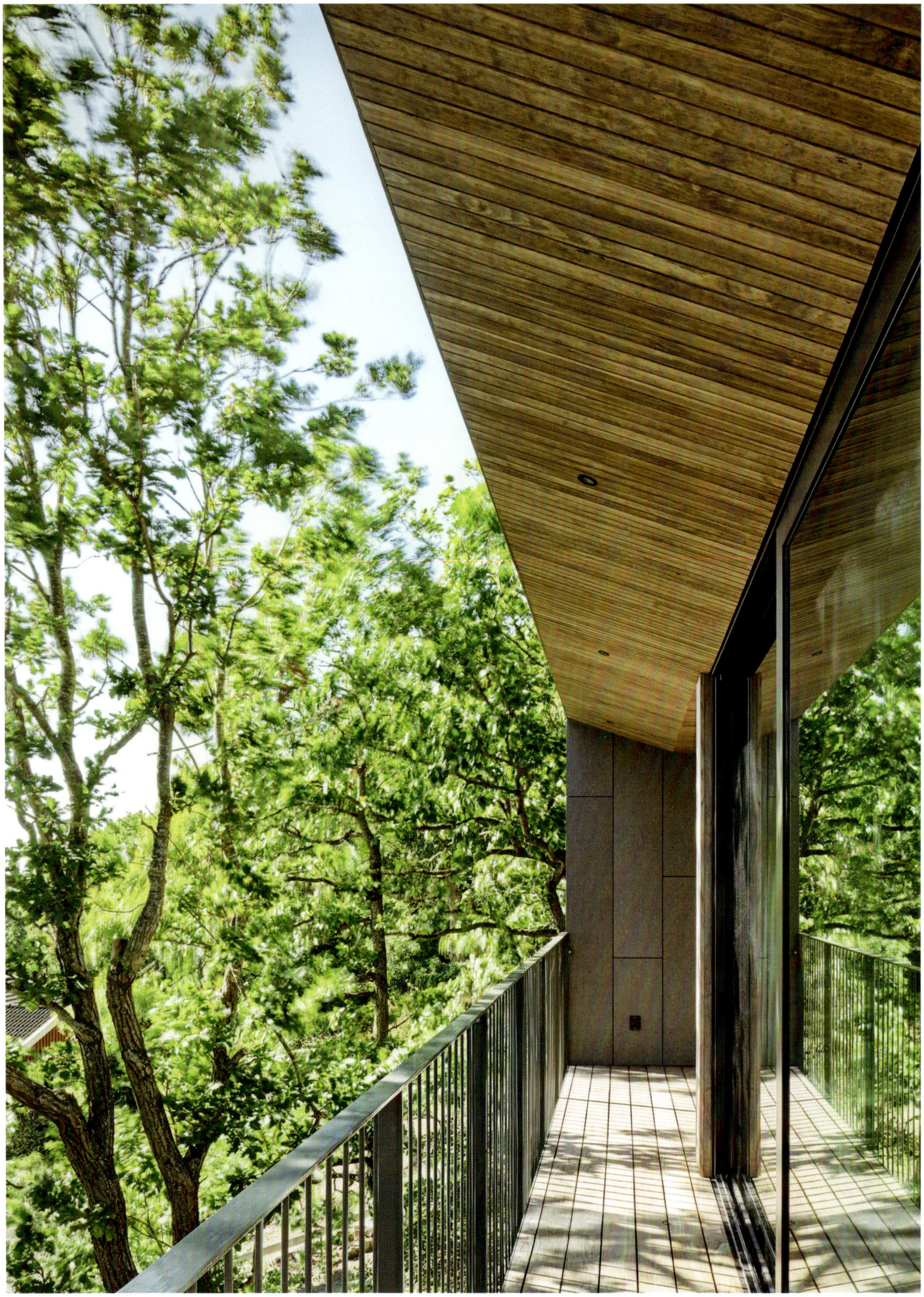

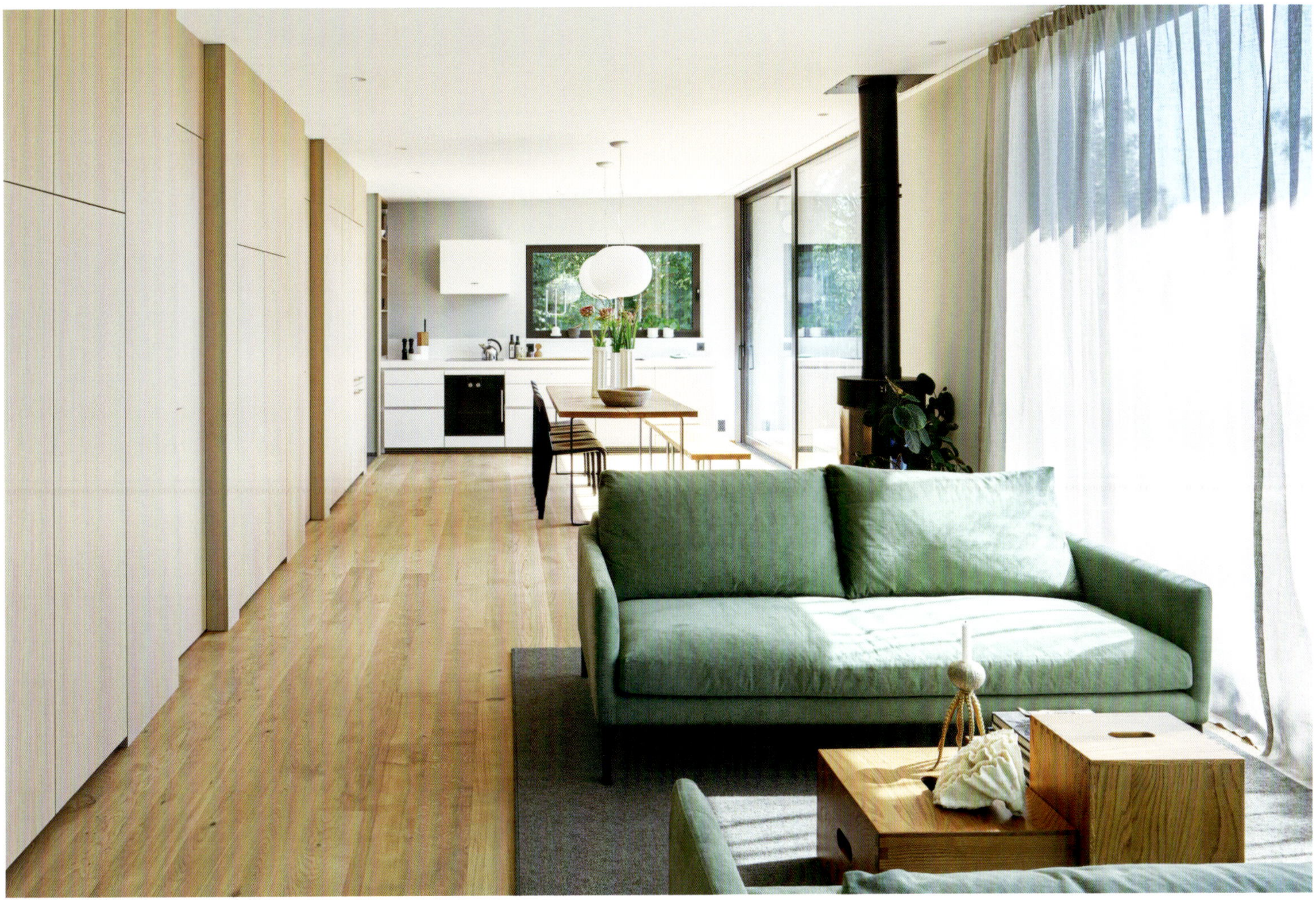

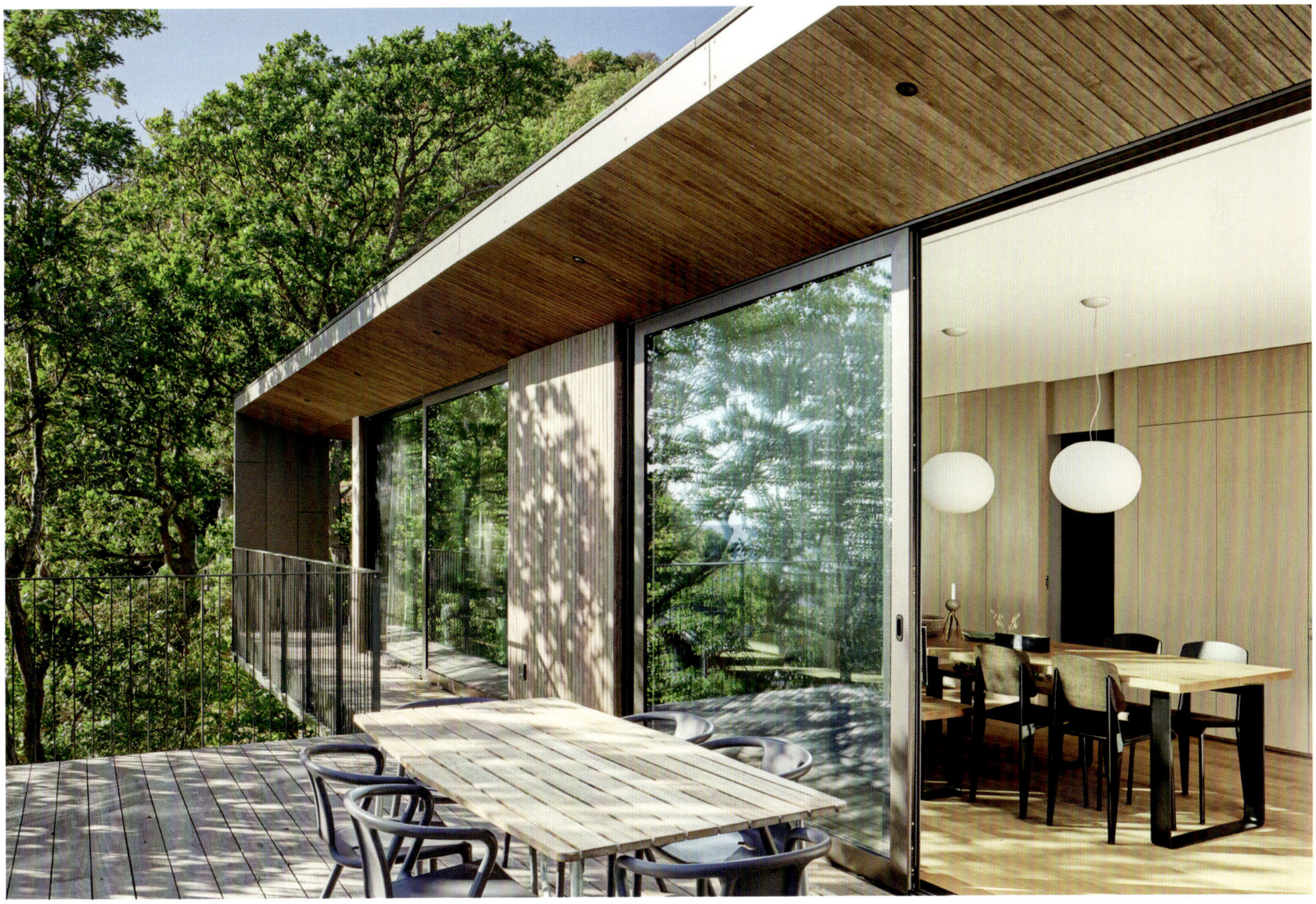

Espen Surnevik
PAN TREETOP CABINS
2018 | Gjesåsen, Norway

Partly inspired by Tove Jansson's tall, conical-roofed "Moominhouse," these triangular stilted cabins in eastern Norway subvert preconceived notions of treehouse design. Their shape is also reminiscent of North American A-frame huts or a simplified version of the pine trees that surround them. From certain angles, it is hard to tell how one enters—no staircase or ladder is immediately visible—but, through the trees, the stair tower and connecting bridge soon emerge. The designers deliberately chose to use man-made materials in order to provide an eye-catching contrast with the surrounding forest, yet they do not jar. The cabins, for example, are clad in oxidized zinc, but its leaflike texture also adds some biomimicry; the dark surface complements the shadows and muted tones of the evergreen forest. Ample glazing is angled to align with the sun's path and to heat the living spaces, and from the outside, the glass reflects the trees, creating a camouflaging frieze of branched forms across the facades. The cabins can accommodate up to six people, and each has a kitchen, living, and dining area, and a mezzanine floor with a double bed and additional fold-down beds. They quietly maintain a surreal sentinel presence amid the forest.

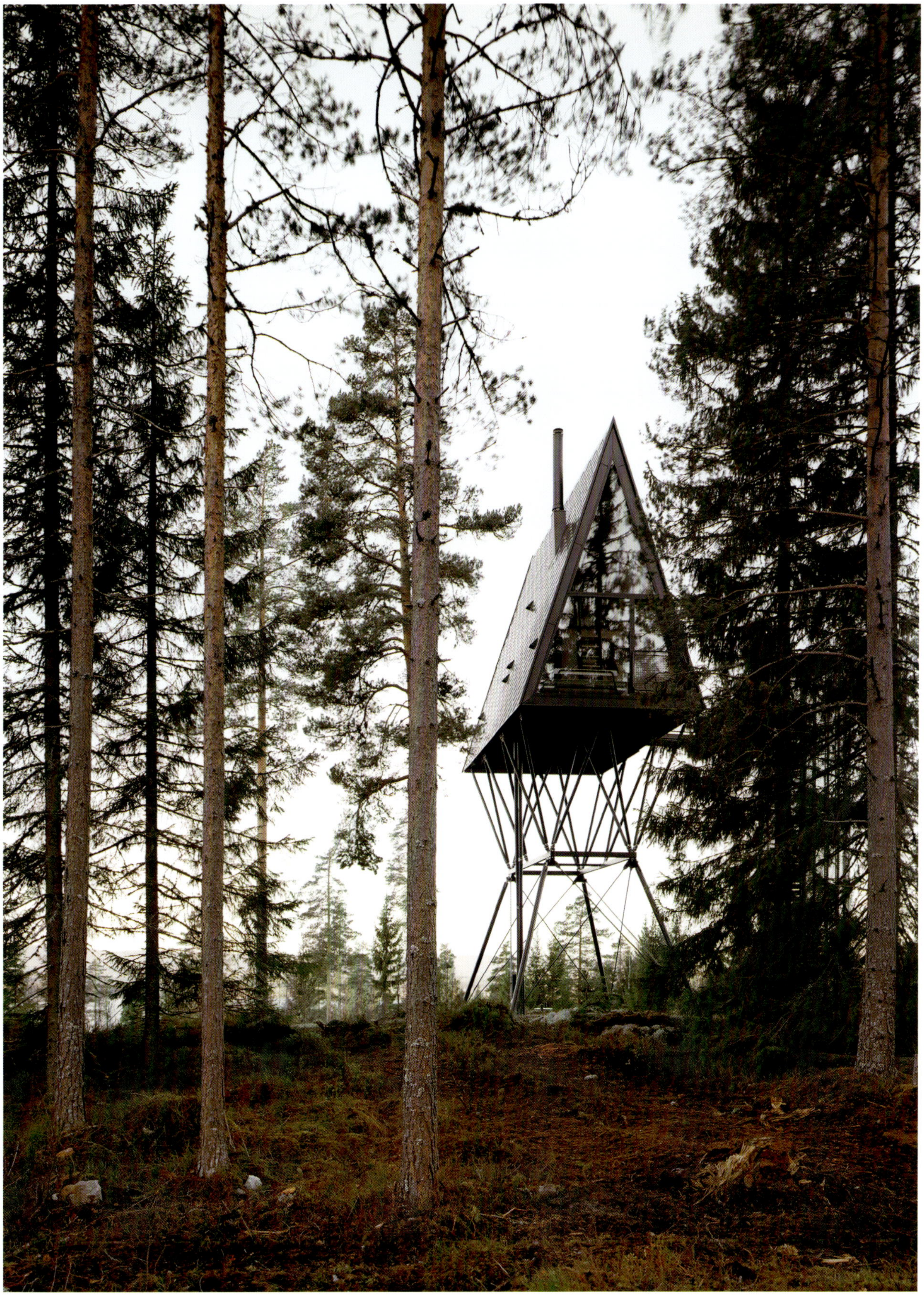

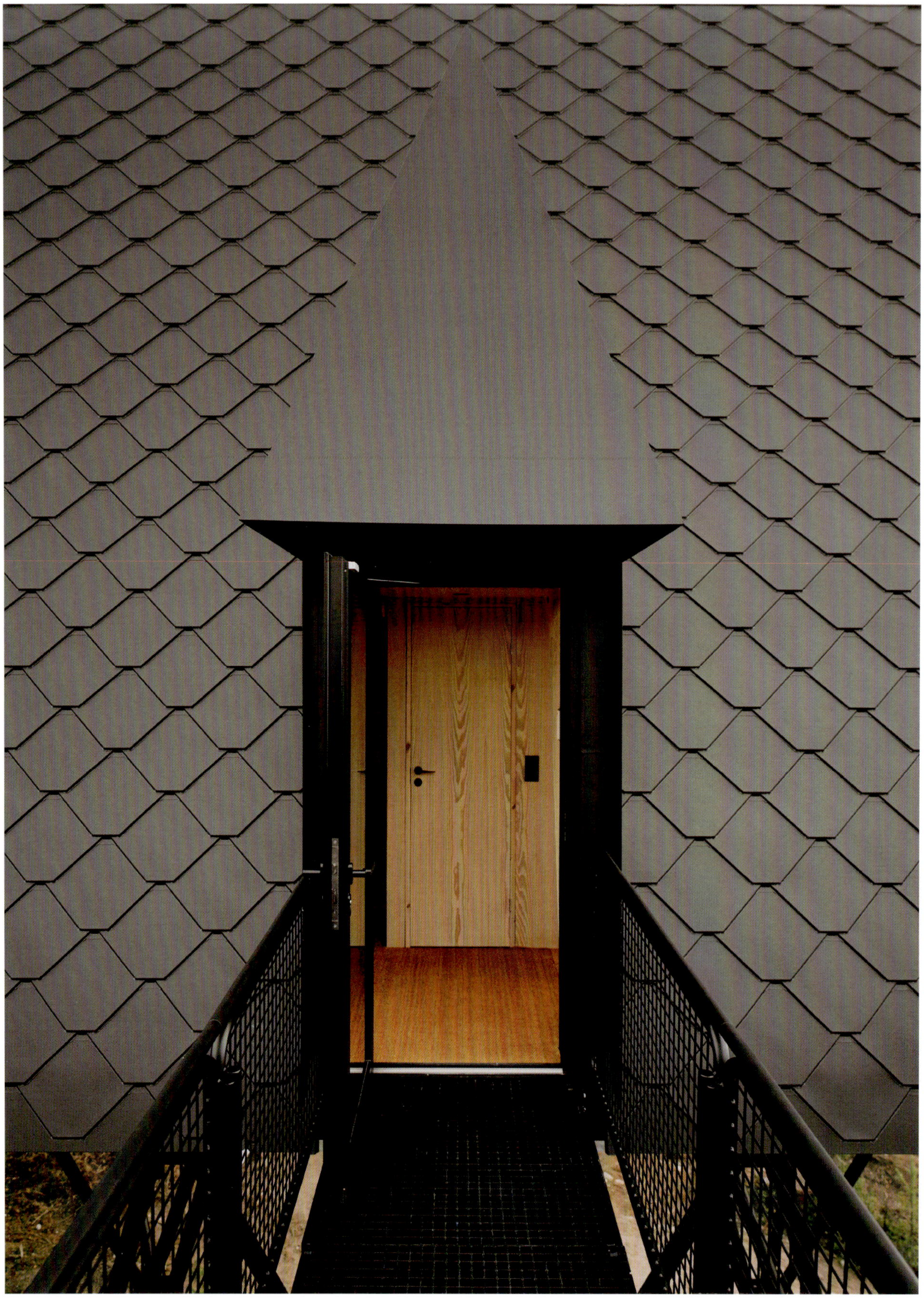

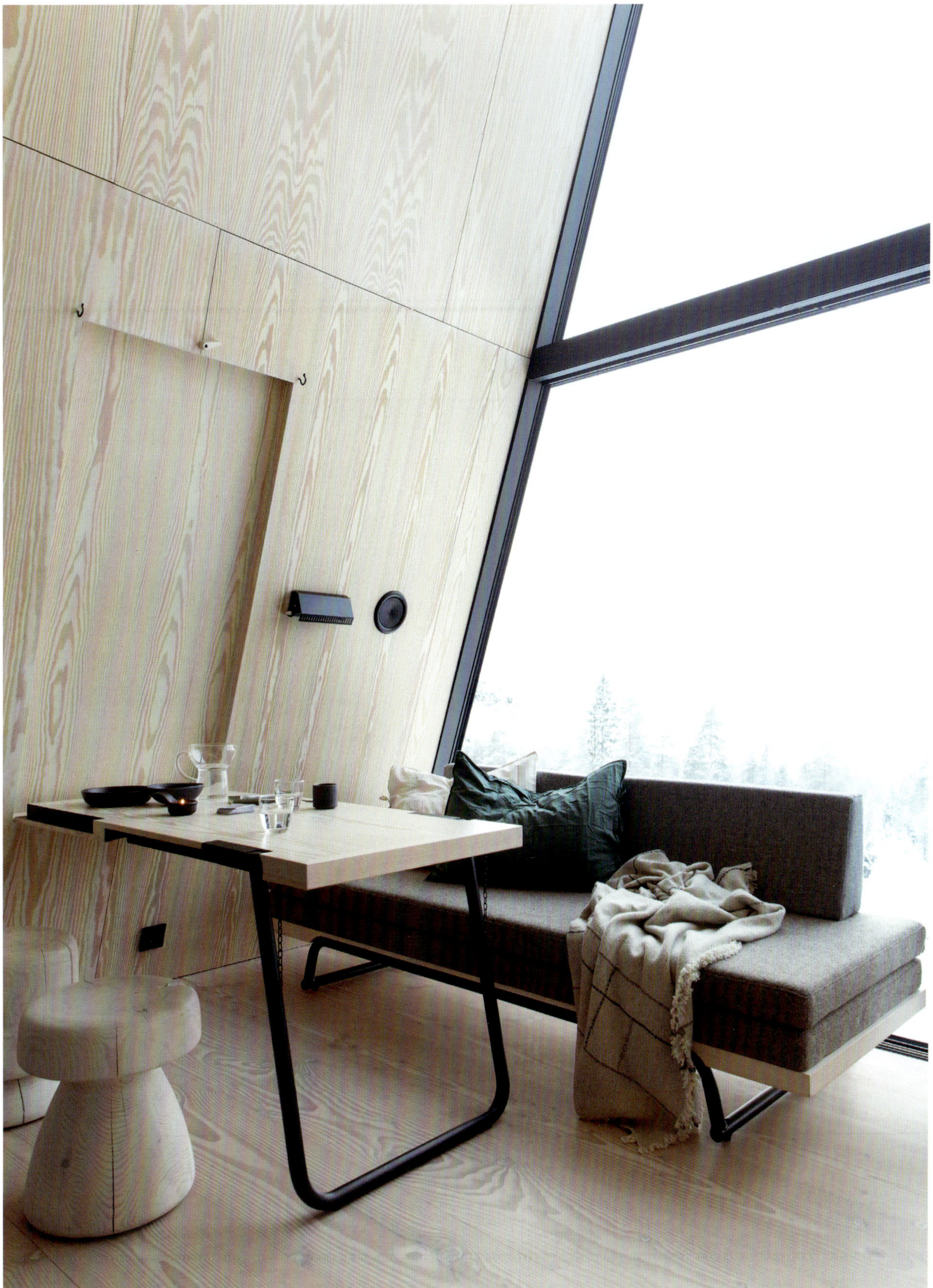

PAN TREETOP CABINS

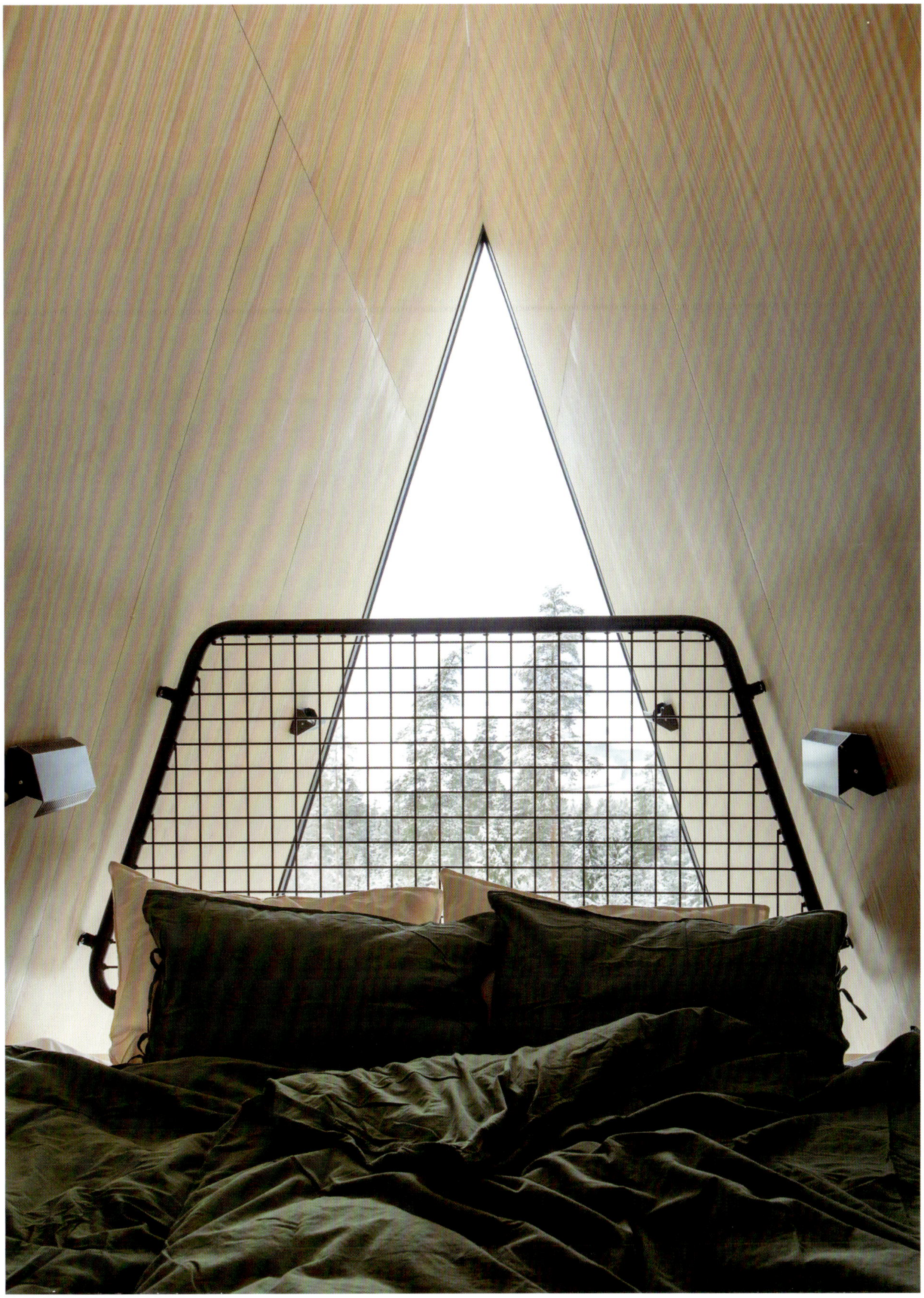

Claudio Beltrame
PIGNA
2017 | Malborghetto Valbruna, Italy

Pigna is the Italian word for "pine cone," and that is precisely what these treehouses, in Italy's oldest forest, are designed to resemble. Nestling amid spruces on a hilly slope, the pods rest on columns with supporting struts and are further stabilized by brackets that attach to the adjacent tree trunks. The houses are reached by footbridges that curve around each one to form an additional structural cage. Insulated from the Alpine winters with breathable wood fiber, their ovoid form is strong, yet retains a sense of fragility and tactility. Each volume is clad in larch shingles to suggest the roughness of a pine cone's surface. Inside, larch also lines the floors and walls, creating a snug, nest-like space. Considering the size and form, each treehouse manages to pack in a surprising amount. On the first floor there are panoramic views of the mountains through large windows, while on the second there is a living area, kitchen, bathroom, more generous glazing, and a balcony. The apex of each "cone" contains a small bedroom, and a skylight above the bed enables nighttime stargazing high among the the snow-dusted trees.

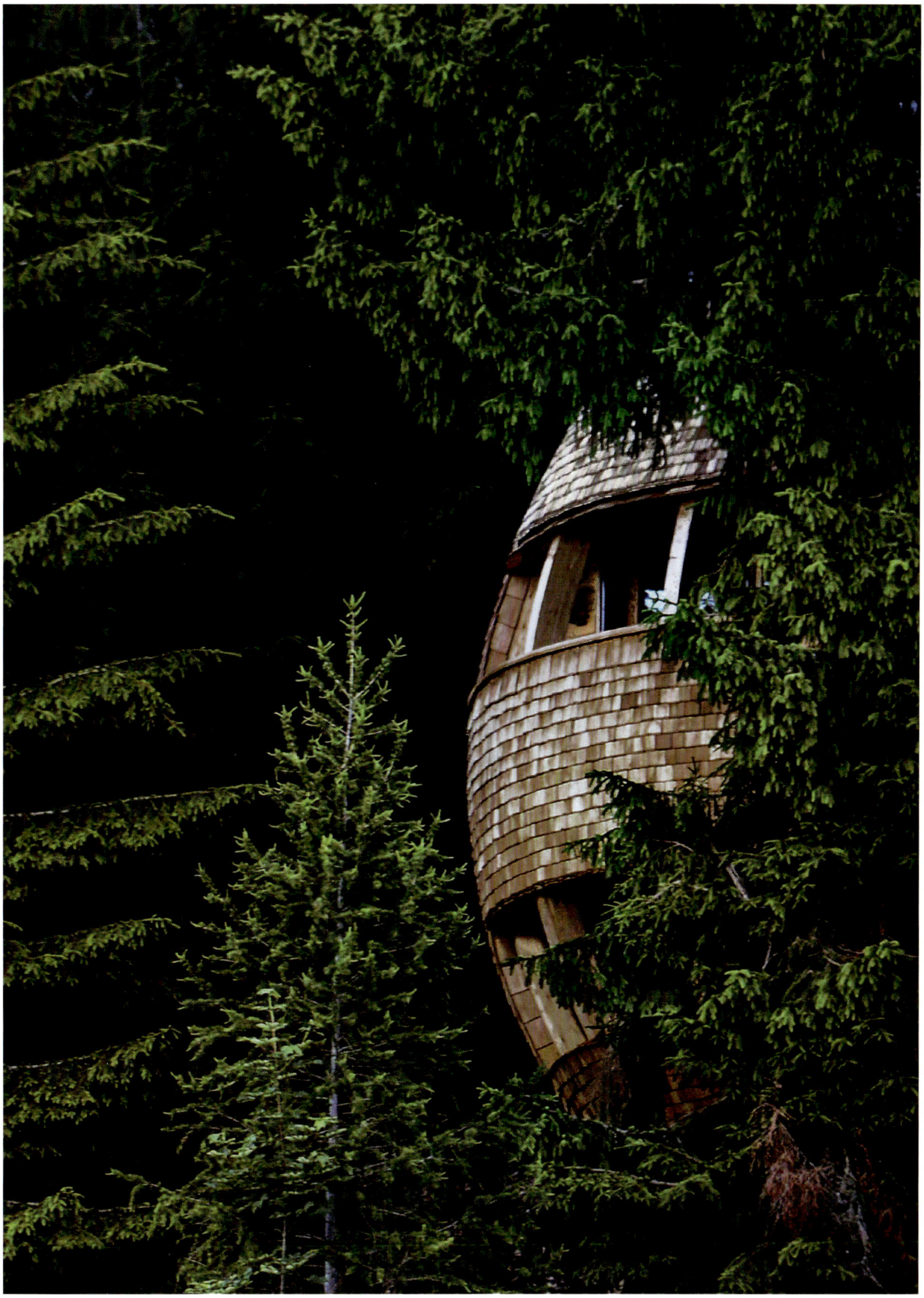

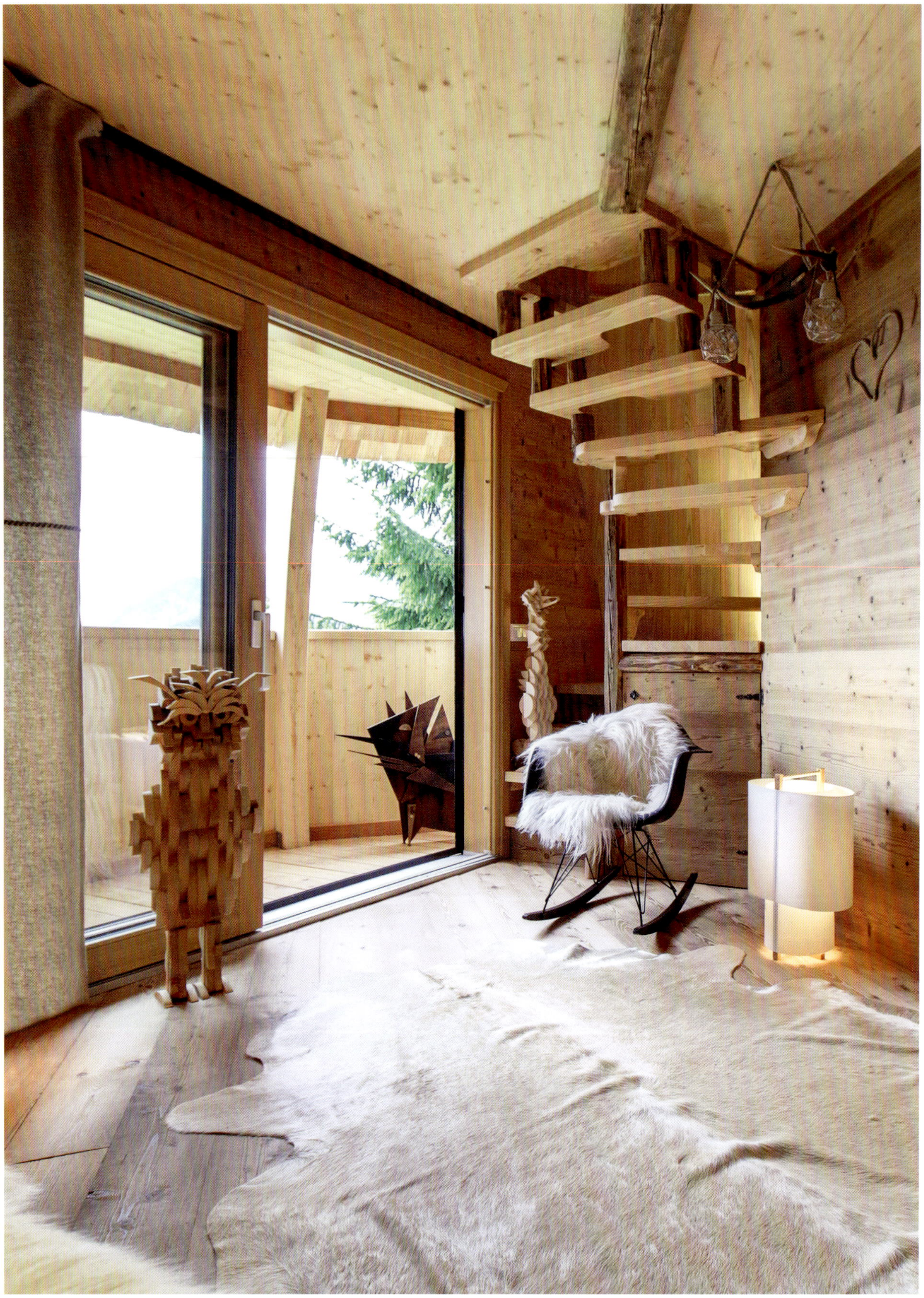

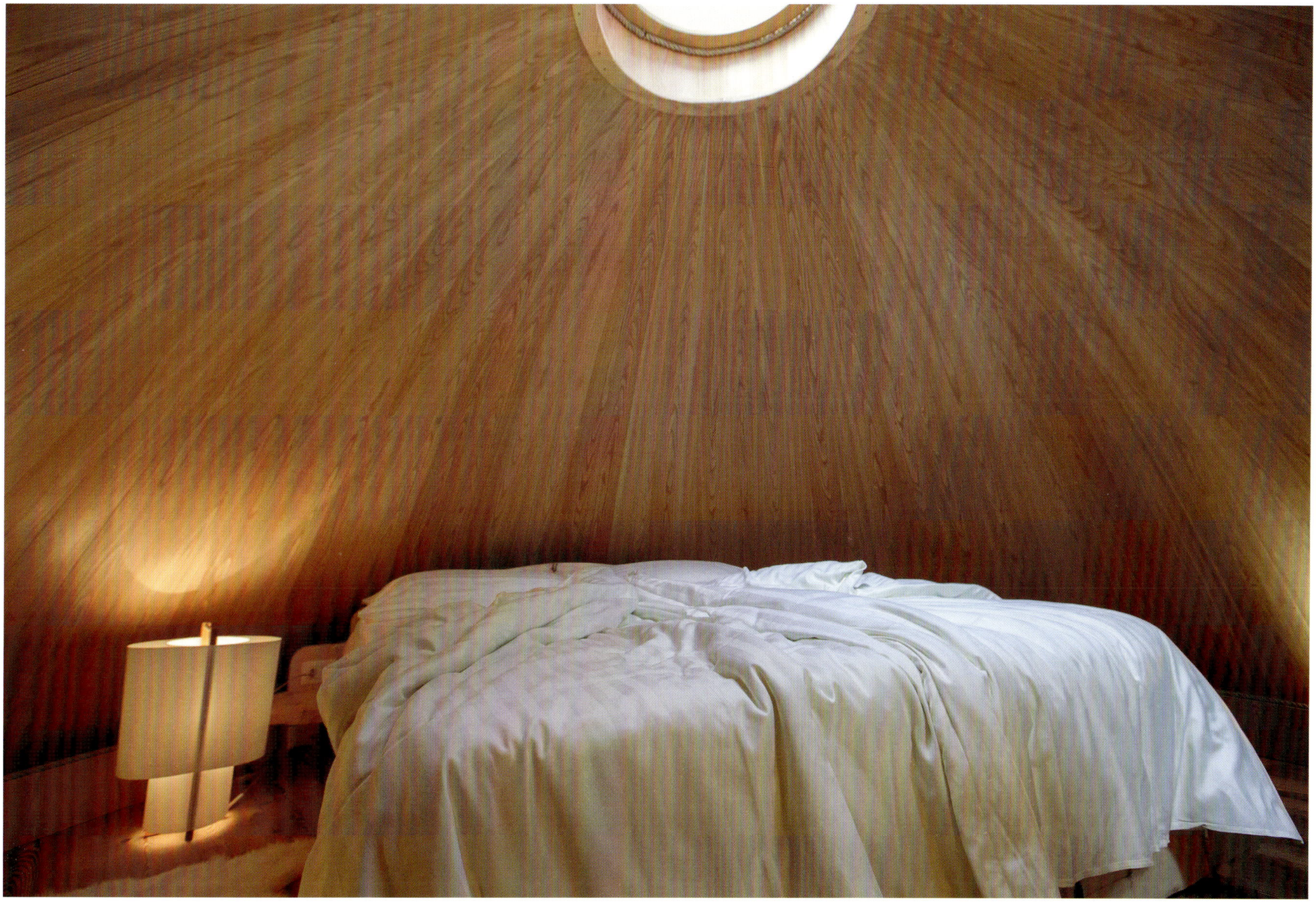

CO-LAB Design Office
TULUM TREEHOUSE
2017 | Tulum, Mexico

An island amid a sylvan sea, this Mexican vacation retreat reaches high above the tree canopy to offer incredible views over the jungle and to the ocean beyond. The four-story retreat is an adaptation of an existing townhouse that had already been added to several times. Tulum-based architecture studio CO-LAB totally reconfigured it to make the flow between rooms more logical and to forge a stronger connection to the outdoors. The intention was to entice guests outside in myriad ways: decks and open-sided dining areas were added, and every one of the five bedrooms has its own terrace with showers and hammocks. CO-LAB's design also made the encircling palm and mangrove trees an integral part of the house. On the lower levels, they practically clamor to enter windows and balconies, screening out the sun and casting complex patterns of shade; every opening frames views of acid-green palmate forms. But the polished white concrete of the floors and walls keeps rooms light and bright, and the same material appears on the sleek exterior. Locally sourced dark tzalam wood provides a tonal contrast for door and window frames, flooring, and supporting pillars. The interior is decorated simply with linens, Oaxacan rugs, reed baskets, and wood from local forests. Everything is calculated to create an organic, sensorily rich, and restorative experience.

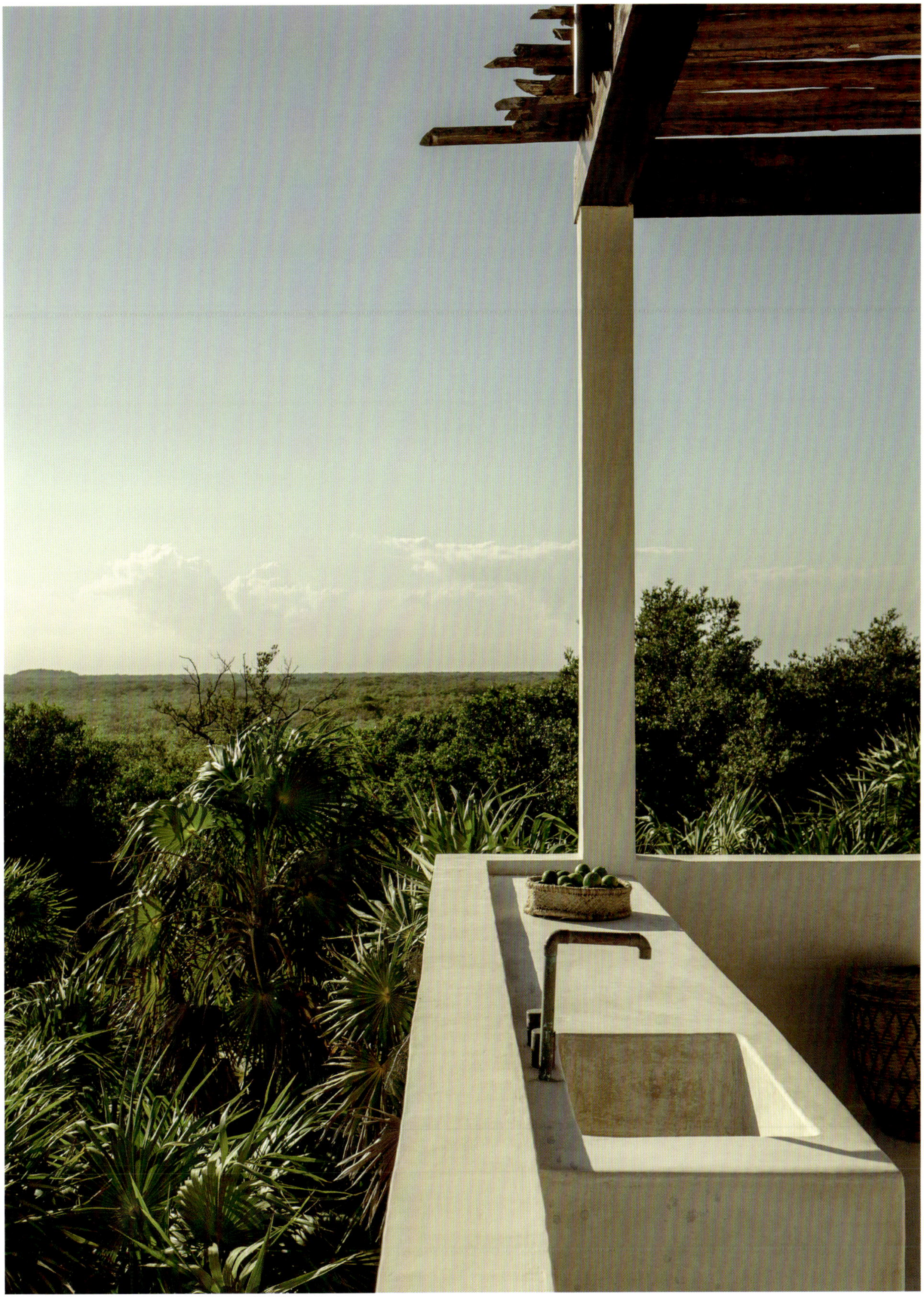

TULUM TREEHOUSE

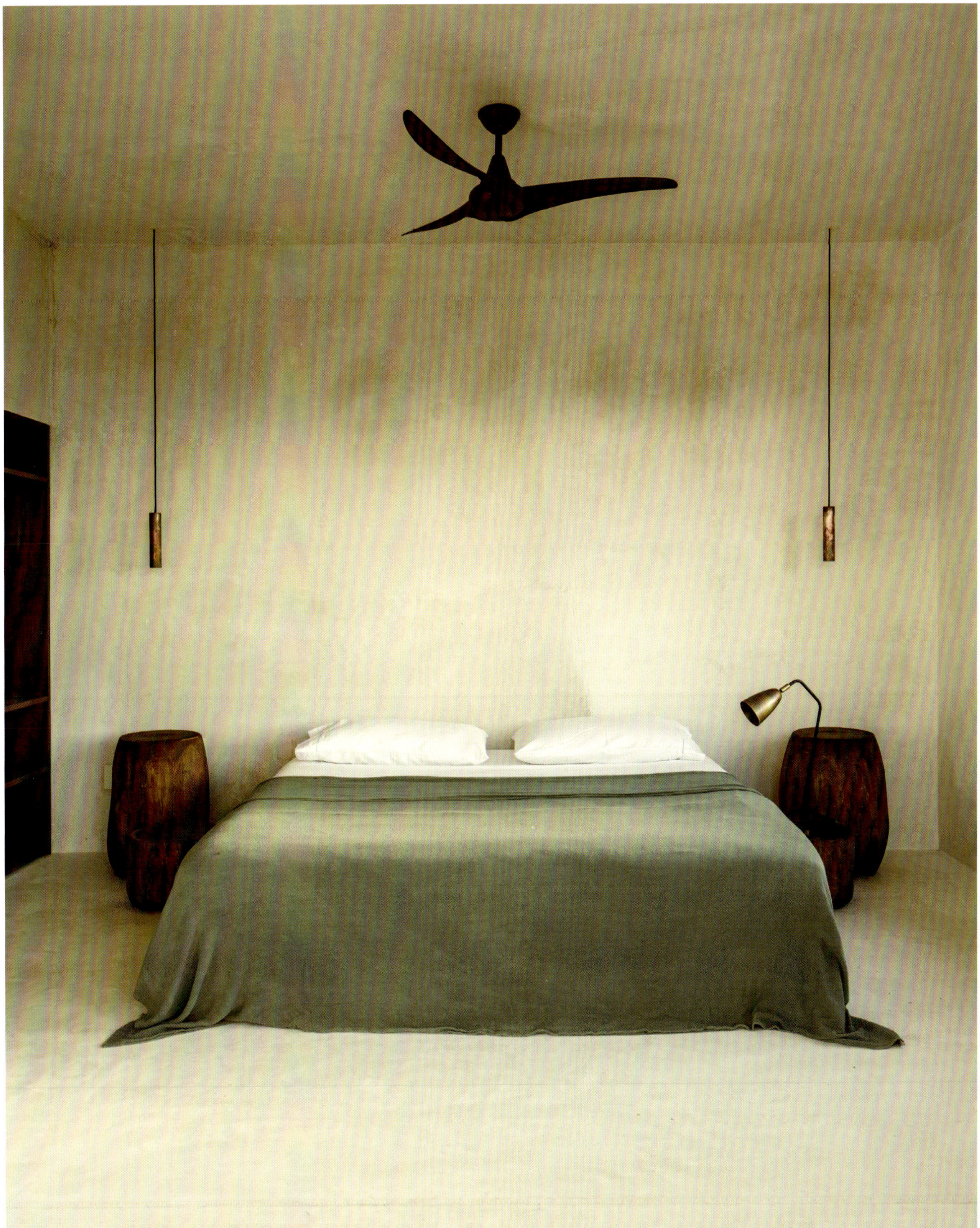

TULUM TREEHOUSE

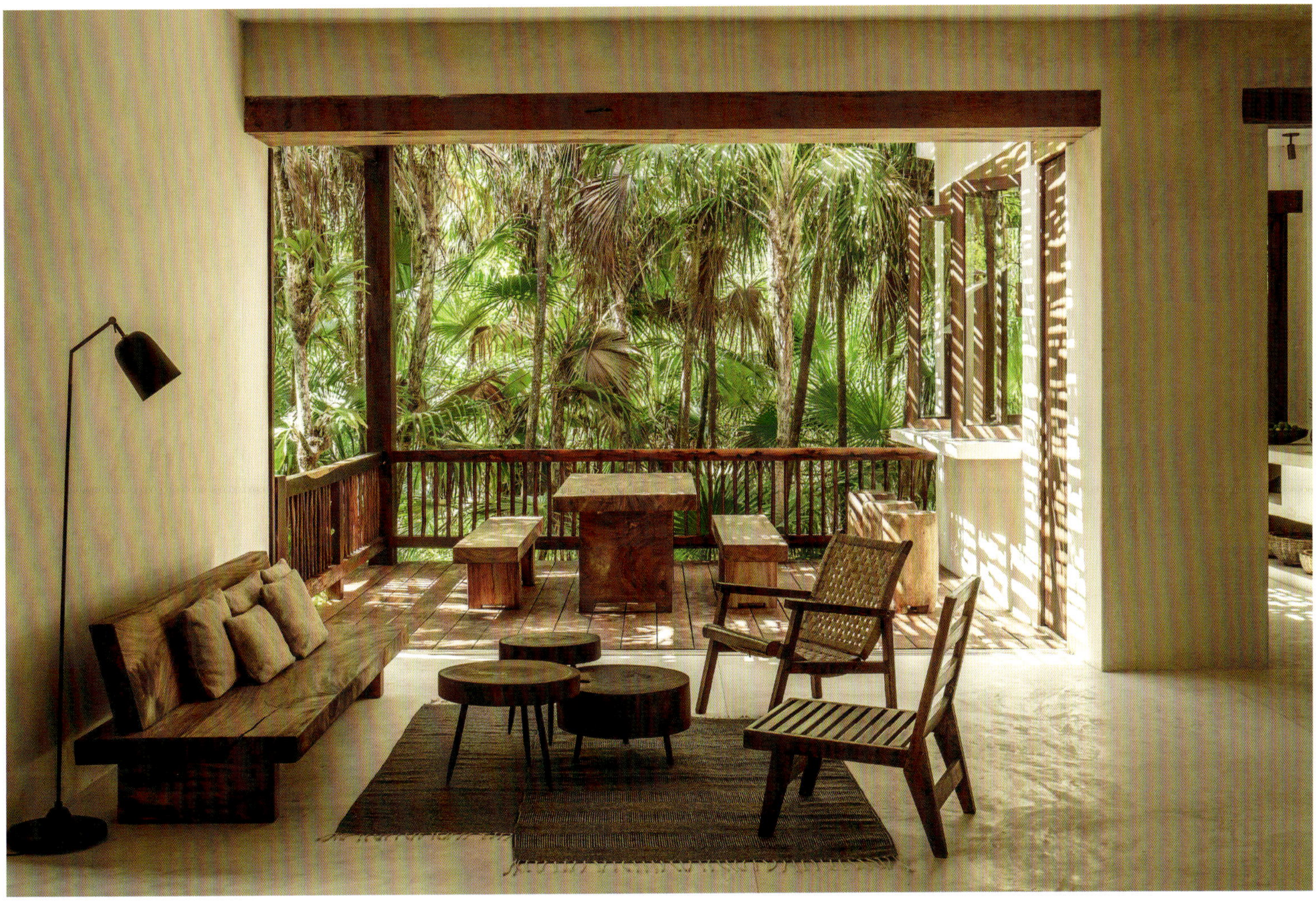

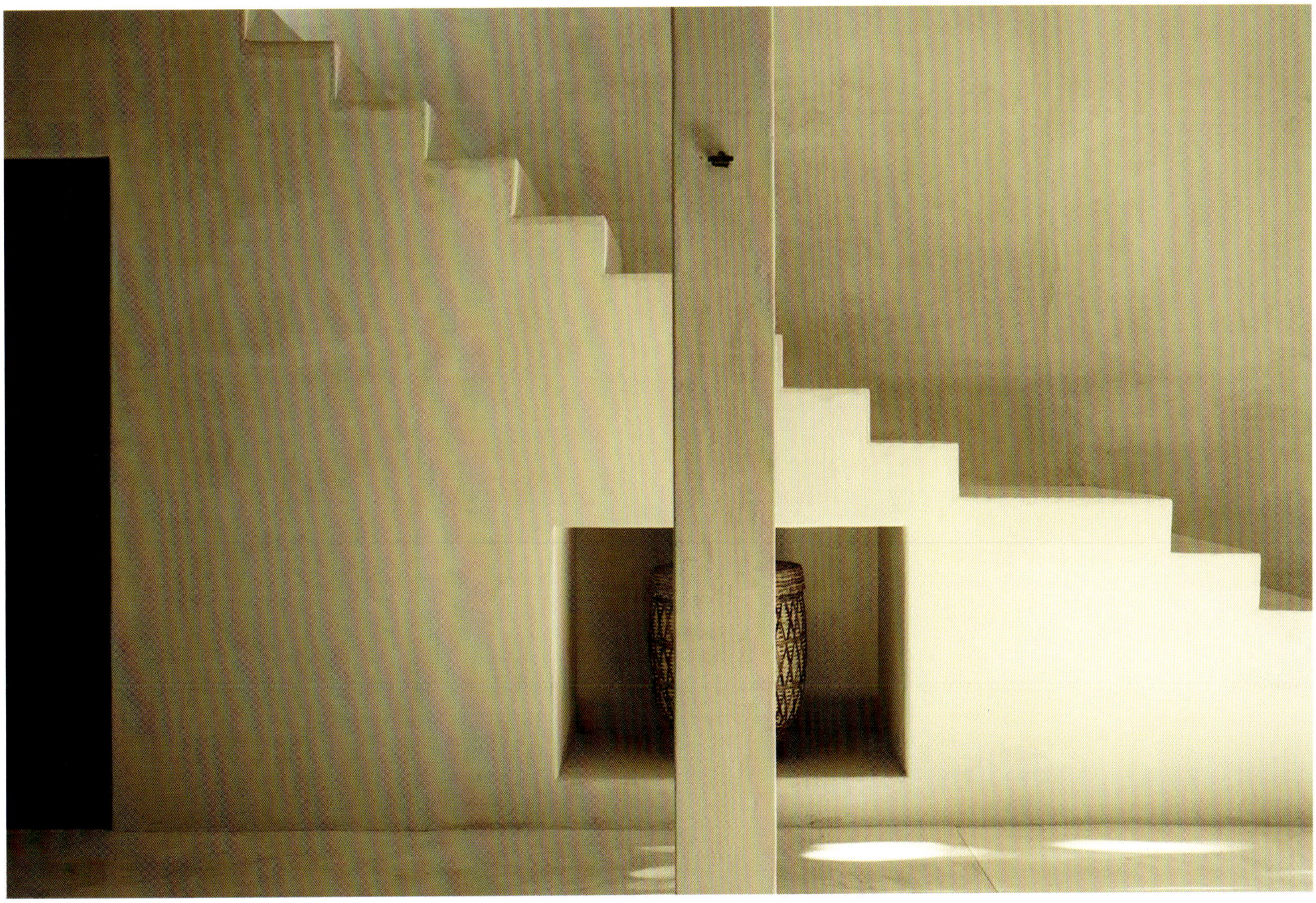

[2] EARTH

80 Studio MK27
CATUÇABA
HOUSE

86 Imbue Design
BOAR SHOAT

90 Architectural Affairs
and Diogo Aguiar
Studio
PAVILION HOUSE

94 Fernanda Canales and
Claudia Rodriguez
CASA BRUMA

100 Rama Estudio
CASA PATIOS

104 Wheeler Kearns
Architects
RAVINE HOUSE

108 Patisandhika and
Dan Mitchell
A BRUTALIST
TROPICAL HOME

114 Mary Arnold-Forster
Architects
AN CALA

118 Alexis Dornier
HOUSE
APERTURE

122 Pérez Palacios
Arquitectos
ACULCO
RESIDENCE

128 Format Architects
BUXTON RISE

132 SPINN Arkitekter and
Format Engineers
VARDEN

According to countless creation myths, human beings were first formed of clay; our affinity with raw earth clearly goes back many thousands of years. Fundamental to our identity, earth is also essential to human life as both an organic medium where things grow, and a material that can be shaped for building.

The designs of the houses in this chapter share a determination to leave as small a footprint as possible, using the natural resources available to form bricks of adobe, walls of rammed earth, or tiles of clay. It is often the sites' isolation that leads to this approach—in remote areas, it is too difficult or unsustainable to have materials transported to the location. This turns out to be an advantage: older construction techniques are rediscovered, forming new idioms in the process. To avoid harming the land, often architects intentionally restrict themselves: building up rather than out, choosing a cluster of single-story dwellings over a multi-level site, or forgoing panoramic glazing to avoid blasting a rocky location.

Many houses here are literally dug into the landscape in order to blend in; most are low-slung and nestle into the earth's curves. Natural materials—green roofs, locally excavated stone, or indigenous wood—are sensitively chosen to complement a woodland, hillside, or ravine. This does not mean that all of these dwellings have a particularly rustic aesthetic. Some retain a sleek urban style that nevertheless harmonizes with the surroundings, such as the retreat in the midst of an American prairie, whose bold linearity blends into the landscape through the use of deep, earthy tones. Another project imaginatively used drone imaging to construct the form of a boulder, creating a new archetype for the mountain shelter. Whether camouflaged or making their mark, each one of these houses is part of a rich and growing seam of environmentally conscious contemporary architecture.

Studio MK27
CATUÇABA HOUSE
2016 | Catuçaba, Brazil

Catuçaba House is wedged discreetly into a steep hillside in a remote corner of São Luíz do Paraitinga. Because of the difficulty of transporting materials to the site, the architects made imaginative use of local natural materials. They excavated soil to create adobe walls and clay tiles for the interiors that keep the house cool in summer. Side walls are made from rammed earth, while eucalyptus is used to provide movable screening on the floor-to-ceiling panoramic windows overlooking the undulating forms of the valley. The roof is covered in native plants to make it blend in with its surroundings. The bulk of the structure was prefabricated using FSC-certified cross-laminated timber to make it easy to assemble in this location. Formally, the house consists of an orthogonal one-story sliver sandwiched between two large, flat planes, one acting as a jutting terrace, the other the cantilevering roof. The site's uneven topography means the house needed to be supported on seven Y-shaped pillars driven into the hillside. Featuring solar panels, a wind turbine, and a rain-collection system, Catuçaba House is completely off-grid. The careful use of nearby wood, soil, and plants makes the residence almost seem to have grown, slowly and organically, from the hillside.

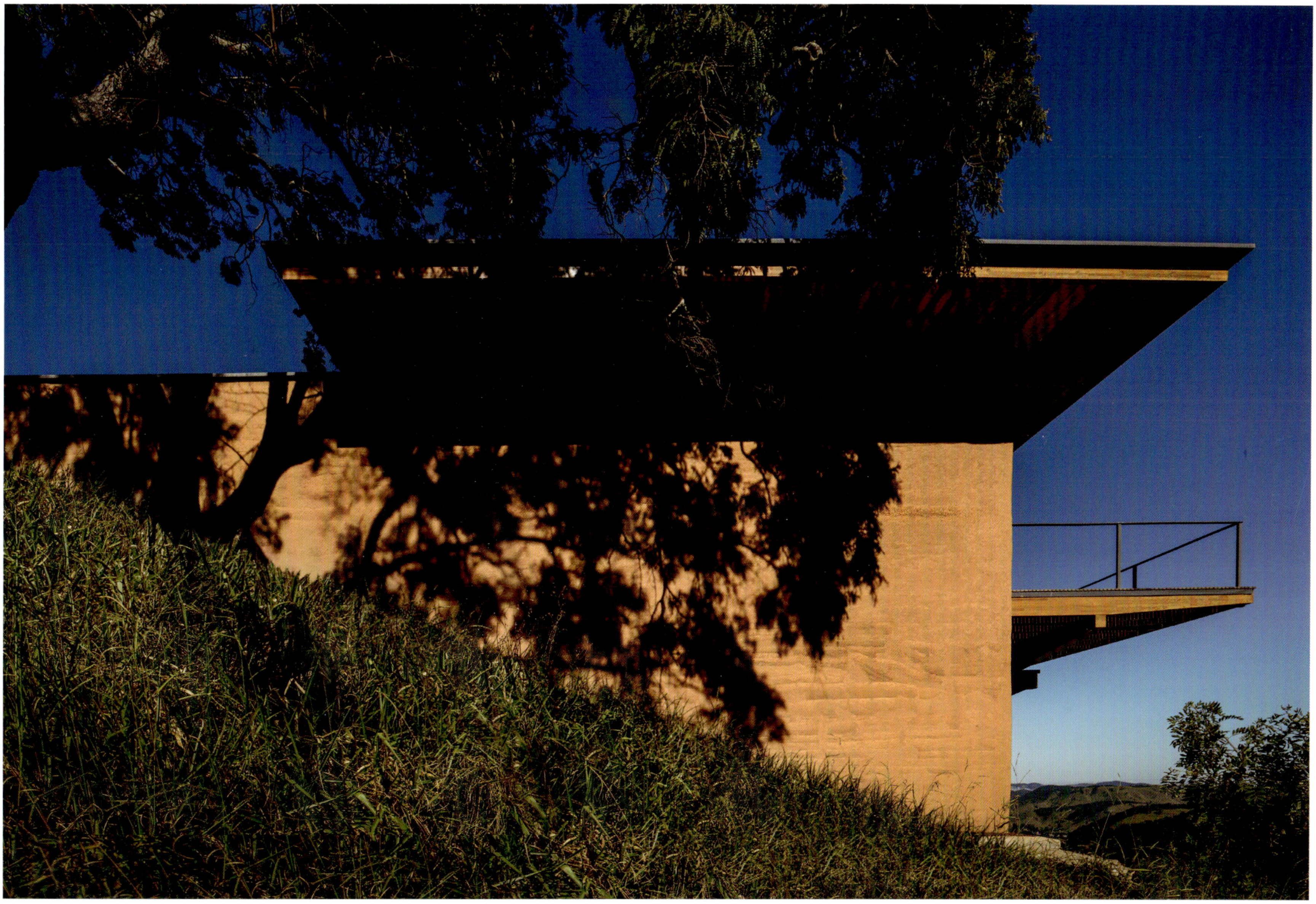

CATUÇABA HOUSE

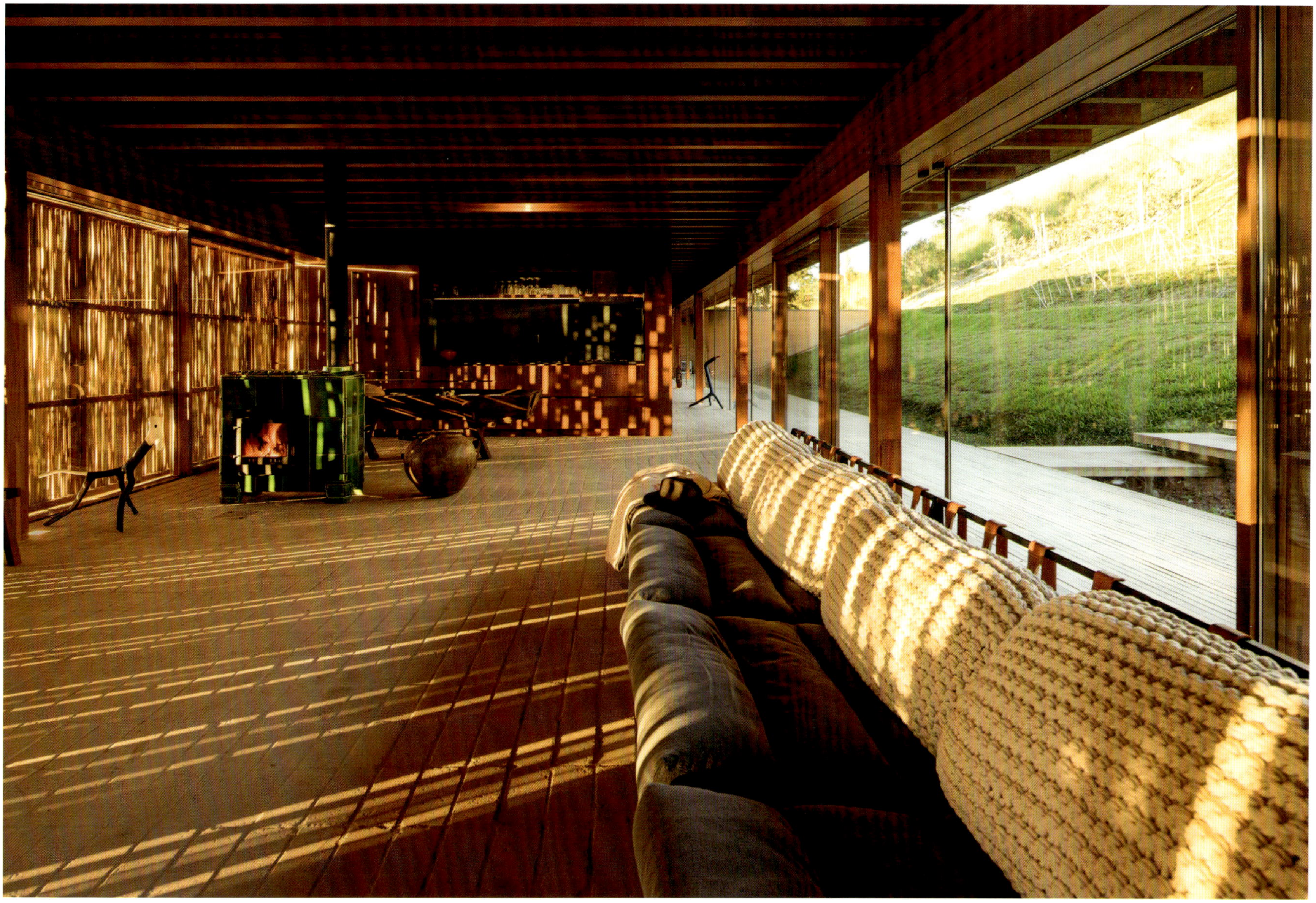

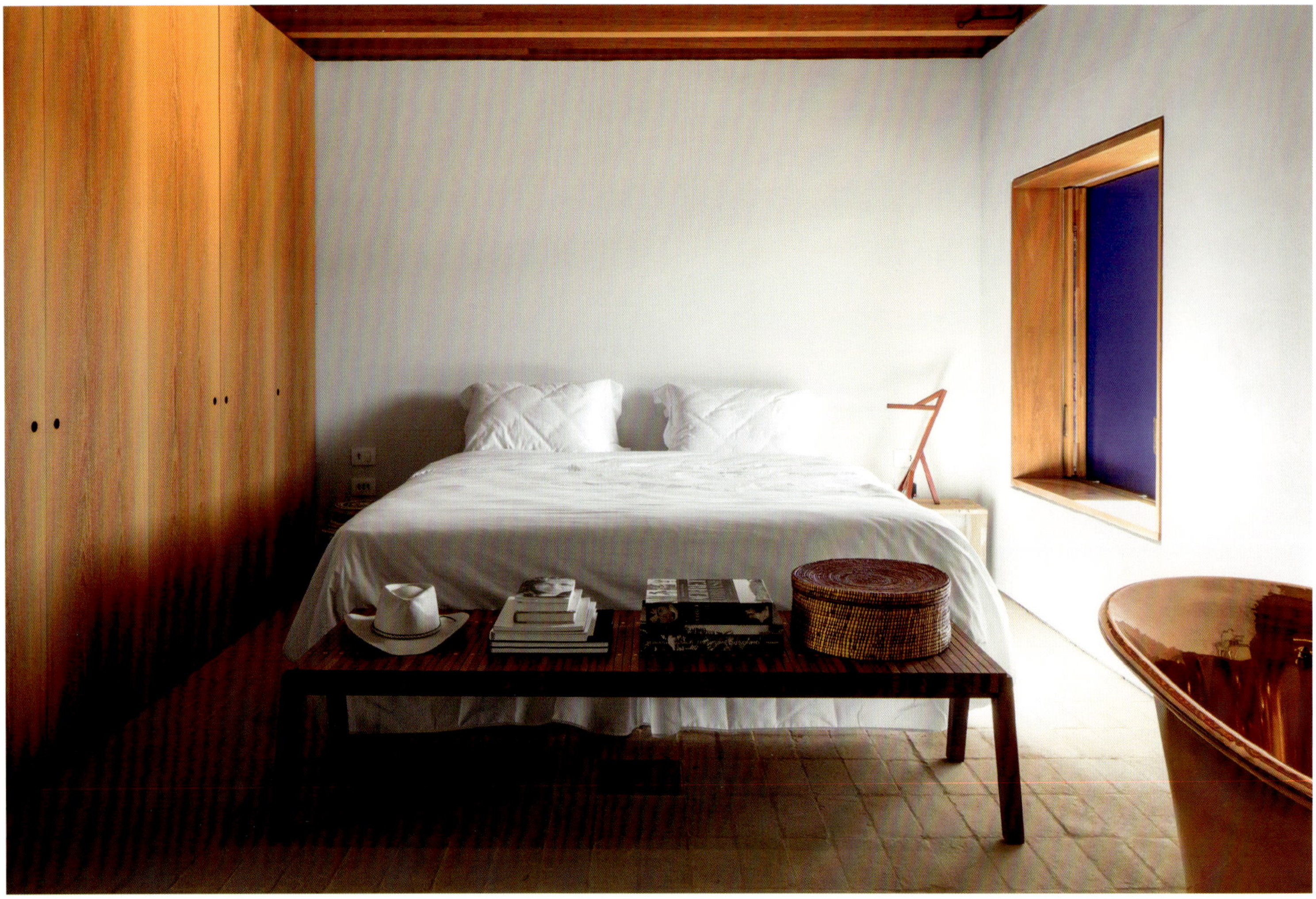

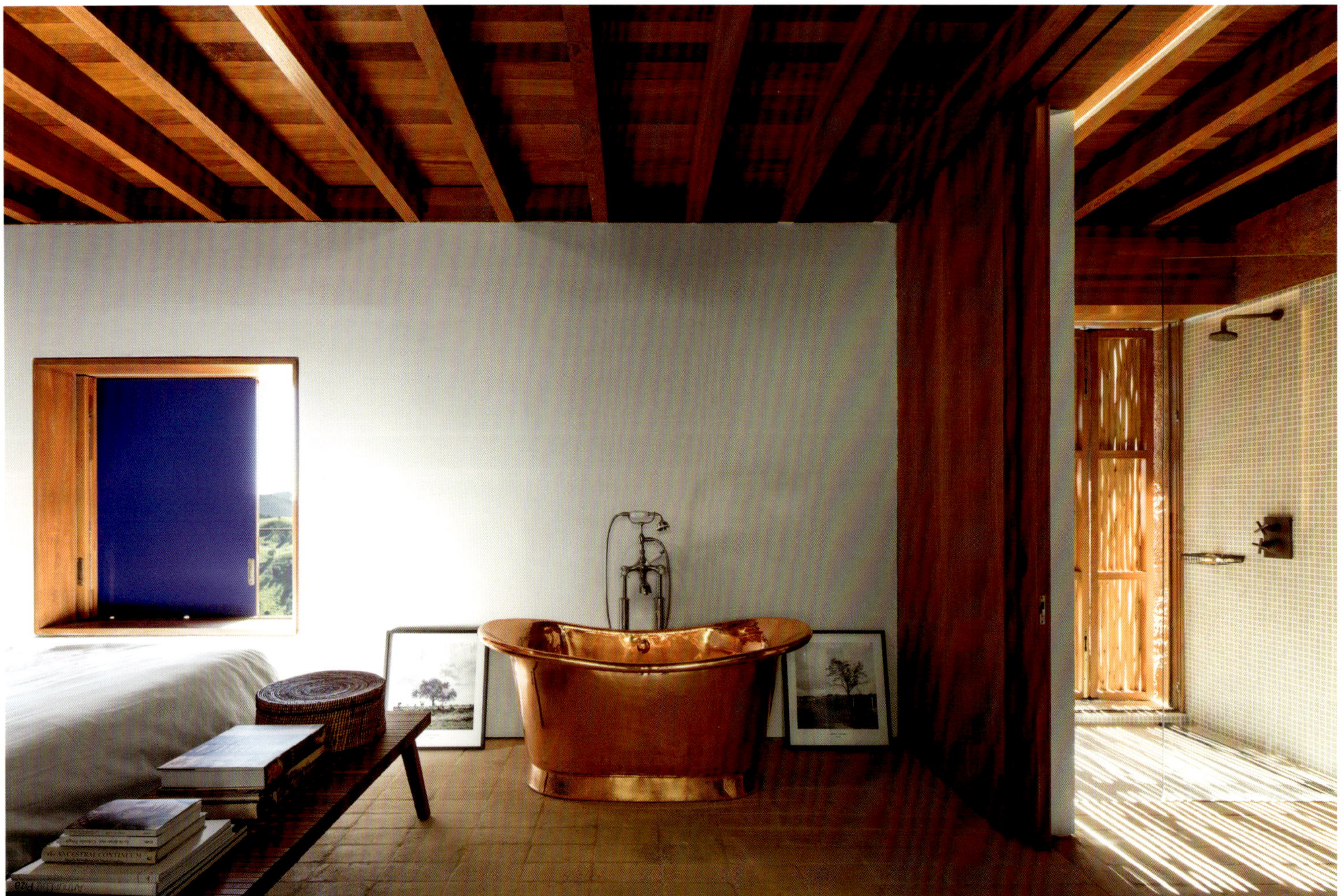

CATUÇABA HOUSE

Imbue Design
BOAR SHOAT
2019 | Bear Lake, ID, USA

Situated on a ridge of the Bear River mountain range in Idaho, Boar Shoat was conceived as a retreat where a family could escape modern life and totally unplug from technology. Although the design is fully in sympathy with the Idaho landscape, it retains a sleek, almost urban aesthetic. Three separate orthogonal volumes—a main residence, guest wing, and garage—are drawn together by a large, flat roof that forms an entry porch, punched through with an oculus to draw in light. The overhanging roof and strong horizontality of the home owe a debt to prairie architecture, but Boar Shoat also has a slightly industrial demeanor, clad in dark-bronze metal panels, whose accordion-like profile causes them to appear multitonal in the ever-changing light. The house makes a bold visual statement, yet its deep earth coloring complements the yellows, fawns, and greens of the hills. There are no utility connections nearby, so the retreat is completely off-grid—photovoltaic roof arrays generate electricity for heating and power, and insulation and sealing techniques ensure a tight building envelope. Topped up by a local supplier, water is stored in an underground cistern. The interiors are simple but luxurious, combining steel, timber, and unfinished concrete that will mark and patinate over time. Touches of leather, wool, and faux fur add luxury and coziness for winter visits.

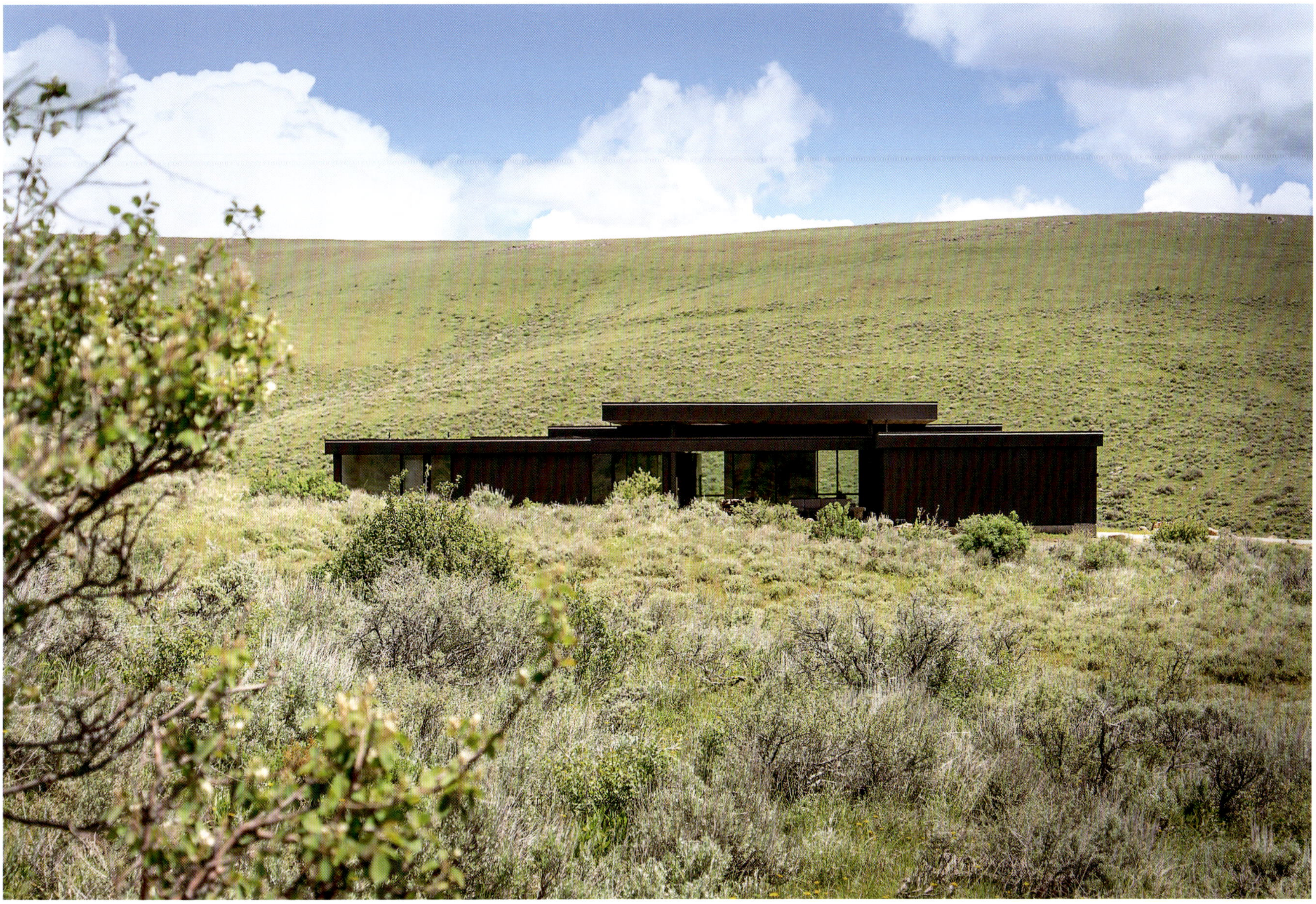

BOAR SHOAT

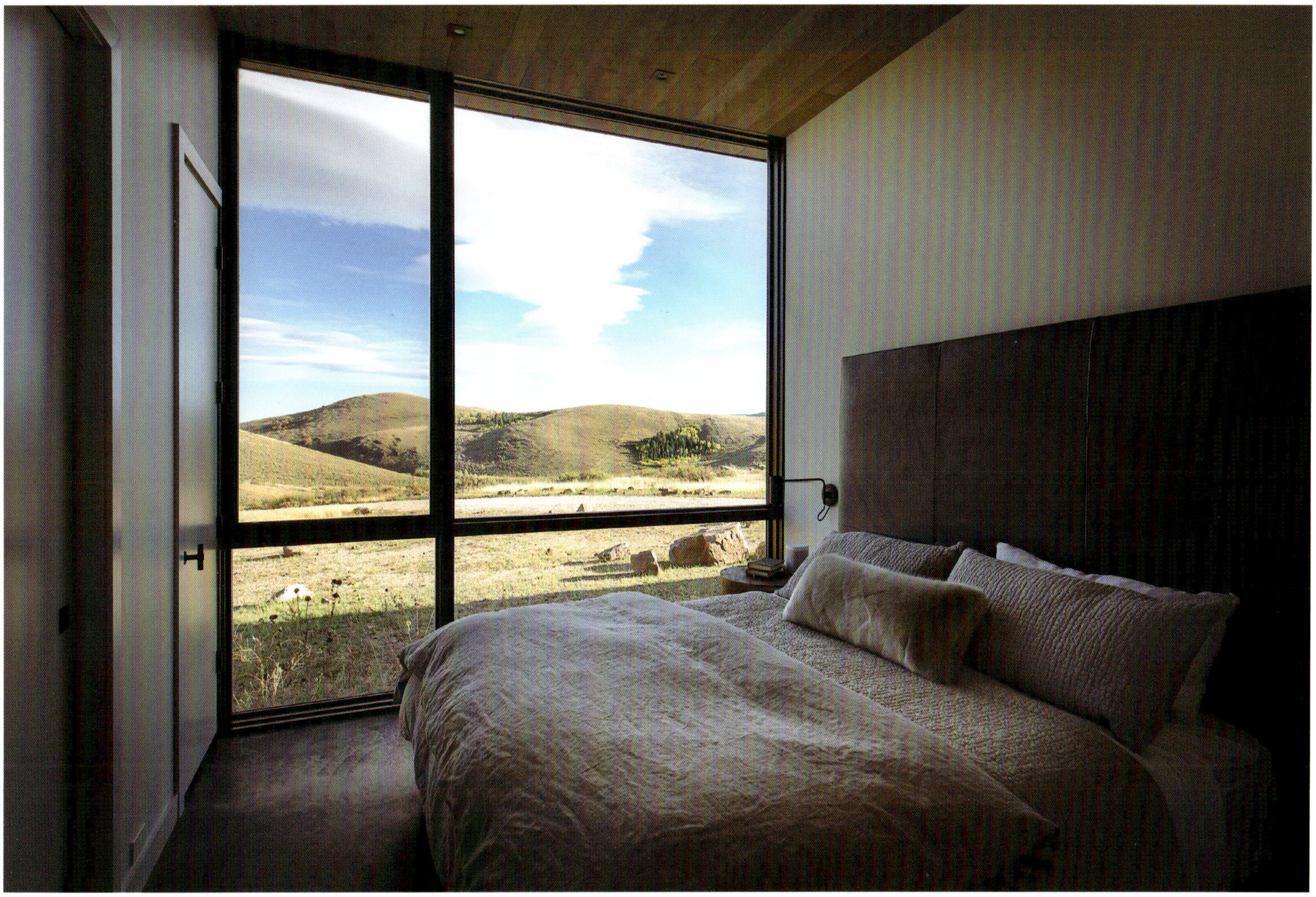

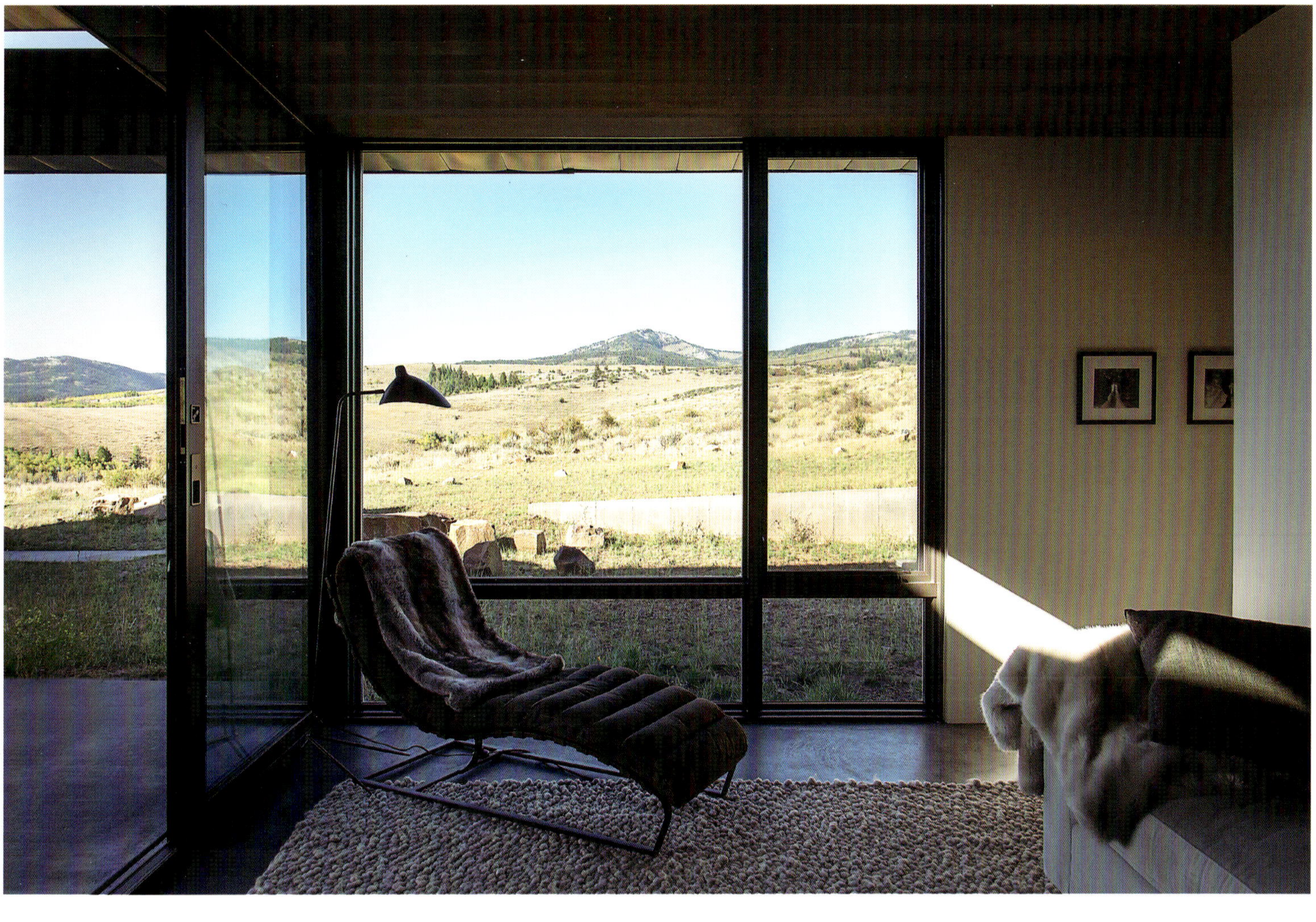

Architectural Affairs and Diogo Aguiar Studio
PAVILION HOUSE
2019 | Guimarães, Portugal

This tiny vacation home in a wine-producing area of northern Portugal was loosely based on the idea of a log cabin but evolved into something far more sophisticated. Surrounded by oak woodland, Pavilion House is sited in beautifully fertile rolling countryside. It rests on an existing granite wine cellar that is built into a hillside. This limits the house's floor plan and lifts the structure so it can enjoy far-reaching landscape views. Far from being a hindrance, the cabin's restricted space was a catalyst for creativity in terms of design. Inside, there is a single open-plan room with seating at its center. When required, the space can convert to a sleeping area when a hidden double bed is pulled down from the wall. Slatted timber bifold doors slide back to reveal a kitchen—this screening is used all the way around the cabin, and the small bathroom is concealed in a similar way. The large windows, one on each side of the building, are carefully positioned to capture particular views—trees and mountain, or vineyard. A skylight cut into the green roof brings in extra illumination. Floors and ceilings are painted black, throwing the visual emphasis on the landscape outside. The base, made of old stone, literally grounds the house in a sense of history, imbuing it with a gravitas that melds surprisingly well with the contemporary aesthetic.

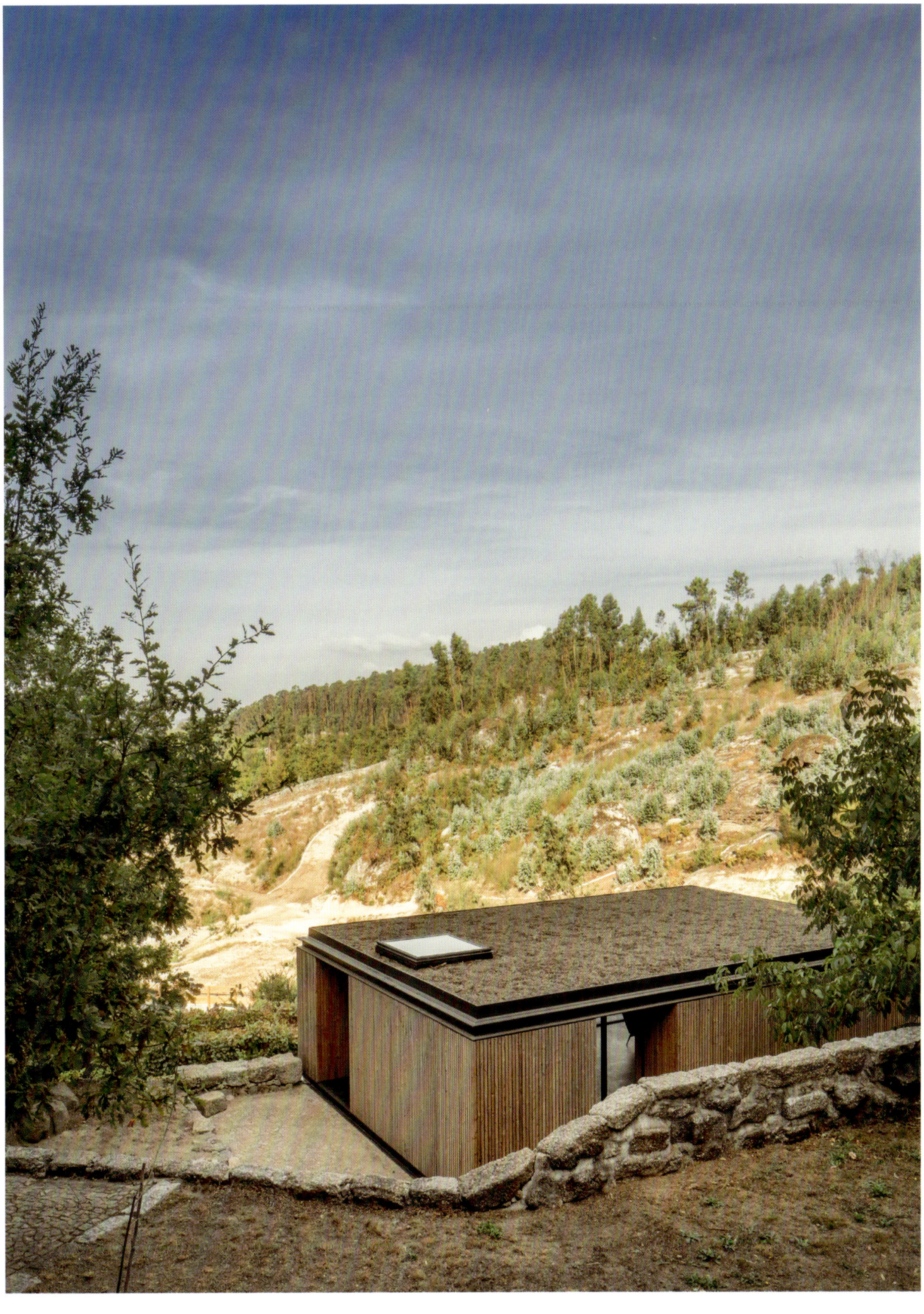

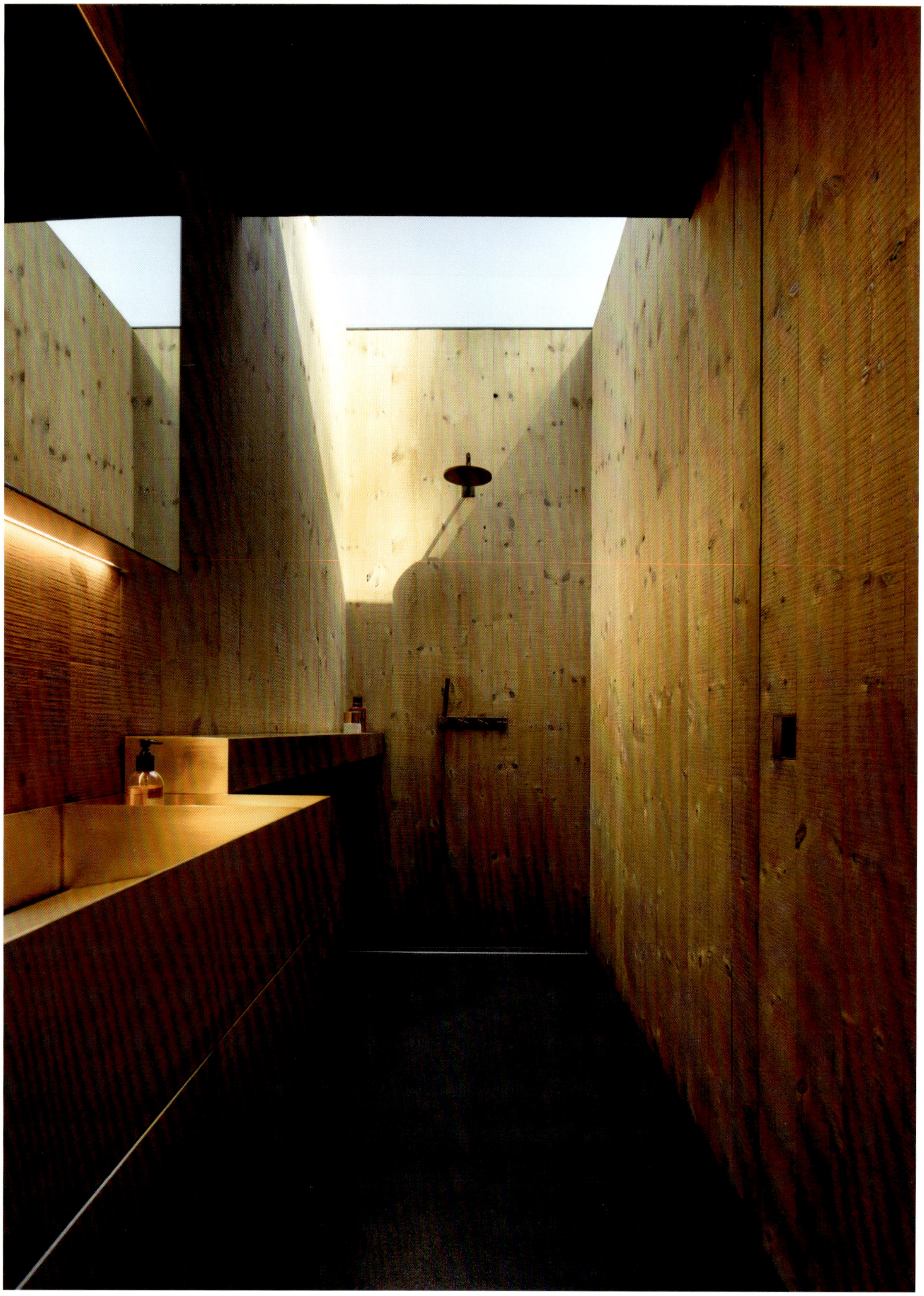

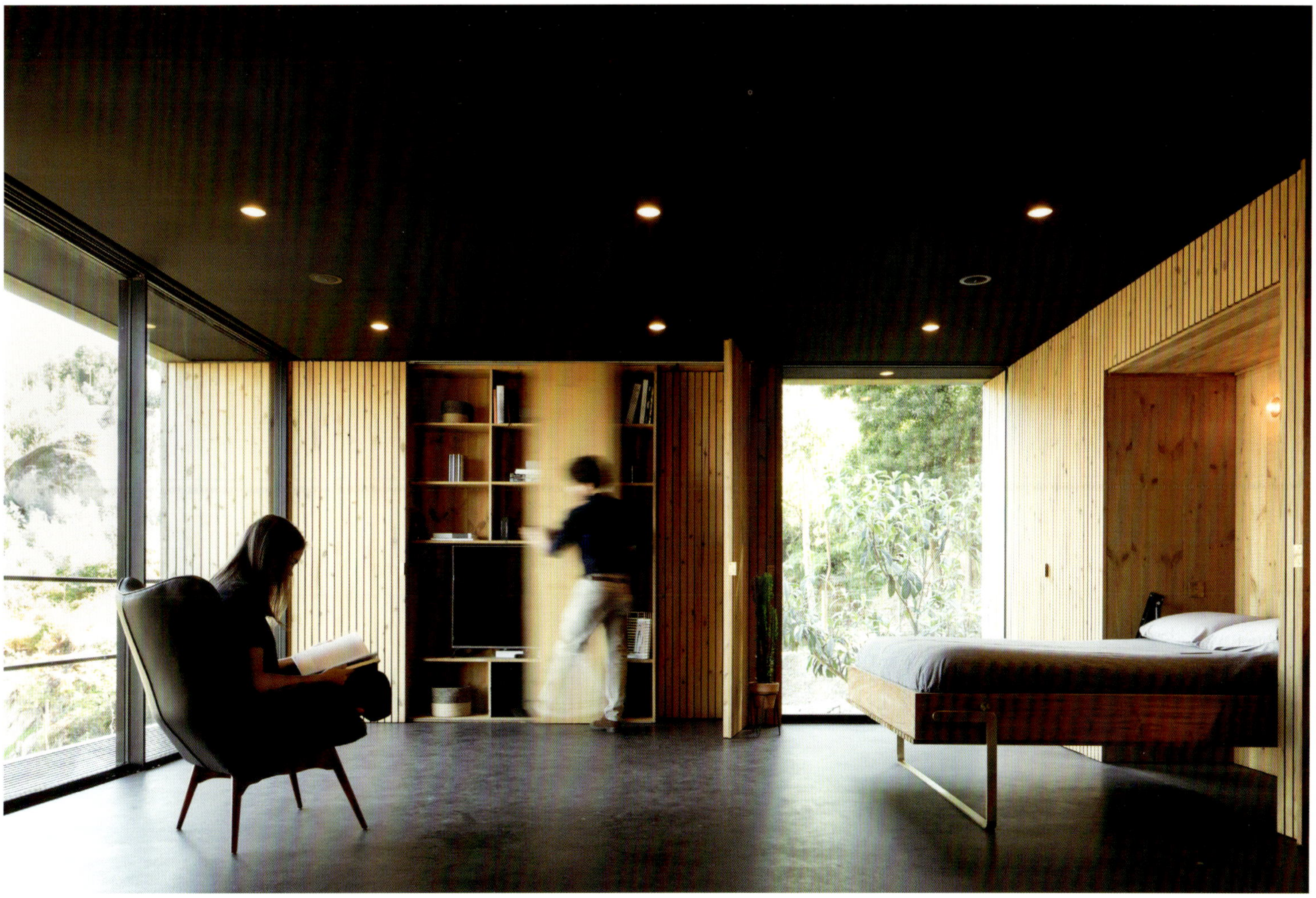

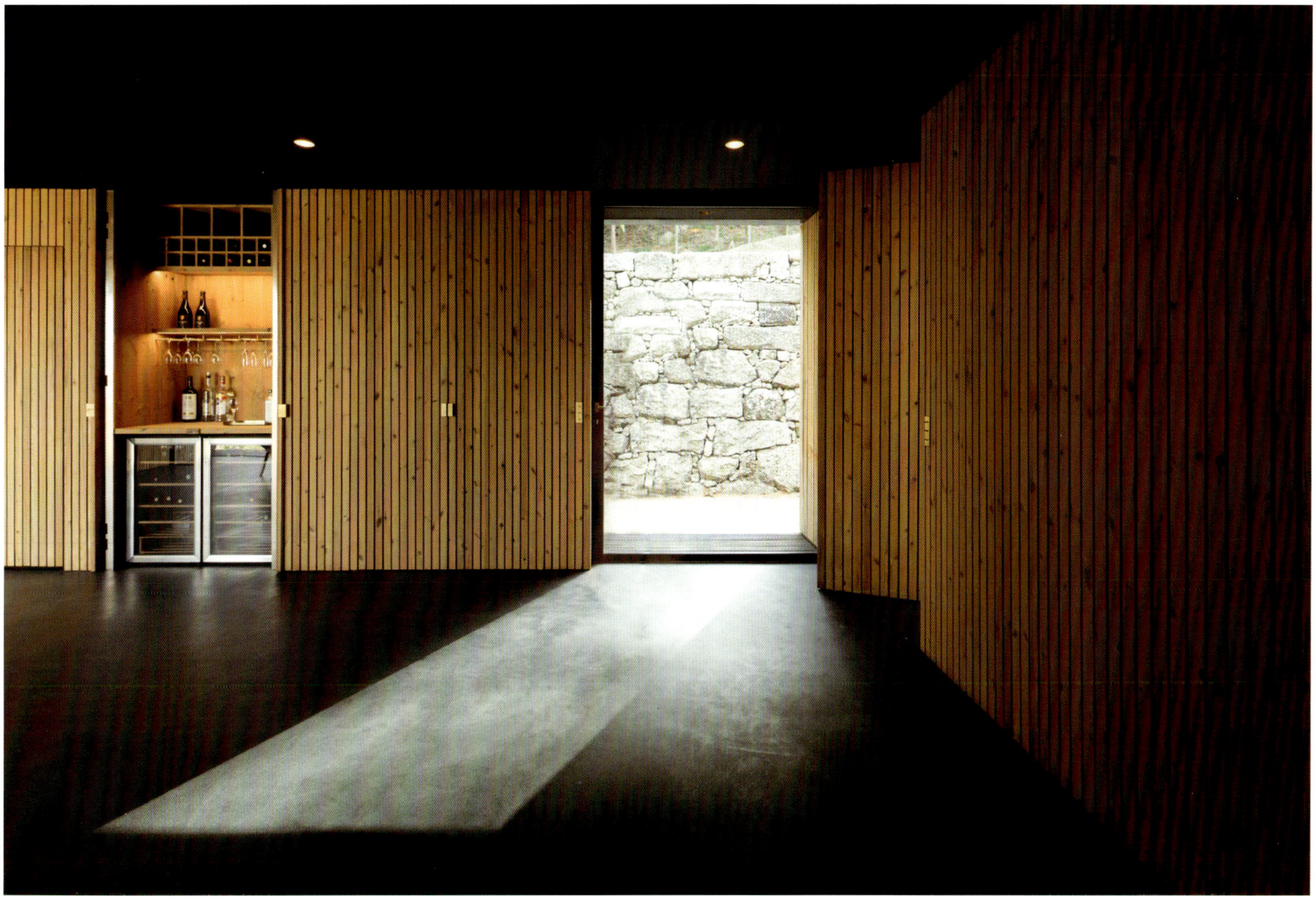

Fernanda Canales and Claudia Rodriguez
CASA BRUMA
2018 | Valle de Bravo, Mexico

At Casa Bruma, the architects' desire to work with nature resulted in a home that is part settlement, part dwelling. Located around 100 miles (160 kilometers) southwest of Mexico City, this "exploded house" is a complex of nine separate rectangular buildings that cluster around a courtyard. The arrangement was chosen primarily to preserve existing trees, but also to achieve the best views and to ensure each space receives enough light at all times of day. The height of each block varies according to the topography, and each has a distinct function—kitchen, dining room, living room, or bedroom. These four units are connected by glazed corridors, opening up views of the landscape as one circulates around the house. There are further blocks for two guest rooms, utilities, garage and a separate caretaker's house. Together yet apart, all face inward toward the courtyard, but on the opposite side, enjoy extensive countryside views. Board-formed black concrete, wood, stone, and glass are the main materials, and their muted tones make the house seem as if it were part of the earth. But green is the dominant color: ferns send tendrils up seemingly monolithic walls, four blocks have plant-covered roofs, and one terrace has a self-contained garden. The village-like huddle of miniature homes fuses a sense of community with a deep empathy for nature.

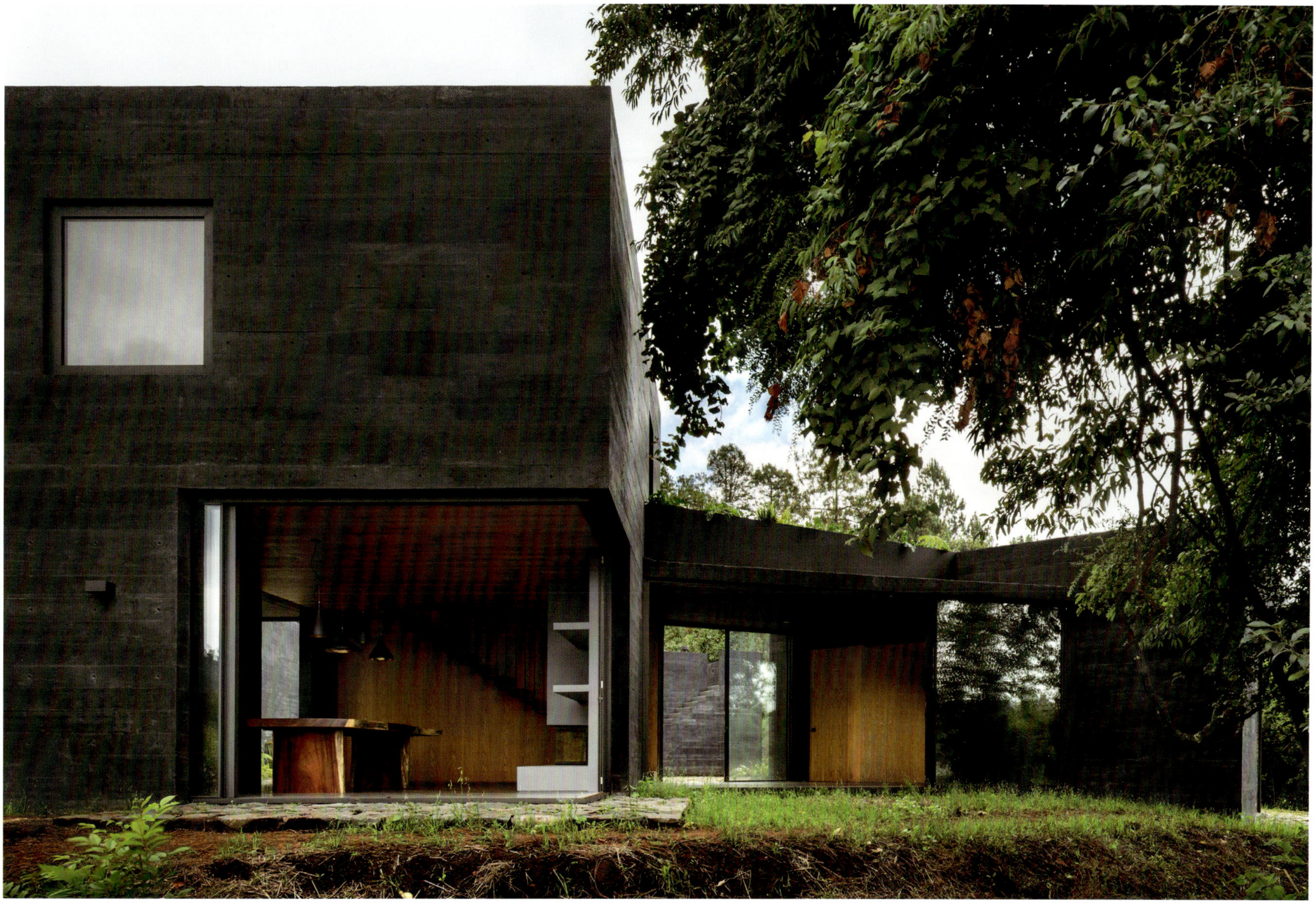

CASA BRUMA

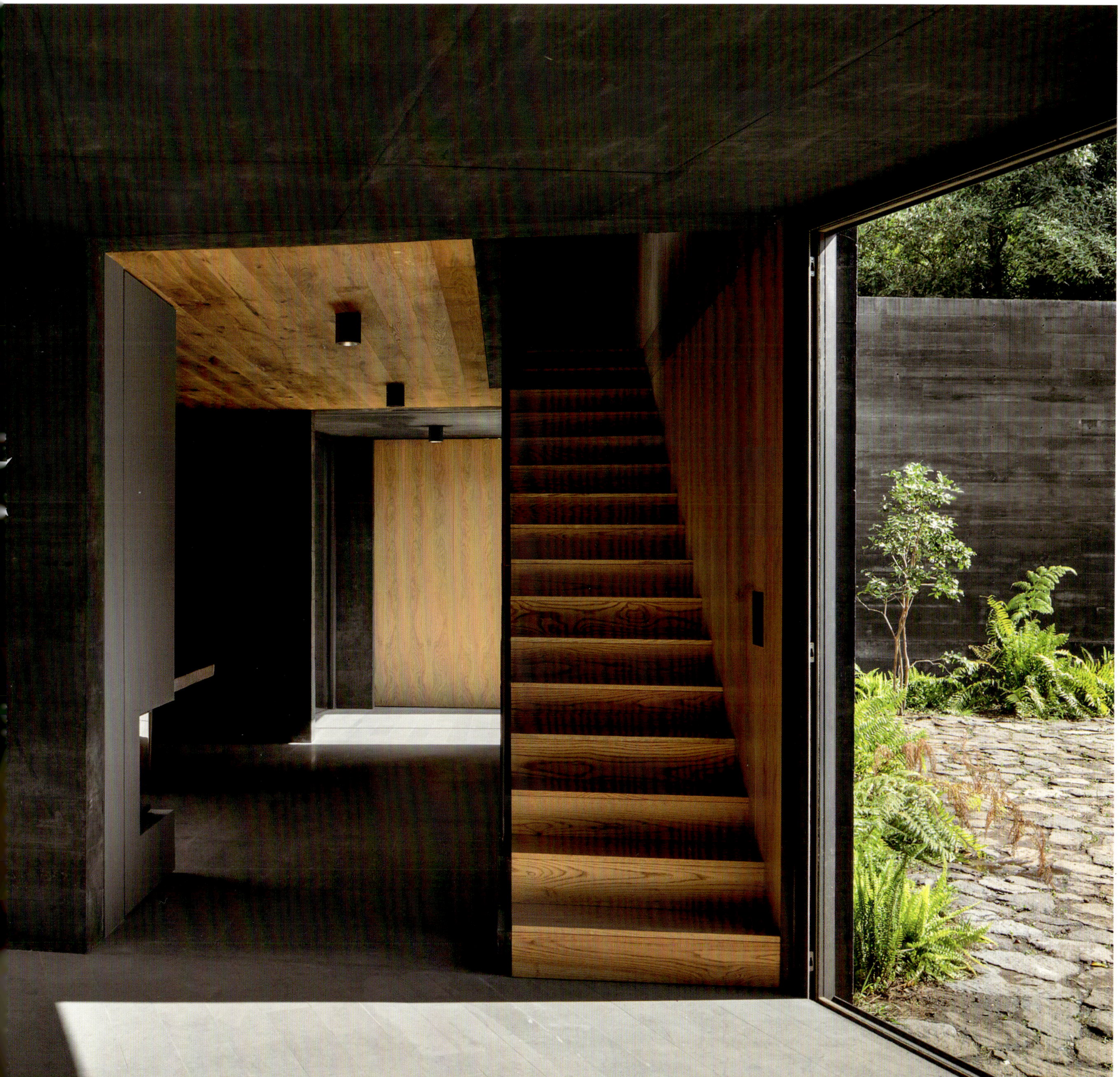

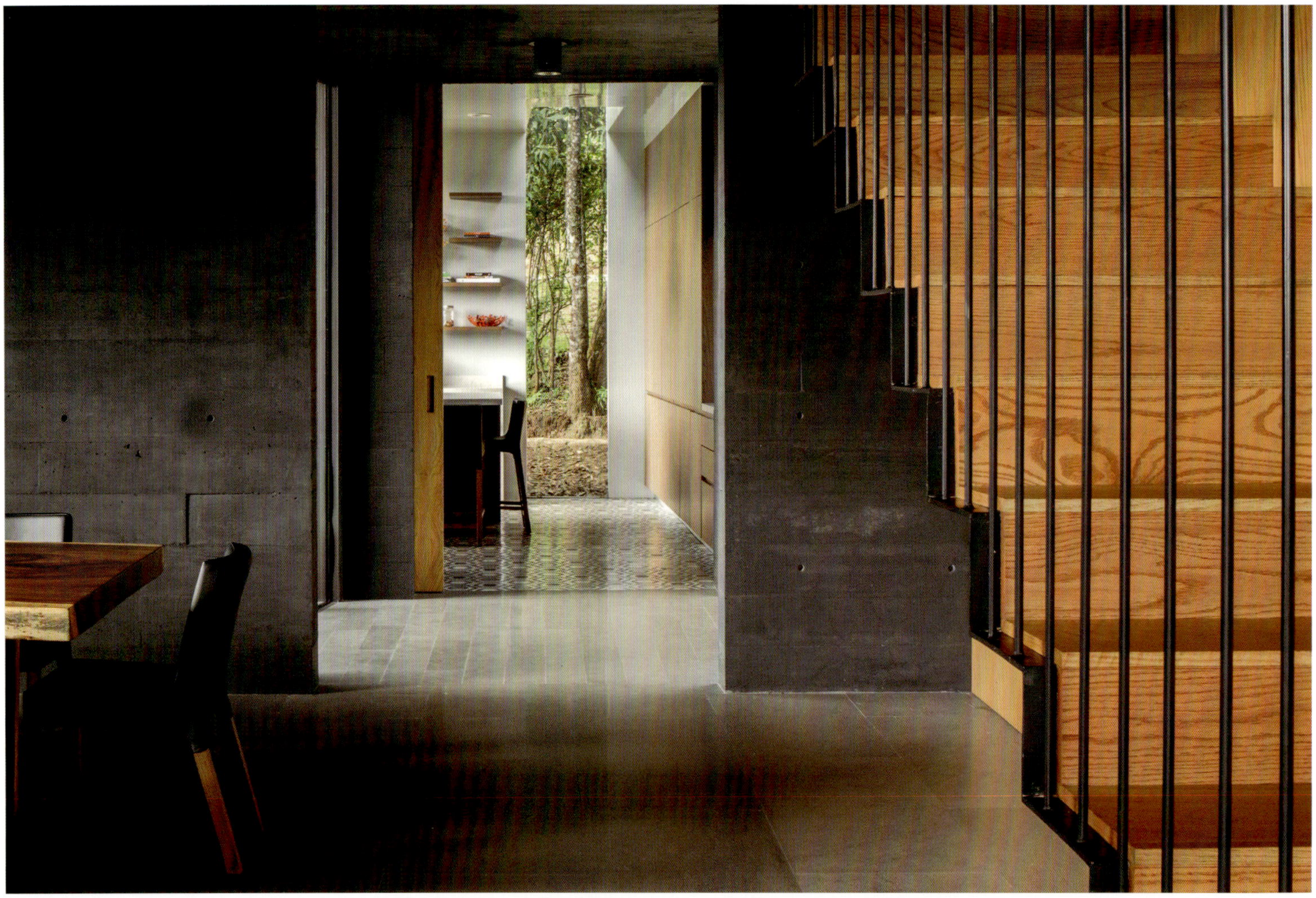

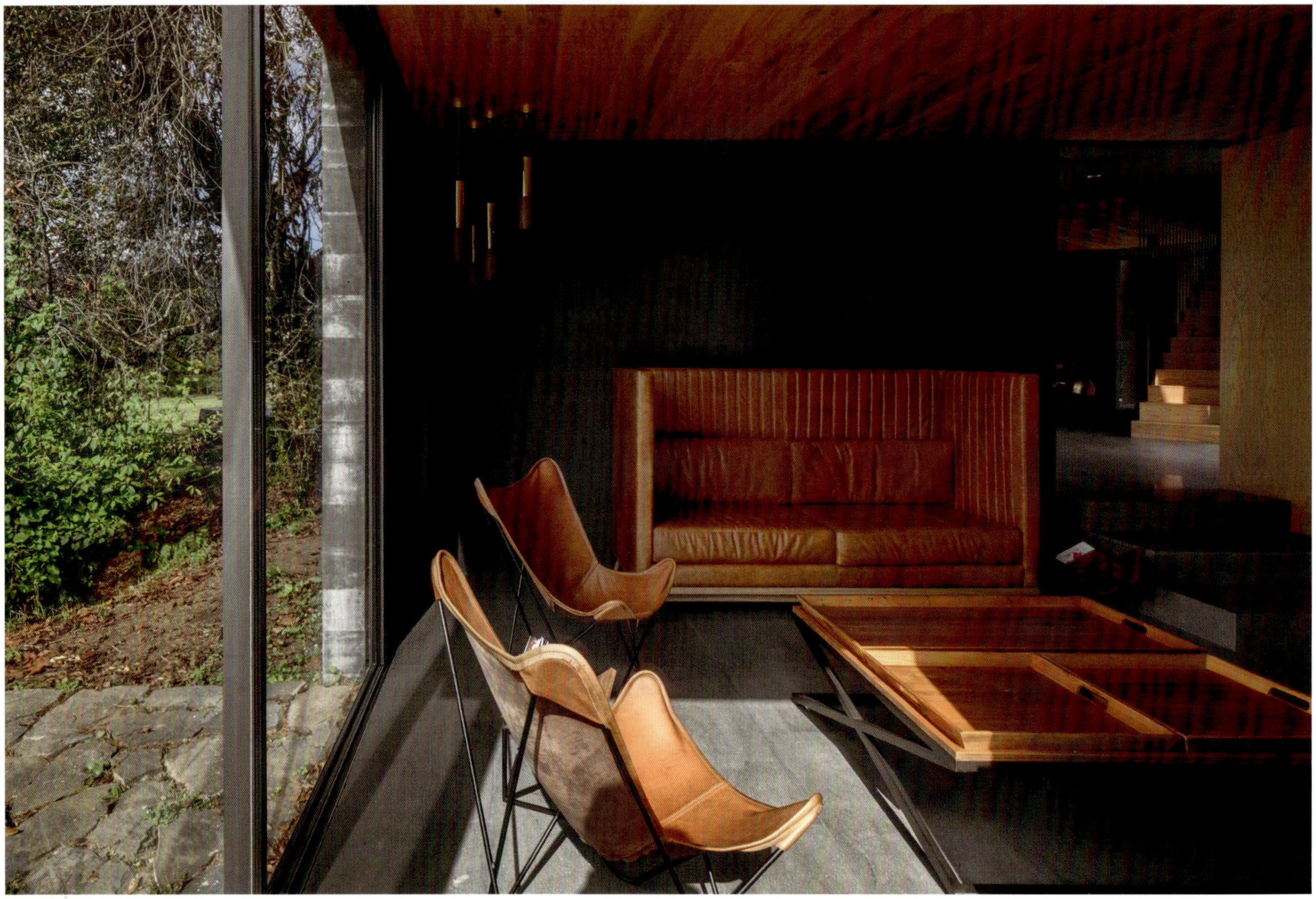

CASA BRUMA

Rama Estudio
CASA PATIOS
2018 | Lasso, Ecuador

This unpretentious second family home in Lasso, Ecuador, is dug into the earth. Casa Patios uses *bahareque*, a building material similar to adobe, for much of its construction; straw and soil from the site were packed into wood-and-metal-mesh frames to form the walls. Outer flanking walls supporting the roof are made of heavy stone, and a green roof helps the architecture further merge with its surroundings. Designed by the Quito-based Rama Estudio, the residence consists of two offset rectangular wings connected by a corridor-like rectangular volume. This H shape creates two patios, which give the house its name. The two wings demarcate separate zones for children and adults, each with bedrooms and places to socialize. The pavilion that connects them houses the main living space: an open-plan room flooded with light from glazing on both sides. Eucalyptus, growing abundantly nearby, has been used for the roof beams and flooring, giving the home a robust, organic feel. The kitchen, which has a Corten-steel ceiling, is zoned off by a wood screen, with a dining area adjacent to a small, unadorned living area. It is possible to walk across the green-roof garden from one side to another, looking out to spectacular views of mountains and woods. Solid, sheltered, and grounded, Casa Patios is totally in tune with the surrounding landscape.

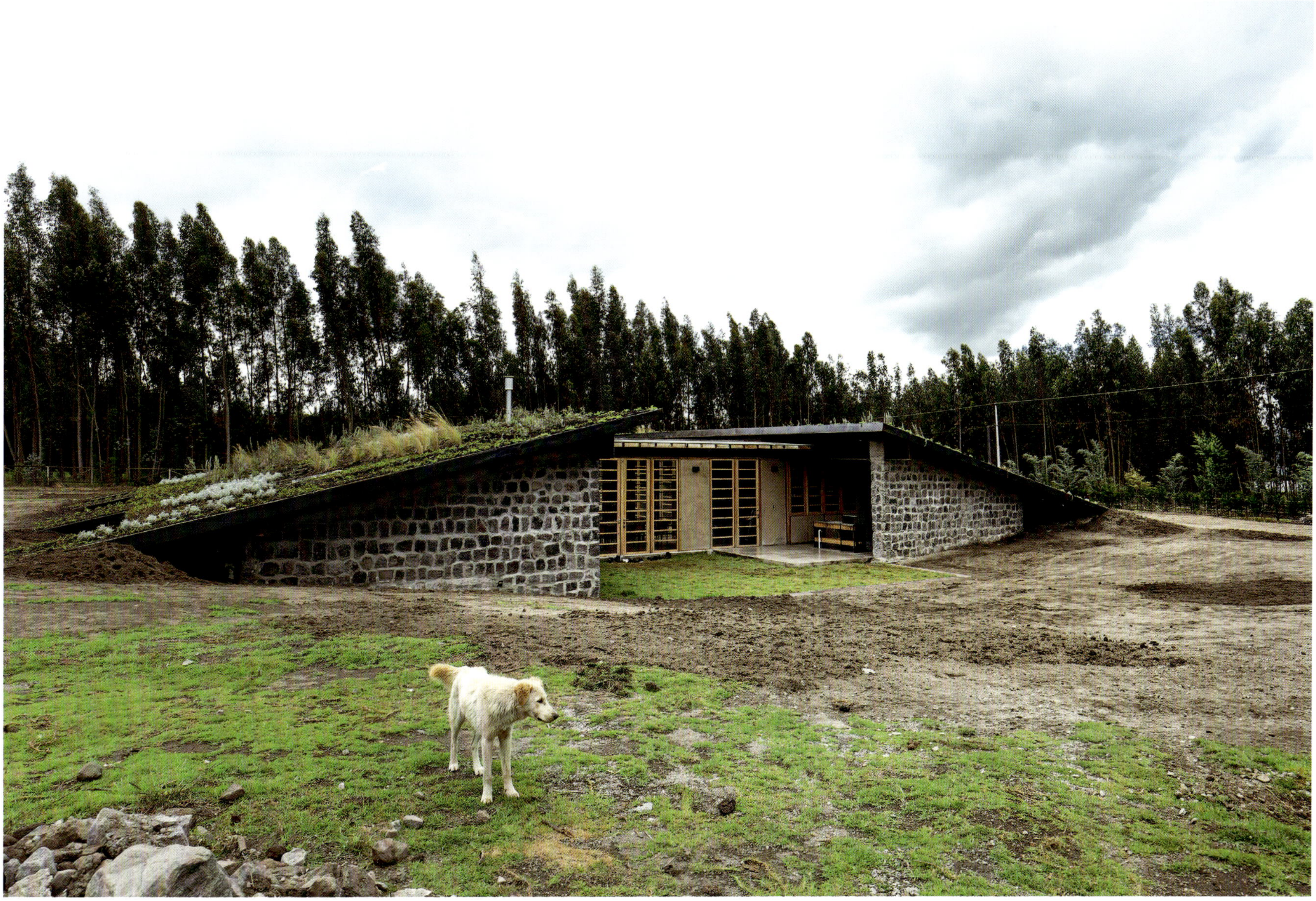

CASA PATIOS

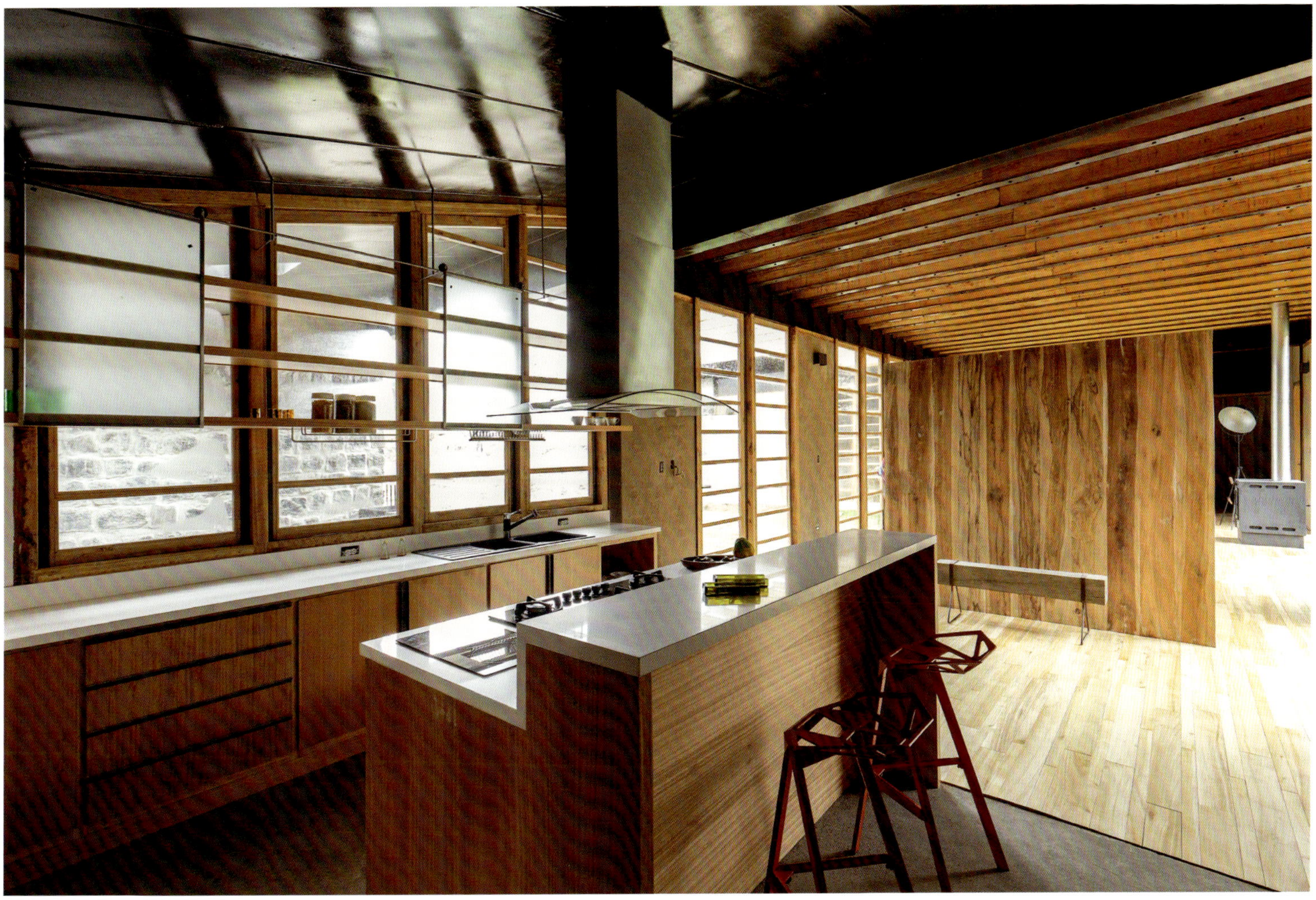

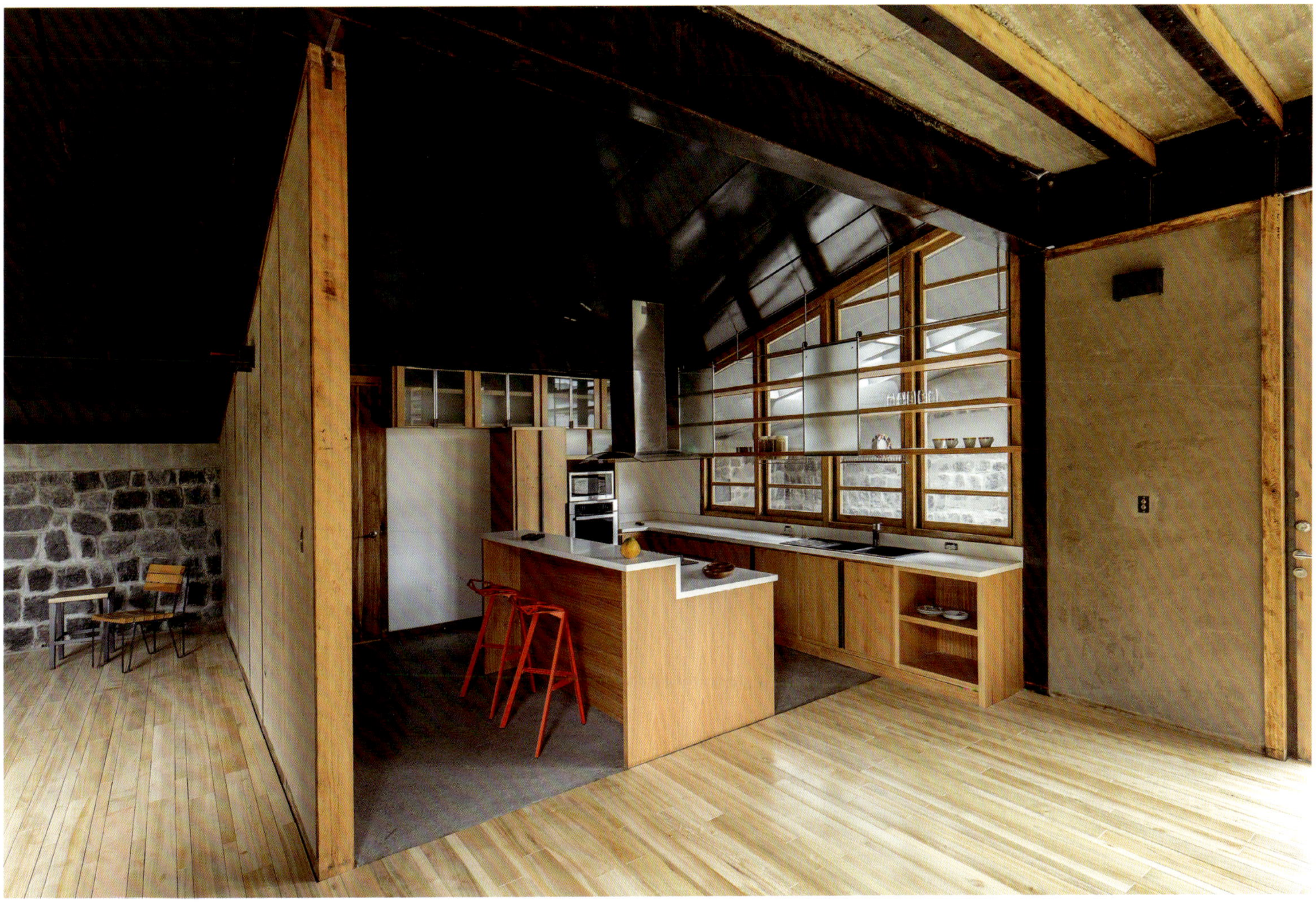

Wheeler Kearns Architects
RAVINE HOUSE
2017 | Highland Park, IL, USA

The ravines of Lake Michigan's western shore, carved by waters that flow into the lake, are unique natural environments. This project was commissioned by a couple who had found a ravine plot where an older brick house had burned down, and wanted the new house to respect the site's gentle slopes and enhance, rather than harm, its ecosystem. Wheeler Kearns responded with this modest, single-story retreat positioned at the ravine's brow, nestling into its woodland. Formally, the house is a dark rectangle from which a corner has been broken off to create a garage and entrance courtyard, thus encouraging engagement with the outdoors. Wood features everywhere, making constant connections with the surrounding forest. Inside, white oak flooring and walnut furniture create a tactile and organic decor, while exterior courtyard walls are clad in black locust timber, more sustainable than widely available jungle hardwood. Even the black steel vertical cladding echoes the form of nearby trees. The home's central hub is its walnut-clad core, around which bedrooms, an artist's studio, and a light-filled kitchen, living, and dining area are arranged. The owners restored the land by eliminating invasive species and replanting with prairie grasses, fruit bushes, and native plants that will self-sow, naturally perpetuating the beauty of the site.

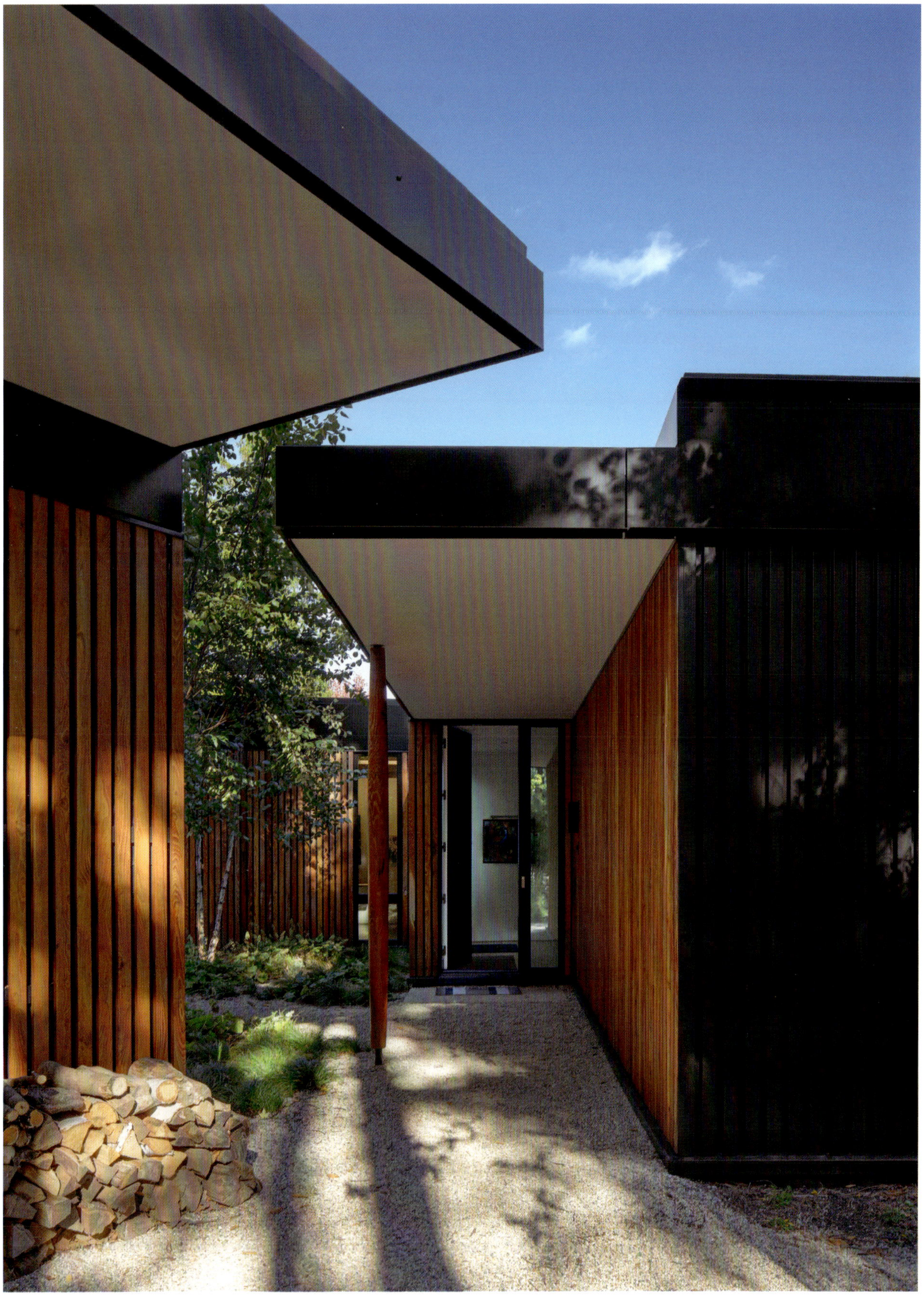

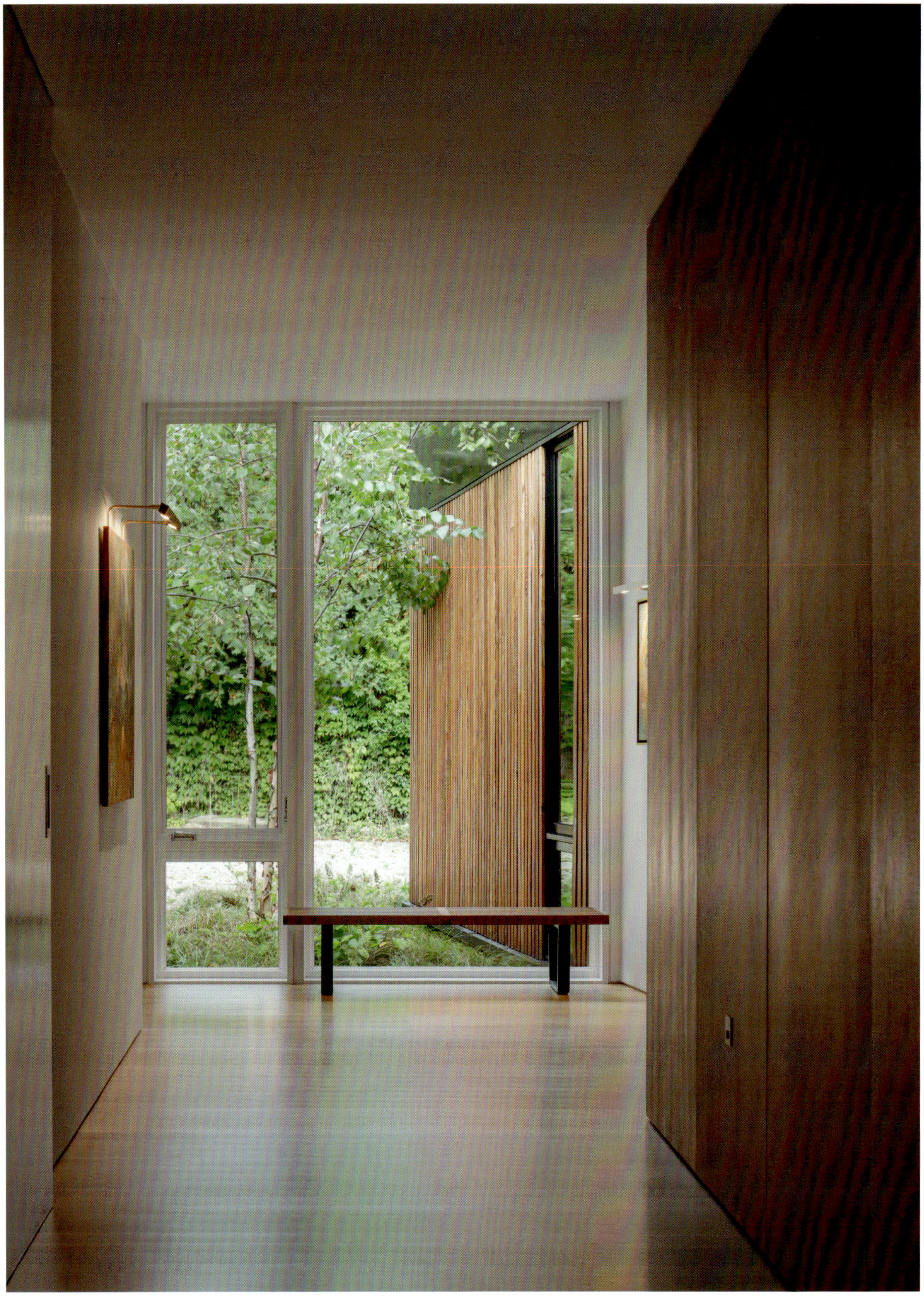

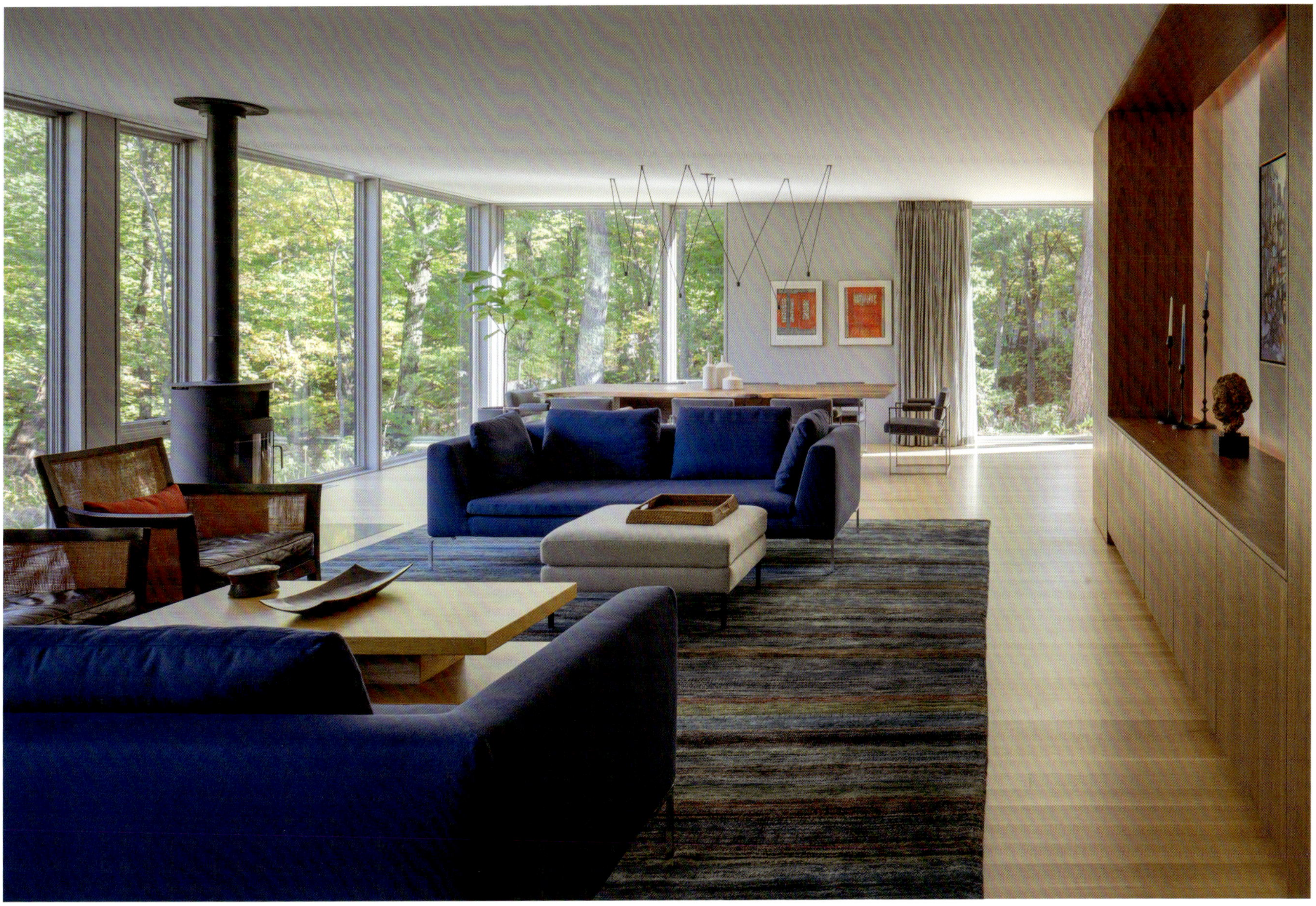

Patisandhika and Dan Mitchell
A BRUTALIST TROPICAL HOME
2017 | Bali, Indonesia

Although constructed predominantly from a man-made material, this concrete house in Bali integrates brilliantly with its natural surroundings, erasing distinctions between inside and out. Concrete suits tropical climates due to its durability, coolness to the touch, and plasticity—it can be molded in various forms to provide shading and ventilation. The architects were inspired by the Kappe House in California and borrowed from its open-plan interior spaces, split levels, concrete, glazing, and wood, as well as its wholehearted embrace of the outdoors. The living room's full-height glazed panels, held within concrete frames, allow light in and open up views of vegetation, but a downside could have been the potential for intense heat gain.

To keep energy usage low, the architects avoided air-conditioning and instead designed a series of horizontal concrete slabs, connected to beams extending from the roof, to overhang and shade the glazing. Foliage and other greenery enter the house at multiple points: there is a full-size tree growing in the living room, and palms jostle to enter from the elegant triangular second-floor balcony. Splashes of color—red and yellow abstract panels leaning against a wall, blue stair risers, yellow built-in cupboards—add vivid contrast to the pale gray of the concrete. The interior is cool, airy, and bright; outside, plants and trees soften the building's crisp forms so that it merges into the landscape.

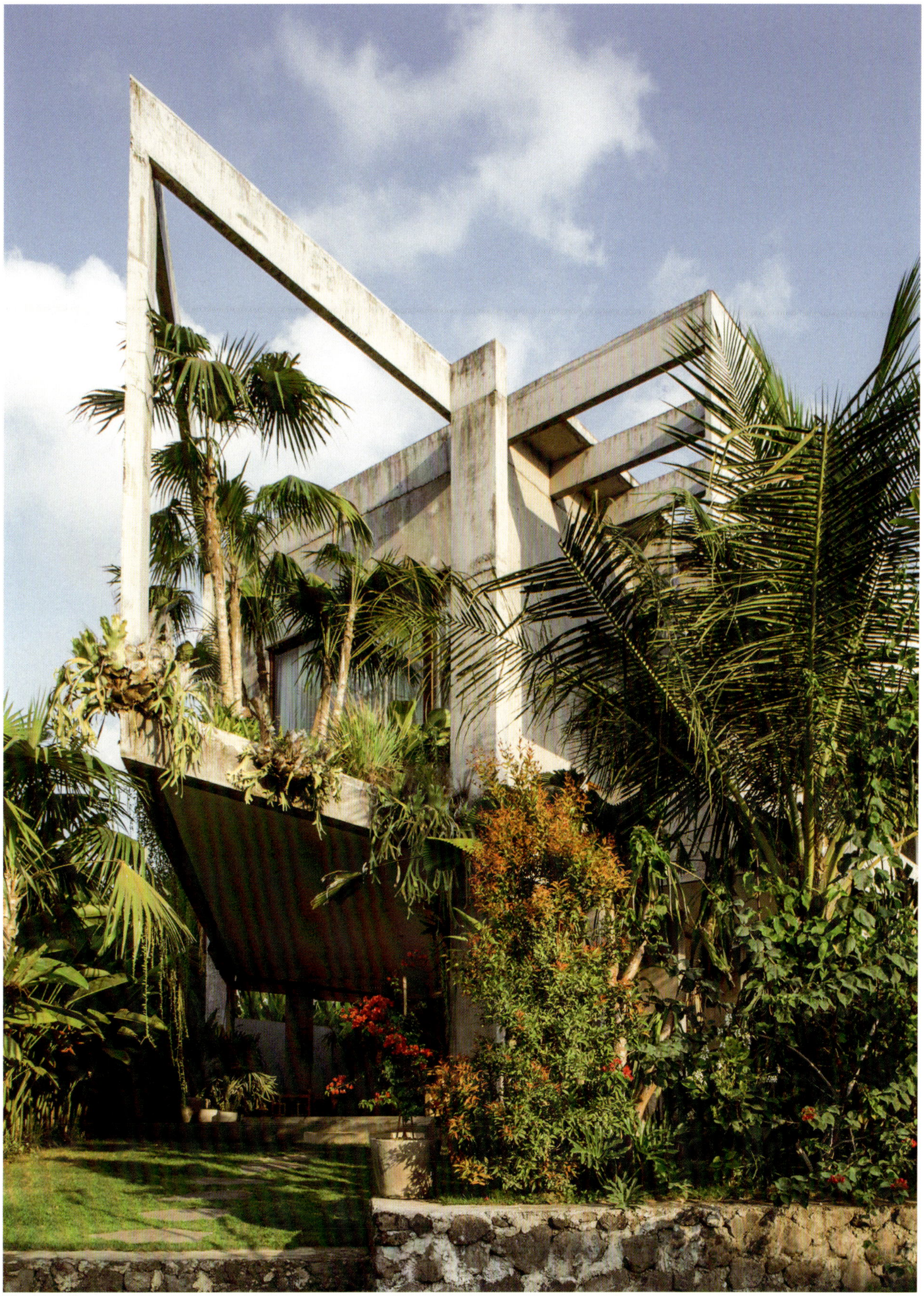

A BRUTALIST TROPICAL HOME

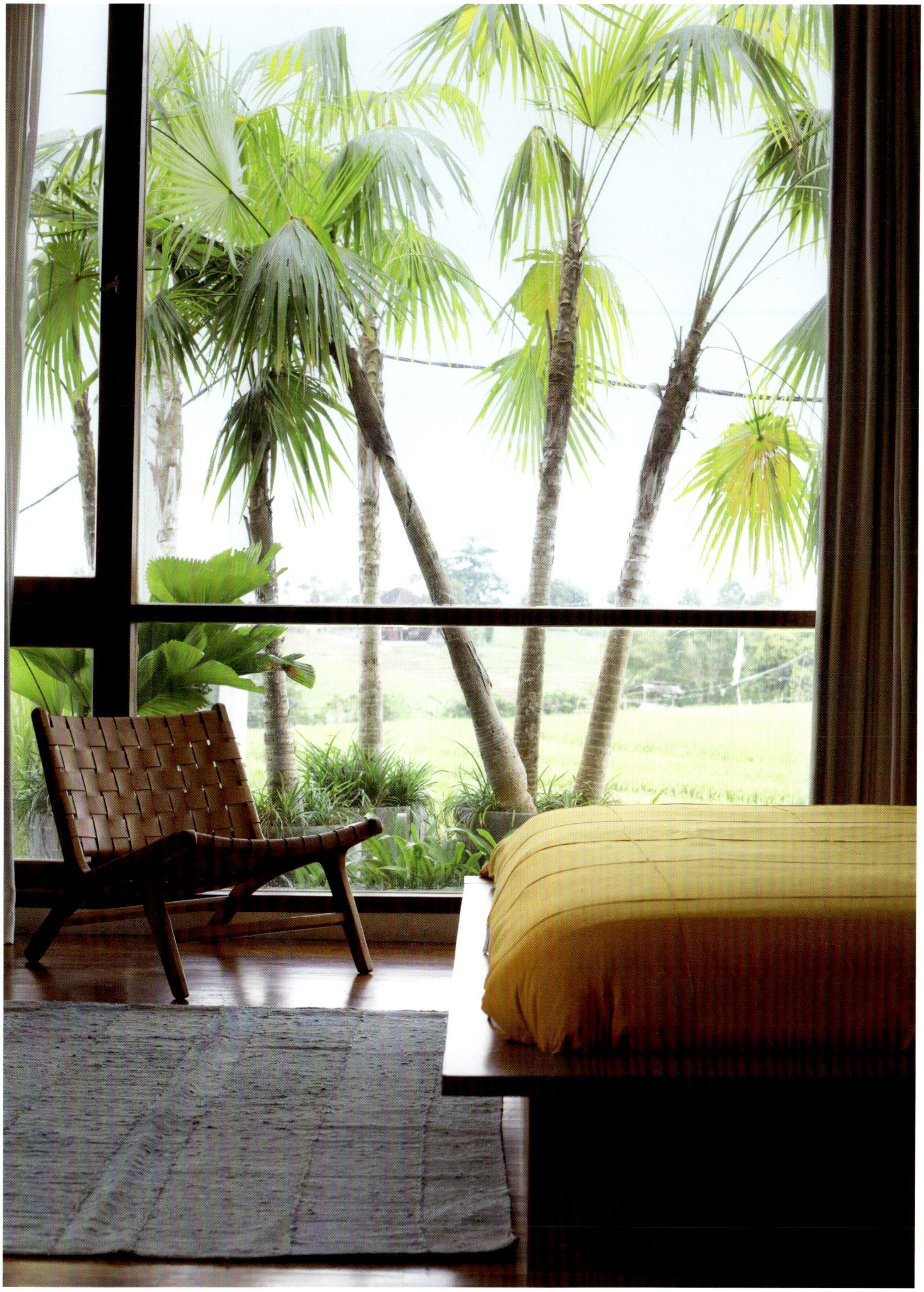

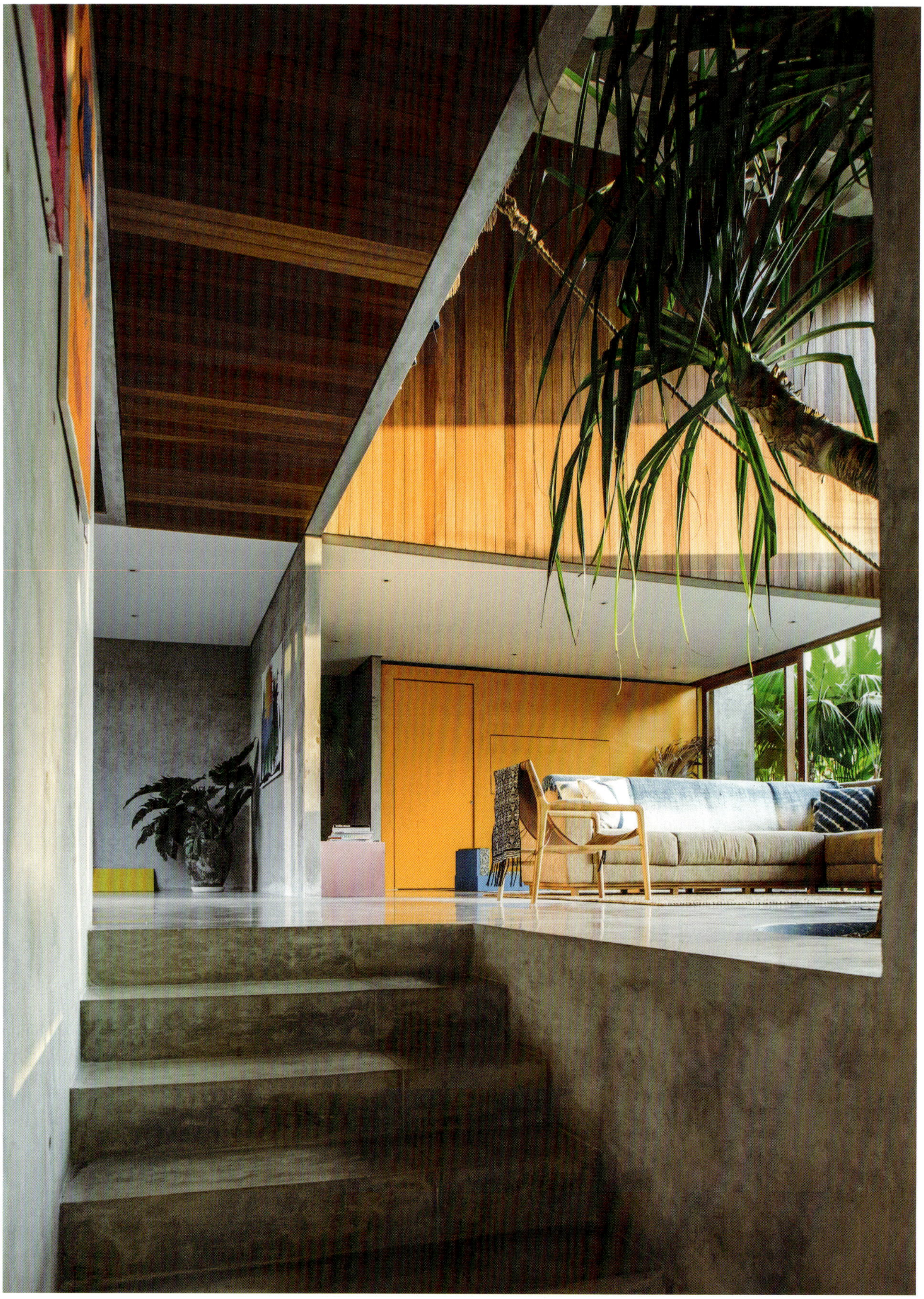

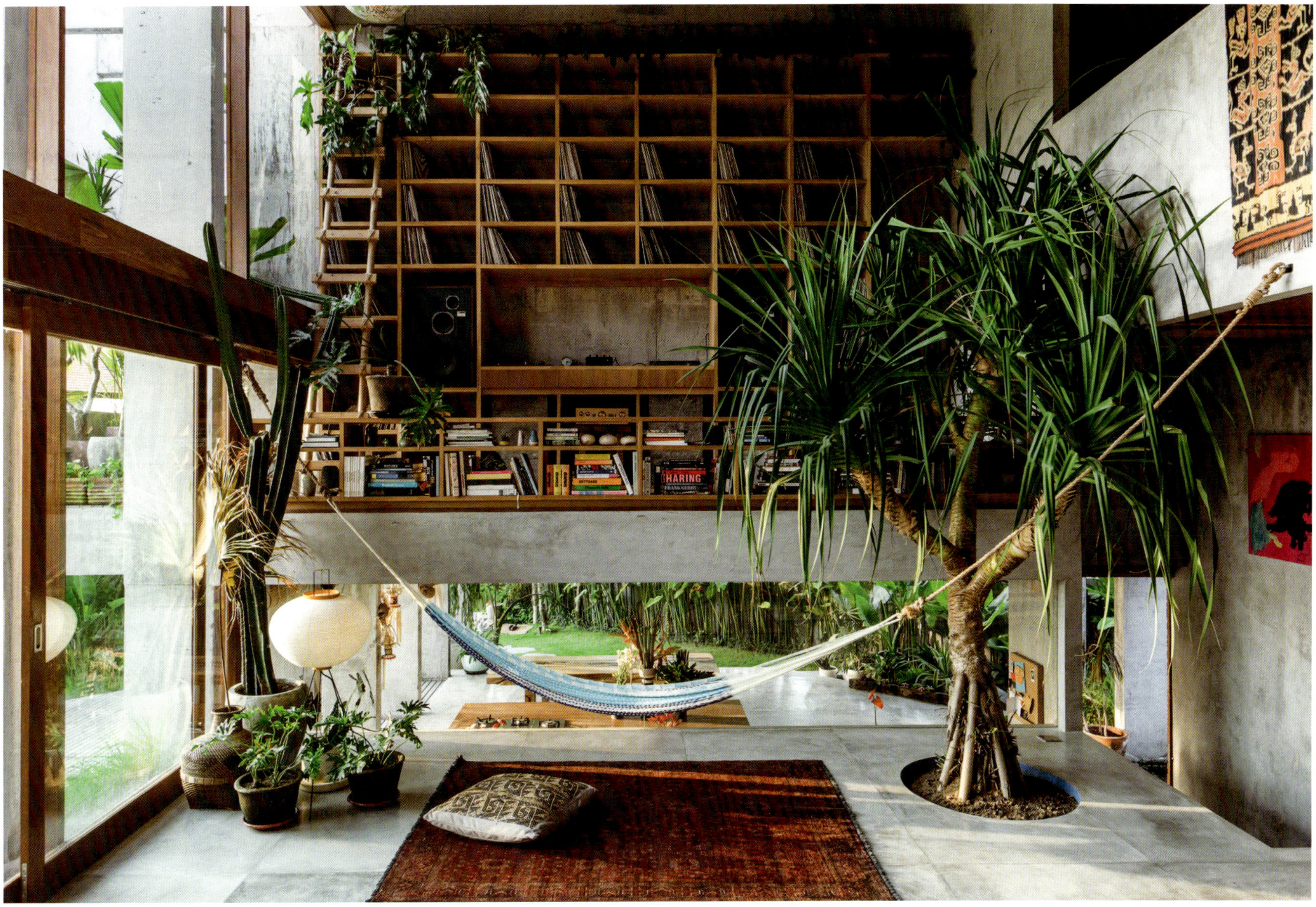
HARING

Mary Arnold-Forster Architects
AN CALA
2019 | Nedd, Scotland, UK

An Cala modestly matches its ambitions to a fragile environment, yet still offers its inhabitants an uplifting experience of the Highland landscape. To avoid having to blast out the rock to widen the plot, the architects tucked the house in between two stony outcrops, with the retreat's long axis running west to east. To reduce further impact on the land, they designed An Cala to be raised on concrete piers and respond flexibly to the topography with its series of interlocking cross-laminated timber modules, the volume of which was dictated by the size of truck that could make it up to the site. From these modules, three "pods" were formed: a living area and two bedrooms with showers. All three pods are linked by a glazed corridor that draws light into the house. A burnt-larch rain screen echoes the tones of nearby birch trees, granite, and peat, thereby gracefully merging the building with its surroundings; the screen also serves as an envelope to insulate the home. Despite the architects' self-imposed restrictions, the living room and main bedroom windows frame spectacular views of the sea loch and the western side of the mountain range Quinag, while numerous other openings around the house offer earthier views of the hillside on which the home rests.

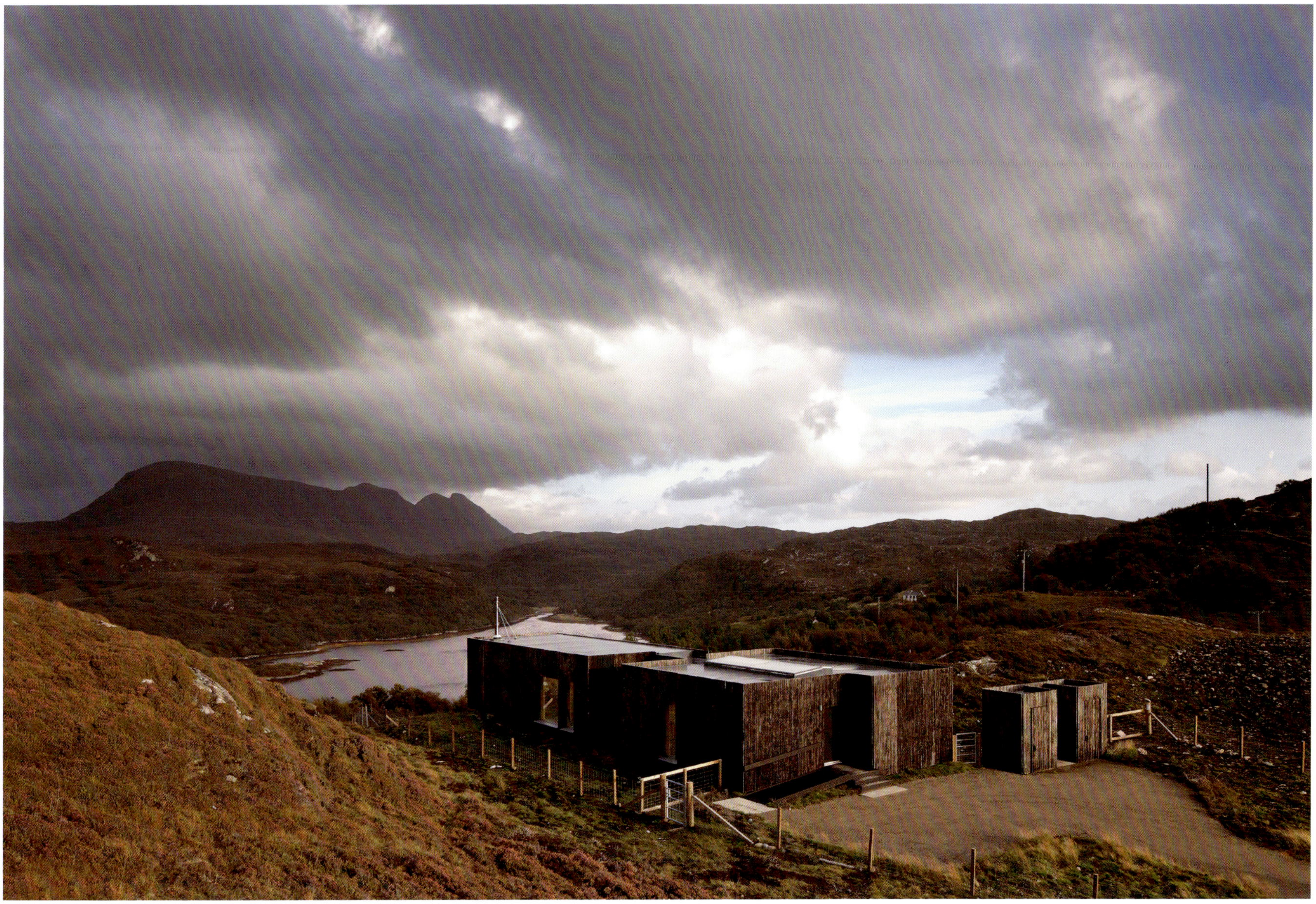

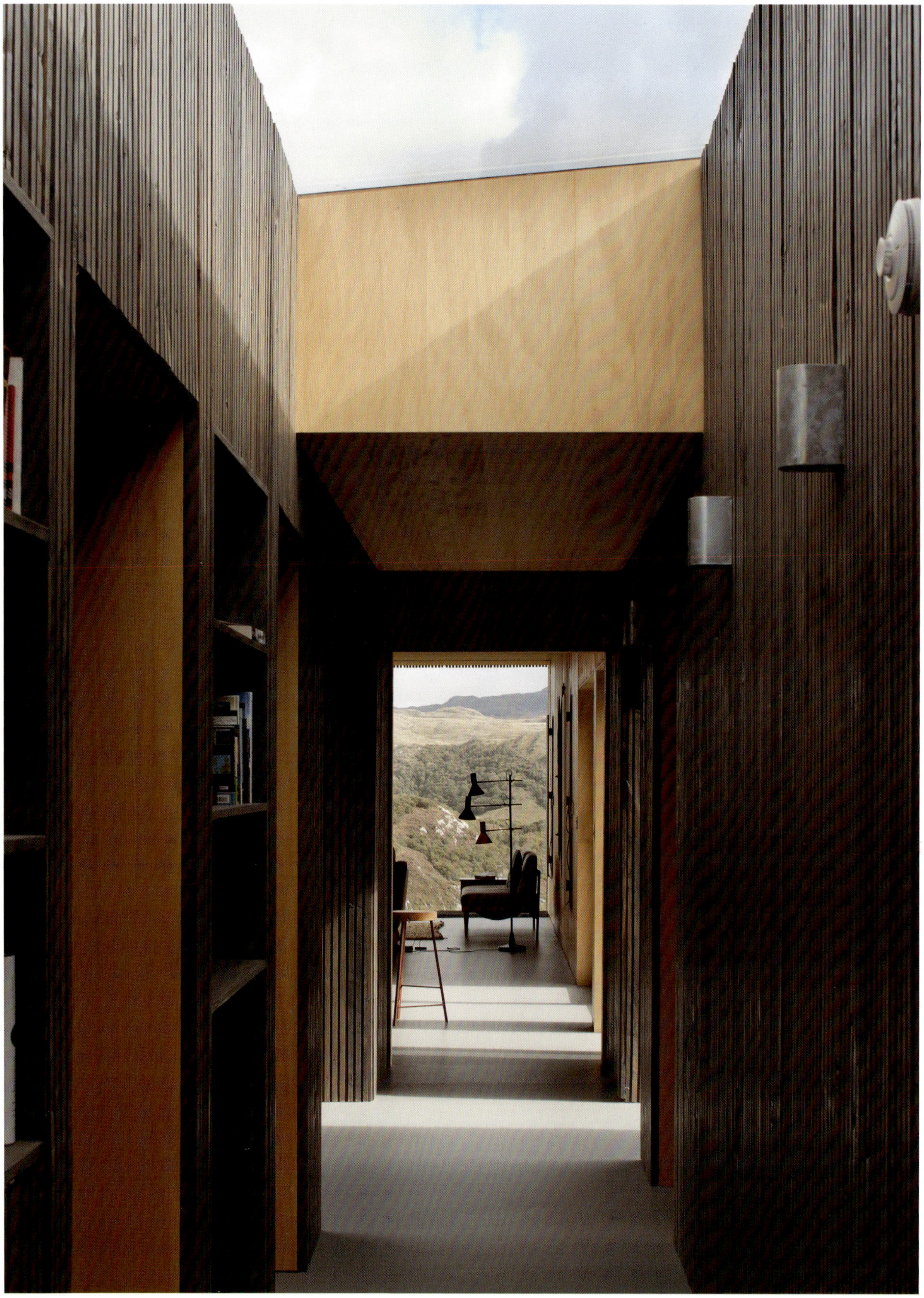

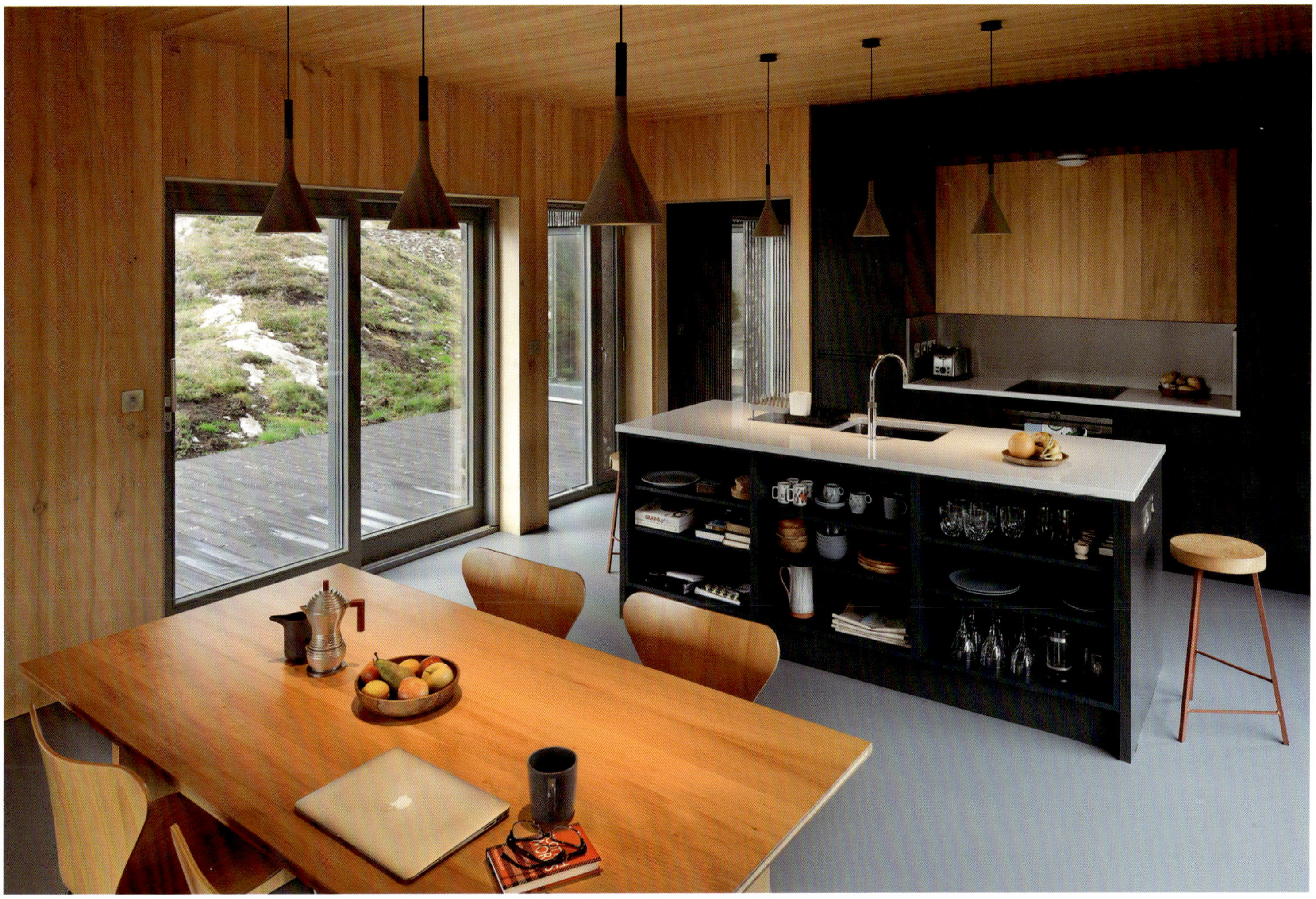

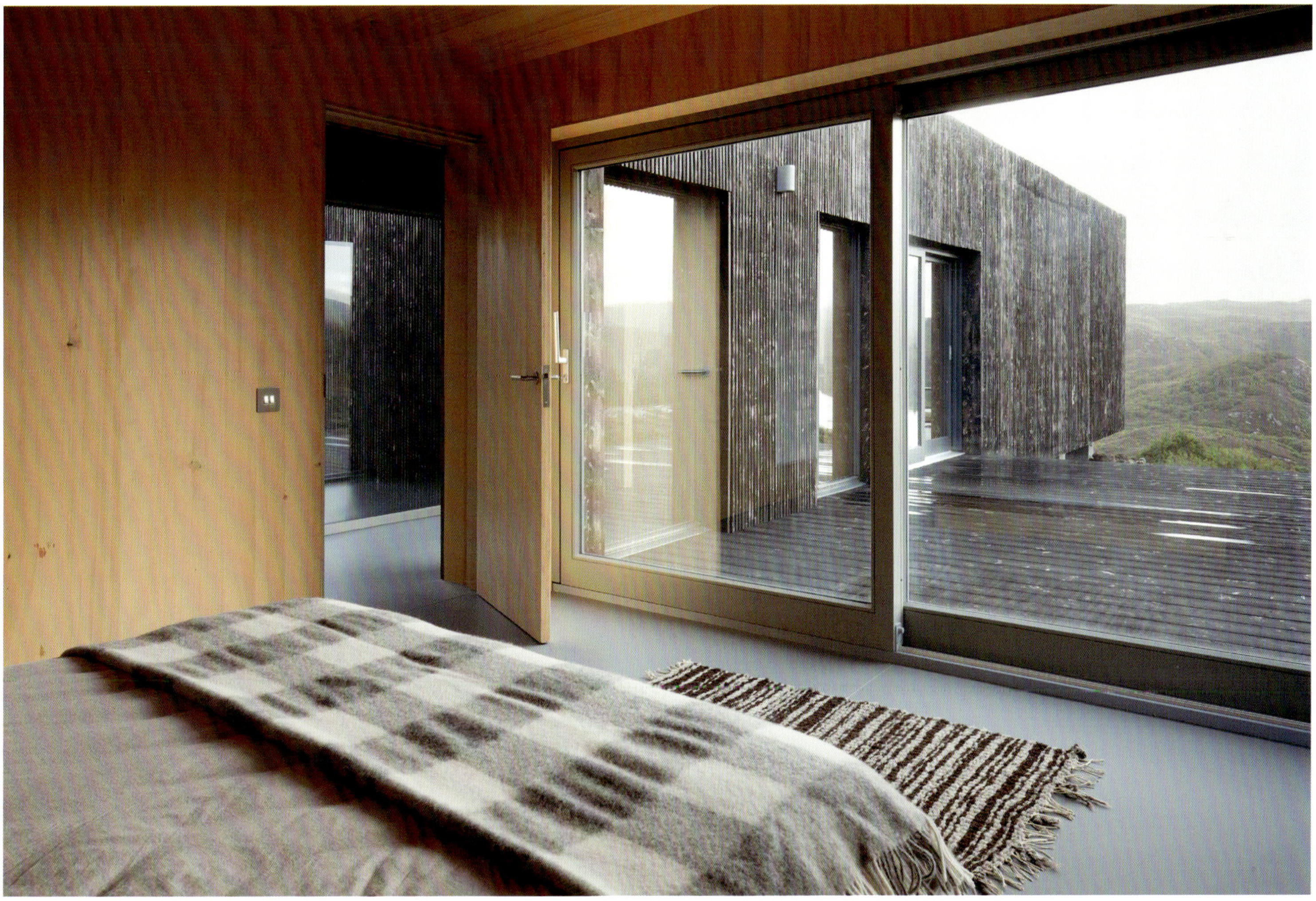

Alexis Dornier
HOUSE APERTURE
2019 | Uluwatu, Bali, Indonesia

Everything in this retreat was conceived with simplicity and sustainability in mind. The box-shaped tower sits amid Uluwatu Surf Villas a small development on the western cliffside edge of Uluwatu in Bali. House Aperture is split-level, built on a slope over three floors. A bedroom opens onto a lush garden on the lowest floor; on the middle story, a living area flows onto a deck with a pool. An additional bedroom and bathroom are on the top level. Master carpenters hand-built the house out of recycled Javanese teak, steel, and glass. Limestone is used widely around the pool and deck areas, and in the sturdy perimeter wall. Blasted from a local quarry, it references Uluwatu's impressive cliff formations nearby. Darker rock clads the lower-level bedroom walls and floor, creating a cool place to sleep. The house's name refers to its openness: sliding glass doors and slatted wooden ventilation on three sides of every floor, shift forward and back to create multidirectional airflow. The ability to move these elements around, like tiles in a puzzle, makes the simple structure a flexible, comfortable, and dynamic living space. It is always open to the elements, and through its sensitive use of materials, asserts an emphatic connection with its context.

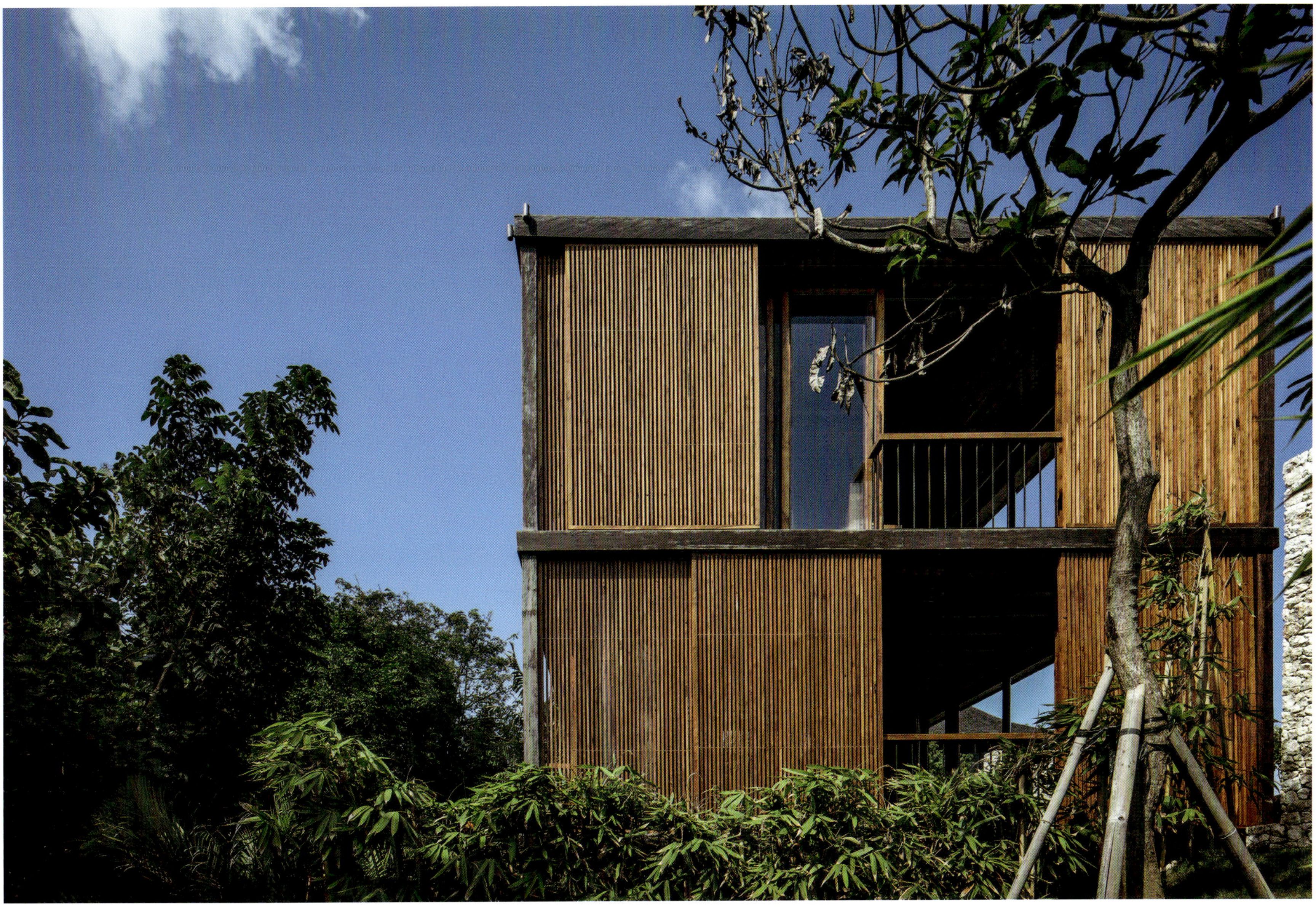

# HOUSE APERTURE

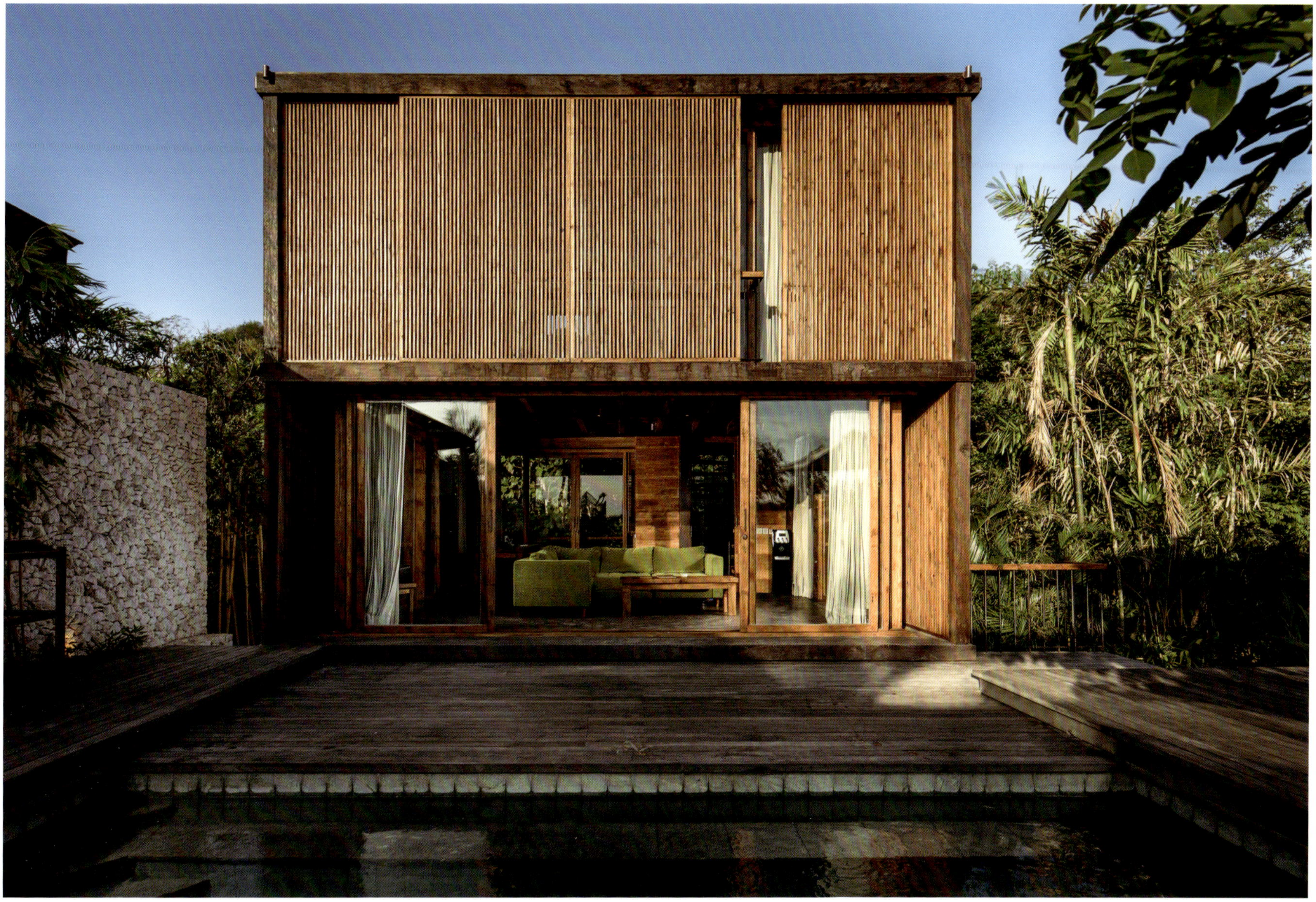

Pérez Palacios Arquitectos
ACULCO RESIDENCE
2018 | Aculco, Mexico

This tiny retreat near Aculco, northwest of Mexico City, resembles a small modernist chapel: the wedged-shaped stone volume has a lofty, light-filled internal space devoid of ornament, shifting the main focus to the surroundings. Built for two brothers in the remote countryside, the isolated plot demanded the use of local materials, and the design was informed by a longing for simplicity, minimal maintenance, and dialogue with the land. The interior divides efficiently into lounge and kitchenette at the home's center, with a bedroom at one end and bathroom at the other. The second bedroom is on a mezzanine above the bathroom, accessed by a wooden ladder. Opening up the house to the elements was key; on all four facades, glazed doors slide open to provide natural ventilation, and three terraces, the largest to the east, more than double the house's footprint. Warm, honey-colored walls, made of stone from a nearby quarry, give the house a sense of gravitas and rootedness in the locality. Clay for the floor tiles and timber for doors and furniture also originate from around Aculco. Left in their rawest state, the materials further strengthen a connection with the earth. Openings frame views of the landscape, transforming the home into a place for looking and quiet contemplation.

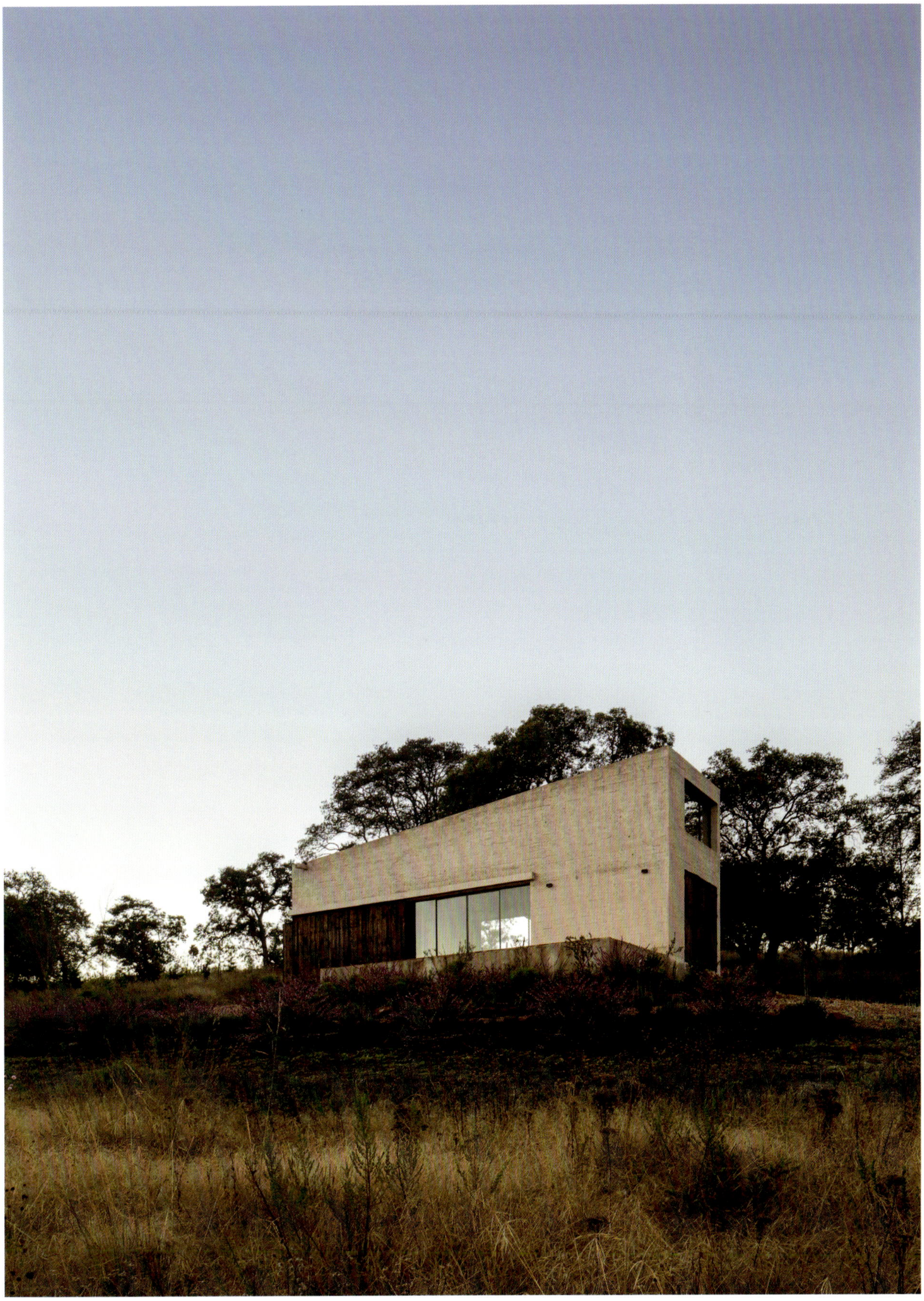

…

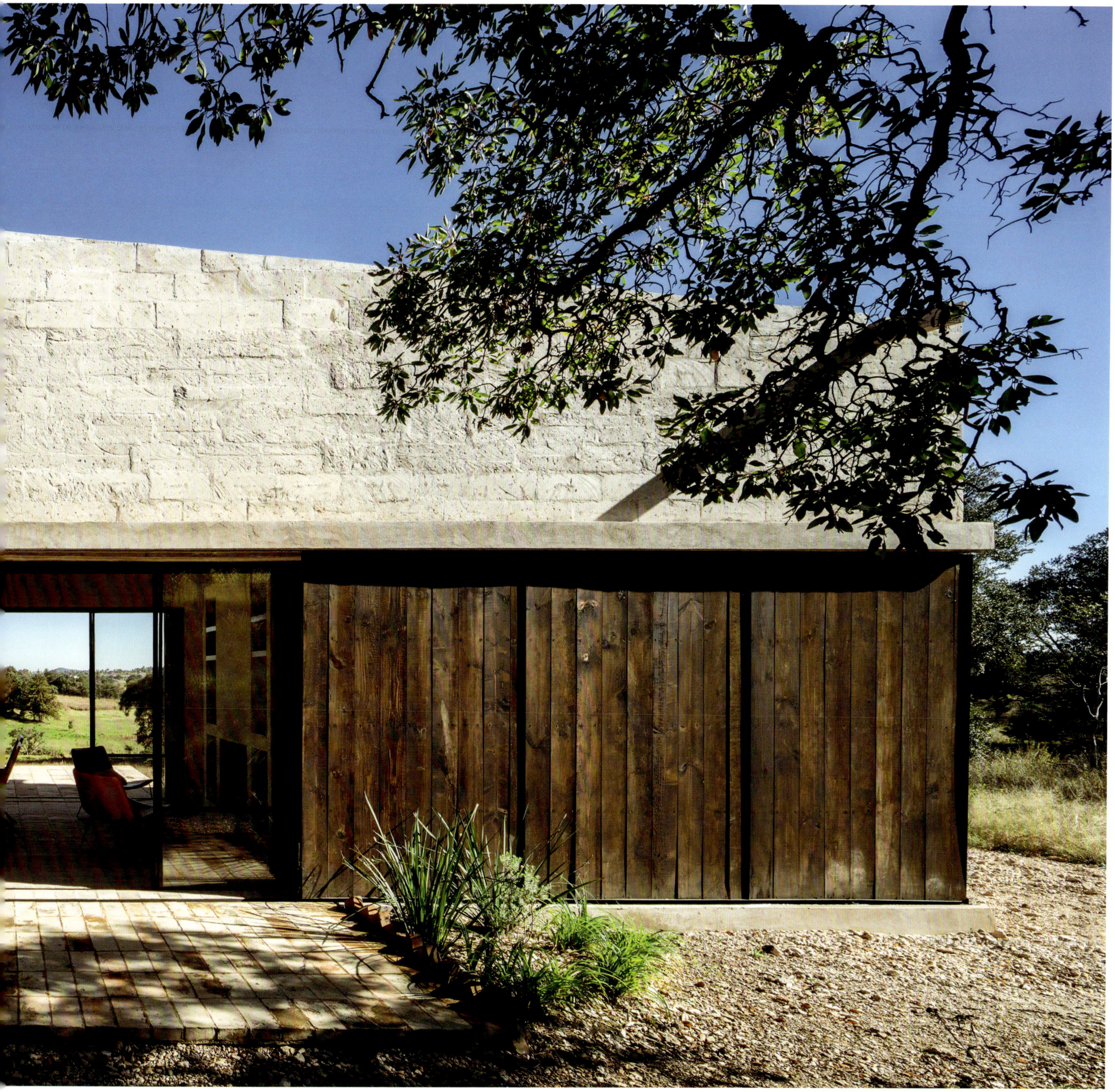

ACULCO RESIDENCE

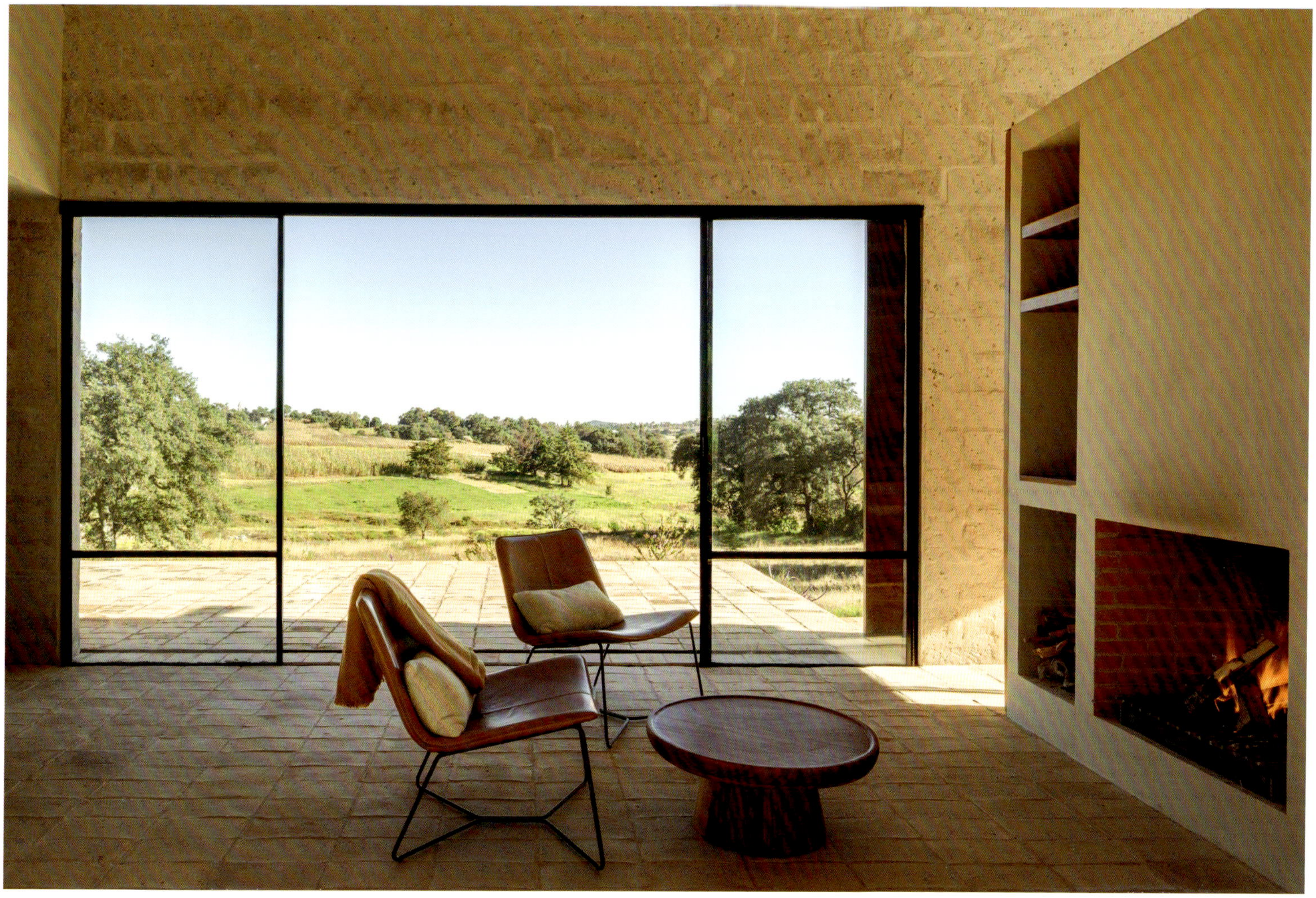

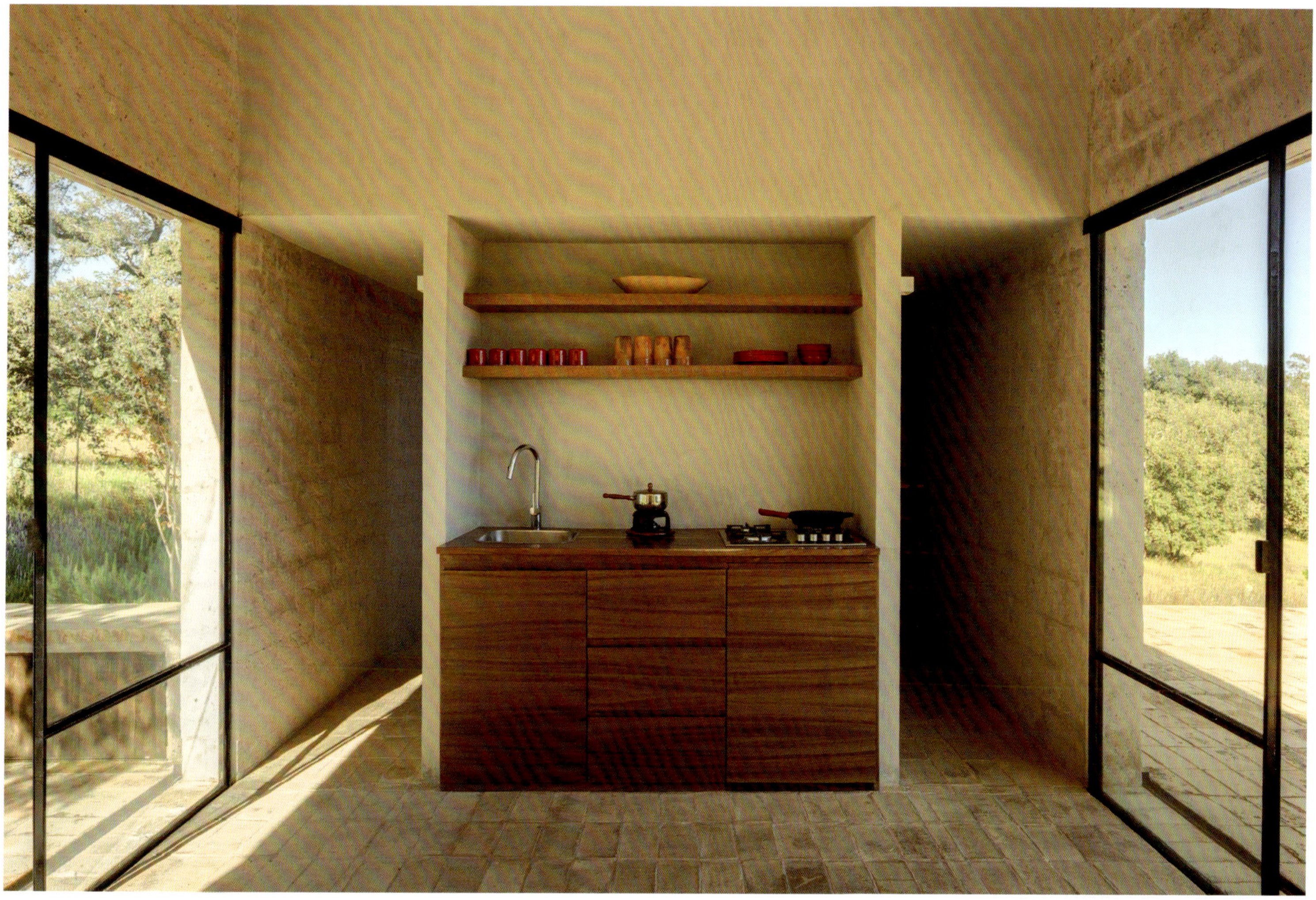

Format Architects
BUXTON RISE
2019 | Buxton, VIC, Australia

Nestled into a hillside, Buxton Rise enjoys a profound connection with the earth. This low-profile family retreat is designed to make a minimal impact on the rural environment while making the most of views of the rolling countryside and a small lake below it. The strongly horizontal house forms a compressed T shape. Looking north down the valley is a glazed volume with an open-plan living and dining area. Tucked behind that, facing uphill, a smaller sleeping volume is cocooned by heavy masonry walls. For this relatively small dwelling, outdoor spaces are as important as indoor ones. Outside areas are shaded by the huge cantilevered roof to the east and west, creating spaces to enjoy both sunrise and sunset. The roof consists of a grid of laminated-veneer lumber beams that are left exposed inside the house to show the texture of the wood. Earth tones in the furnishings further strengthen the connection to the land. Walls are covered by polished plaster with an irregular patina and the polished concrete floors, created using locally sourced river rock and sand, reflect light around the space. Handcrafted cantilevered wood shelving keeps walls uncluttered. The stripped-back but homely aesthetic results in a warm, welcoming retreat that complements the natural environment.

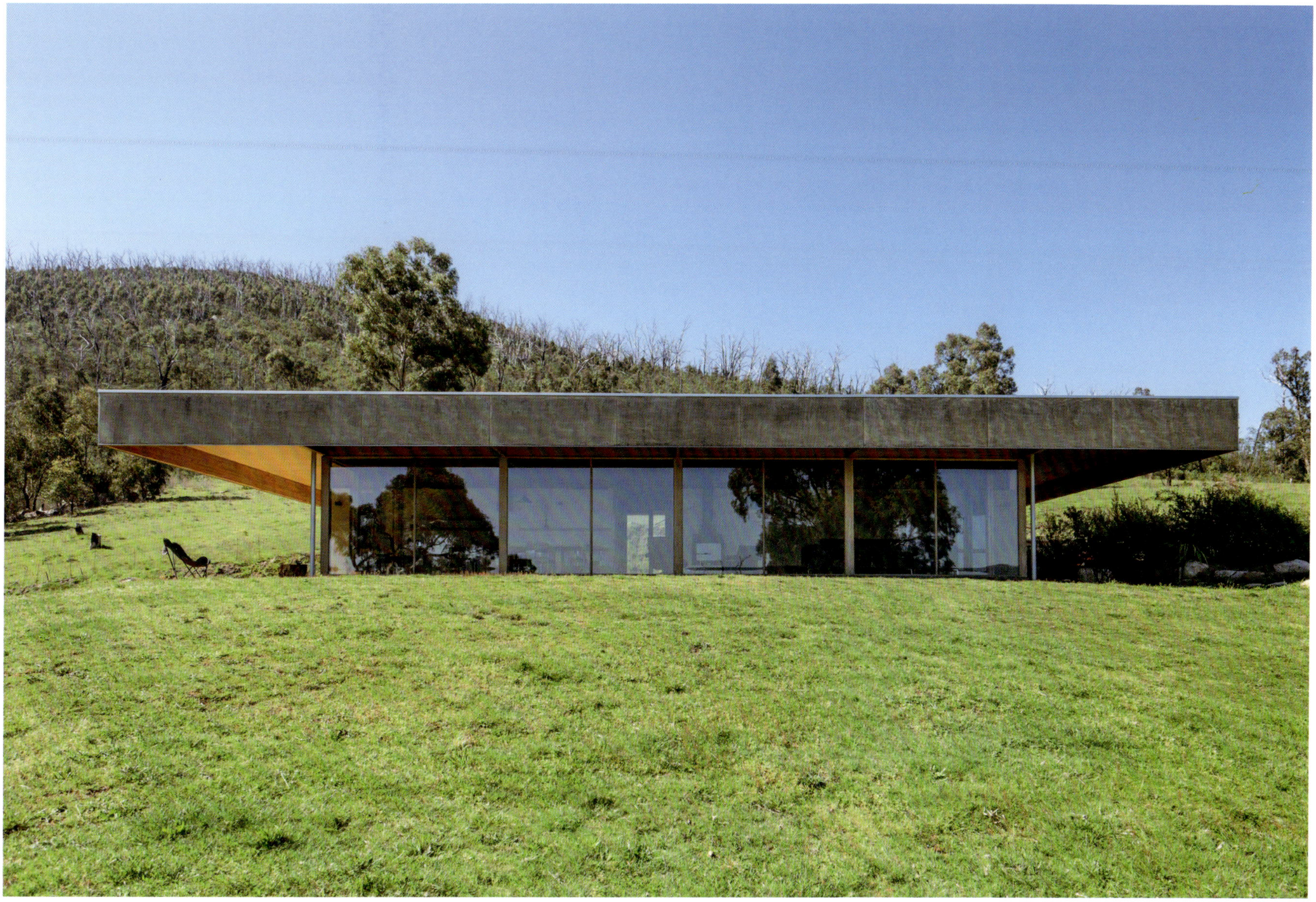

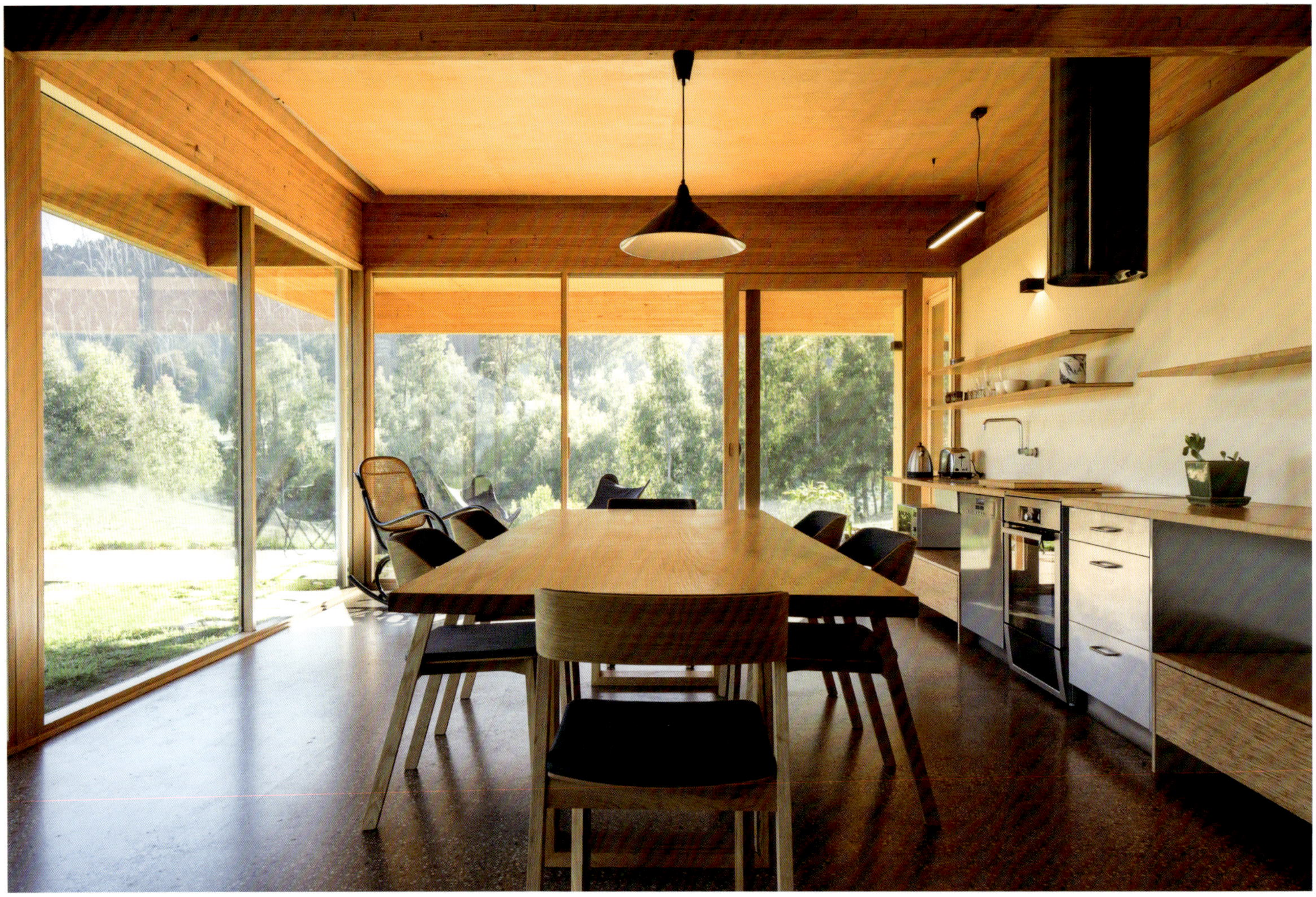

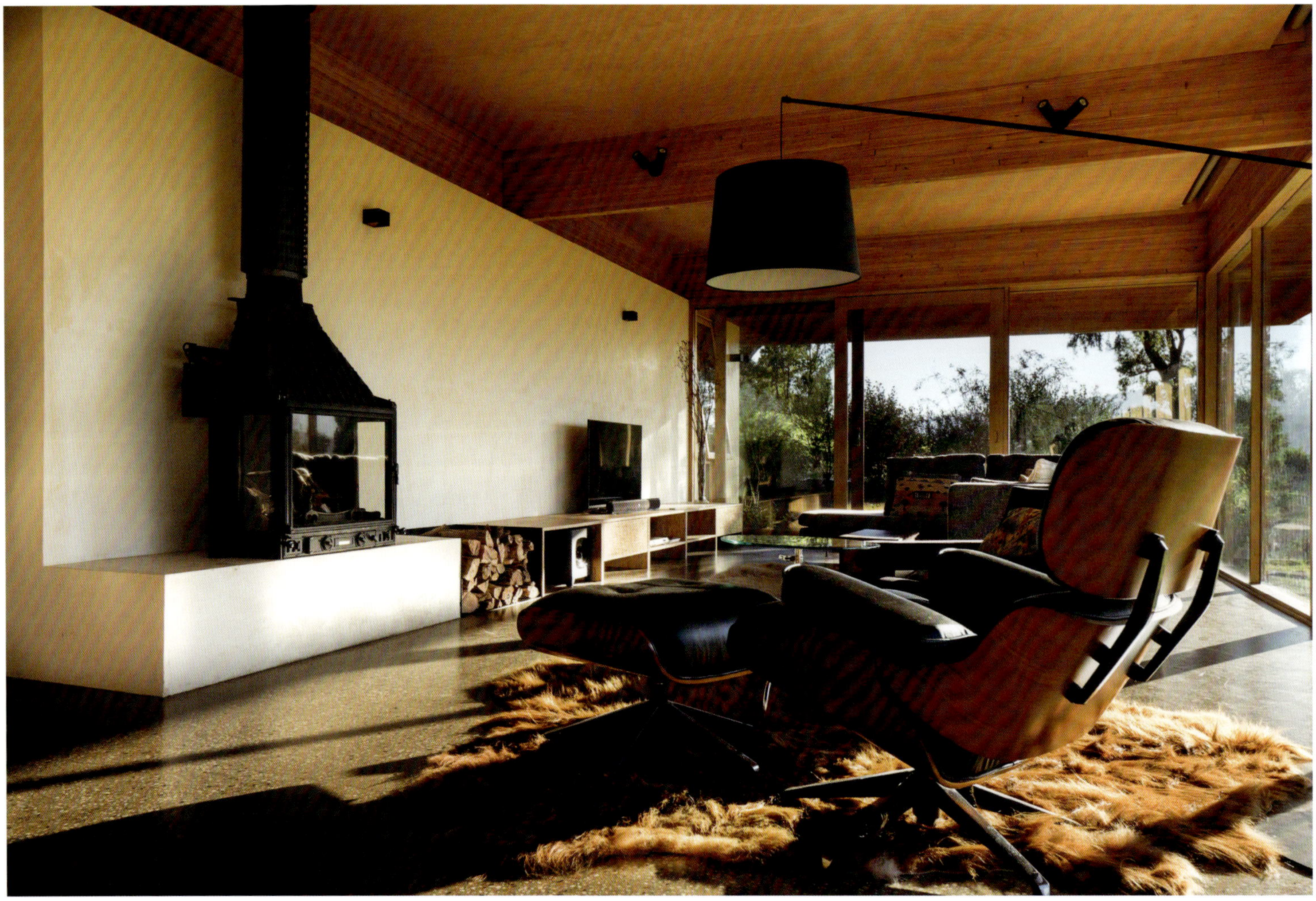

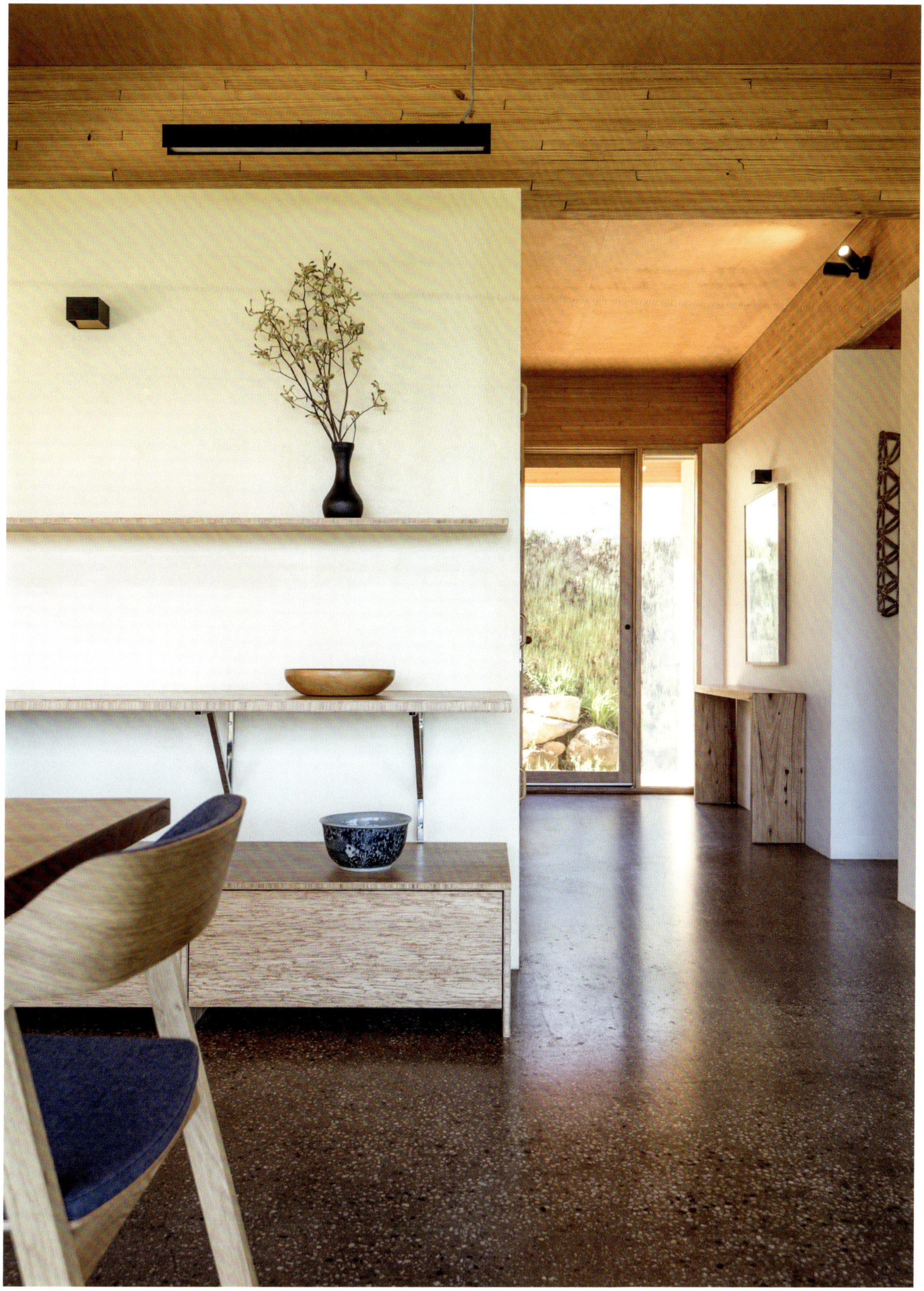

SPINN Arkitekter and Format Engineers
VARDEN
2019 | Storfjellet Mountain, Norway

The form of this multifaceted mountain cabin is inspired by its rocky environment. The Norwegian Trekking Association wanted to promote hiking in Hammerfest—famous as a place to see the northern lights—by providing an eye-catching, efficient, and welcoming rest stop for walkers at the peak of Storfjellet Mountain. The site was first mapped by drone using photogrammetry software, building up a baseline collection of forms that could fit together to form the hut's structure. The result, Varden, has a timber shell with seventy-seven unique panels that interlock like a jigsaw puzzle. To figure out how each part would fit together, 3-D printing was used and the shell was tested for wind resistance and snow-bearing ability. Prefabricated in a warehouse, it was split in two and reconstructed on the mountain. Rooted in community engagement, Varden was crowdfunded and built by a group of volunteers. Only the foundation laying and application of bitumen to waterproof the cladding were done by professionals. Inside, the cabin is a single open-plan space, with built-in furniture and a stove; it is sturdy and sheltering, with soaring views over the mountains, town, and fjord. It is a naturally inspired, yet unearthly shape watching over Hammerfest.

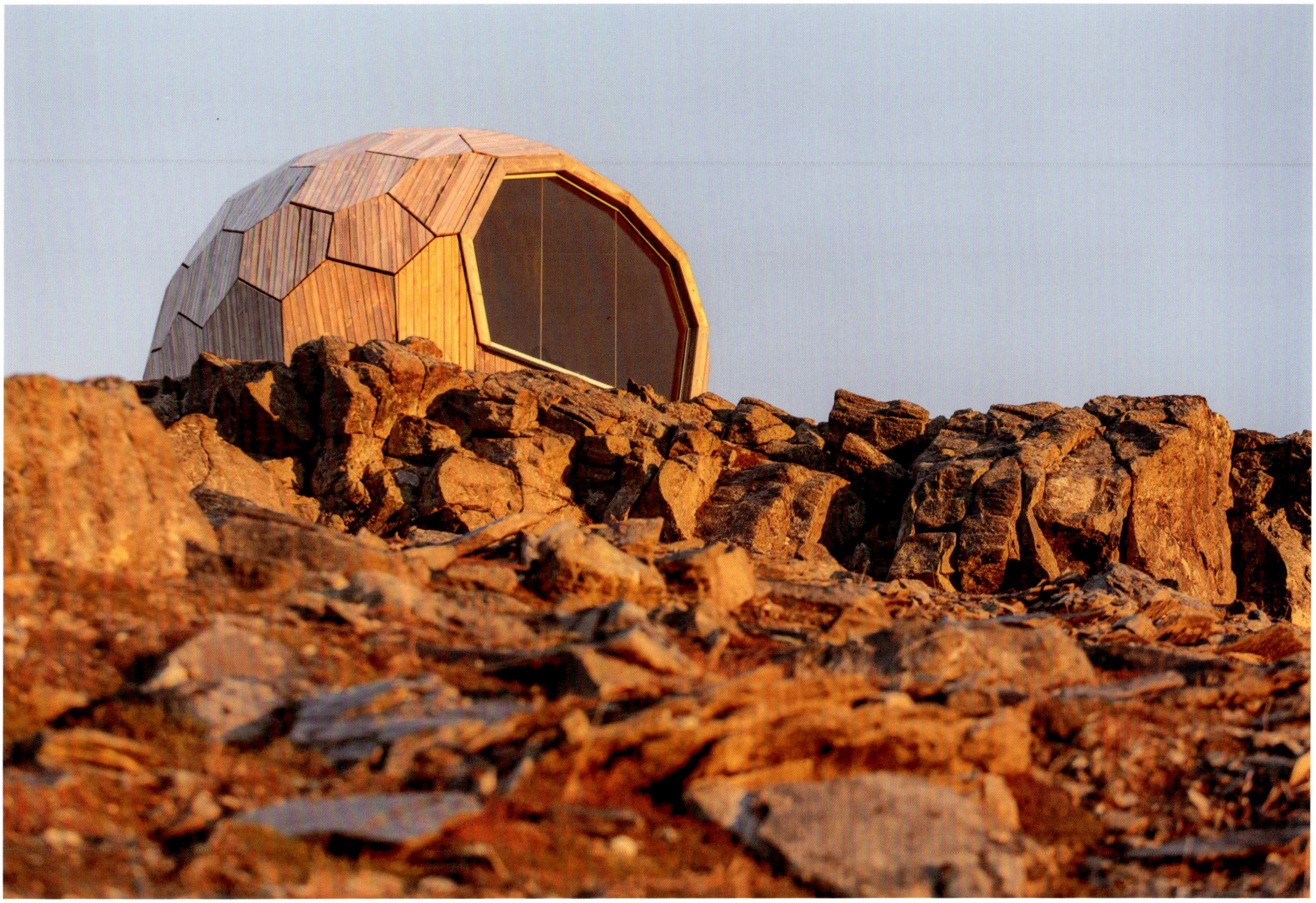

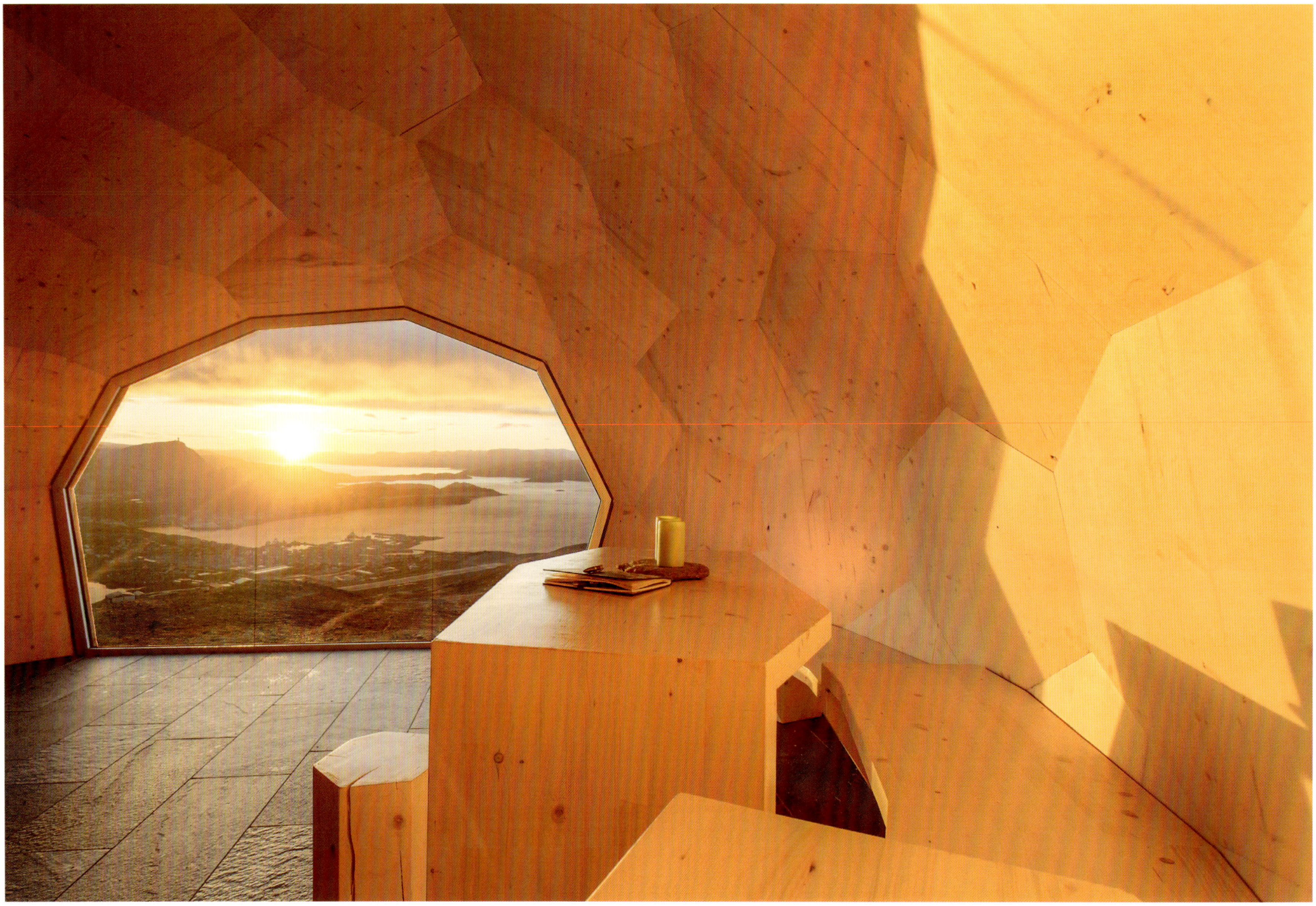

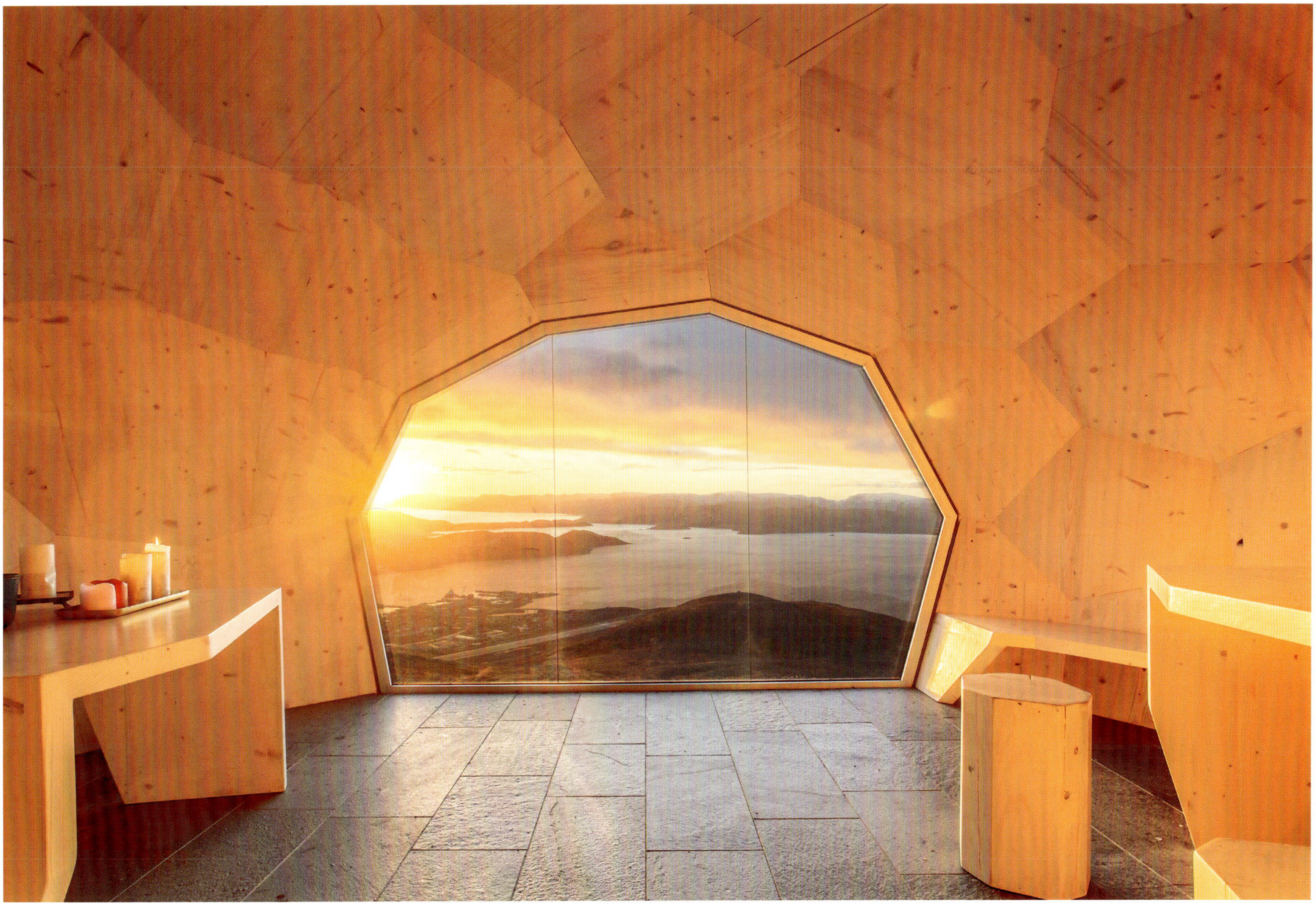

[3] FIRE

140 Luciano Giorgi
CASA FALK

144 Hacker Architects
HIGH DESERT
RESIDENCE

148 Olson Kundig
HALE LANA

154 Ampuero Yutronic
CASA HUALLE

158 K-Studio
VILLA MANDRA

164 Weber Arquitectos
SAN SIMÓN
CABINS

168 Cohesion
FOLLY CABIN

172 Formafatal
ATELIER VILLA

178 Faulkner Architects
LOOKOUT
HOUSE

182 DUST
CASA CALDERA

Extreme heat—whether from the sun or volcanic magma—is, to humans, both a danger and a draw. Experiencing such elemental forces in action evokes a sense of wonder, awe, and fear. We marvel at landscapes that have been scorched, dried out, charred, or formed from layers of molten rock and yet are still inhabited by humans.

This chapter explores architecture that seeks to turn the inhospitable into somewhere to thrive. It looks at several dwellings that are built surprisingly close to active volcanoes, like Stromboli in Italy, or on land scarred by eruptions, such as a jagged lava plain in Hawaii. Other locations are pounded by incessant heat: the arid Arizona desert, a tropical jungle in Costa Rica, and a sultry Greek island.

The demands of these extreme conditions often bring a certain congruence in architectural forms—for example, low, sturdy, compact cubic volumes with flat roofs that convey a sense of fortitude and protection. The houses in the following pages are often very simple, reduced to essential elements, but there are occasional noteworthy touches of luxury, and frequently, exquisite craftsmanship. Materials suggesting intense heat or volcanic activity such as charred wood, black concrete, rust-red aluminum, "lava-concrete," lava stone, and red-orange glass are used in abundance. Methods of keeping cool passively are often ingenious: a traditional "zaguan" passageway becomes a corridor to effectively channel breezes through the middle of a desert house. There are perforated metal screens in the jungle and thick, heavy walls in the Mediterranean. Overhanging roofs pull air currents inside; pergolas and verandas give some much-needed respite. These buildings fire the imagination, yet take care not to harm the environment. Nature has always involved cycles of desolation and regeneration and this eternal principle is what these superlative houses excmplify.

Luciano Giorgi
CASA FALK
2008 | Stromboli, Aeolian Islands, Italy

Although its landscape has been shaped by violent natural forces, Casa Falk projects a sense of absolute calm and fortitude. It is wedged between dark volcanic cliffs and the Sciara del Fuoco, a blackened lava scar caused by eruptions running down the volcano Stromboli's northern flank. Its abstract sculptural forms are typical of Aeolian architecture: pristeen white stucco, sloping walls, separate parts huddling together like a miniature casbah. The house is a former residence of Swiss artist Hans Falk. Architect Luciano Giorgi simplifed its original configuration, improving the flow between its components and its openness to nature. Terraces, external staircases, passageways, and patios connect the four volumes to make a single dwelling. The upper floors are devoted to private suites with sea and volcano views; the ground level is conceived as open social areas, with a kitchen and dining room, studio, library, spa, and large living room. A dazzling monochrome palette illuminates the interior: white walls and black lava-stone flooring sourced from Mount Etna spills outside onto terraces and paths. Dark bronze window frames will naturally oxidize, showing elemental processes at work. Other materials, such as chestnut wood from Sicilian forests and marble from Carrara, add to the restrained opulence. In one suite, a giraffe-necked concrete-and-lava-stone fireplace that Falk made has been thoughtfully restored.

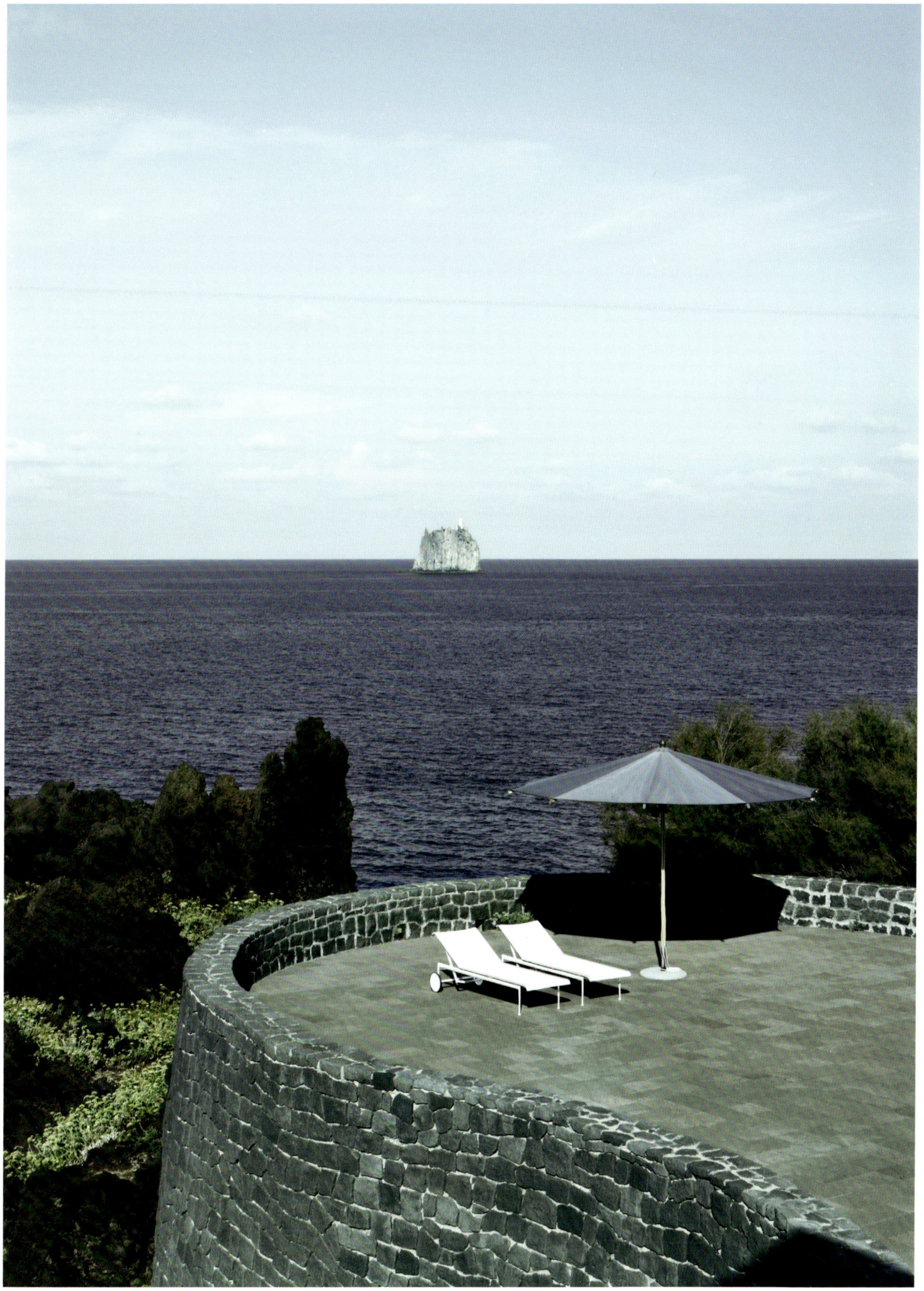

CASA FALK

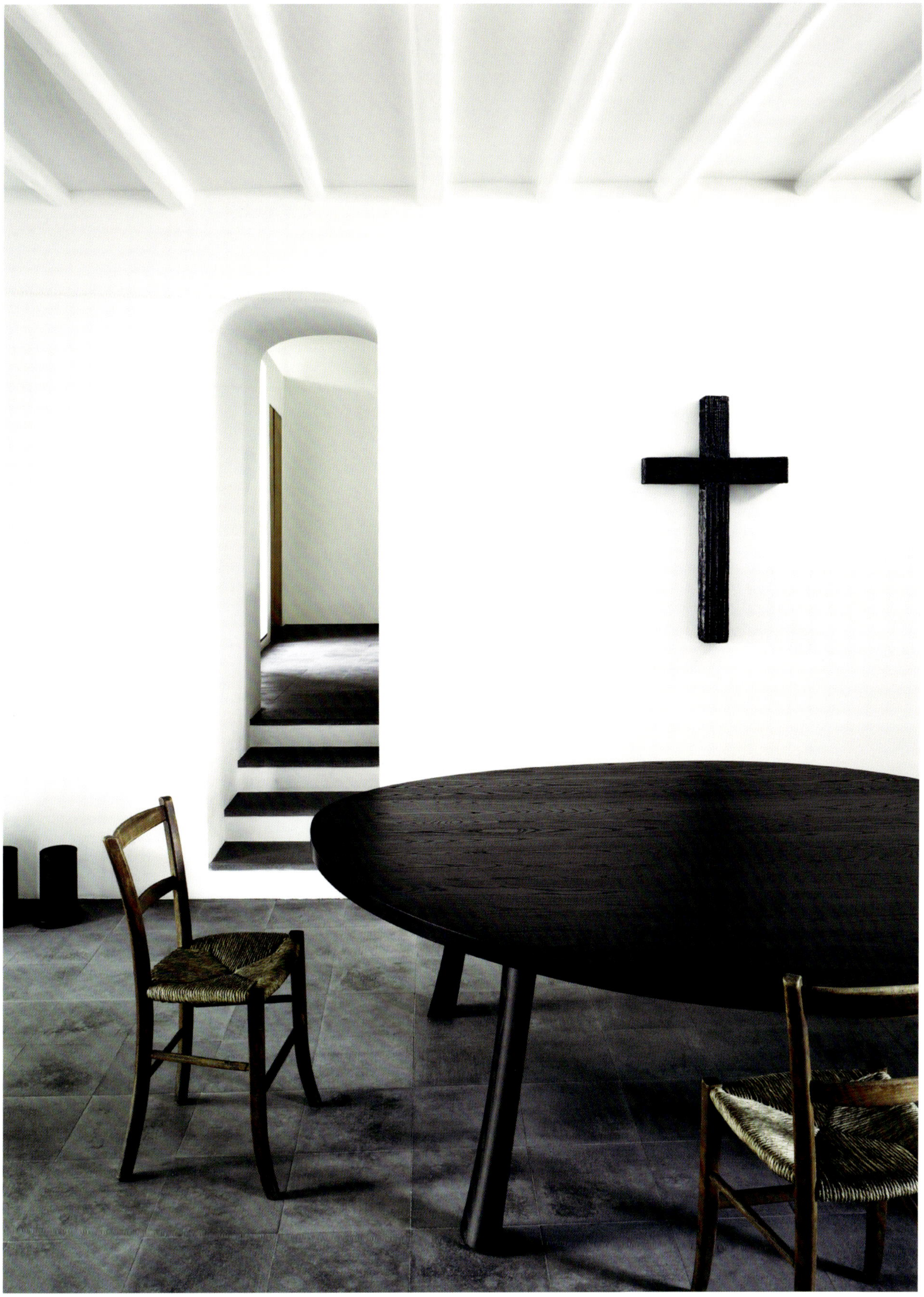

Hacker Architects
HIGH DESERT RESIDENCE
2018 | Bend, OR, USA

This boldly conceived weekend escape in Oregon's high desert near the city of Bend took the landscape itself as a starting point—the architecture is in the service of looking. The resulting house has far-reaching views and a seamless connection with the outdoors. The design takes elements of the box form and articulates them, turning the composition into a series of cubic volumes with opaque and transparent facades. This creates apertures through which to gaze at the desert and the sky, with filled-in areas made of swathes of cedar to create privacy. Stained a warm gray to reflect the tones of desert plants and shadows, the wood is also used widely inside, fostering a sense of continuity between outside and in. Terraces and decks encourage inhabitants to immerse themselves in a desert landscape that has a range of climatic conditions, including snow and golf-ball-sized hail as well as fierce heat. In the summer, oblique bars of shading from pergolas provide relief and animate the spaces with shifting abstract patterns. The views constantly change too, making this a home that is at once restorative and charged with the pulsing energy of the desert.

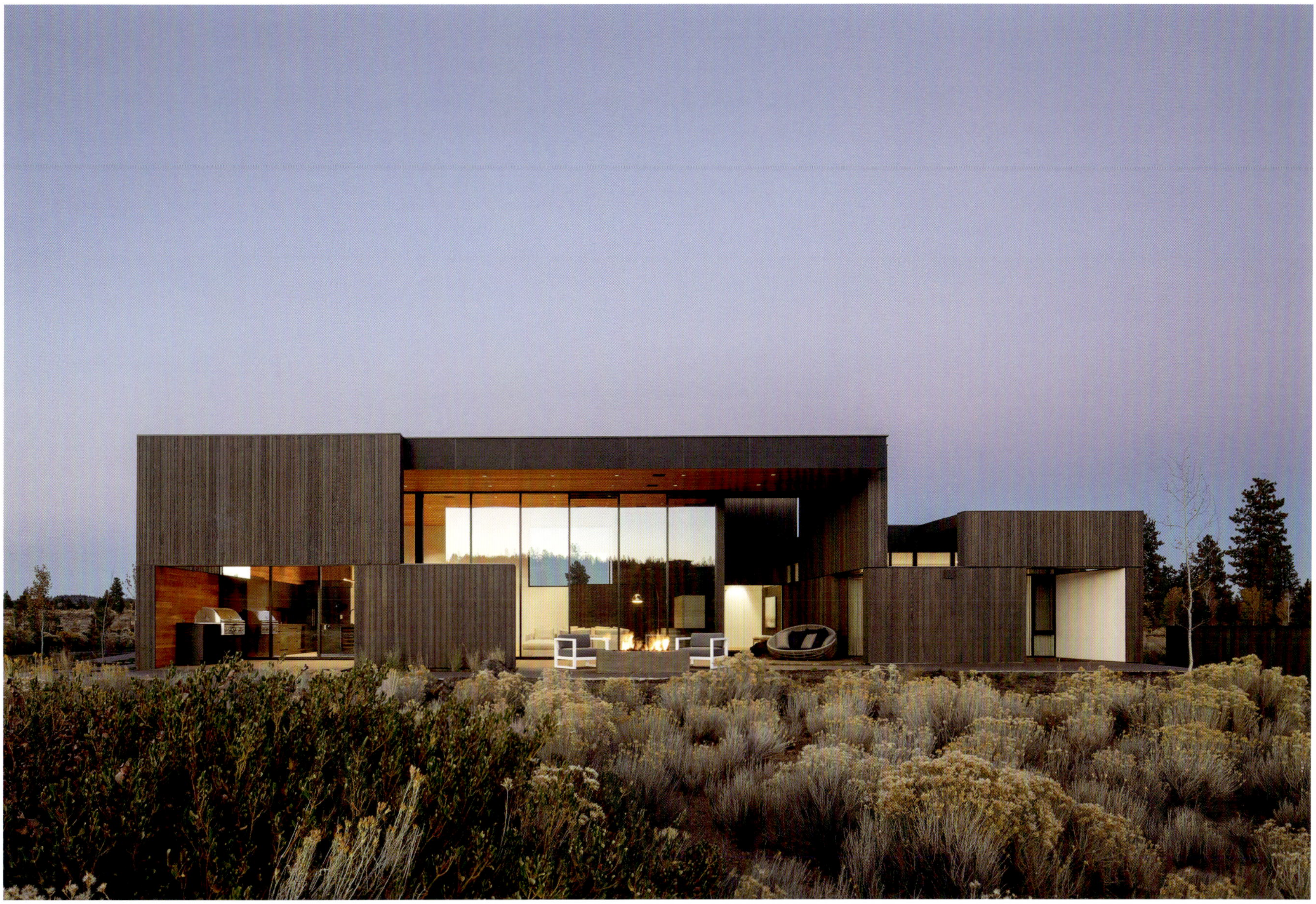

HIGH DESERT RESIDENCE

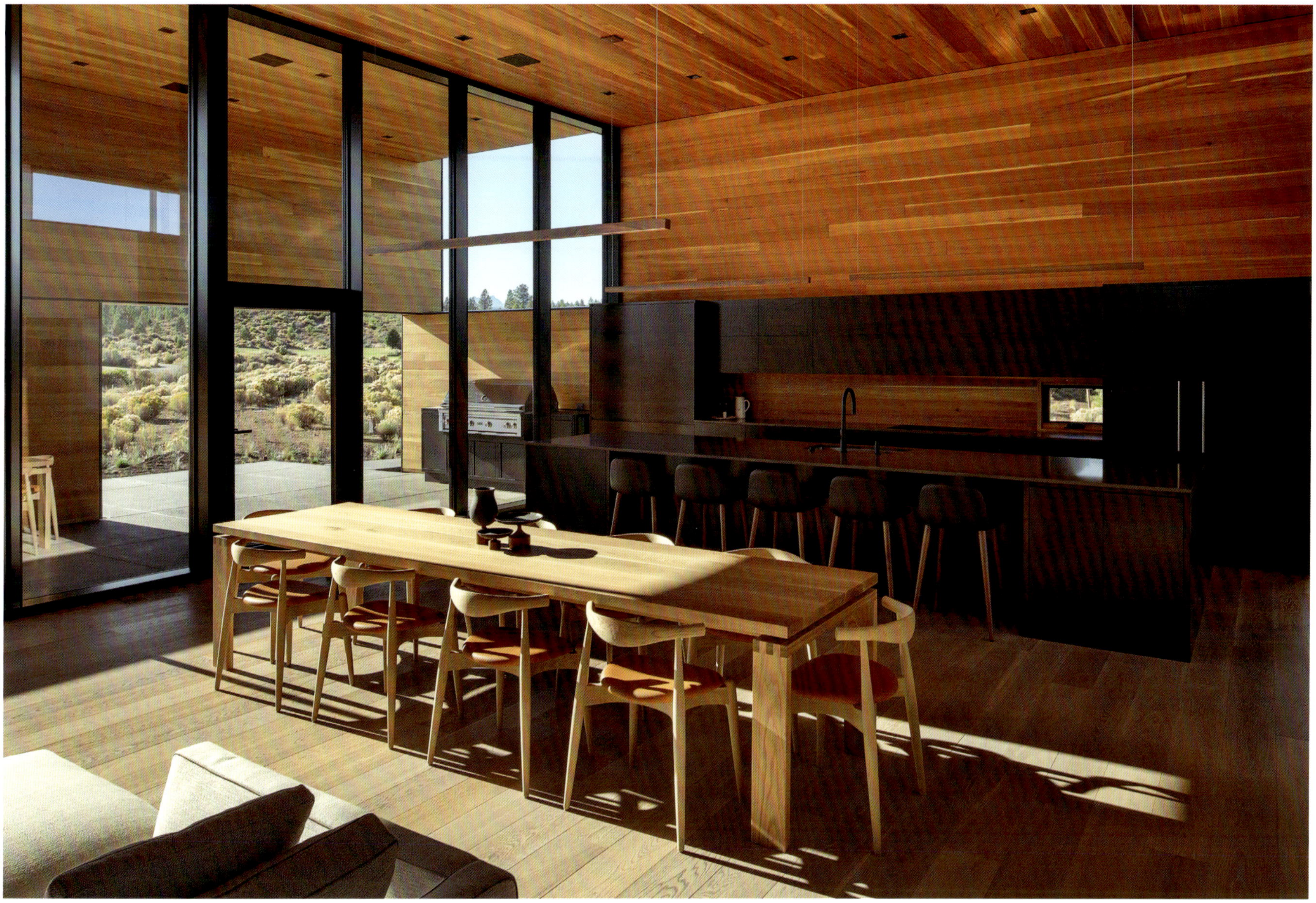

Olson Kundig
HALE LANA
2018 | Kona, HI, USA

Surrounded by piles of red and black volcanic rock, this residence sprawls elegantly across a lava plain in Kona, a coastal region of Hawaii. Olson Kundig conceived the house as a collection of five pavilions, whose double-pitched roofs subtly mimic the forms of the low mountains behind. The firm referenced the Hawaiian vernacular style of large overhanging roofs, which tame prevailing winds, transforming them into cooling breezes to ventilate interiors. In this house, however, the corrugated metal canopies are strongly exaggerated: their bladelike forms balance lightly on glazed walls and give the house a distinctive, dynamic form. The main living and social pavilion and "cabana" for drinks and dining meet at right angles around a slender pool jutting out into the lava field. To the rear are guest suites. Connections between the separate volumes are made by way of a series of lanais, or covered verandas, in cedar and ipe that snake between the pavilions. Wood is used throughout—for roof overhangs, flooring, and walls—to create continuity between the elements. The main bedroom and attached terrace has pride of place overlooking the volcanic escarpment. Hale Lana (which means "floating home") is an island of coolness and serenity resting on a once-burning landscape.

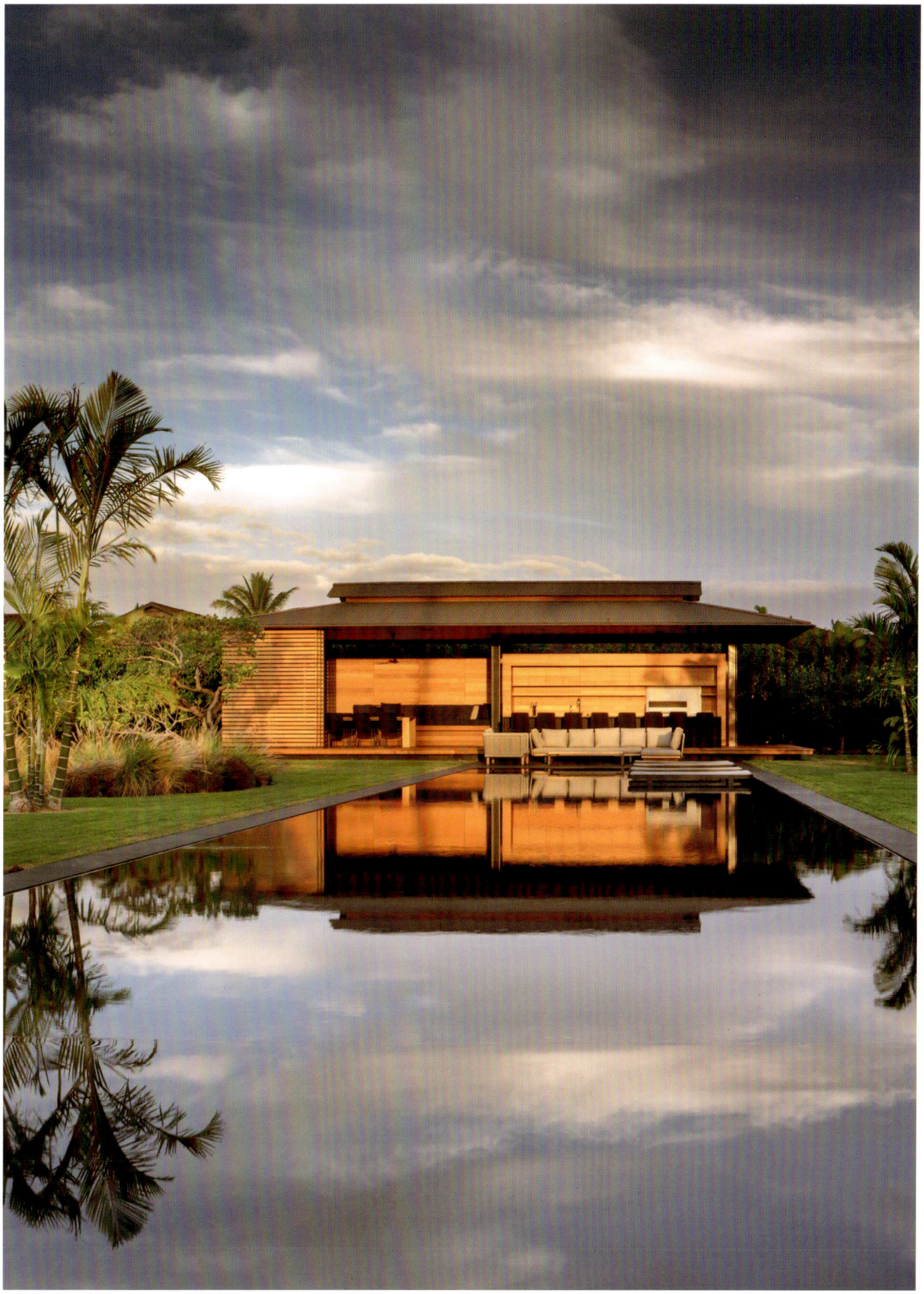

HALE LANA

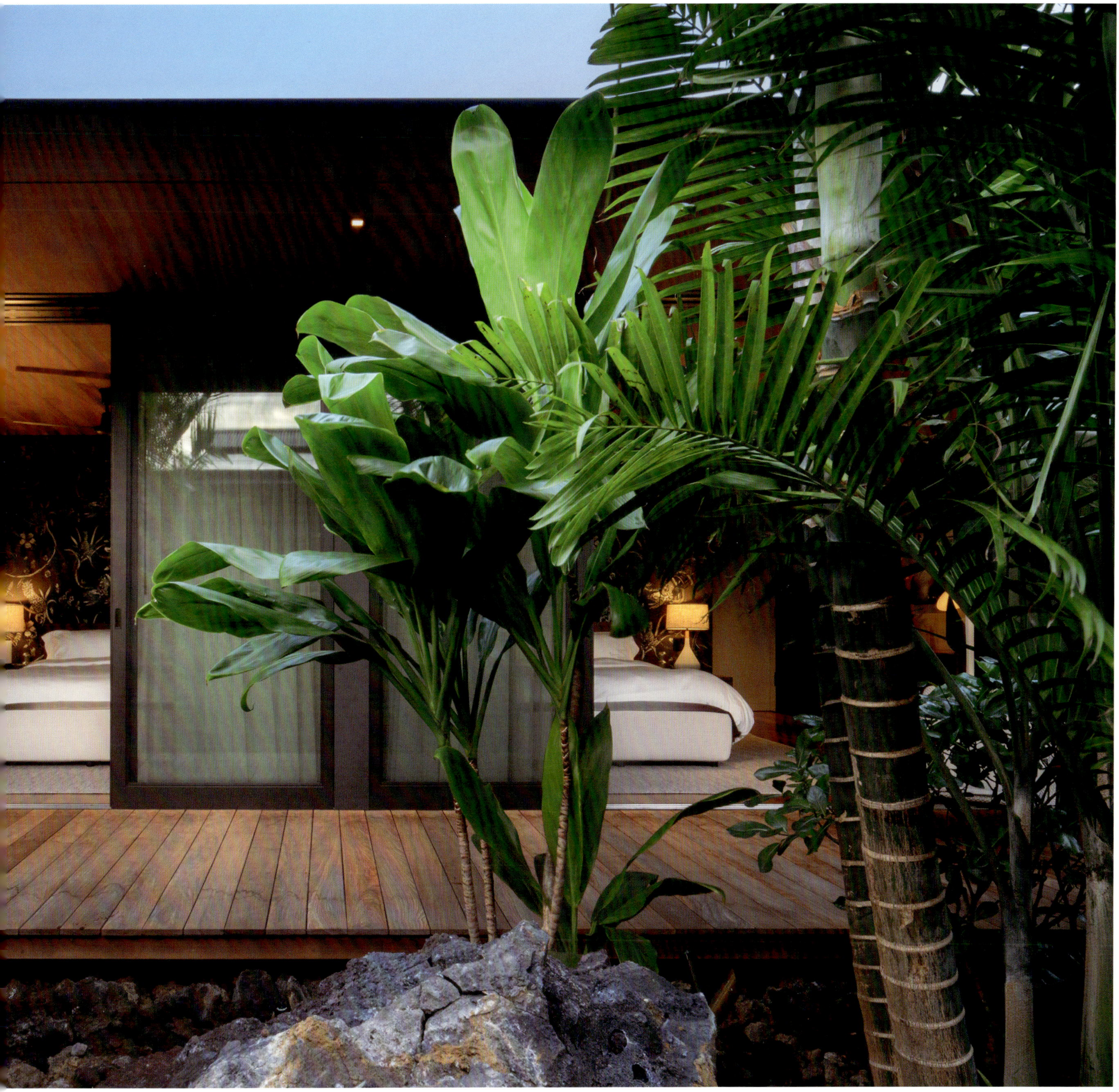

HALE LANA

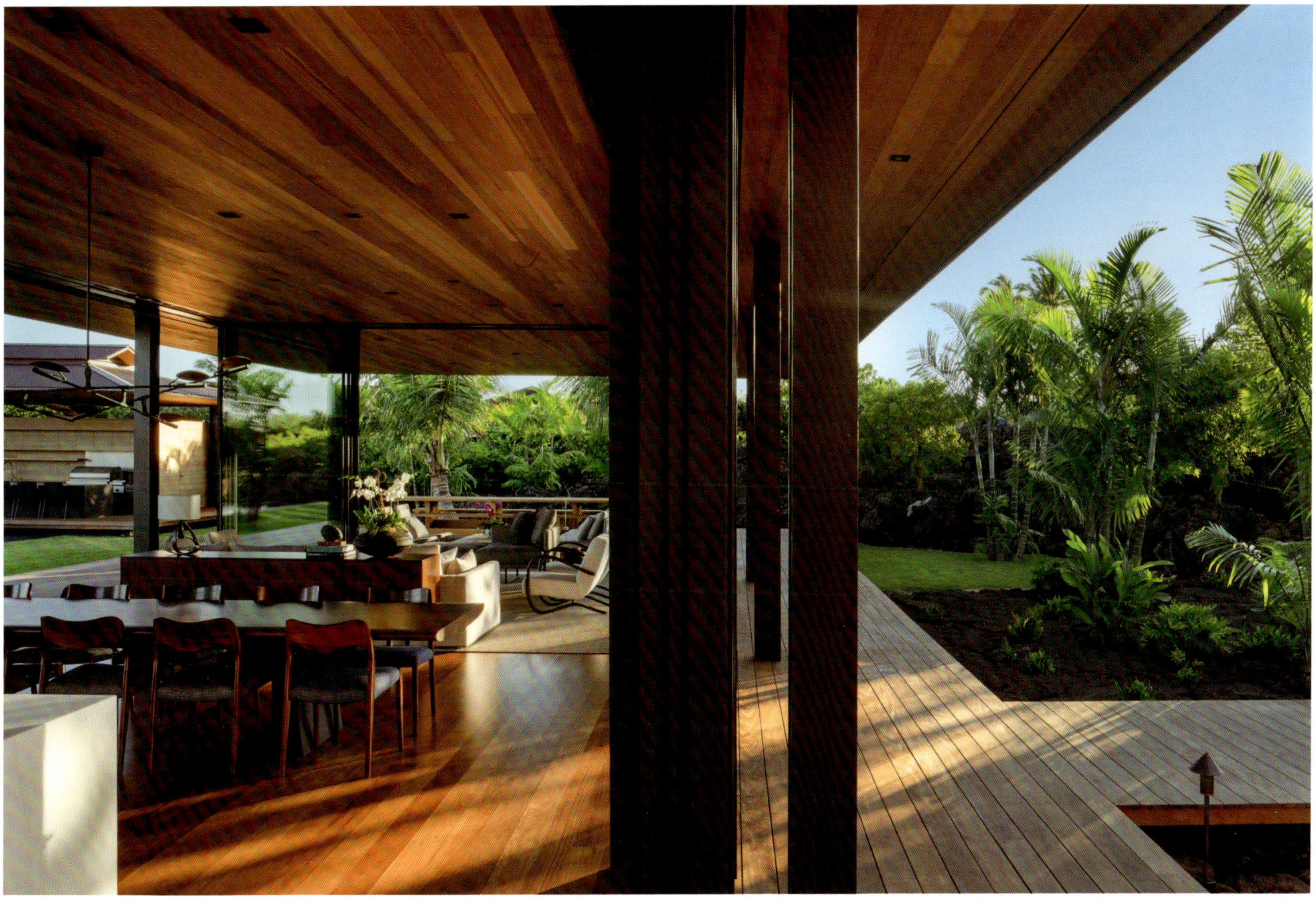

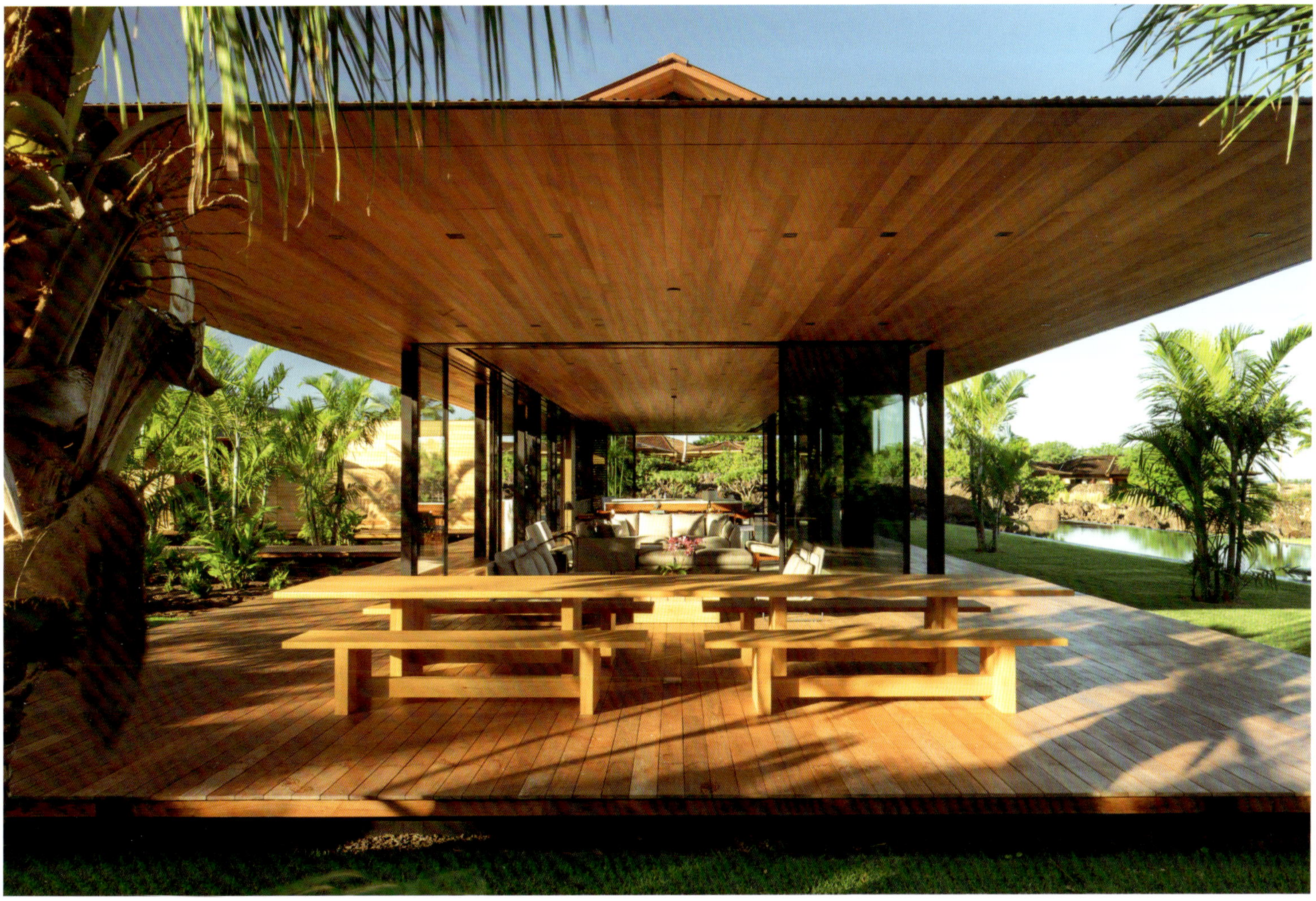

Ampuero Yutronic
CASA HUALLE
2017 | Pucón, Chile

The monolithic form of Casa Hualle boldly interrupts the landscape of Chile's Araucanía region, which is known for its geothermal activity, far-ranging vistas, and lakes. With views of Villarrica, one of Chile's most active volcanoes, the two-story house is wrapped in slender dark-stained softwood slats that reference the black lava stone commonly used to clad houses in Pucón and its surrounding area. The dark tones intentionally contrast with the washed-out landscape hues of brown, blue, and green. Approached from the road, the house resembles a regular pitched-roof agricultural shed, similar to many nearby. But a closer look soon reveals that Casa Hualle is far from straightforward: its roof is faceted, and its overall form is characterized by a series of geometric folds and cut-outs, one of which highlights the main entrance. From the exterior, the windows in the facades appear randomly placed, but they are intended, from inside, to frame the best views of Villarrica and the massive Chilean plain. When someone enters the house, the interior provide a startling contrast with the dark exterior: the stained plywood walls are pale, almost white. They transform the house, with its double-height central living area, into a gallery-like space, where views of the land "hang" like paintings on the blank walls. The design references geothermal forces again indoors: the exposed-concrete floors incorporate black volcanic ash. Following the roof's geometry, the ceiling folds sinuously along the length of the house.

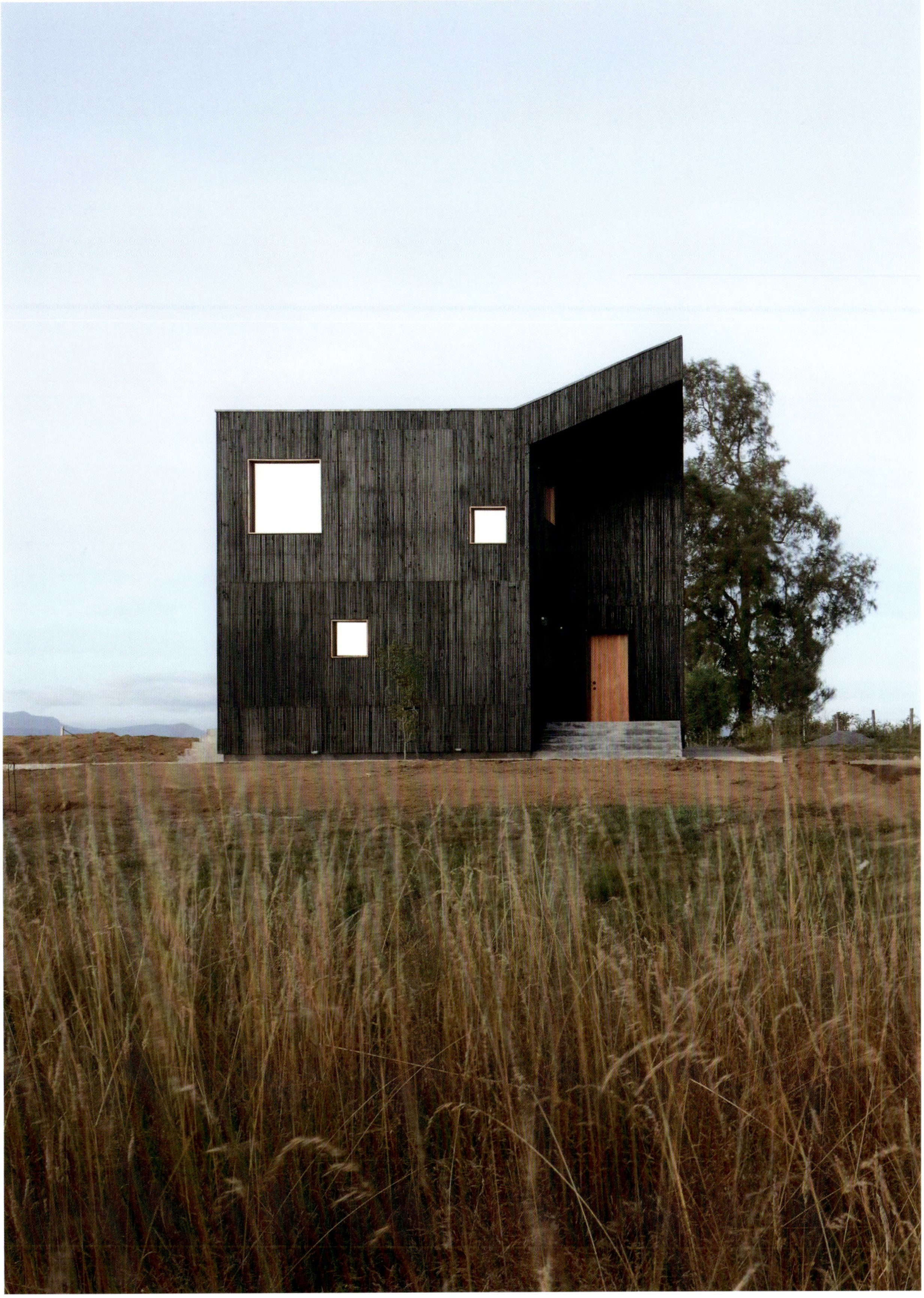

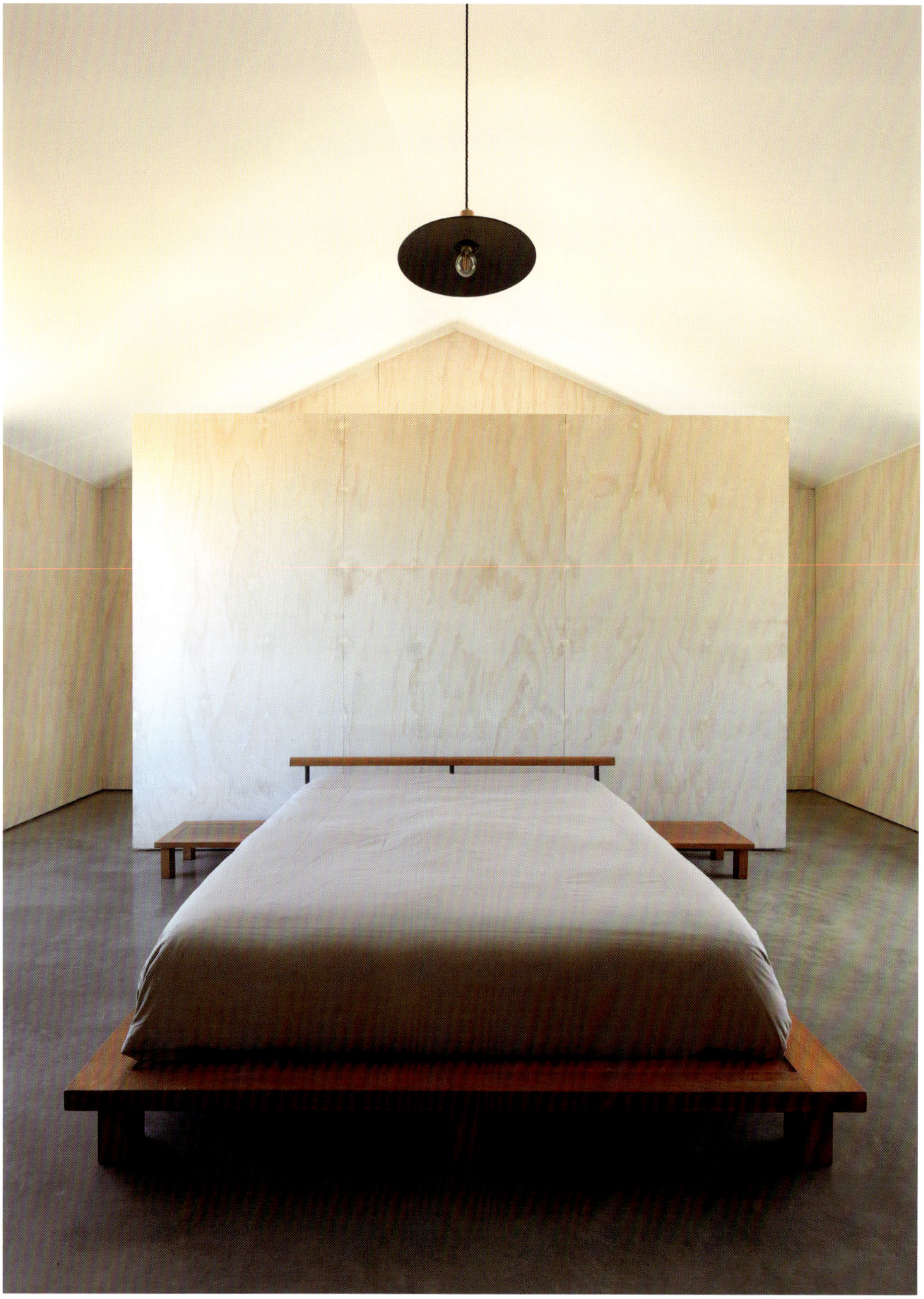

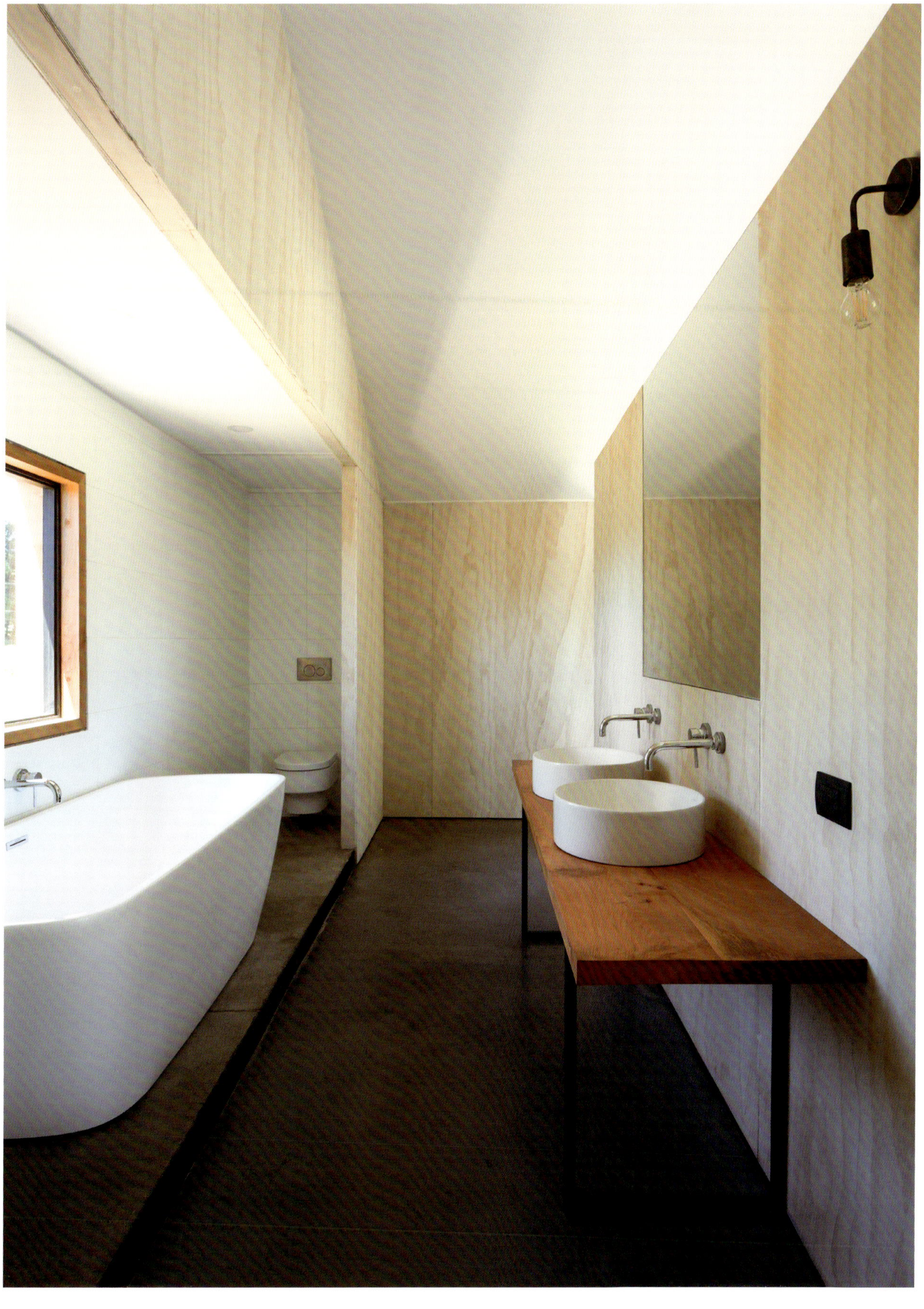

K-Studio
VILLA MANDRA
2019 | Mykonos, Greece

High on a ridge in Aleomandra on the Greek island of Mykonos, surrounded and hidden by a hefty stone wall, this low-lying complex was built for a young couple to enjoy with family and friends. The upper level—two simple cubic volumes connected by a central covered courtyard—is devoted to living, eating, and socializing. Down the hillside, in a quieter and more secluded area, a rectangular volume with a roof garden houses six bedrooms. The project's overriding aims were to achieve protection from the fierce Mykonos heat and create spaces where people could comfortably relax outdoors all day. Villa Mandra employs many typically Cycladic architectural features to deal with the climatic challenges. The nexus of the house, the courtyard, is shaded by a traditional Greek chestnut pergola, reinforced with a network of glulam beams. Walls are hand-built from hunks of locally excavated rock—a third of which is from the site itself—which keep the house cool. Stone flooring is used throughout, and also features in details such as door lintels and window frames. Exterior walls are limewashed to deflect the harsh sunlight, and shutters keep out the intense heat. The low-hunkering buildings and perimeter wall also protect the inhabitants from the notorious *meltemi* wind. These vernacular elements, reinterpreted with a contemporary slant and employing high standards of craftmanship, are crucial in creating the villa's shaded and serene spaces of rest, reflection, and refreshment.

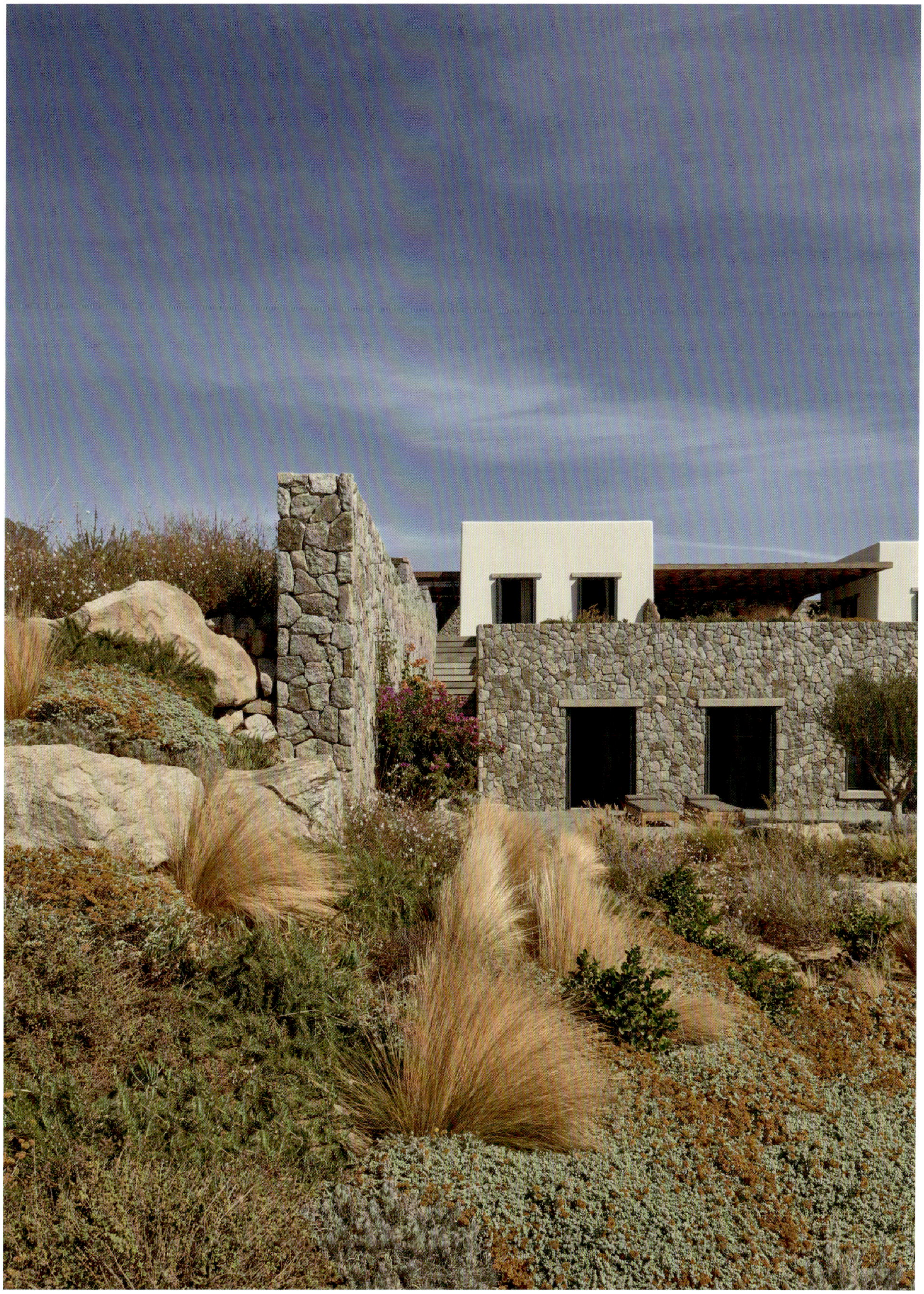

VILLA MANDRA

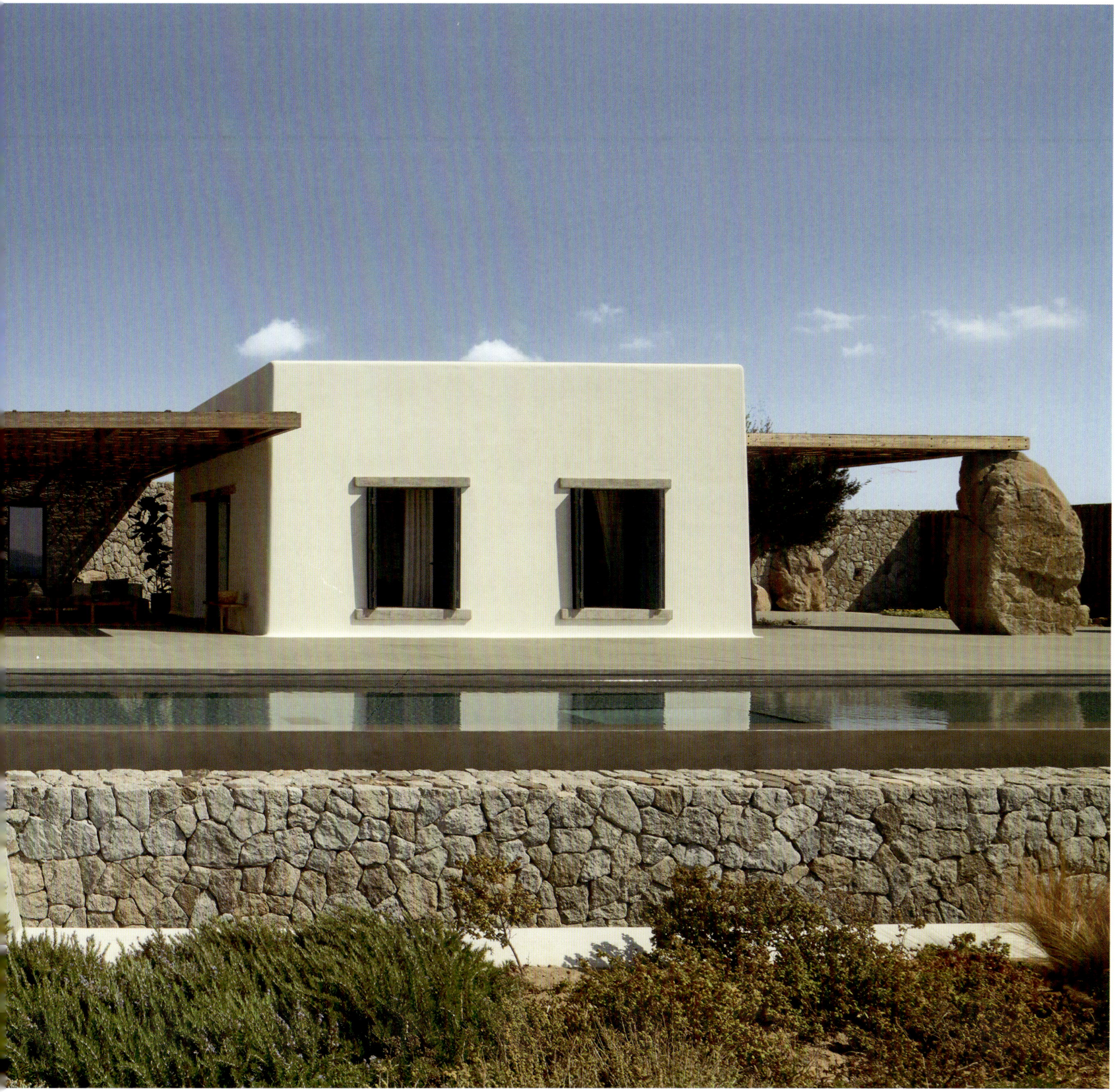

VILLA MANDRA

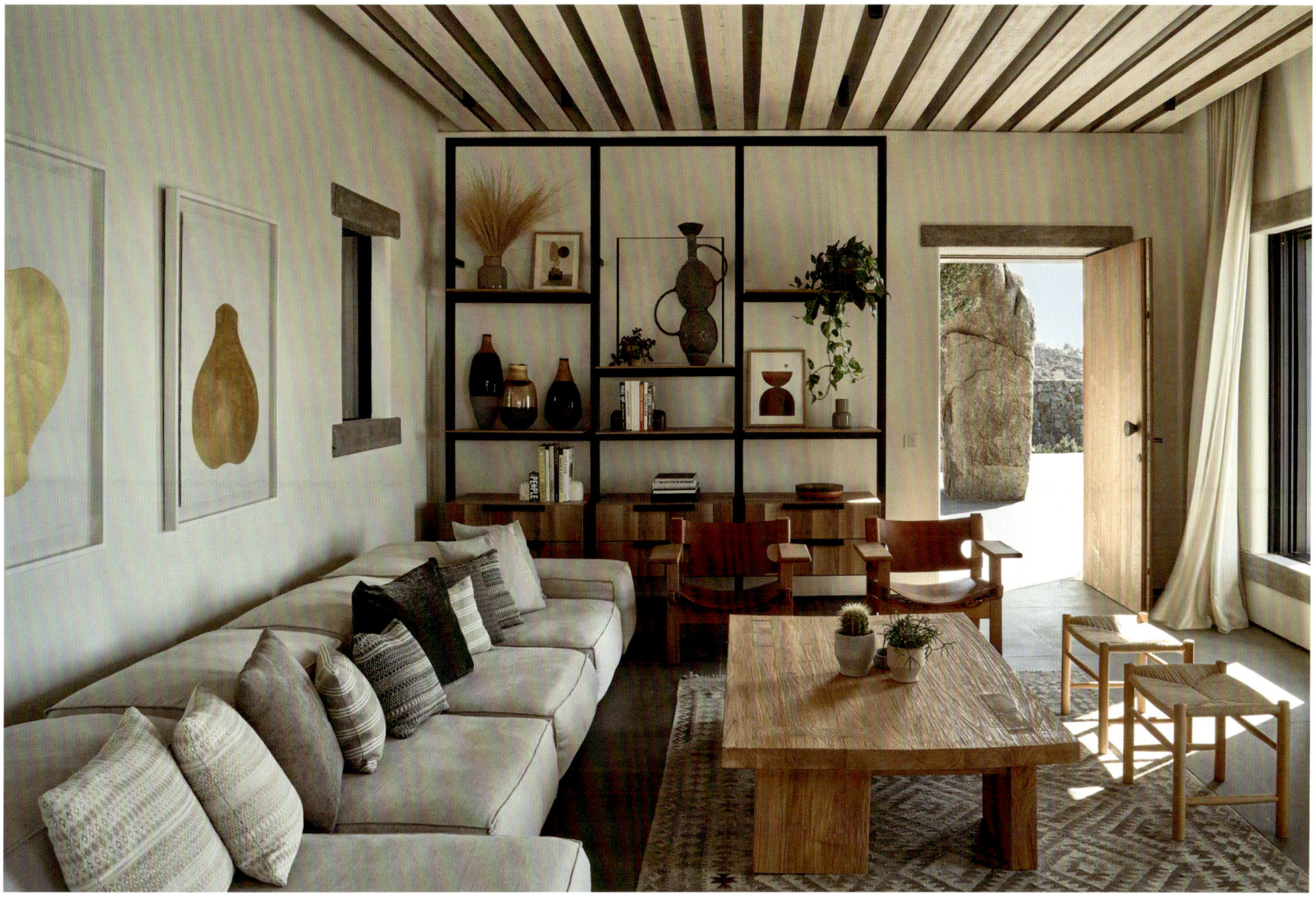

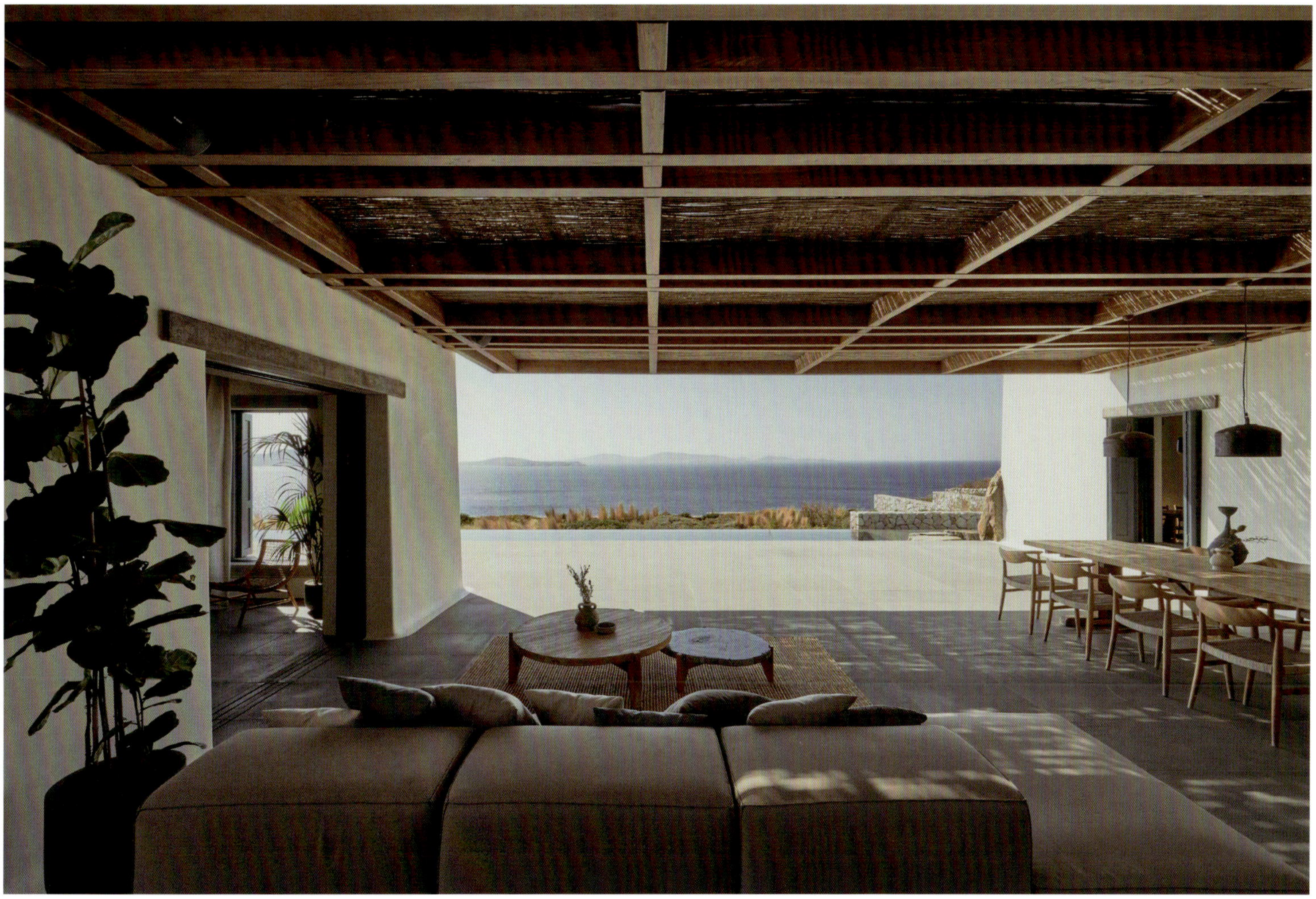

Weber Arquitectos
SAN SIMÓN CABINS
2019 | Valle de Bravo, Mexico

Situated in lush woodland near Valle de Bravo, all of these cabins, forming one single complex, are made of gray volcanic stone. The area is part of Mexico's central volcanic belt, and the landscape has been scarred by violent eruptions that took place thousands of years ago. The complex has been designed this way to avoid harming existing trees and keep the whole project's footprint light. One house is the main residence; there is a separate recreation and social space, as well as three guesthouses. Each cabin has sloping roofs and is elevated on a base made of volcanic stone. Their design is simple, with minimal ornamentation and substantial areas of glazing. A strong connection with the outdoors is central to the ranch's ethos, and each cabin's bathroom has an interior patio filled with plants and a front-facing terrace shaded by an overhanging canopy. Inside, tones are muted and dark to match the somber exterior colors. The recreational cabin features a full kitchen, a living and dining area, pool and poker tables, and a sunken outdoor patio; there is a stone jacuzzi in the nearby woods. The project reflects the area's geology, resulting in a high-end vacation retreat with sharp, clean lines. It is luxurious, but retains an air of restraint and respect for nature due to the sensitive choices of materials and design.

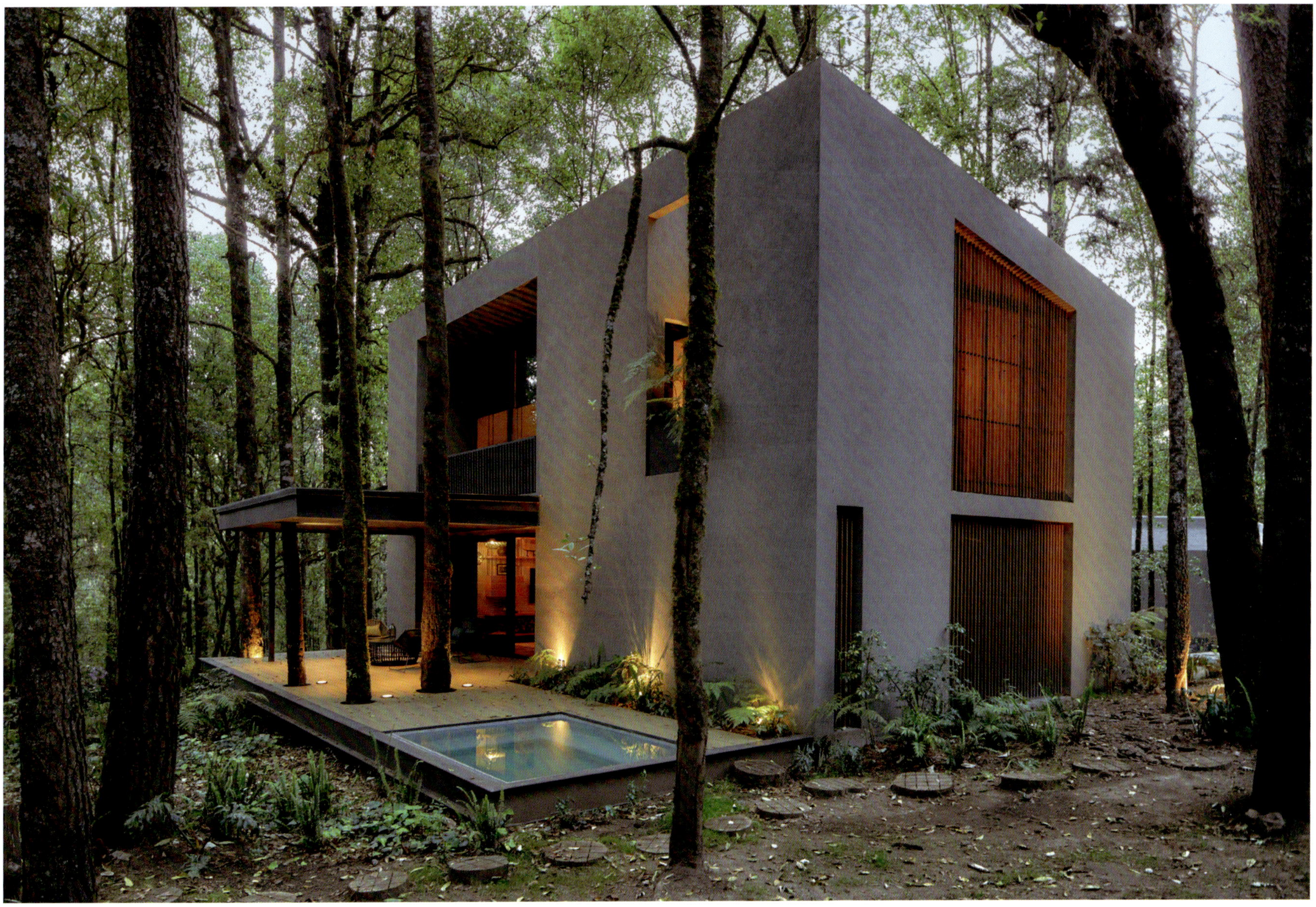

SAN SIMÓN CABINS

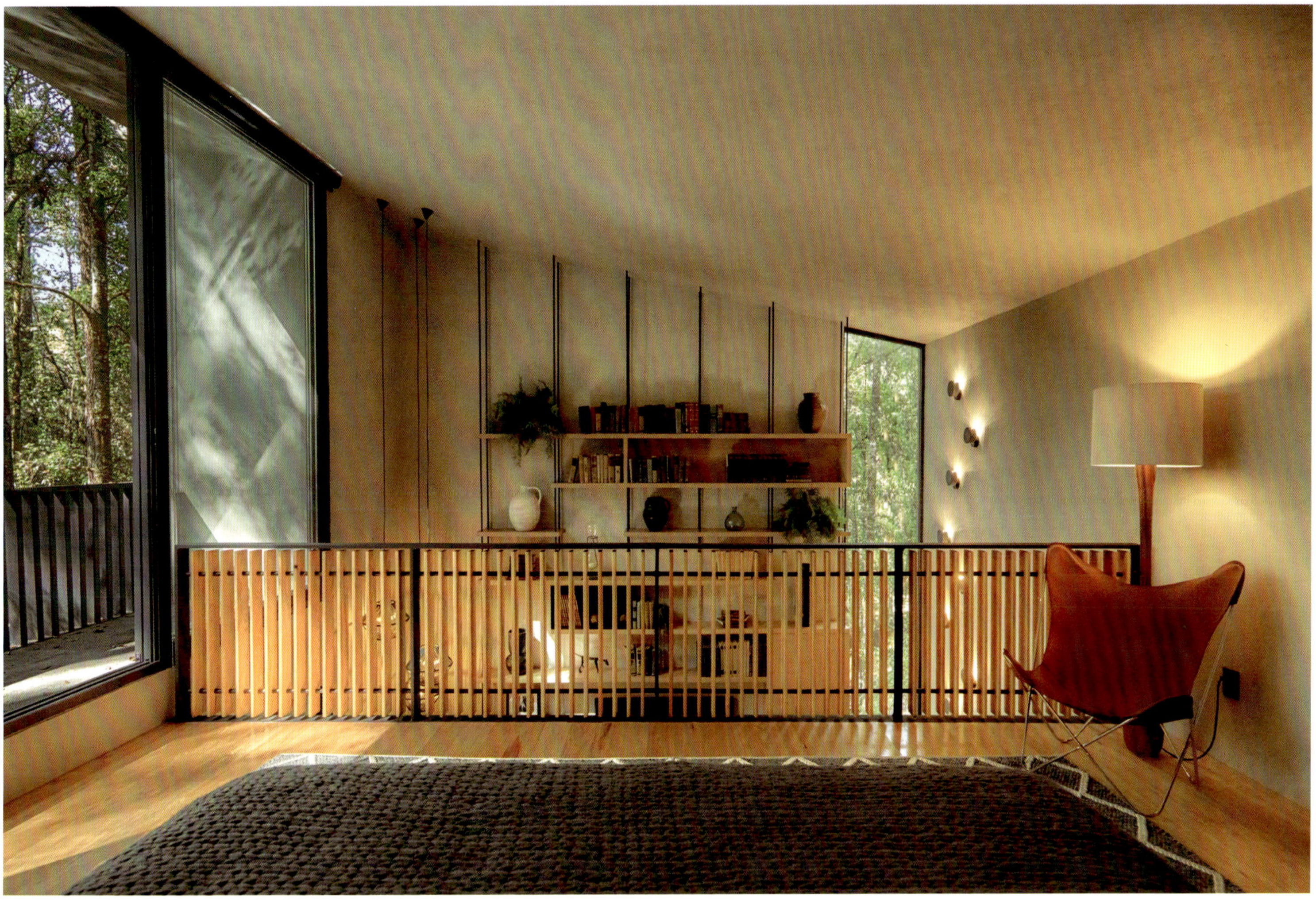

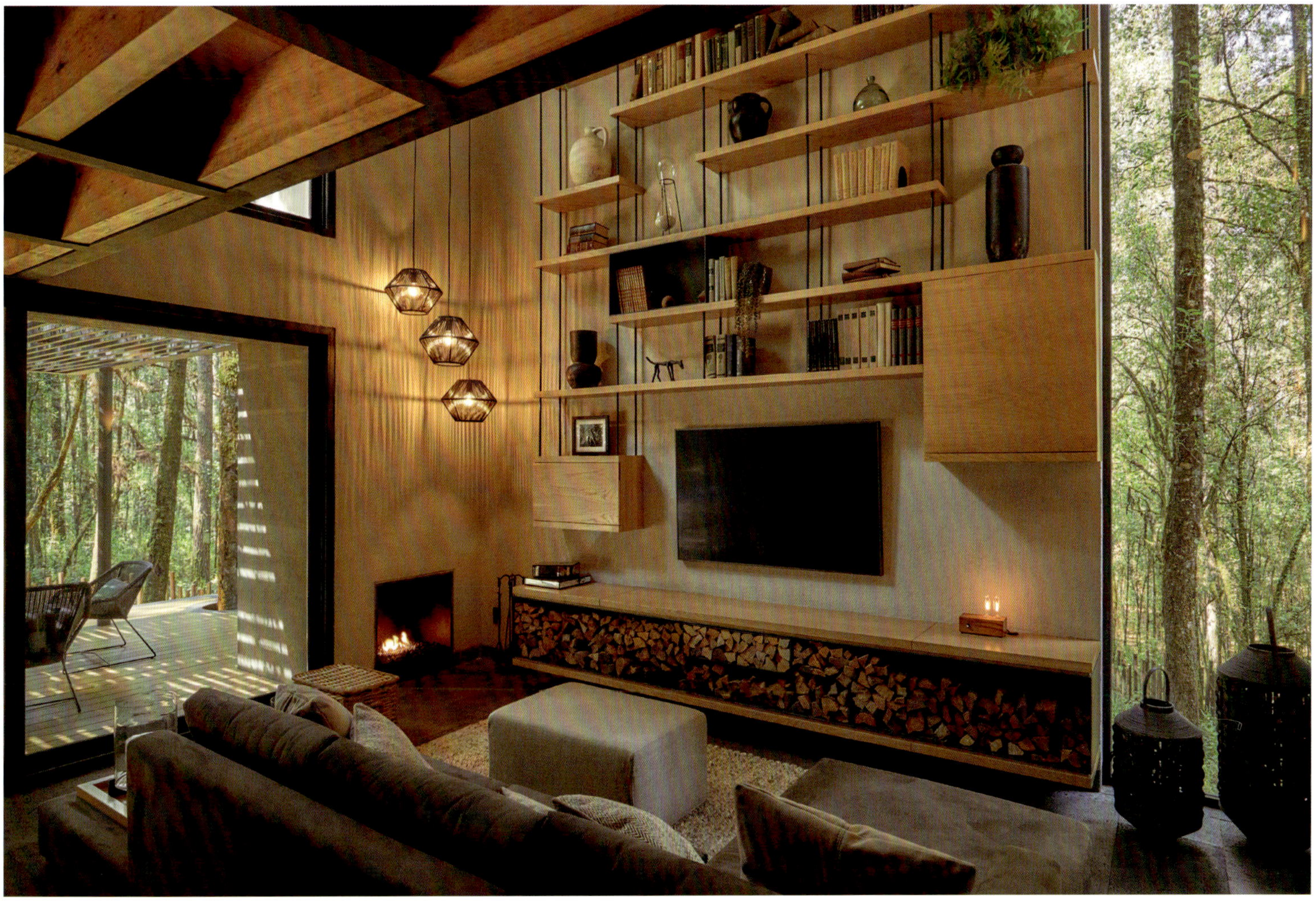

Cohesion
FOLLY CABIN
2018 | Joshua Tree, CA, USA

This rust-red folly looks like a house that has been sliced in two: a witty and surreal sight amid the desert landscape. Each volume has distinct functions, and the two combine to offer a unique wilderness experience. The larger unit is a living space, with a kitchen, living room, and sleeping area; the other serves as a storage space and—enchantingly—a "stargazing portal." Cohesion's principal, Malek Alqadi, found a dilapidated homestead in Joshua Tree National Park in Southern California as a site for a prototype dwelling, reusing the existing slab to keep a small footprint. He designed an archetypal house form, with a tall pitched roof that accommodates more living space than the original cabin, and crucially, allows hot air to vent out through solar-powered roof skylights. The living space, which is lined by raw plywood—contrasting with the burnt-orange reclaimed-steel outer cladding—squeezes in a kitchen, lounge, and mezzanine bedroom. Accessed by a metal ladder, a terrace cut into the roof of the second volume is the stargazing portal, which features some luxurious touches, such as a bioethanol fireplace and a heated queen-size bed for chilly nights outside. A short distance from this building is a photovoltaic-array "solar tree." As opposed to a roof array, this configuration allows the panels to "breathe" and makes them more efficient, and it is suitably elegant and sculptural for this house.

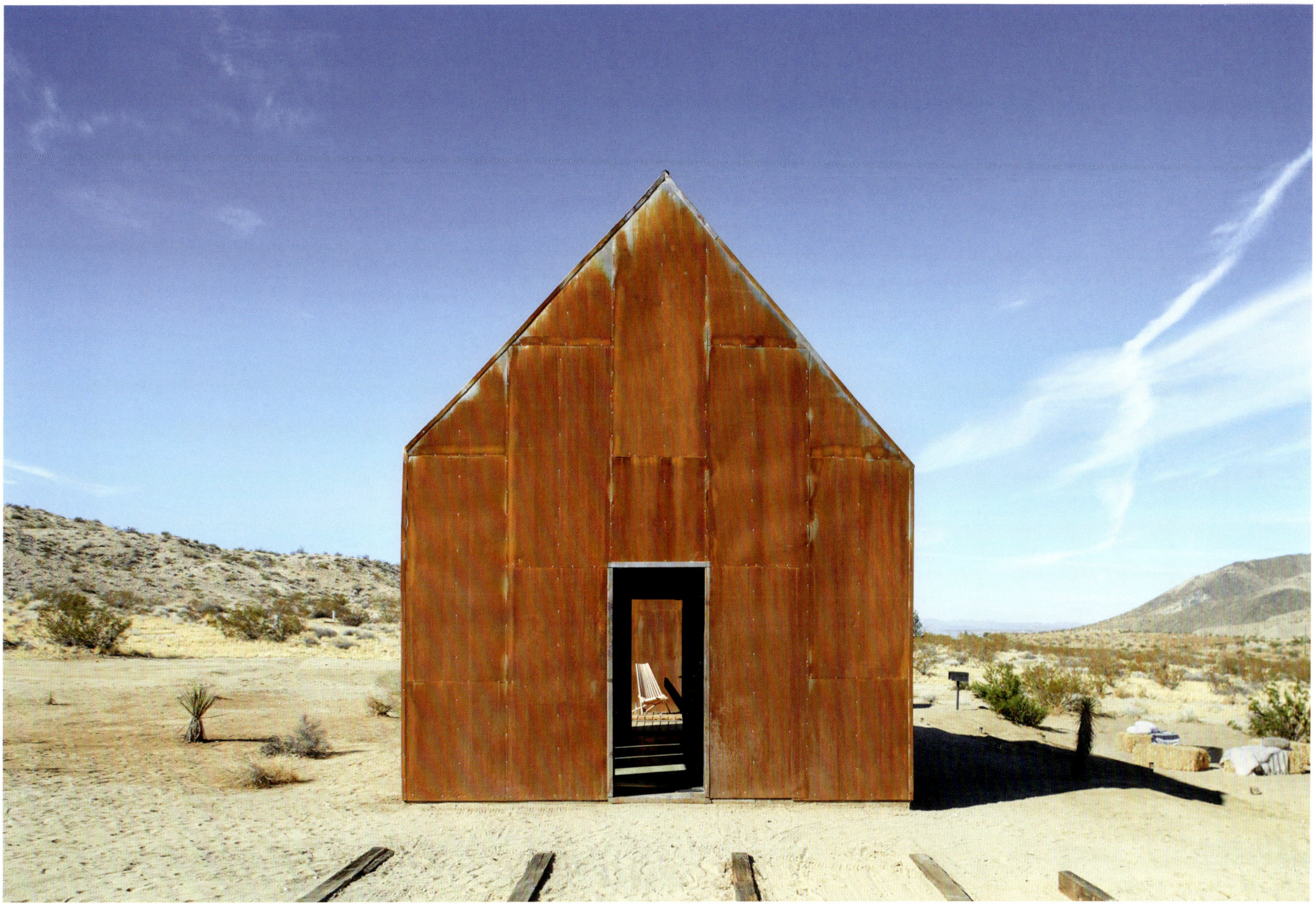

FOLLY CABIN

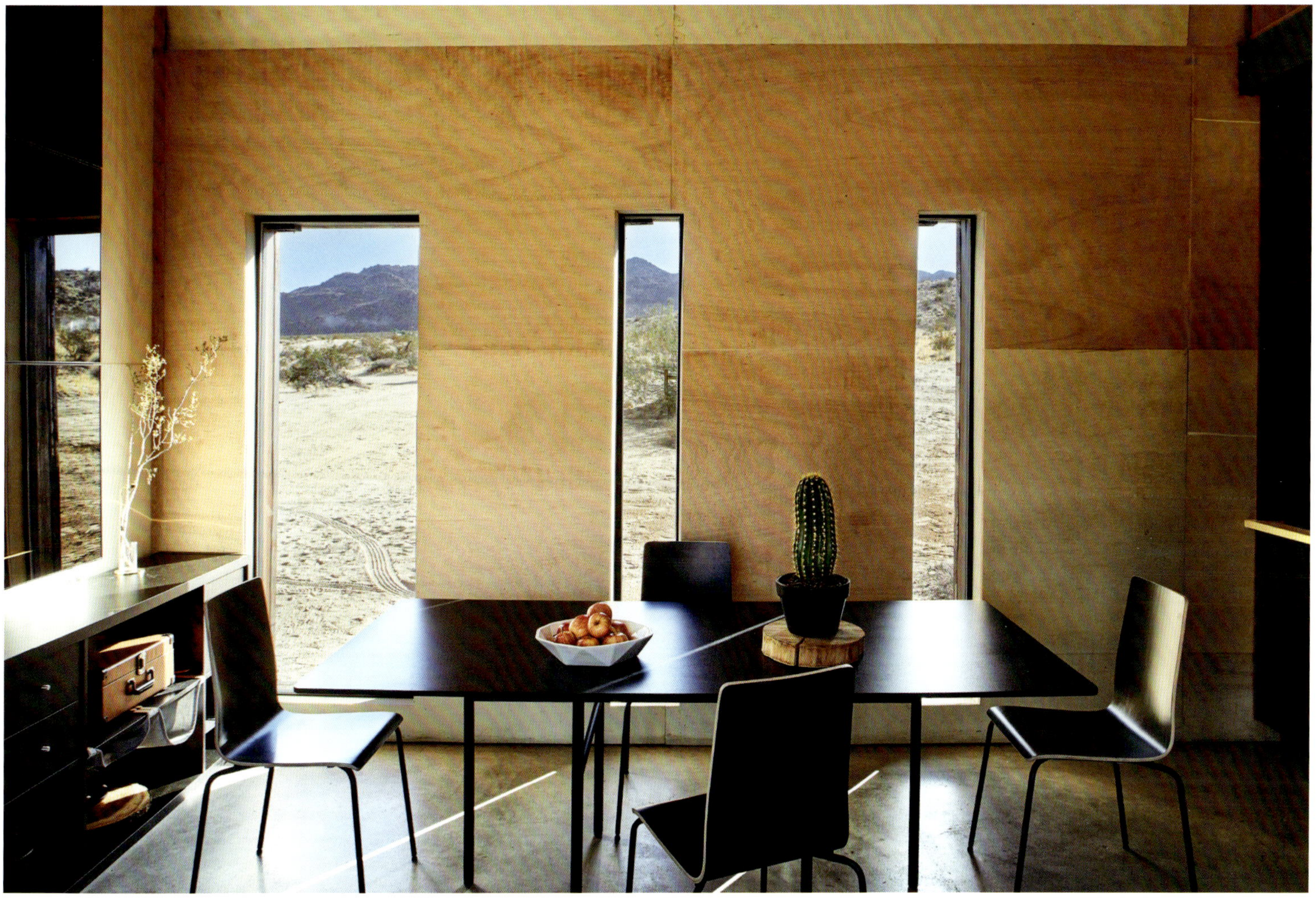

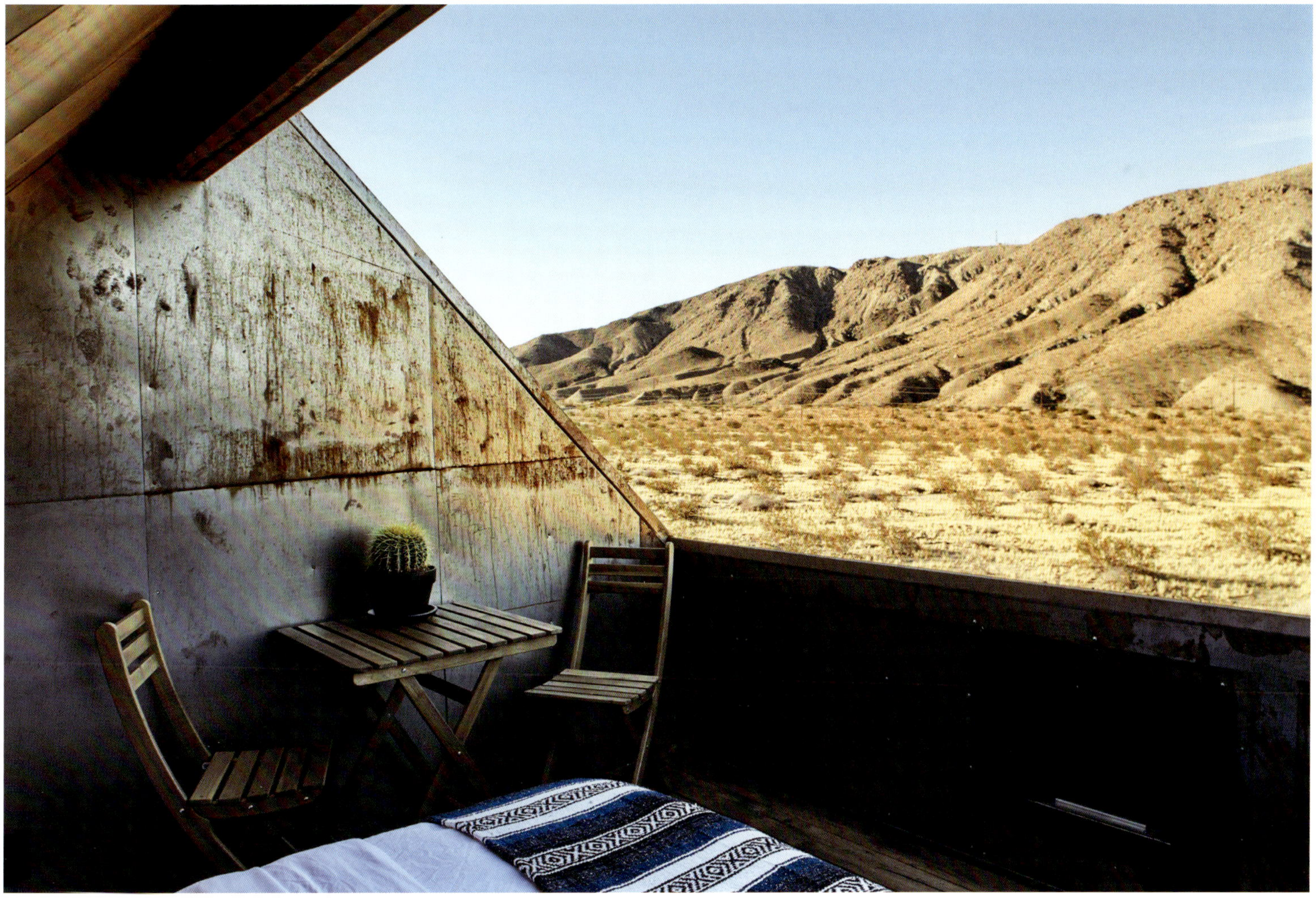

Formafatal
ATELIER VILLA
2020 | Puntarenas, Costa Rica

The Japanese method of weatherproofing, *yakisugi*—in which wood is charred in fire and then oiled—is an unusual but logical response to the tropical climate of the Costa Rican jungle. Czech design studio Formafatal used this technique on a wall at the rear of this vacation retreat; a simple horizontal volume on short stilts. The black wall is totally windowless to screen the house from its neighbors, apart from openings at one end that slide back to reveal an indoor-outdoor swimming pool. Materially, the rest of the villa is dramatically different: perforated rust-red aluminum screening makes it visually porous on all three sides. The screens provide shading and ventilation, and they can open, close, or pivot back as required. Each panel has a unique pattern of piercing and was forged using intense heat. Like the burnt timber, they recall Costa Rica's fiery, volcanic geology. Inside, living and sleeping space is fully flexible; screens can be shifted to expand or divide rooms. The roof of the retreat, accessed by a metal ladder, is covered by a thick layer of grasses, palms, and flowers, creating a strong visual connection with the surrounding jungle.

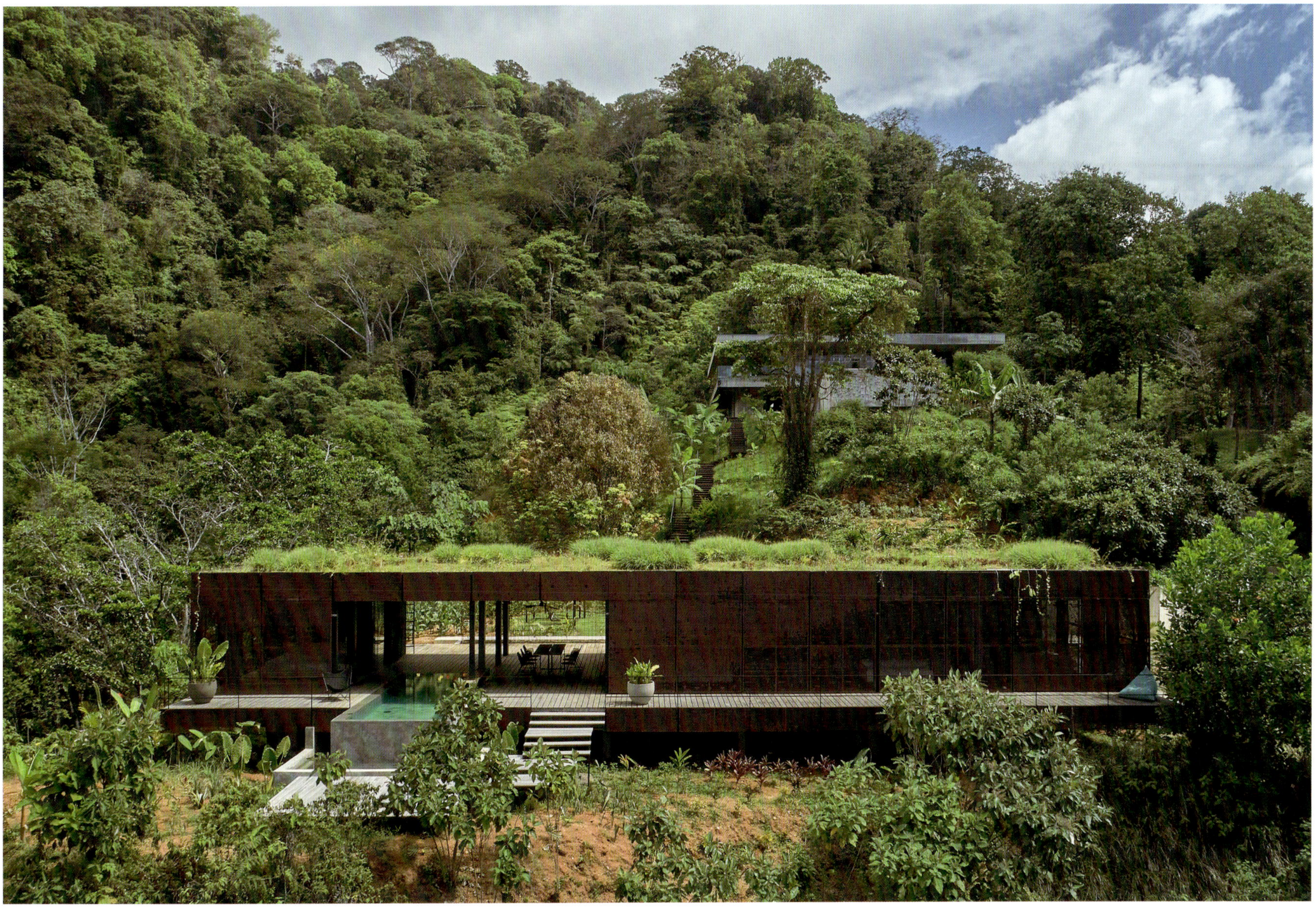

ATELIER VILLA

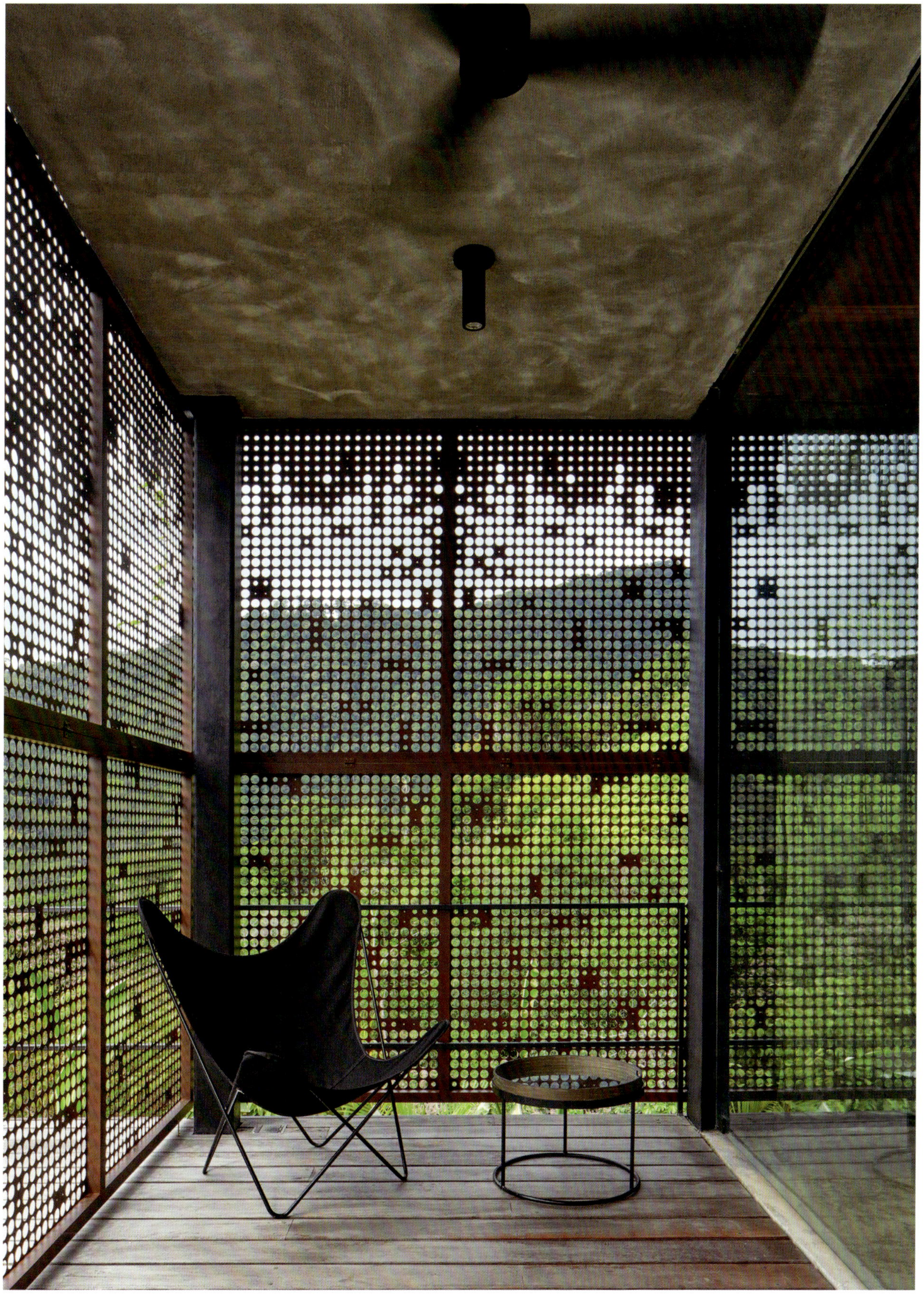

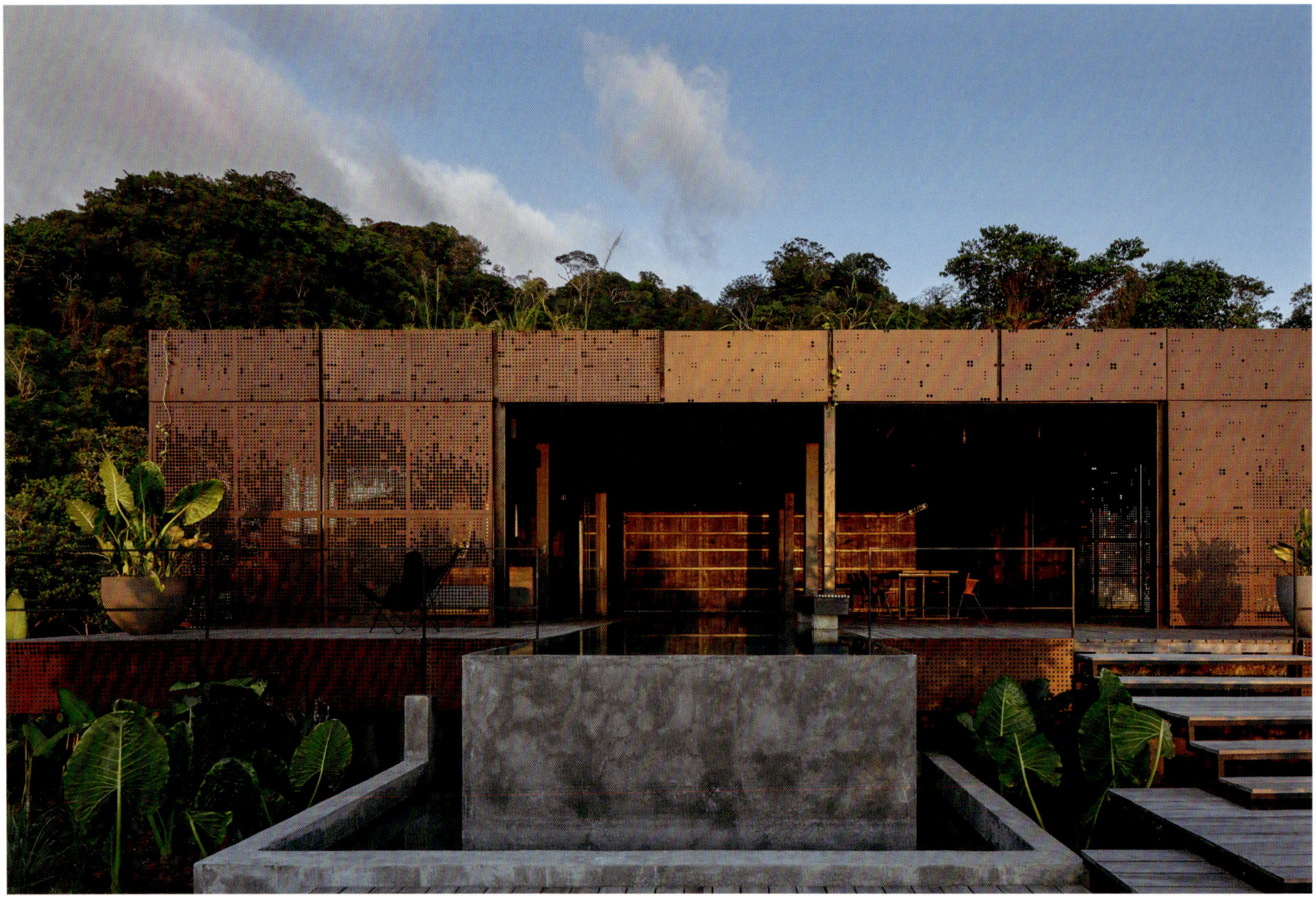

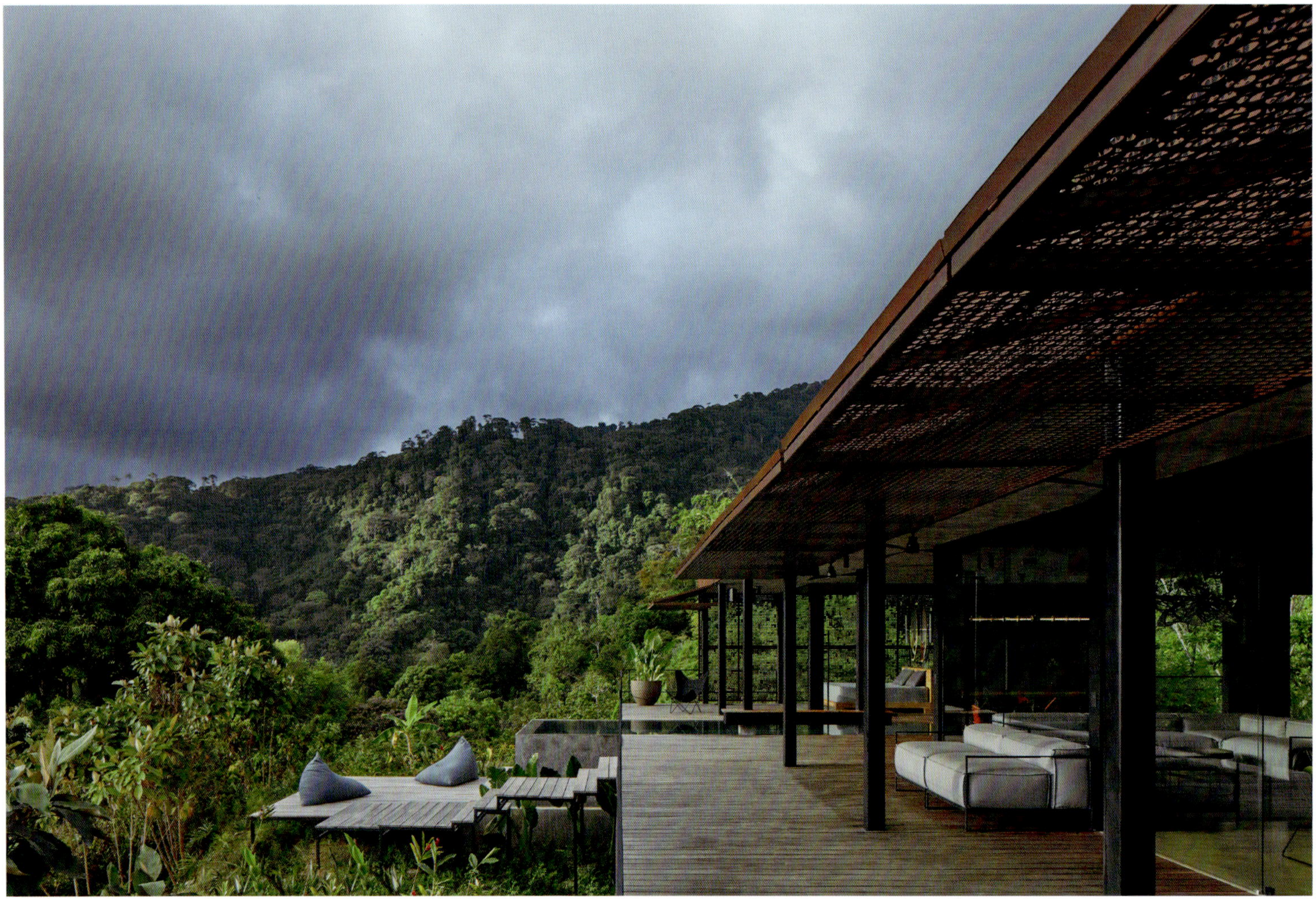

ATELIER VILLA

Faulkner Architects
LOOKOUT HOUSE
2018 | Truckee, CA, USA

Situated near the base of a three-million-year-old volcano, Lookout House is a low-slung composition of concrete volumes easing down a slope like a cooled lava flow. It occupies a privileged spot amid a stand of dramatically tall Jeffrey pine and white fir trees, and the site consists of volcanic sediment from ancient flows and huge basalt boulders. The house is divided into various zones as it descends: the uppermost part for the main bedroom, the next level for guests, and finally, at the front, an area for living and dining. The living block is distinguished by its black steel (the other two are a pale gray concrete) and features cantilevering overhangs to provide shade and shelter from the elements. Extremely thick walls throughout absorb scarce rays and heat from the sun. In places, the house features red-orange glass to suggest volcanic magma. Interior walls are also concrete, and they are combined with glass, steel, and walnut detailing and flamed basalt floors, creating an organic yet sleek modernist aesthetic. High ceilings and continuous spaces give a sense of easygoing grandeur, while cozier areas have been created using more subdued lighting.

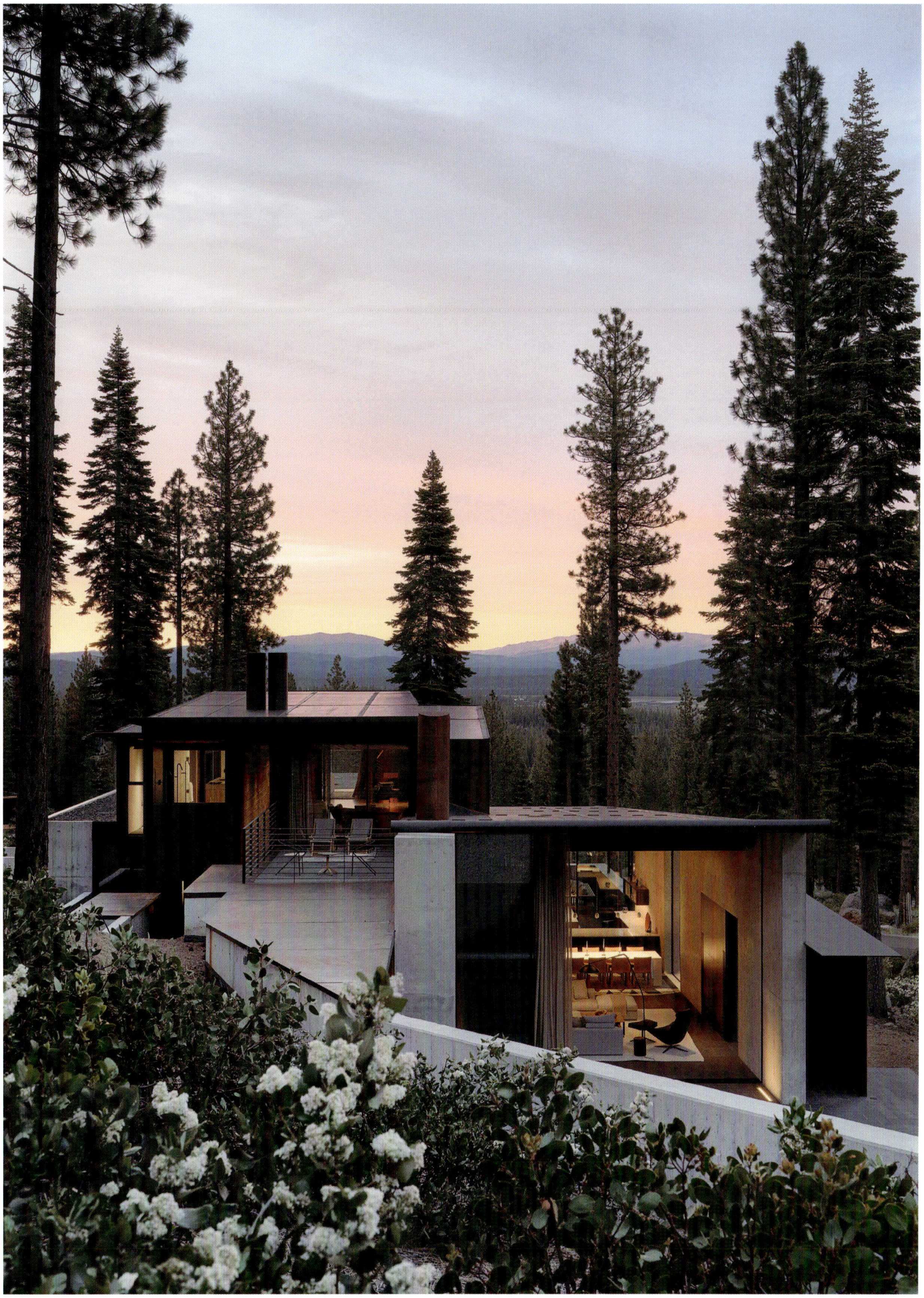

LOOKOUT HOUSE

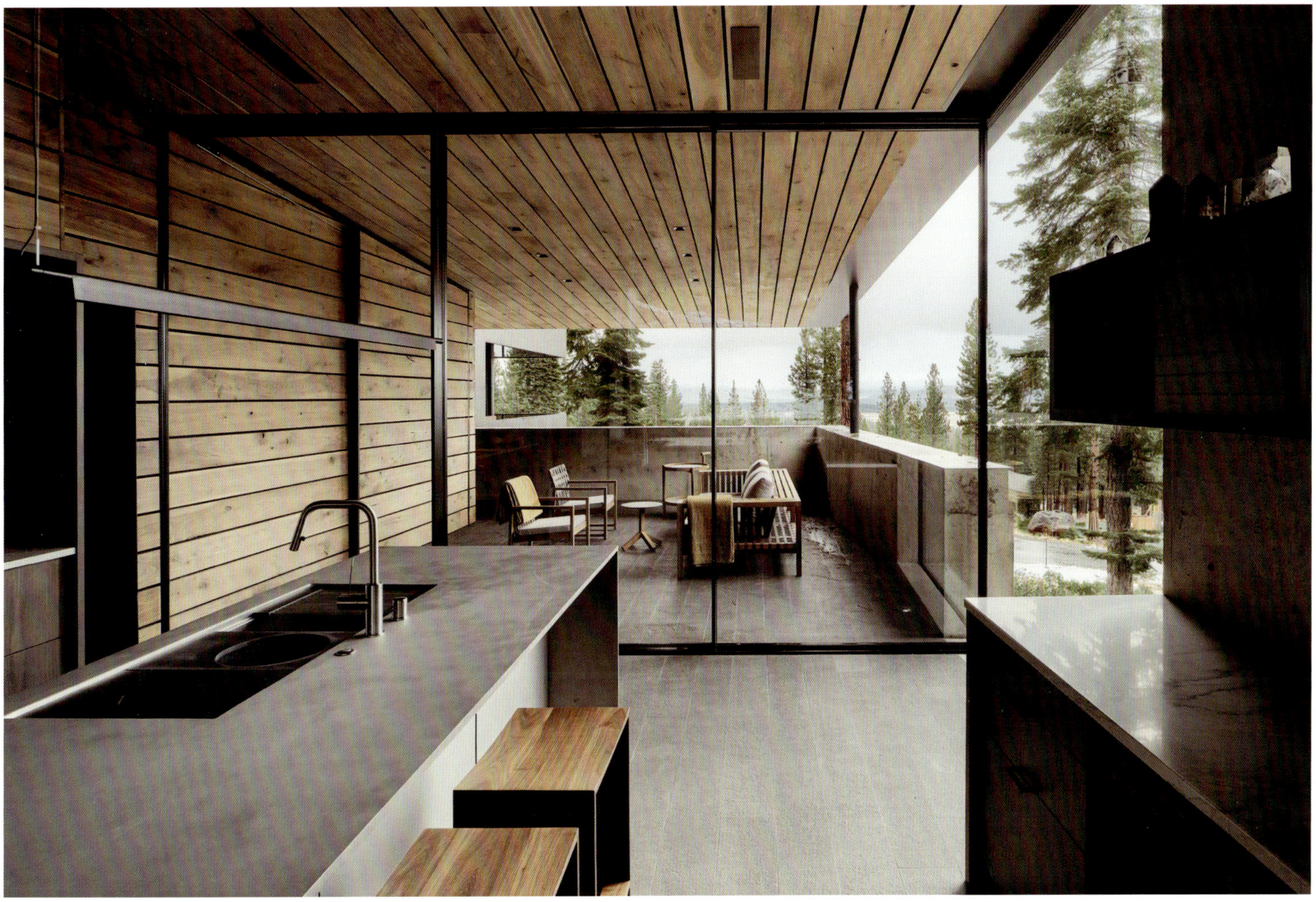

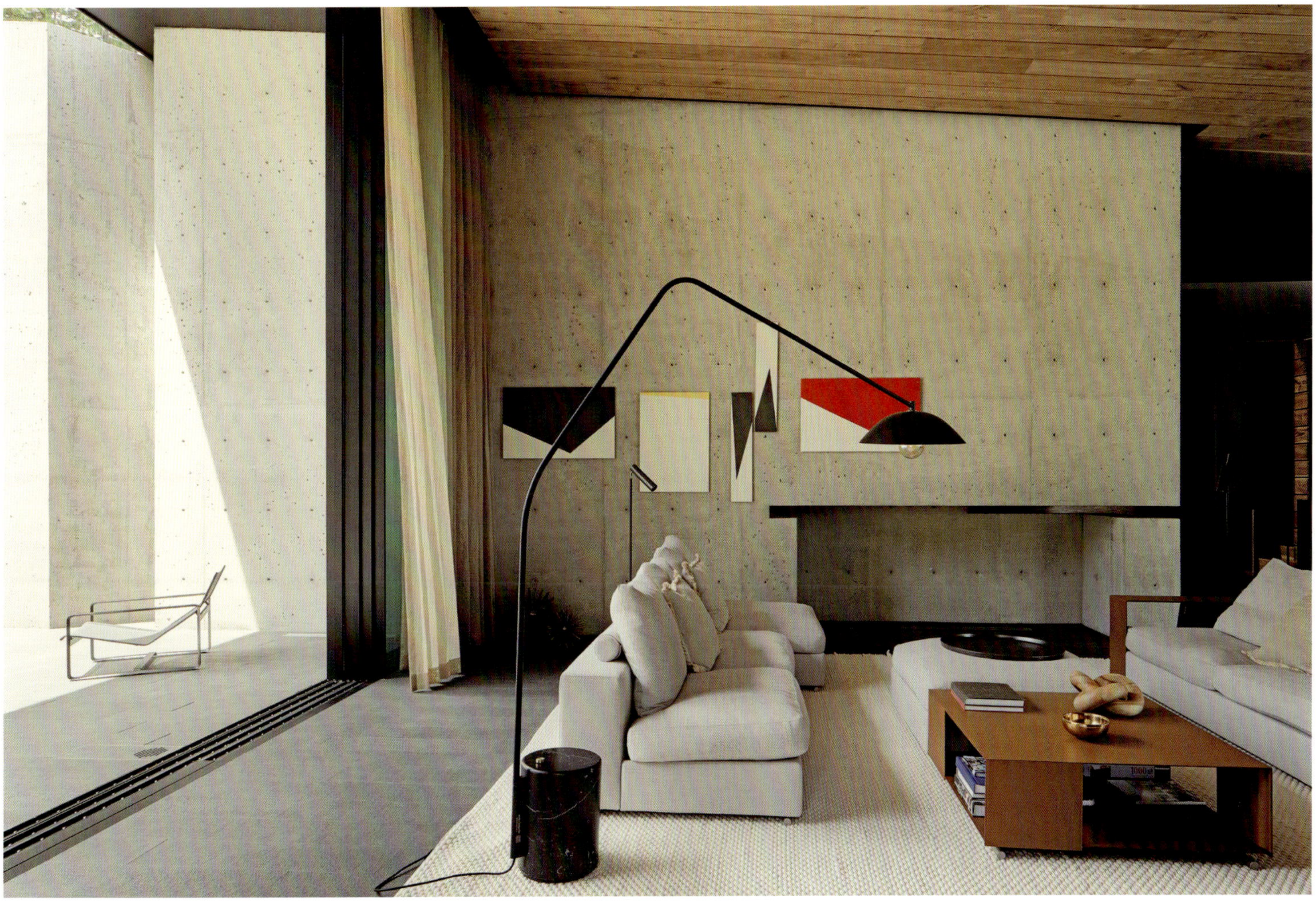

DUST
CASA CALDERA
2015 | San Rafael Valley, AZ, USA

Both tiny and monolithic, the walls of this Arizona desert retreat in the Canelo Hills are made of a compound of red pulverized lava rock, cement, and water, making an emphatic connection with the earth beneath. Two rectangular volumes—one for sleeping, the other for living—are arranged around a central space called a zaguan, a passageway bisecting the building. This corridor, a feature of local, historic desert architecture, draws breezes through the house and provides a shaded, sheltered spot in which to sit and watch the landscape as the sun tracks across the sky. The living and kitchen area to one side of the zaguan has expansive windows that bring in light and ventilation. In a warm contrast to the rough lava-concrete walls, golden sassafras wood is used for bedroom doors and lines the ceilings, glowing gently as sunshine penetrates the zaguan. The house has excellent insulation, thanks to its robust, thick walls, and the fireplace in the living room provides heat during colder winter months. The retreat is completely off-grid, drawing water from its own well and using the desert's fierce, abundant solar power for electricity. Two huge, rusted metal bifold doors at either end of the zaguan can be used to direct airflow, and when the owners leave, they can be closed to create an impenetrable barrier. Though diminutive, Casa Caldera maintains a fortresslike aura, an indomitable presence amid the wilderness.

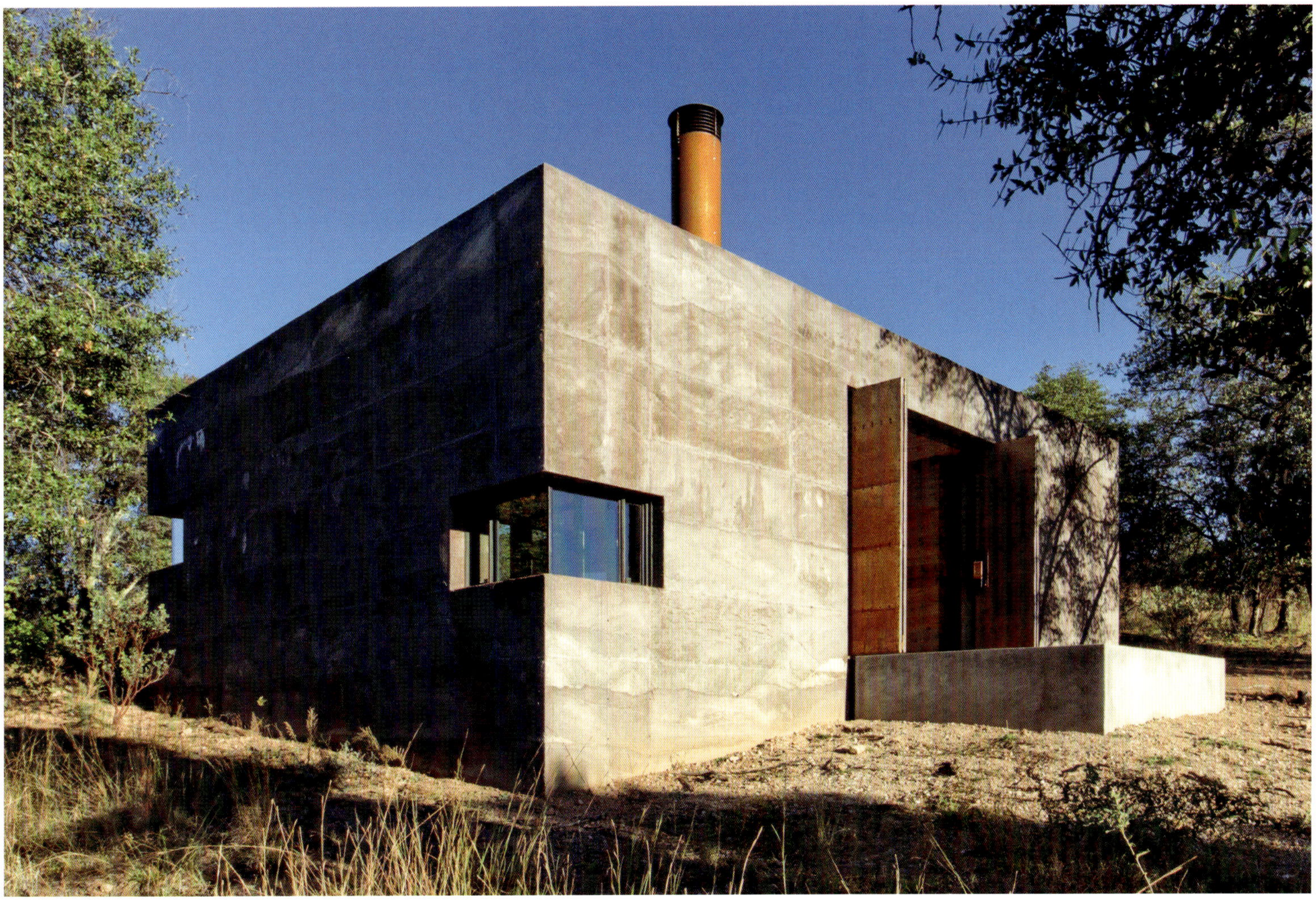

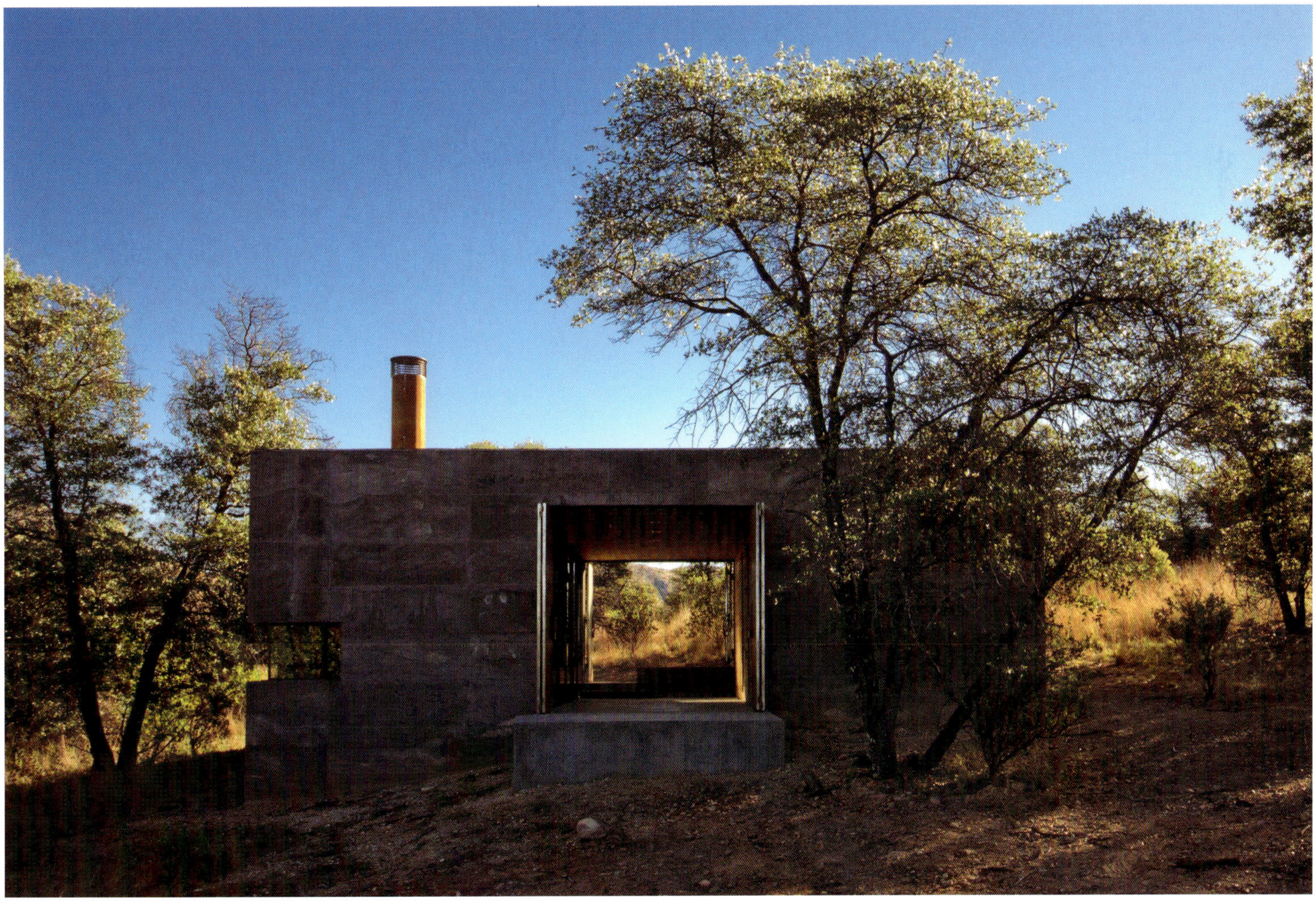

CASA CALDERA

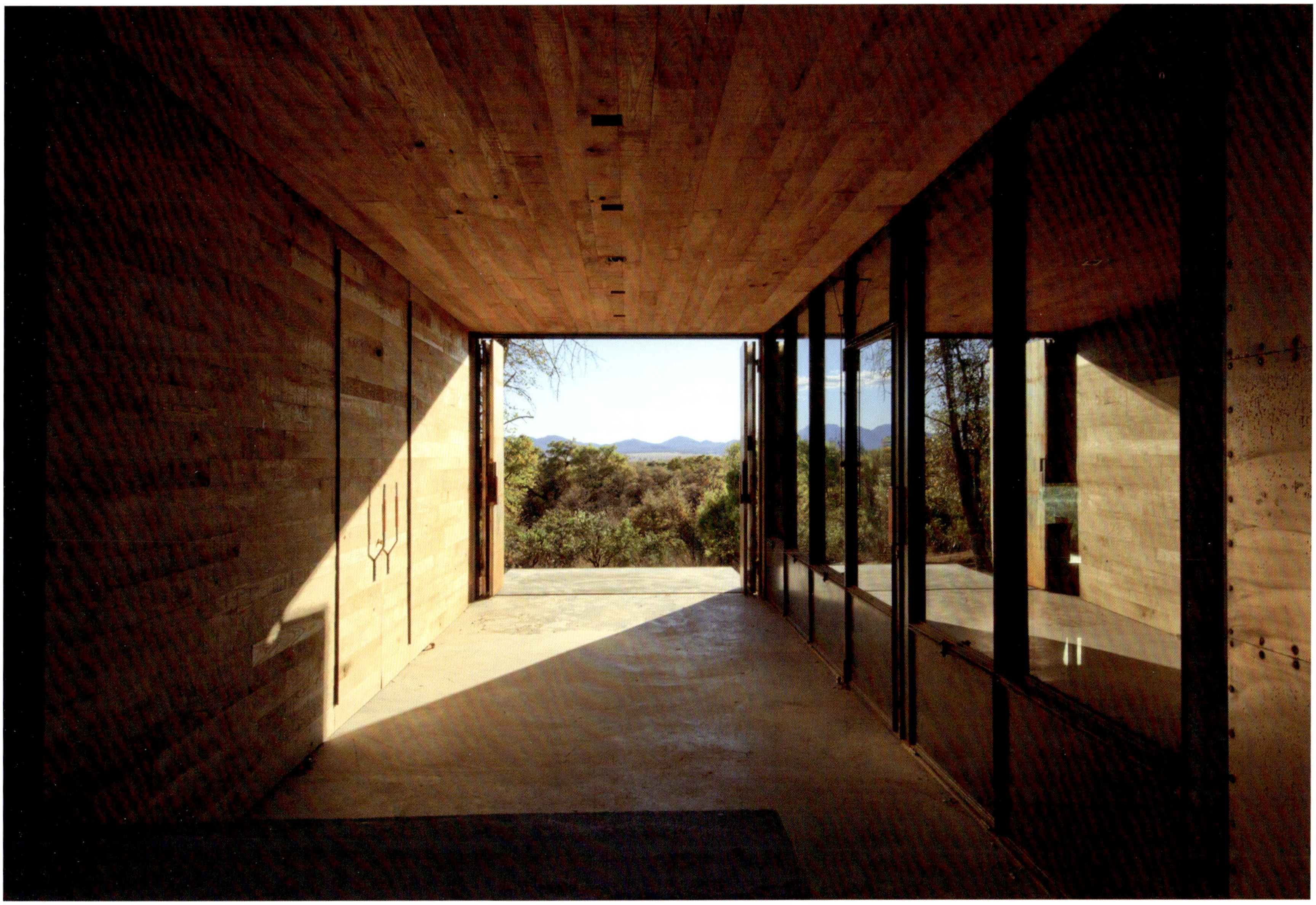

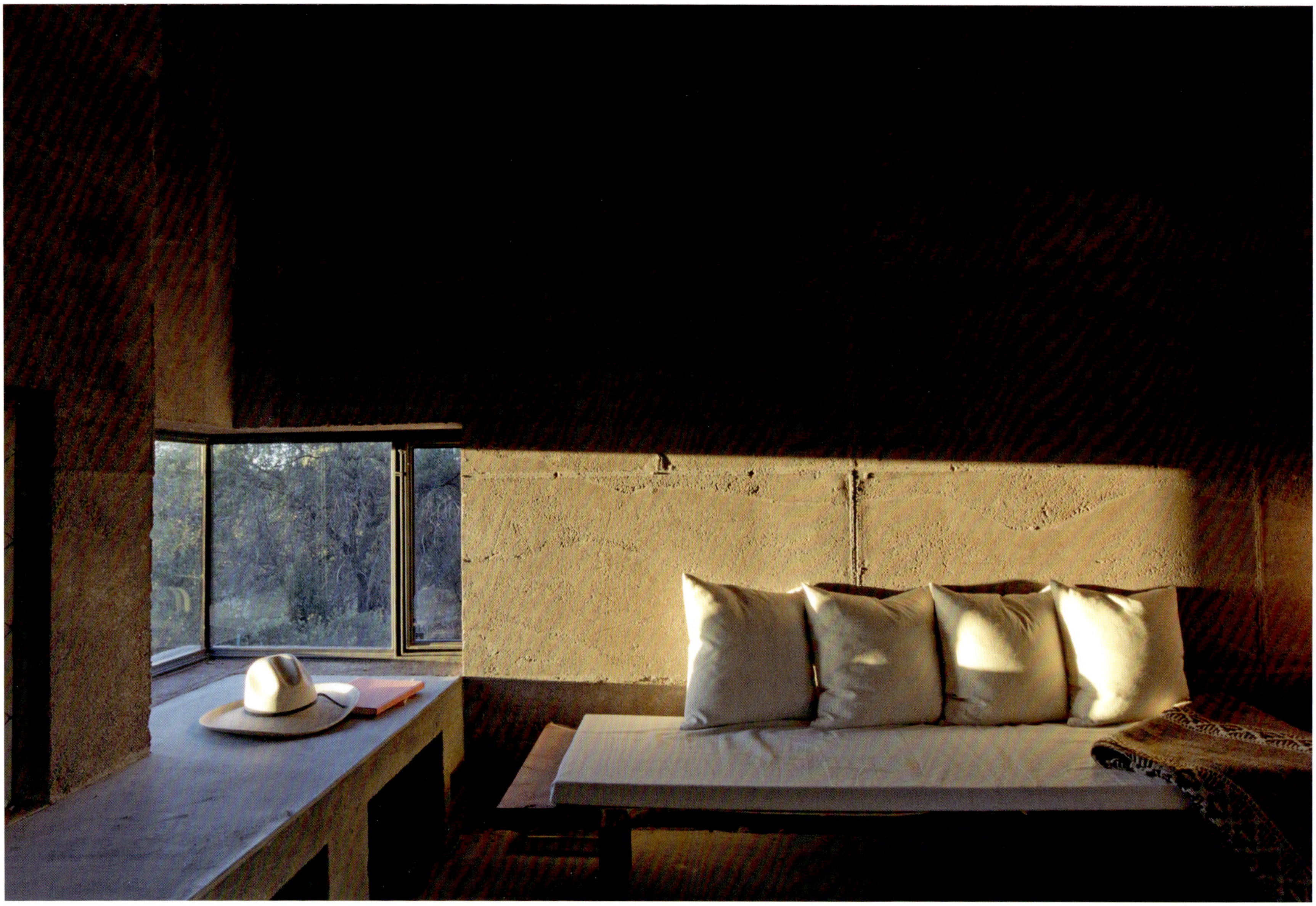

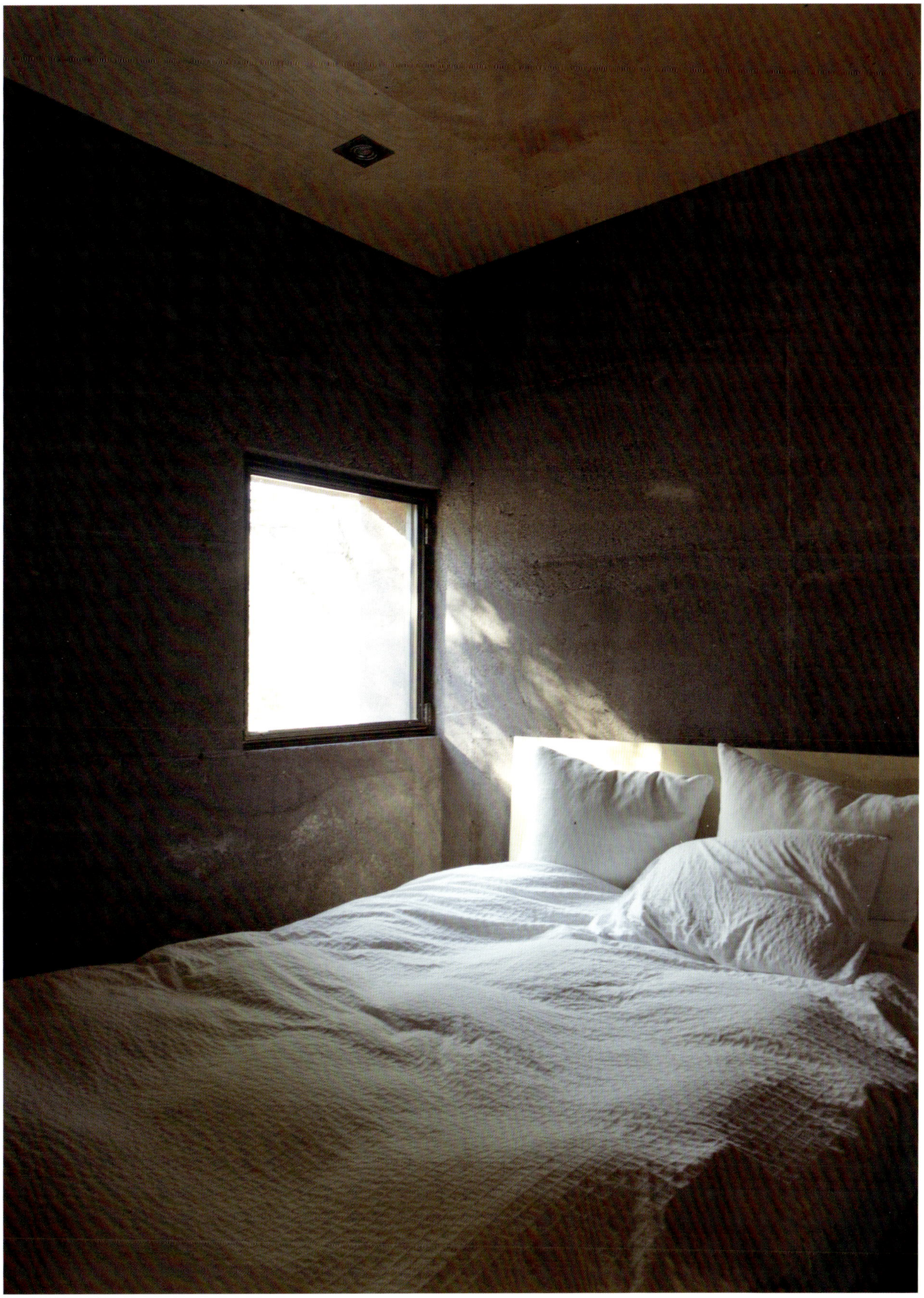

[4] WATER

192 Rob Mills Architecture & Interiors
OCEAN HOUSE

198 Anne Carrier Architecture
RÉSIDENCE LE NID

202 Dualchas Architects
BORERAIG

206 Kapsimalis Architects
VILLA DROP

210 Austin Maynard Architects
ST ANDREWS BEACH HOUSE

214 Building Arts Architects
KAWAGAMA BOATHOUSE

218 D'Arcy Jones Architects
DEEP COVE HOUSE

222 1+1>2 Architects
STRAW HOUSE

226 Kazunori Fujimoto Architect & Associates
HOUSE IN AJINA

230 Aleksi Hautamäki and Milla Selkimäki
PROJECT Ö CABIN

236 Grove Architects
BUNDEENA BEACH HOUSE

240 TAOA Design
LANDSCAPE HOUSE

244 Vandkunsten Architects
MODERN SEAWEED HOUSE

248 John Pardey Architects
NARULA HOUSE

Two-thirds of the earth is covered in water, yet to live close to it is still a fantasy for many. Whether water is invigorating or calming, wild or still, we are drawn to it. The psychological benefits of living near it are undisputed; it simply feels good to enjoy lake breezes or river swims, or to gaze out over a shimmering ocean.

The selection of houses in this chapter reflects water's ever-changing, dynamic qualities. Many of them are second or vacation homes, but they could not be more varied in terms of climate and topography—locations include a small man-made Scottish lochan, the vast Pacific Ocean, Quebec's meandering Saint Lawrence River, and a serene Vietnamese lake. For most religions, water has a special symbolism, and that significance is central to two houses here: one built for a Buddhist in Scotland, and another in Japan that is specially designed to highlight views of a Shinto torii gate that seems to float on a lake. Both are contemplative spaces formed through loving craftsmanship; both exude a quiet dignity.

Water exerts its own influence on spatial design, and some homes featured here have no designated room plan at all, favoring free-flowing flexibility. Simplicity is also key—while several watery retreats are fairly luxurious, most of them embrace a more basic and frugal way of being. That is sometimes unavoidable due to a remote location, as was the case for a Canadian boathouse unreachable by road. Materials tend to be more conventional in this chapter, but one house makes ample use of seaweed to embody the very sea it is surrounded by. Brutalist homes are rare on the Australian coast, yet there is a superb example here, and concrete has very practical advantages specific to that location. Wherever these inspiring houses happen to be, the experience of living by the water, even for a short while, is immersive, sensorially rich, and restorative.

Rob Mills Architecture & Interiors
OCEAN HOUSE
2012 | Lorne, VIC, Australia

Clinging to a steep hillside just off Australia's Great Ocean Road, this retreat was built as a home for architect Rob Mills and his family. He originally designed it as a timber shack, but after a period of bush fires and a change in planning laws, he embraced the creative possibilities of concrete. The rectangular pavilion of the house is constructed of wood and glass, but rests on a concrete base and connects to a cylindrical concrete tower. Concrete gave Mills a more sculptural material to experiment with: the residence features circular bedrooms and porthole windows, elevating it above much beach-house architecture. Ocean House has six bedrooms, with various indoor and outdoor social spaces arranged over three stories. Glazing on both sides of the pavilion gives it great transparency, allowing uninterrupted views through to the sea at the front and the forest behind. Inhabitants can throw open the doors to feel the cross-ventilation and hear the sound of the ocean, which is critical to the sensory experience of living here. The interior's monochrome simplicity keeps the focus on sea views: timber walls and ceilings, and velvet-smooth polished floors and walls are the palest of fawns and grays. Rather than being austere, all the concrete contributes a coolness and a tactility that works with, rather than against, the surrounding nature.

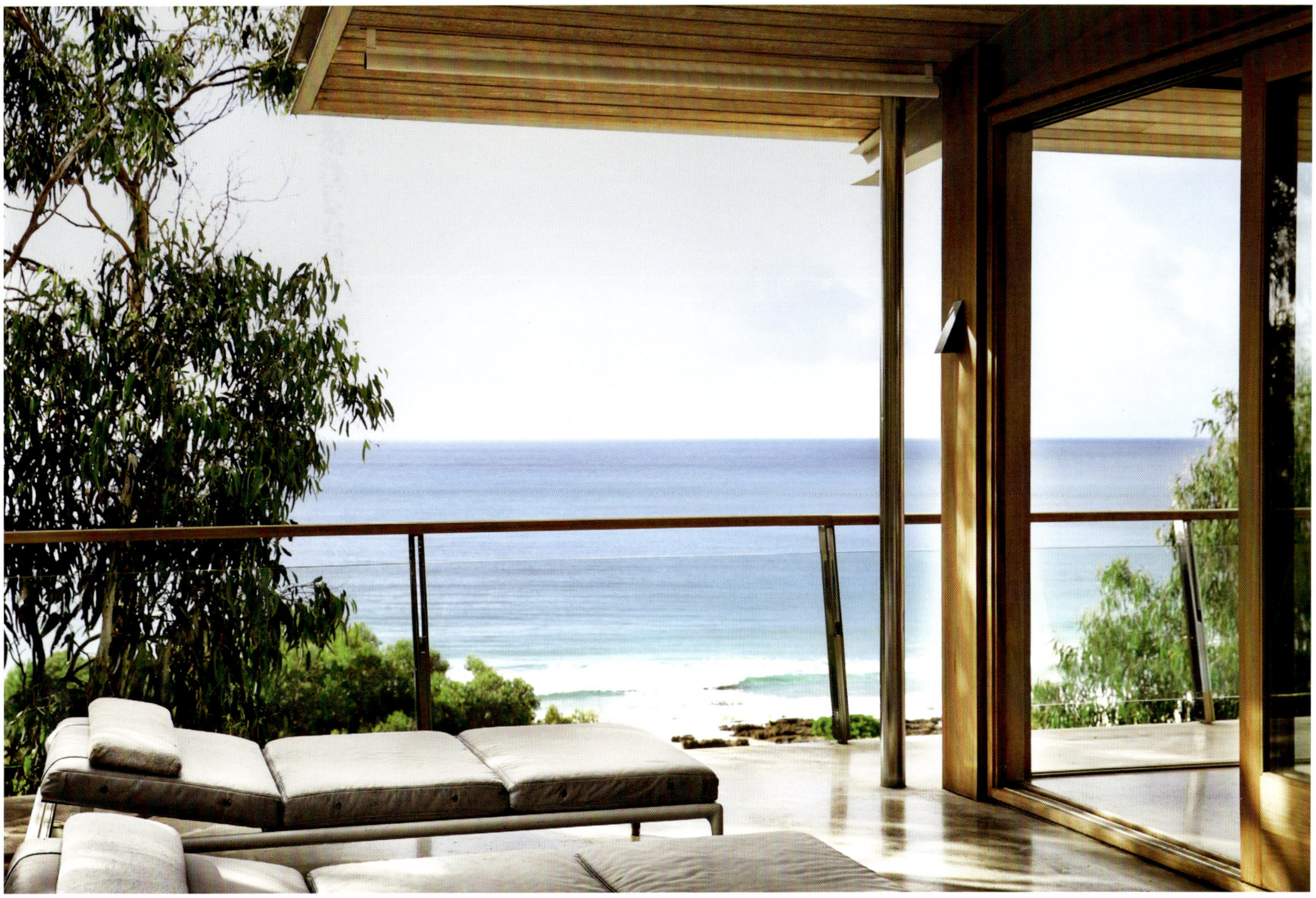

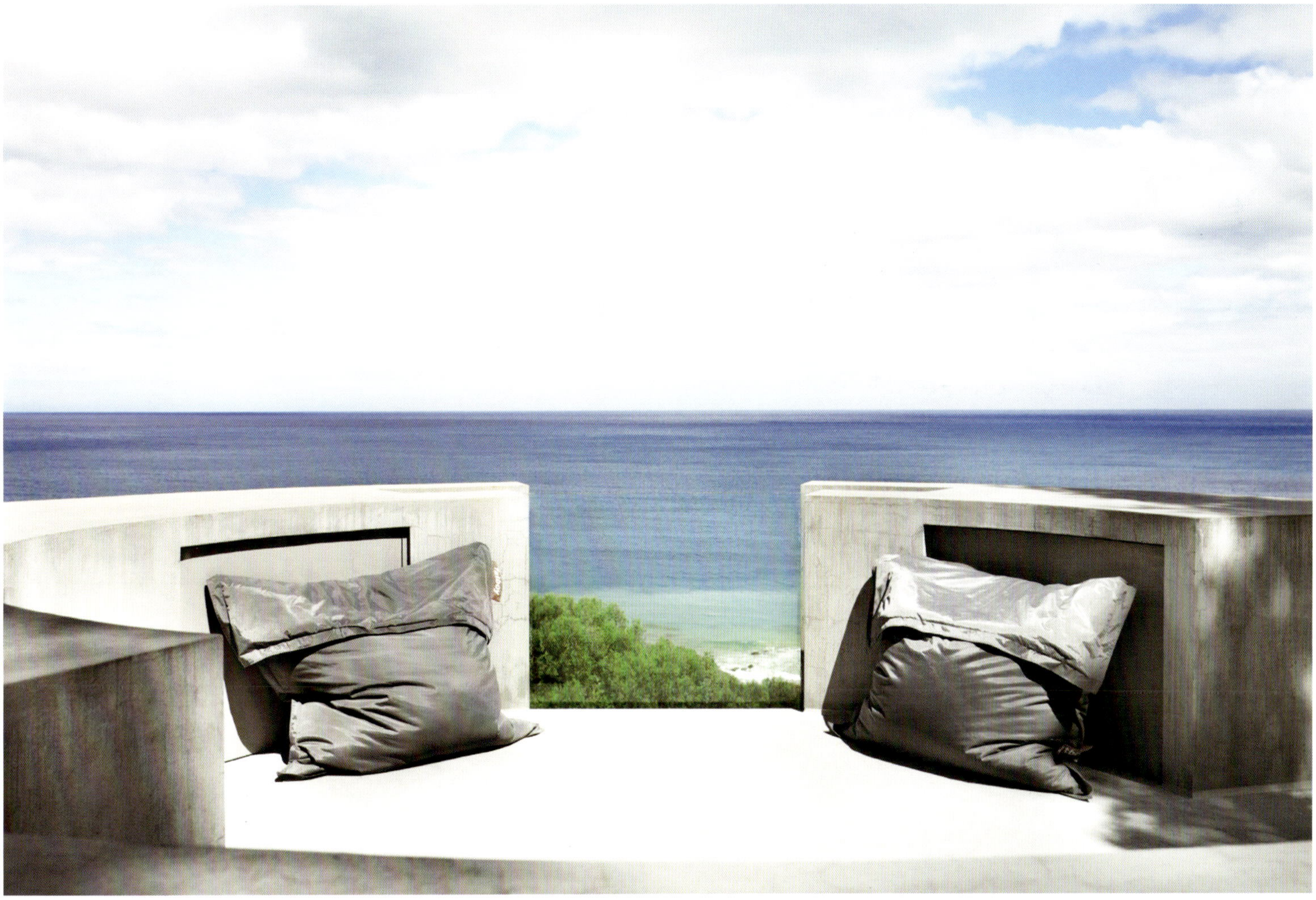

OCEAN HOUSE

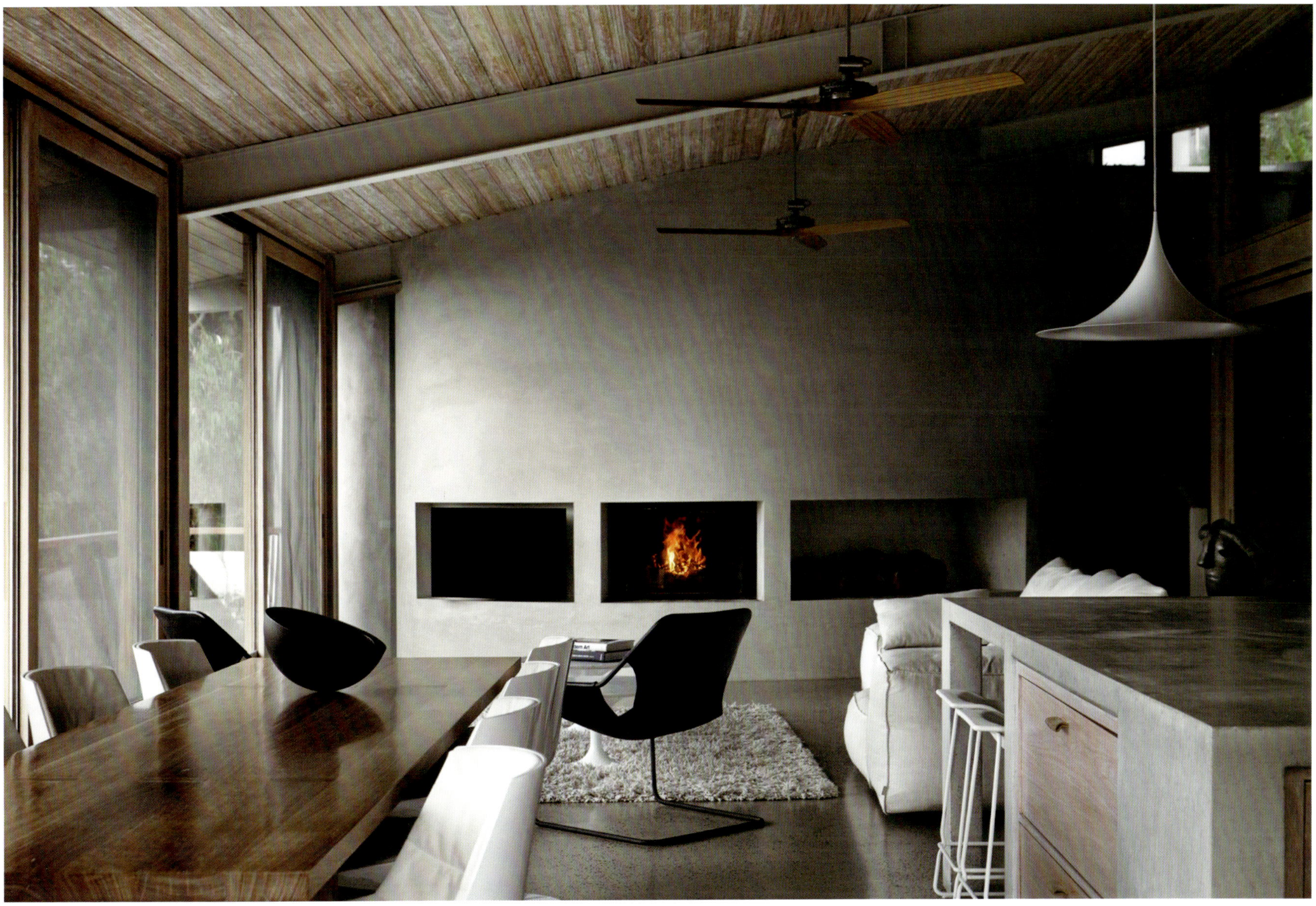

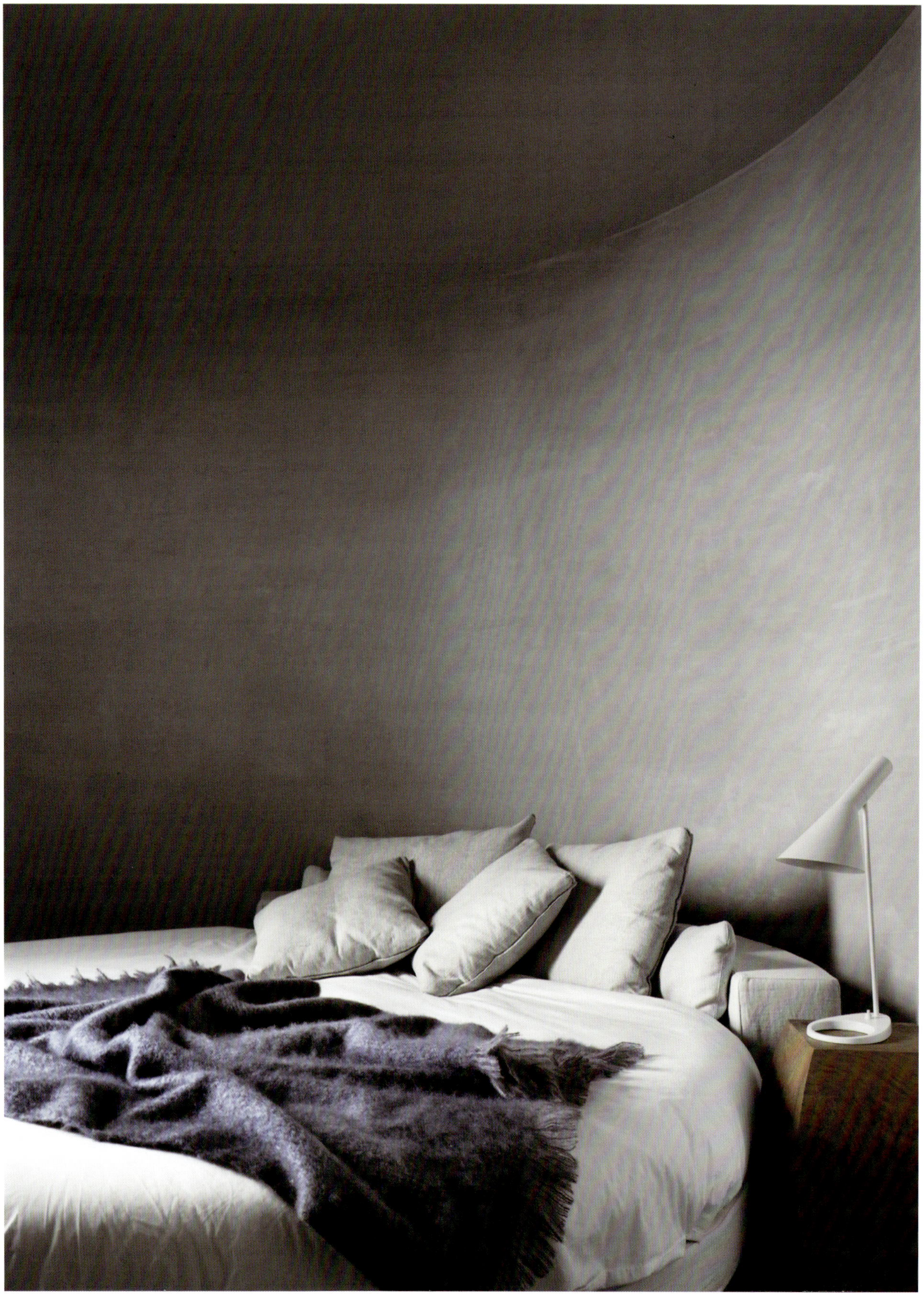

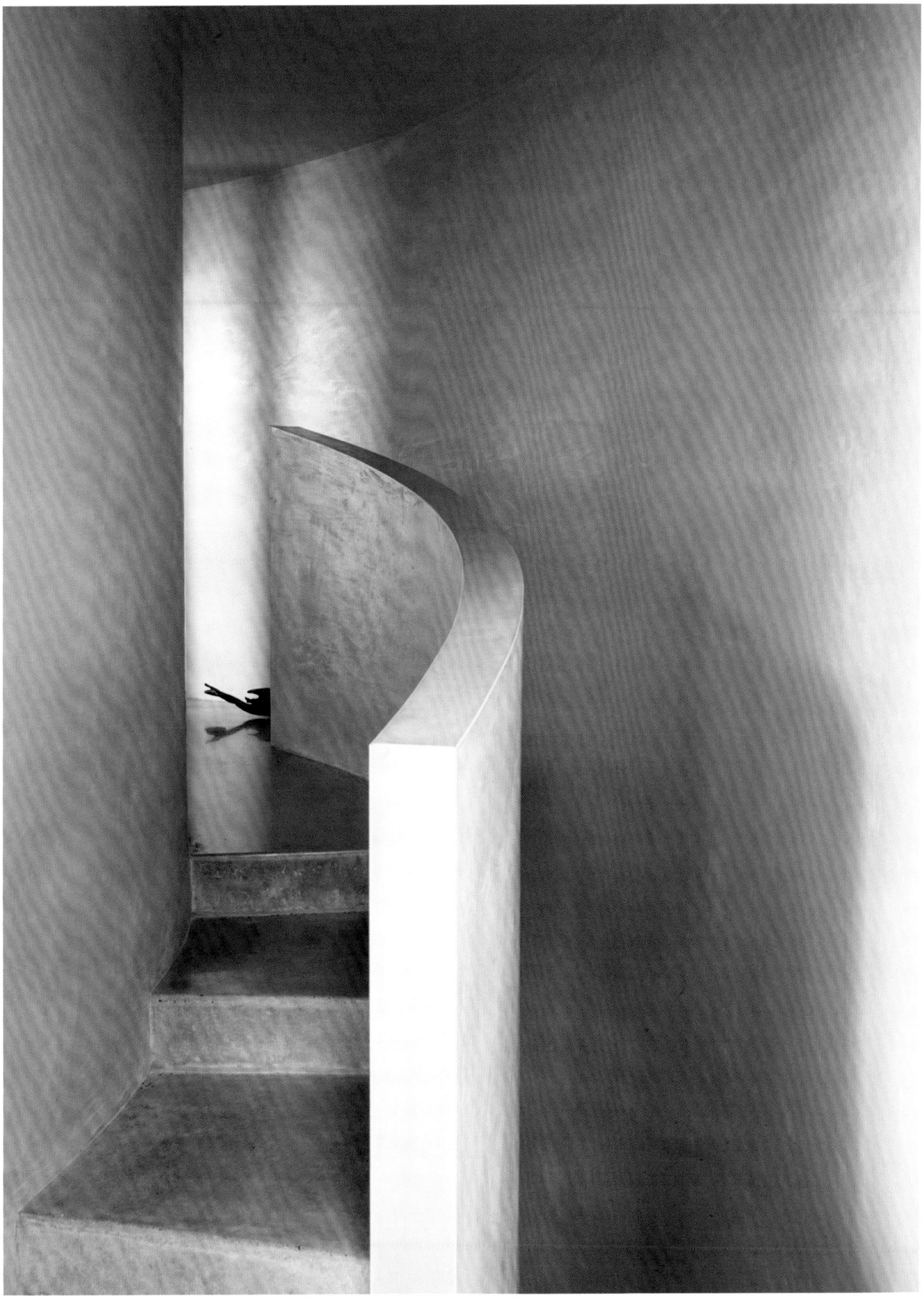

Anne Carrier Architecture
RÉSIDENCE LE NID
2017 | Baie-Saint-Paul, QC, Canada

Résidence Le Nid is designed around a succession of framed views of Quebec's vast and majestic Saint Lawrence River. The architect wanted the experience of being in the house to be like inhabiting a constantly changing artwork. Formed of two interlocking rectangular volumes, the building is in an elevated position and rests on a narrow escarpment. A cedar bridge connects to the upper level and the home's main entrance, where one enters directly into the living area. Floor-to-ceiling glazing in this room creates a deluge of light and provides panoramic views of the river and nearby towns. In addition, lateral bay windows to either side of the main view create a triptych of alternative outlooks. The lower volume is clad in dark spruce, the upper in pale cedar. It cantilevers outward, appearing to float without visible support, its balcony wrapped with overhanging screening. This is the part of the house referred to as *le nid* (the nest), and it is a sheltered yet dramatic portal through which to view the flow of water below. Two terraces provide further spaces to relax and gaze outward, and the palest wood interiors ensure that views are the main focus. Le Nid's architecture is enigmatic yet functional; every part of the house is concerned with the simple act of looking.

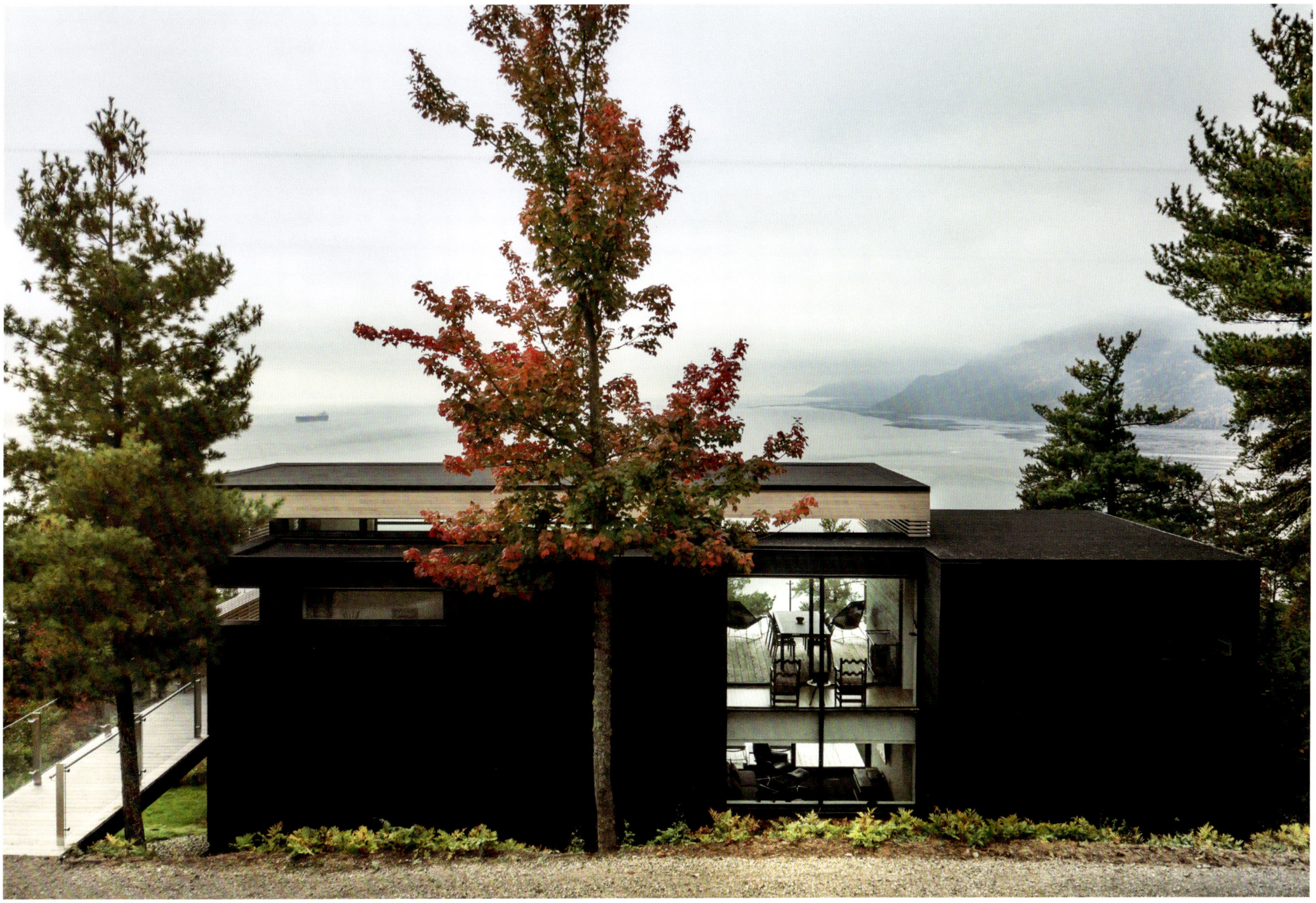

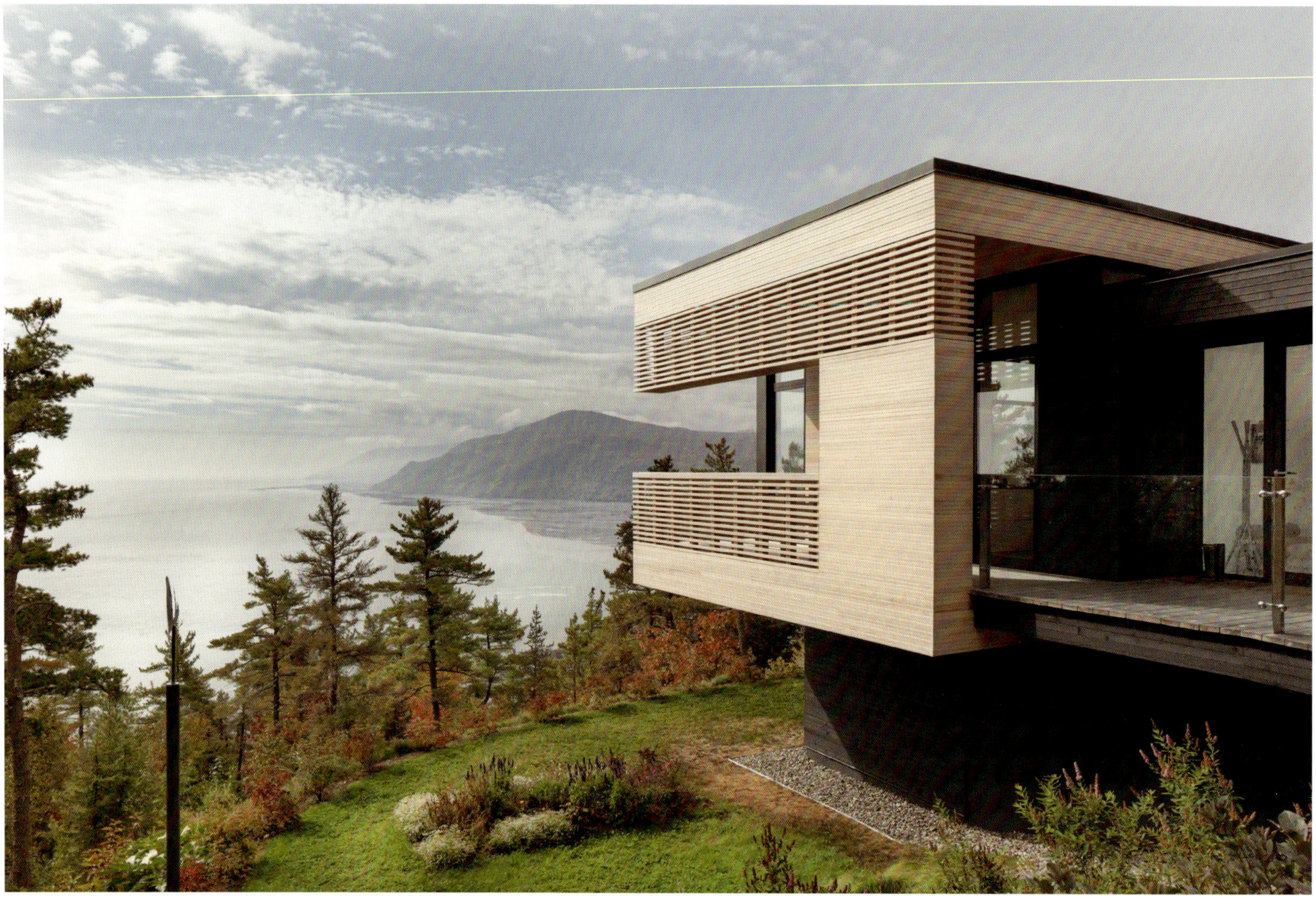

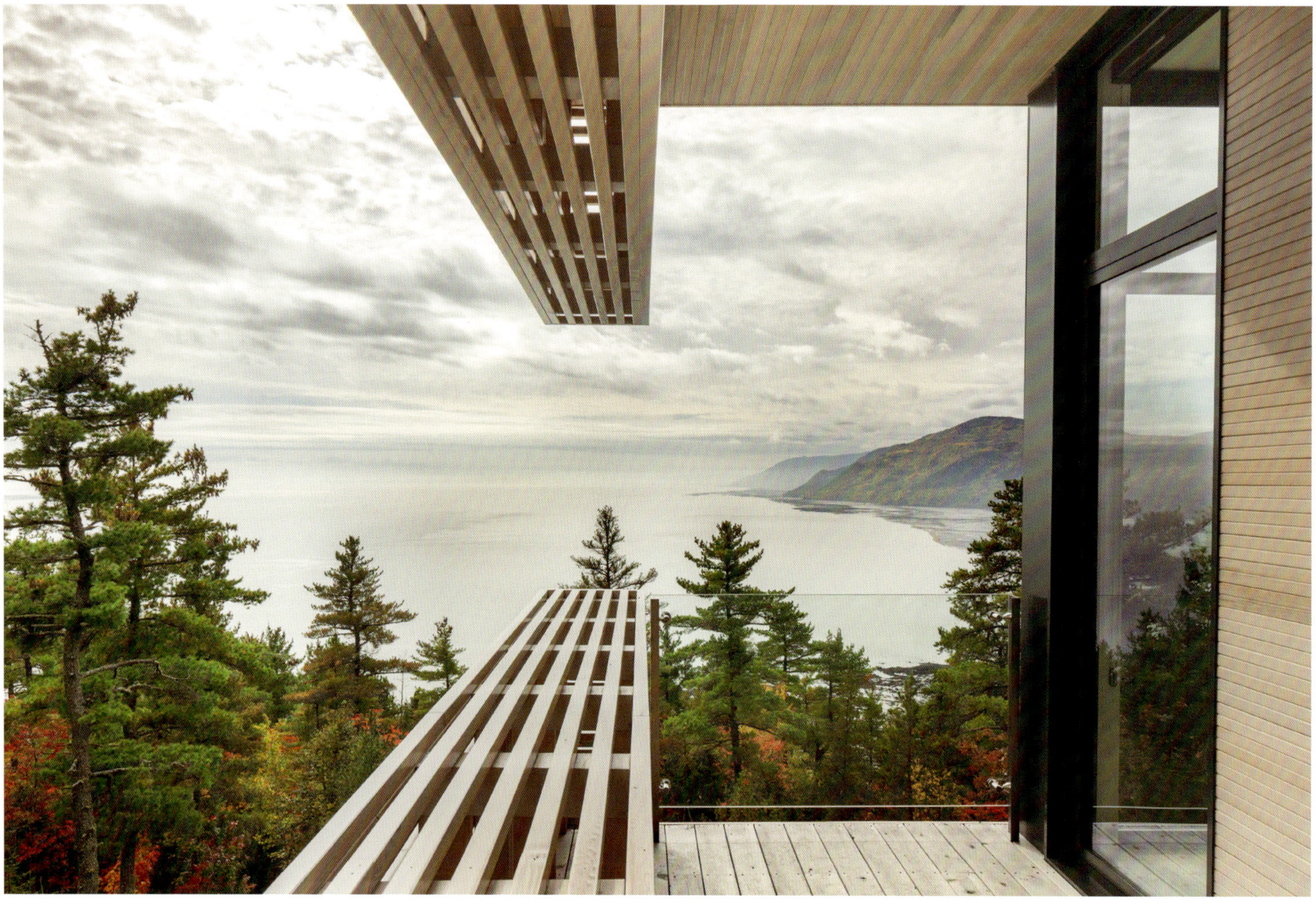

RÉSIDENCE LE NID

Dualchas Architects
BORERAIG
2011 | Isle of Skye, Scotland, UK

Boreraig is rooted in the archetype of the black house, a traditional stone- and turf-roofed Scottish cottage, but embraces modern, abstracted forms. The house hunkers close to the earth and is divided into three volumes: the living and sleeping areas are in two staggered rectilinear volumes connected by a glass corridor, and there is a separate studio hut. Originally, the plot had not been on the water's edge, but a natural bowl in the landscape was turned into a lochan (a small lake) by damming the nearby streams. Now, water contributes to the house's peaceful ambience: the living and dining space and main bedroom are filled with views of the lochan, with the sea beyond. Much of Boreraig's unique sense of serenity is due to the craft of its detailing. Each material, natural and locally sourced, is designed to envelop the house in tranquility, both inside and out. Sloping drystone walls protectively embrace the buildings. A larch rainscreen, echoing the larch fences commonly found on crofts, is crisply linear, and matte Caithness stone floor tiling provides grounding earth tones. Interior walls and ceilings are clad in expanses of warm, tactile oak. Free of distraction or ornament, all elements synthesize into a simple, meditative space.

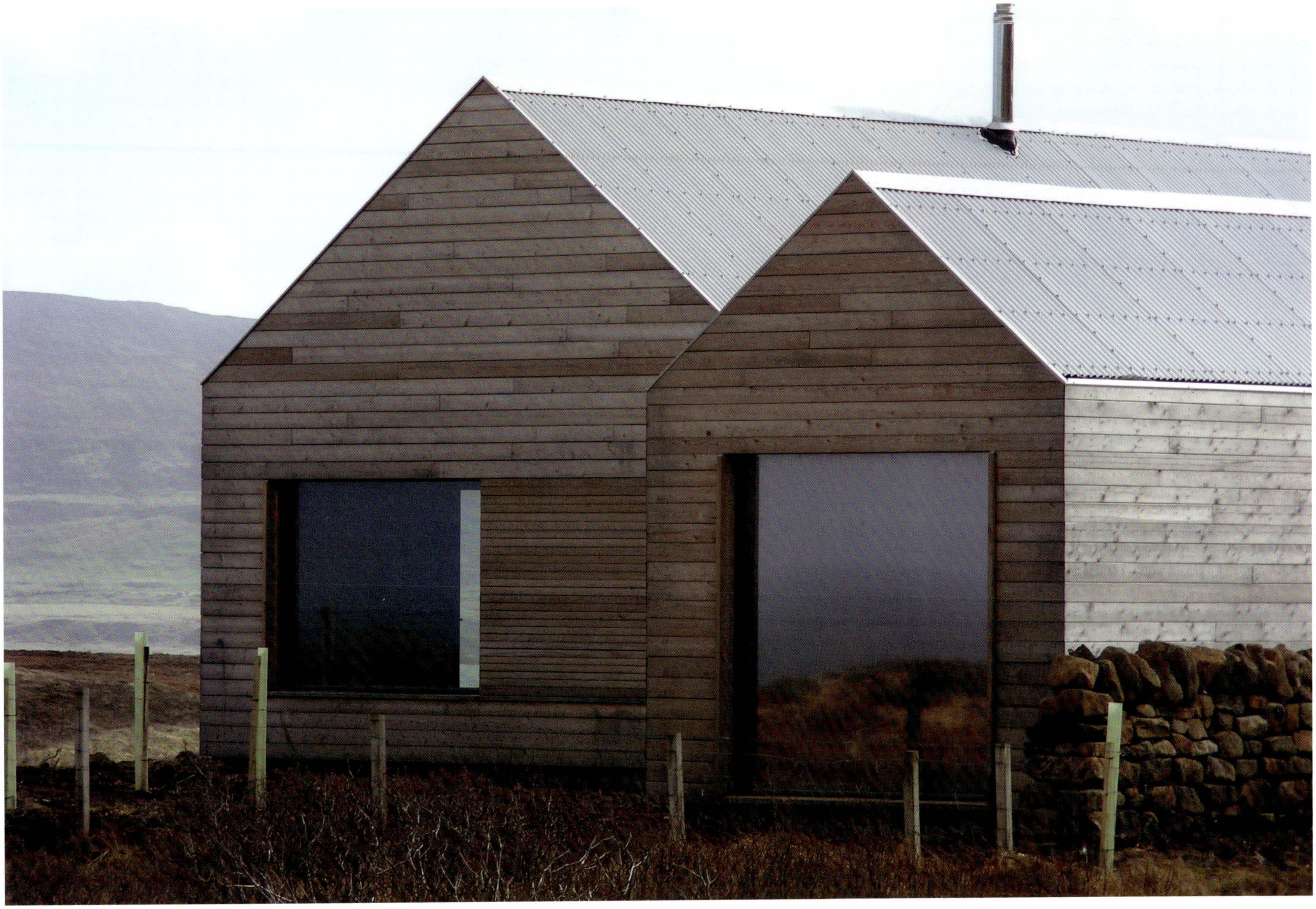

BORERAIG

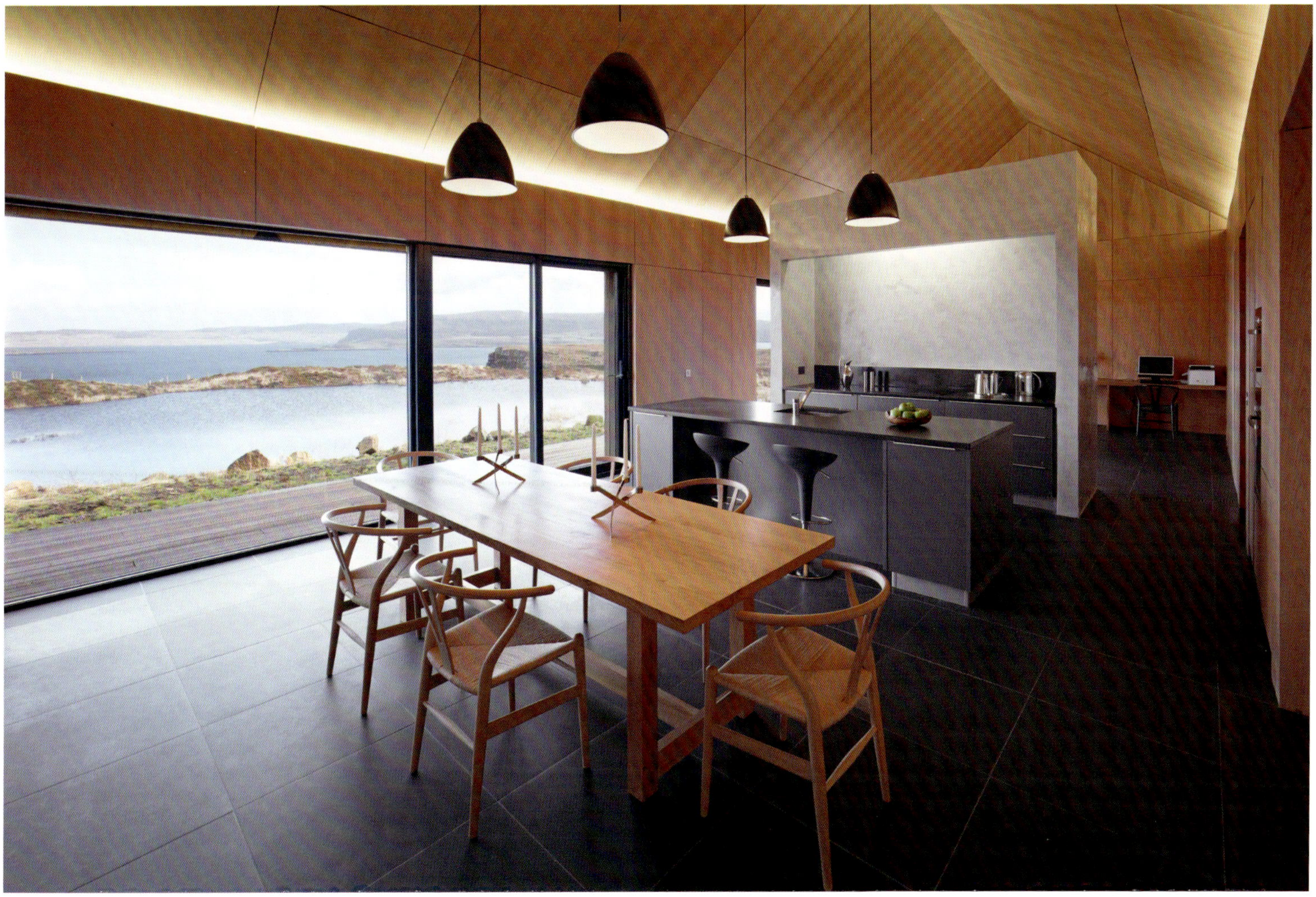

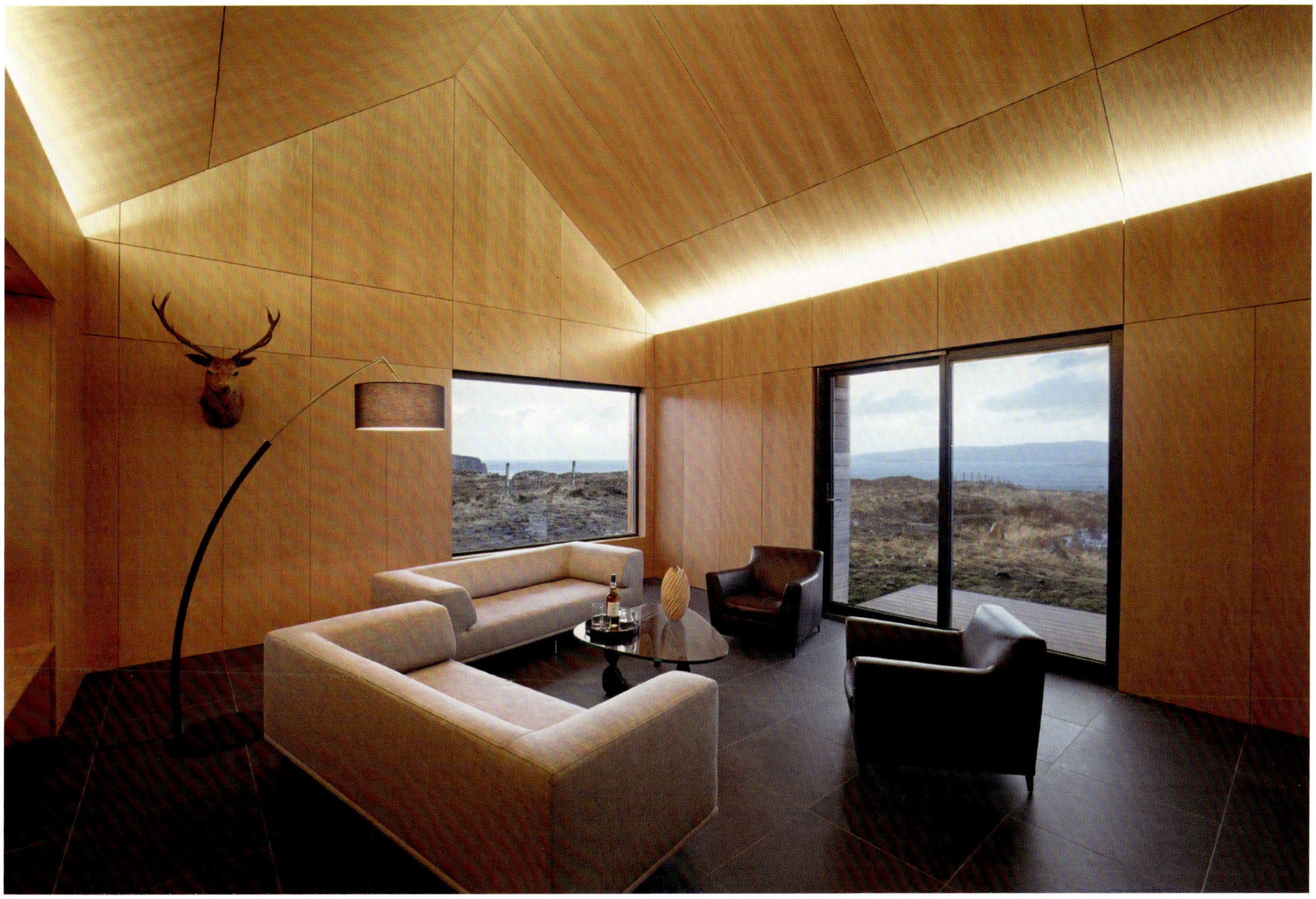

Kapsimalis Architects
VILLA DROP
2019 | Fira, Santorini, Greece

On the vertiginous slopes of the Greek town of Fira, this bijou vacation home faces west out to sea, with an enviable view of the volcano Santorini. The extremely narrow plot—only 13 feet (4 meters) wide—is squeezed in between two houses and backing onto another. Access to the house is via a road below. A few steps lead up to the lower floor of the retreat: a long, narrow open-plan space divided into a sitting area, bedroom, kitchenette, and bathroom. On the upper level, there is a tiny bedroom and bathroom accessed by an external flight of stairs. This opens onto a sun terrace with an elevated plunge pool—a necessity, since the sea is a long drop below—treated to panoramas of the southern Aegean Sea dotted with ships. Because the dwelling is sequestered between other houses, its main sources of natural light are the doorways into each volume. Therefore, the interior decor is as bright as possible, with brilliant white plaster coating walls, and pale-gray polished concrete on the floors. Throughout, construction and craftsmanship are masterly, and the design eschews the typical rounded corners of Cycladic architecture in favor of the most angular, cubic forms. Everything is simple, scuptural, and flawless.

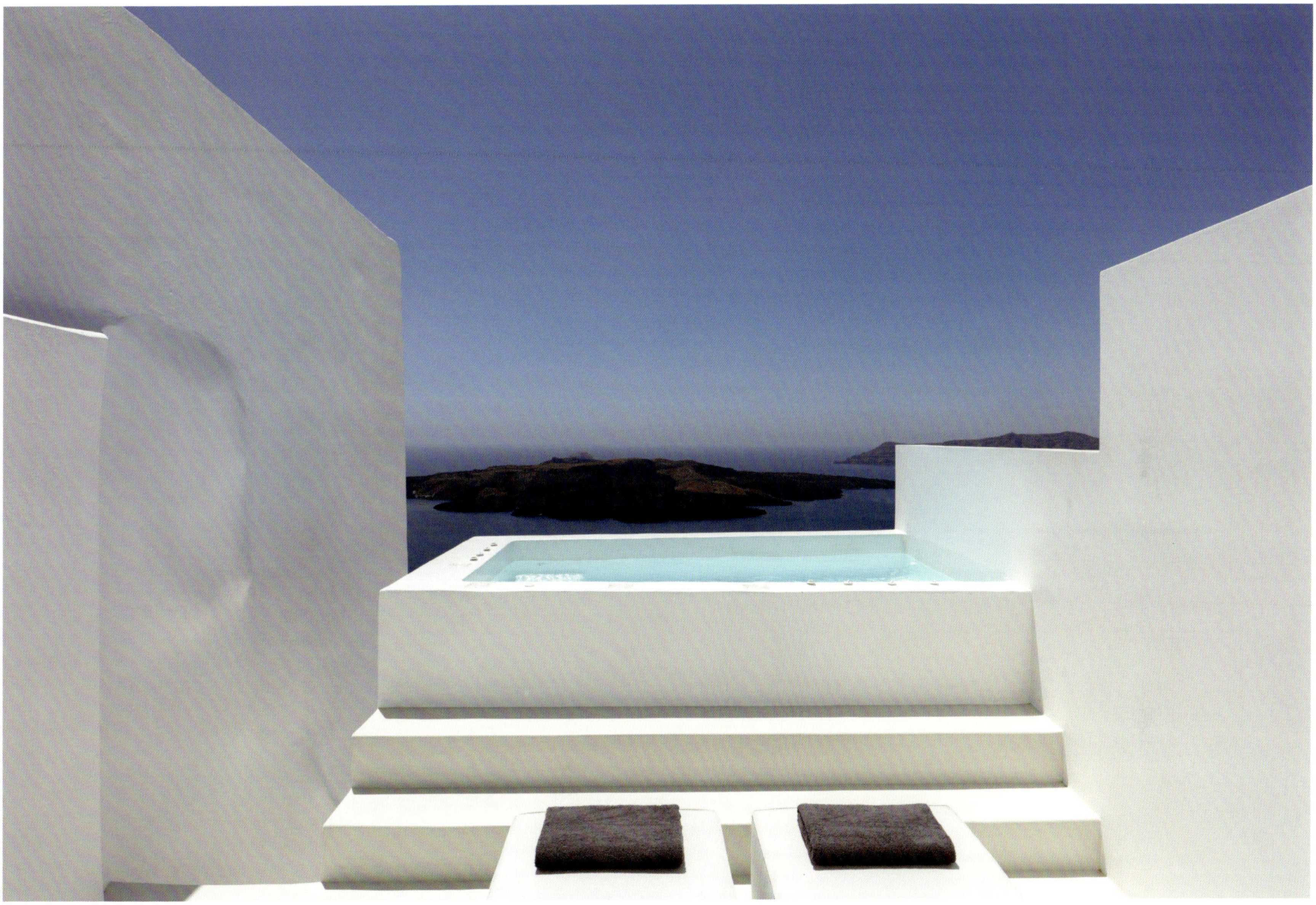

VILLA DROP

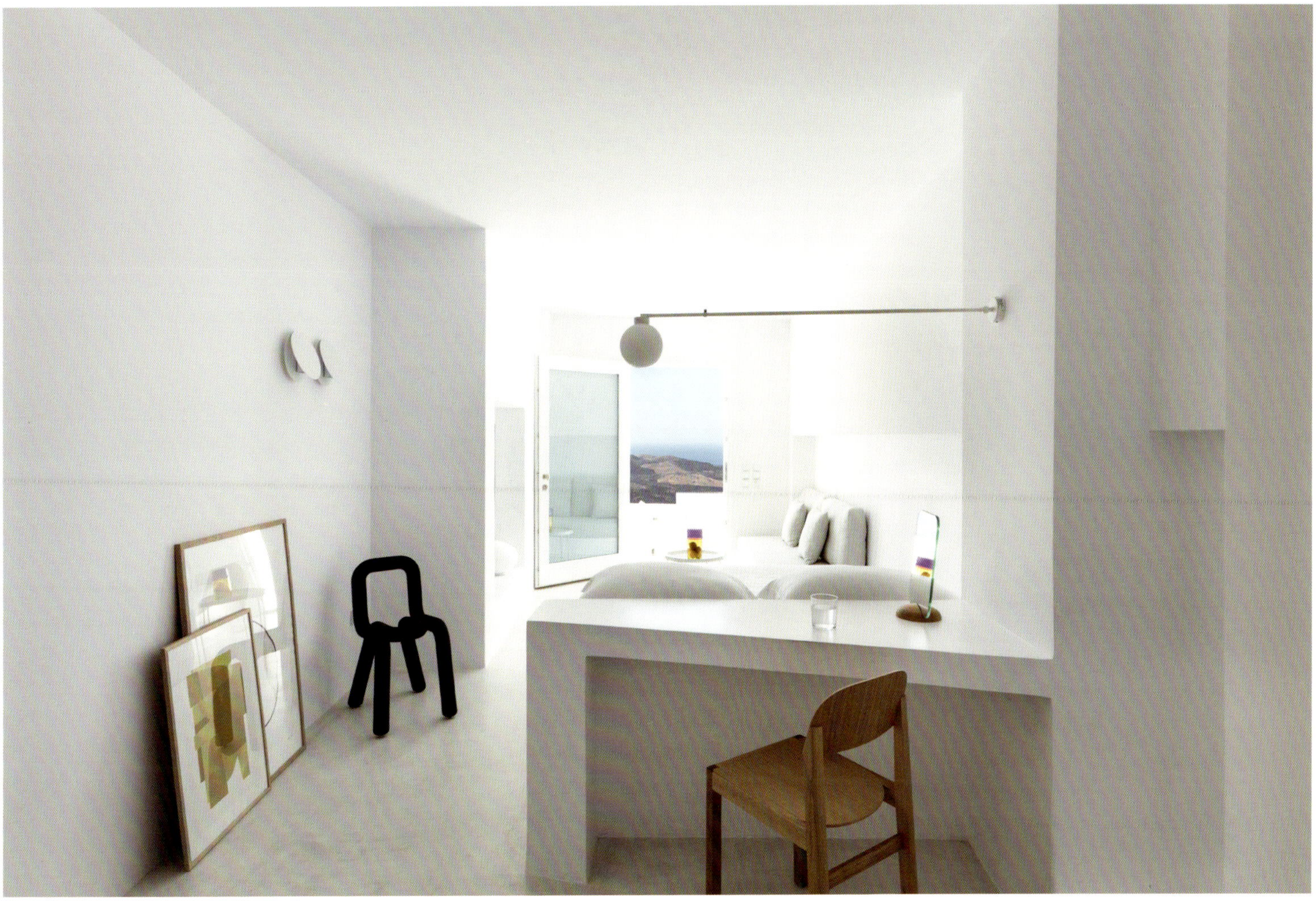

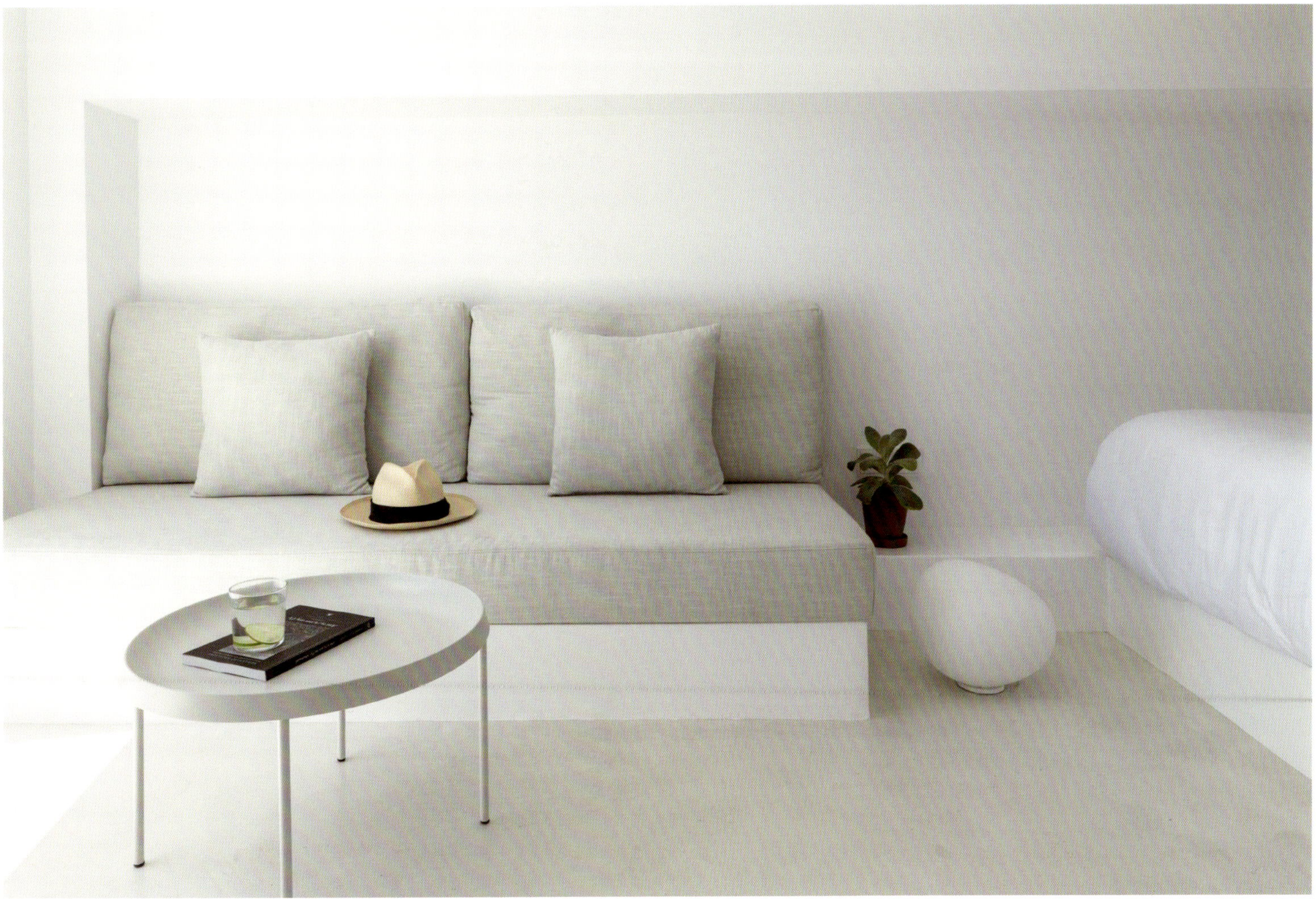

Austin Maynard Architects
ST ANDREWS BEACH HOUSE
2018 | St Andrews Beach, VIC, Australia

Vacation retreats in Australia are often quite spacious, with conventional suburban design, but this stunning location on the Mornington Peninsula—a particularly remote area with very little development, close to a national park—required something more modest. The client wanted a bach (a New Zealand term for a simple shack retreat) in this fragile place of dunes, wild bush, and scrub. No neighboring houses meant no requirement to fit in with existing architectural styles. Achieving great views in all directions, especially over the water, was a key priority of the design by Austin Maynard Architects. This two-story drum-shaped house has a tiny footprint but, as it lacks corridors, every part of it is meant as livable space, and instead of having a conventional deck or veranda, bifold doors slide back to create a terrace within the house. The kitchen, living and dining room, and laundry are on the first floor. On the second level, reached by spiral staircase, flexibility takes priority over privacy or luxury: the space can be configured as bedrooms, separated by curtains, as a second living area, or as a games room. External timber cladding will weather to blend in with the surroundings. Solar panels provide energy, while collected rainwater is used for plumbing and watering the garden. The intention is that the hideaway's unconventional form and relaxed layout will liberate visitors to embrace new ways of being.

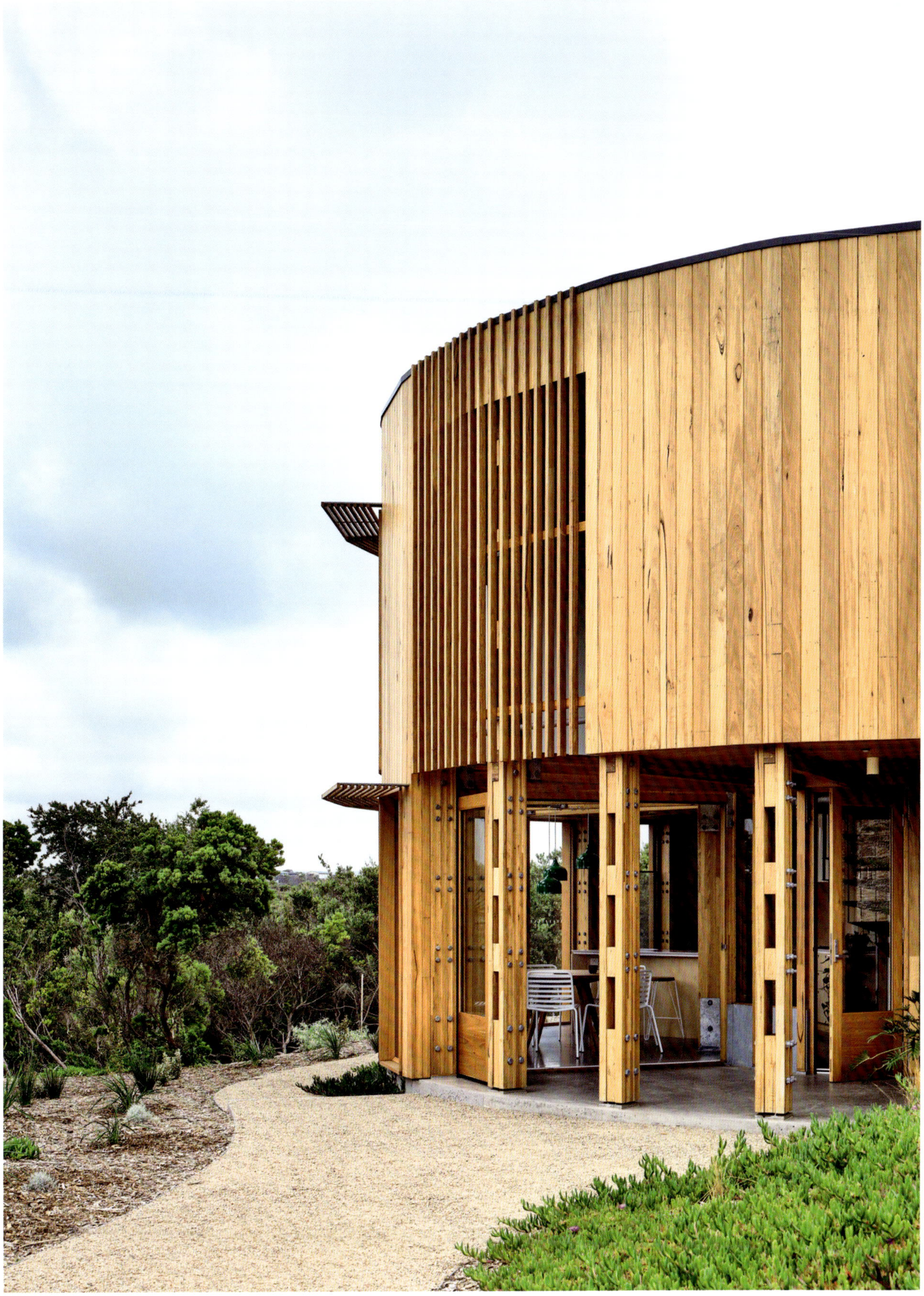

ST ANDREWS BEACH HOUSE

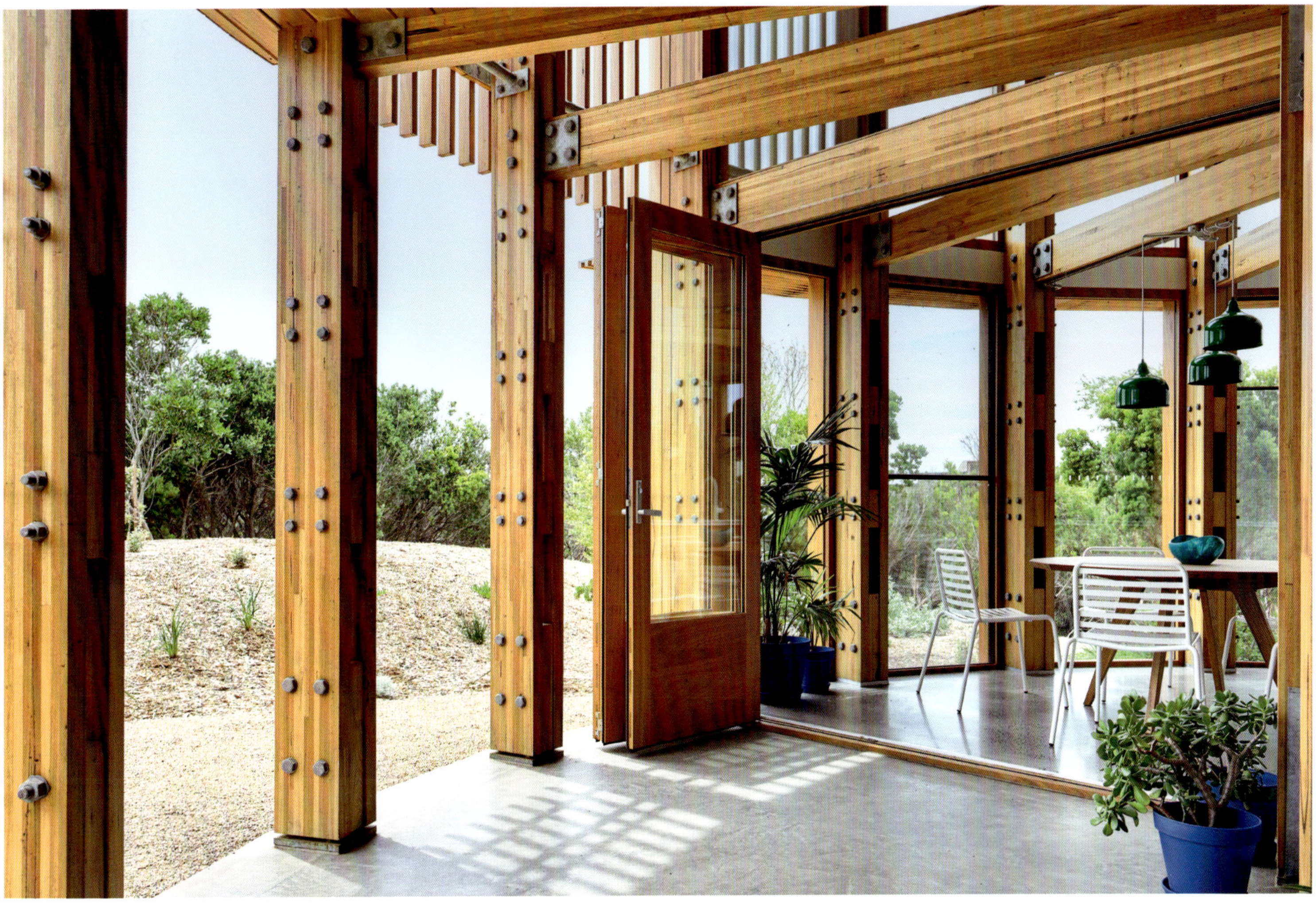

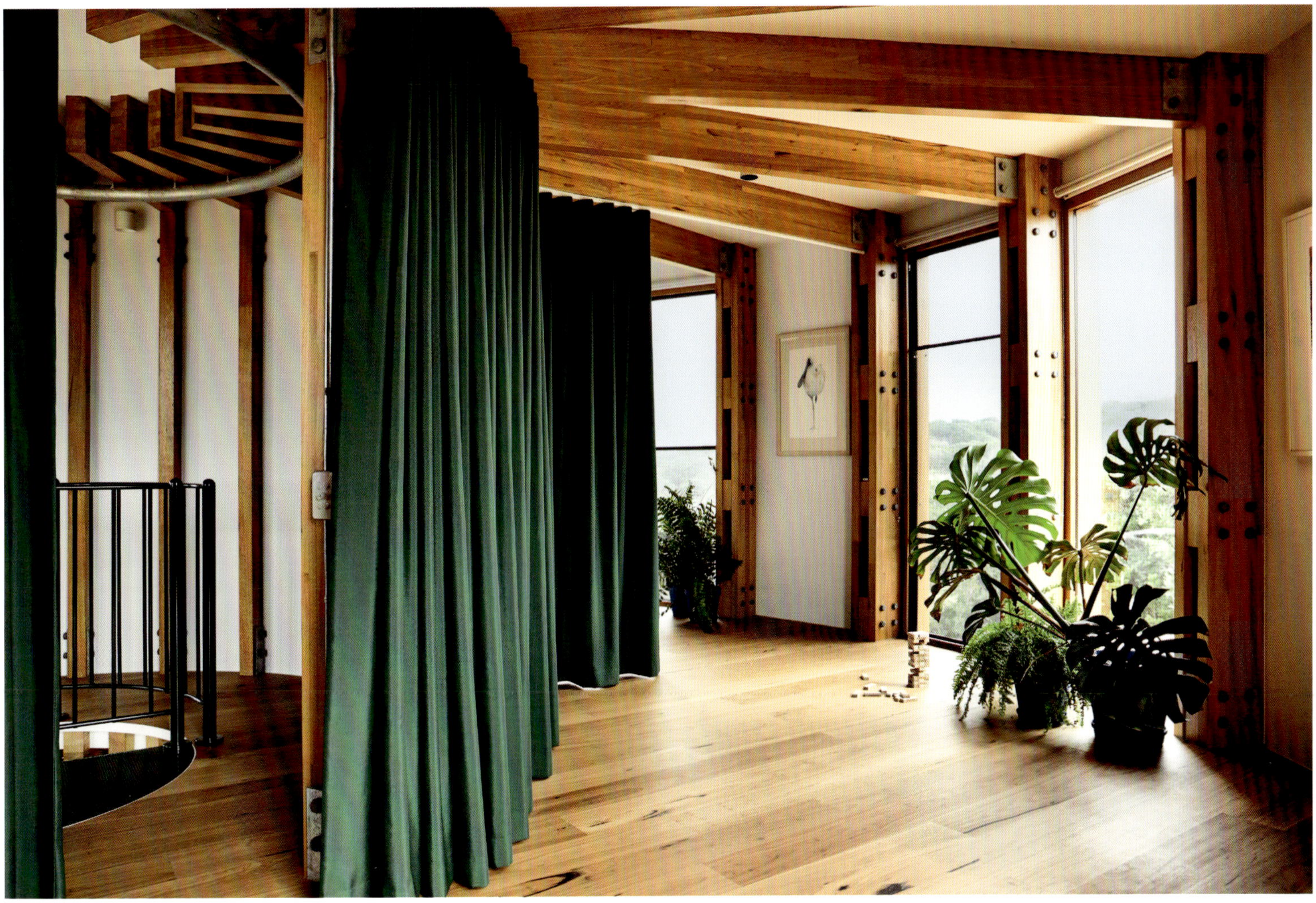

Building Arts Architects
KAWAGAMA BOATHOUSE
2019 | Dorset, ON, Canada

Reachable only by water, this boathouse offers slow and simple living. Perched on a hilly forested plot on the shores of Ontario's Kawagama Lake, it serves as a guesthouse for a larger cottage nearby. Building the boathouse was a patient process that took two years; the major components were prefabricated on land and transported by boat. The house was designed for all the elements to be light enough to be handled by only two people, and simply bolted together. The habitable top floor, resting on steel pillars, hovers over the lower-level boat store. There is no kitchen—just a refrigerator—and there is no bathroom or other indoor plumbing (planning laws prohibit it so close to the lake), just an outdoor faucet—staying here is not for the fainthearted, but what the house lacks in luxury and facilities, it more than makes up in craftsmanship, thoughtful design, and the restorative experience of waking up so close to the water. A stone-floored living space is separated from the bedroom by storage units. The upper floor is almost entirely wrapped in floor-to-ceiling glazing, so residents can focus on gazing out at the panorama of water, birch, maple, and pine. The lack of distraction creates an almost monastic space for contemplation, rest, and enjoyment of the natural world.

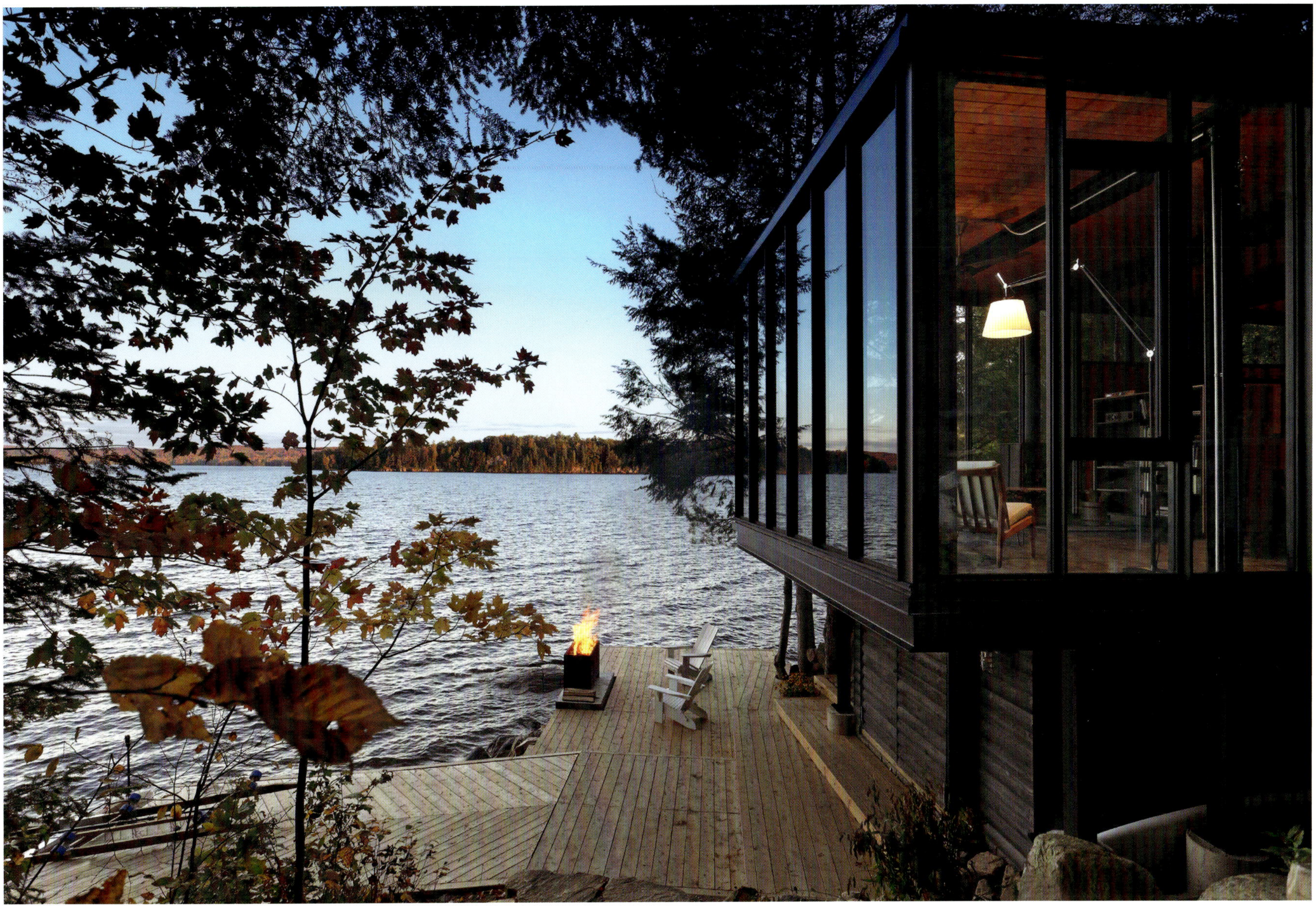

KAWAGAMA BOATHOUSE

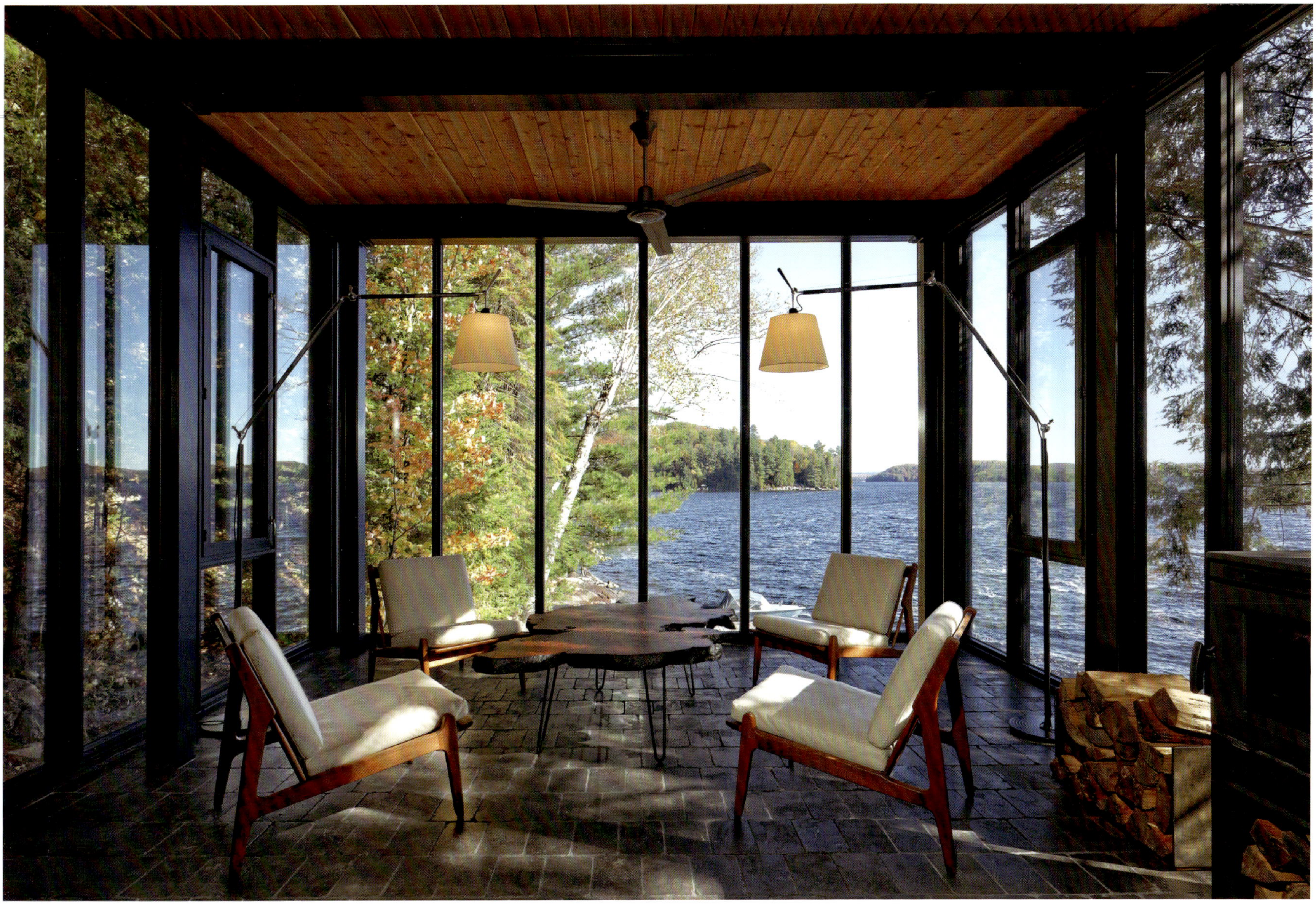

D'Arcy Jones Architects
DEEP COVE HOUSE
2019 | Vancouver, BC, Canada

This clifftop family home in a suburb north of downtown Vancouver overlooks an ocean inlet where ships, kayaks, and even whales can be spotted. Stepping down a cliff, the house is spread over three stories. The front, on street level, has no windows at all to ensure privacy and a sense of self-containment. Entry is via the top floor, which has a bedroom and a hallway at the front, and a kitchen, dining room, and living area at the rear to maximize enjoyment of the stupendous views. The clean angular lines of the facade give it the appearance of a lookout tower—and gazing out over the water is the home's organizing principle. In the top-floor living area, long horizontal windows wrapping 180 degrees around the building ensure that the view of the ocean is a constant presence in the house. Inward-sloping facades reduce sun glare and keep rain off the wraparound windows. Clad in red cedar, the house has an H-shaped plan: its "pinched waist" creates two courtyards to the east and west, giving additional views of inlet and forest, and intriguing outlooks from one wing to the next. The windows are positioned in such a way that when inhabitants sit or lie down, the rest of the suburban environment is edited out, so all that can be seen is the surrounding nature—trees, sea, and sky.

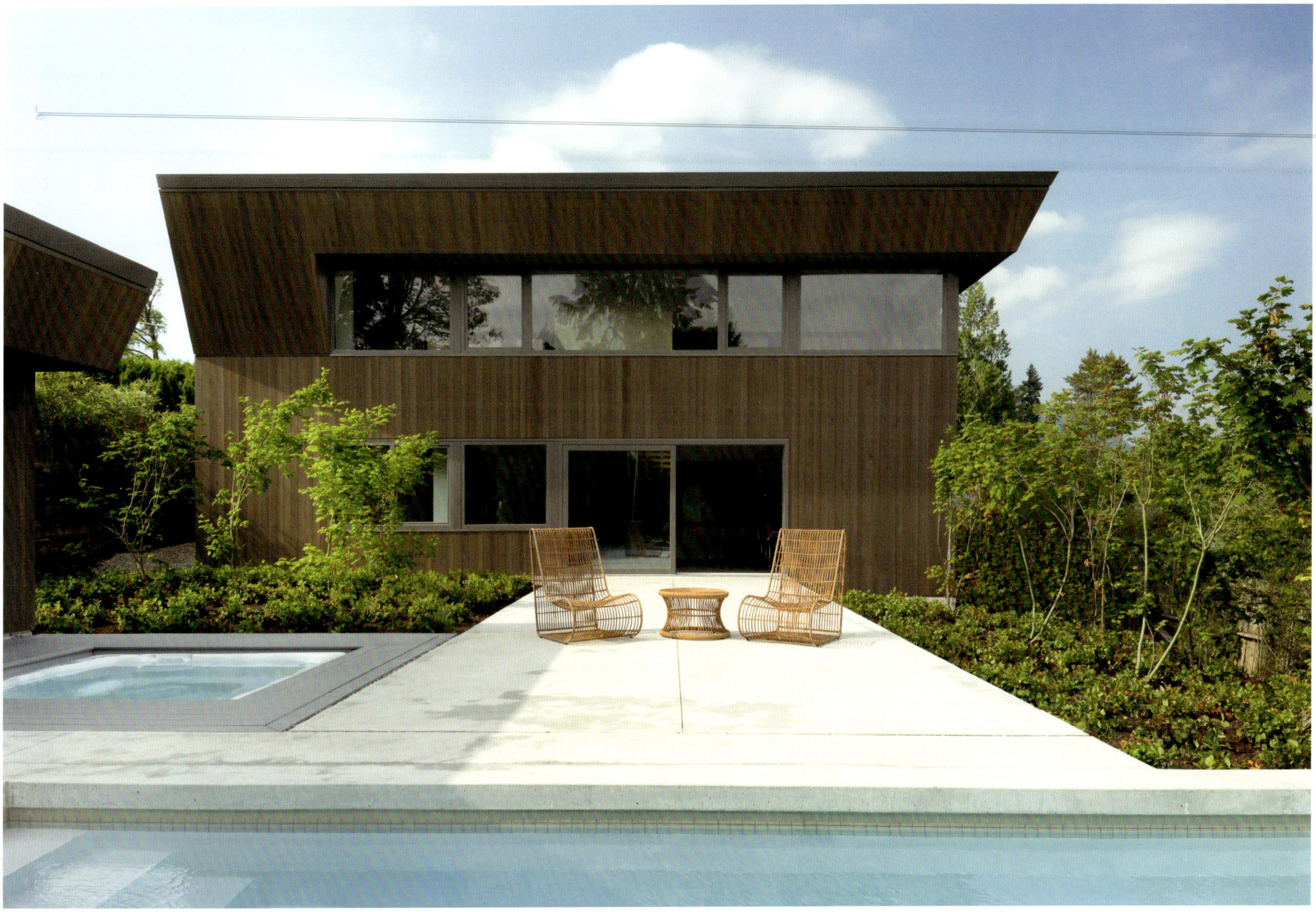

DEEP COVE HOUSE

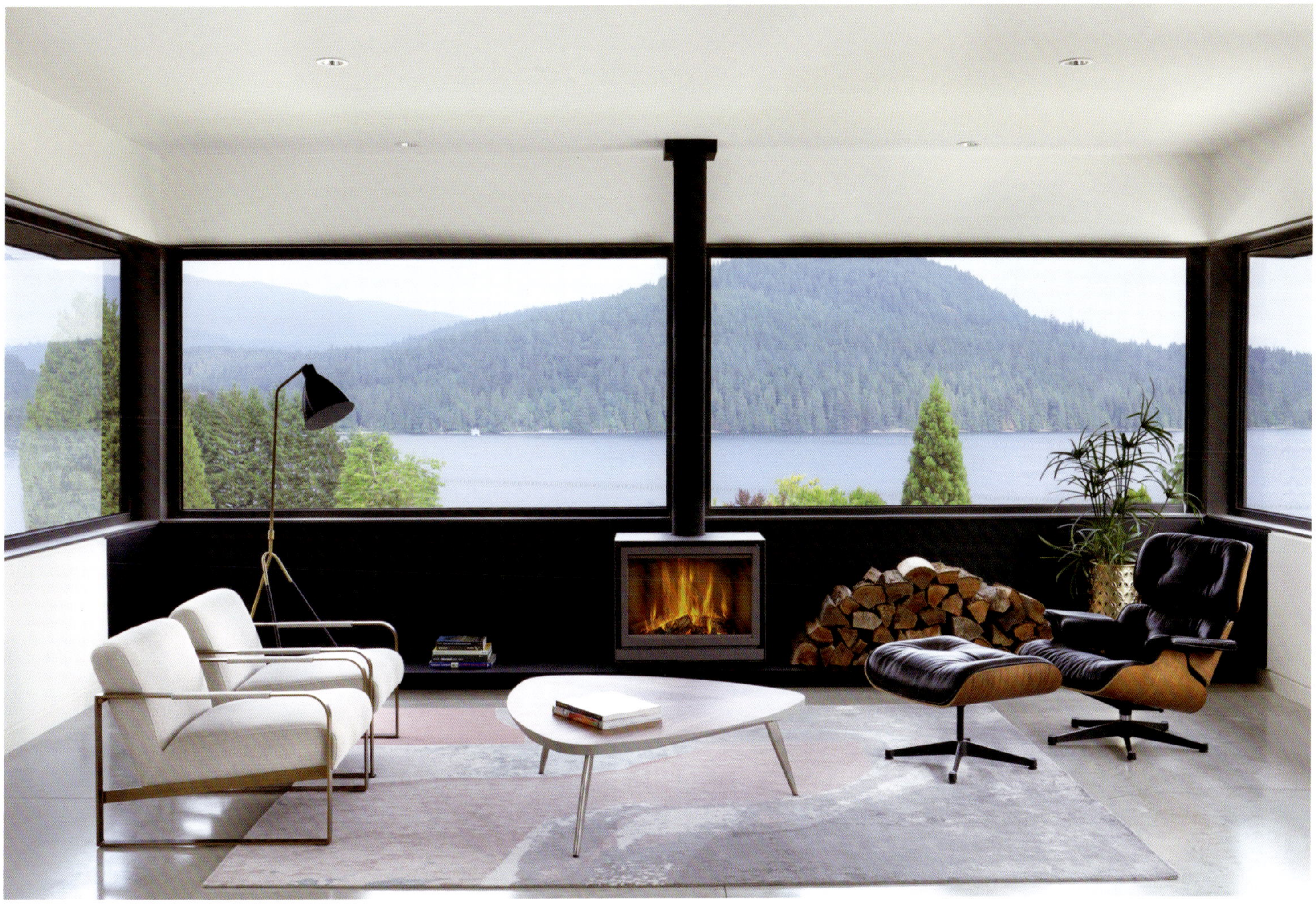

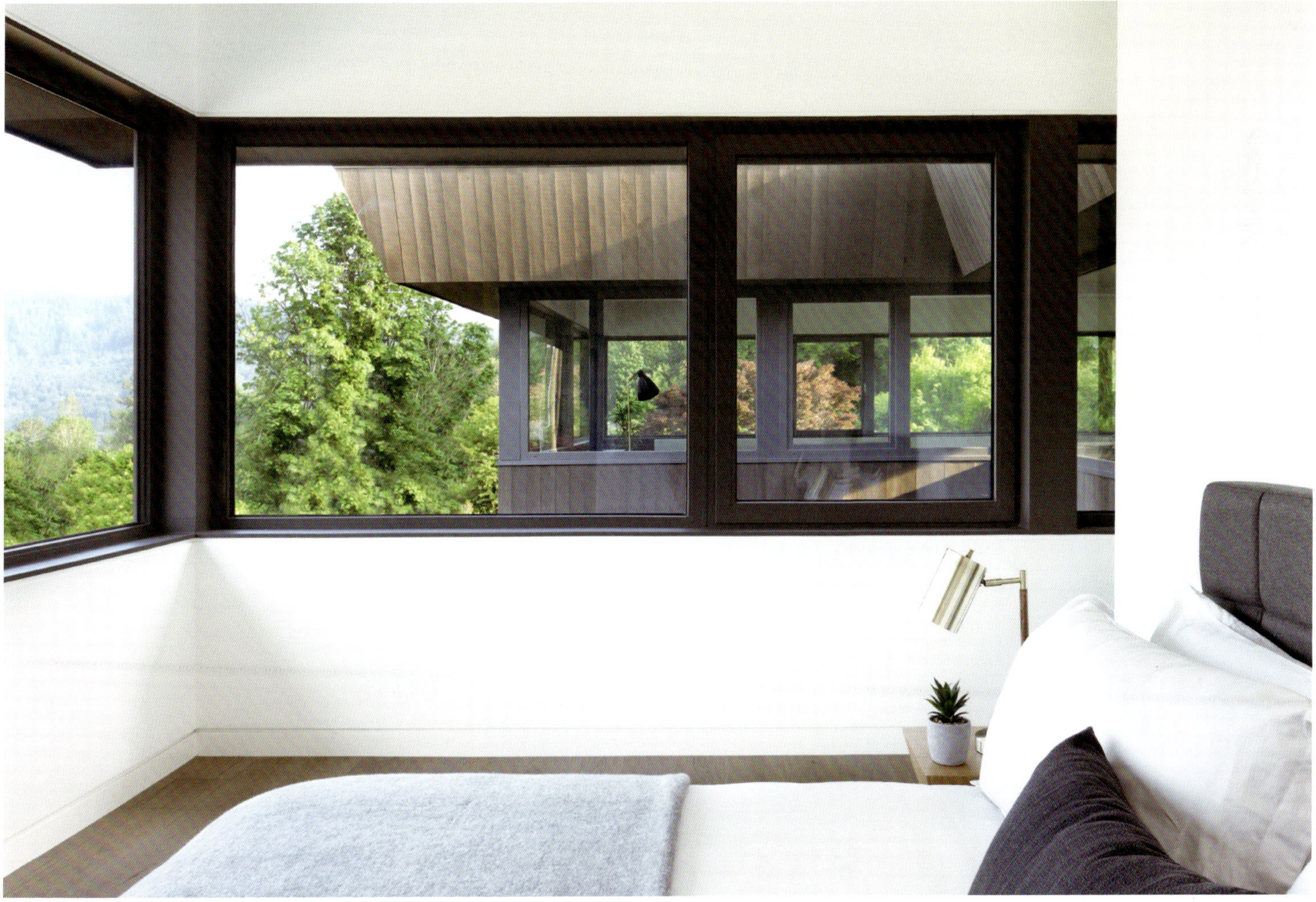

1+1>2 Architects
STRAW HOUSE
2019 | Son Tay, Vietnam

This lakeside house in a suburb of Hanoi, Vietnam, has distinctively organic curves. With a massive thatched roof and adobe-brick structure, the building's materiality reflects its environment. In harmony with the topography of the site, the house orients itself with the lake, almost inclining toward it and stretching out along its shoreline. The residence rests on stilts to protect it from termites and dampness, and to allow rain to run off the slope naturally. Its thatched roof provides shading and soundproofing, and keeps the house cool, hanging low in thick fringes over most of the facade—in doing so, it frames views of the lake with soft curves and arcs, rather than predictable straight lines. There is ample glazing, but this does not dominate with a wall of glass, as in much contemporary architecture. Locally excavated earth is a major building material, and the house is also constructed of wood, bamboo, concrete, and stone. Grapefruit and jackfruit trees huddle closely around the walls, and existing plants were retained even within the building's footprint: a full-height tree occupies the courtyard, penetrating a hole in the roof. Taking care to tread lightly on the earth, the Straw House sits serenely beside the lake, in total symbiosis with nature.

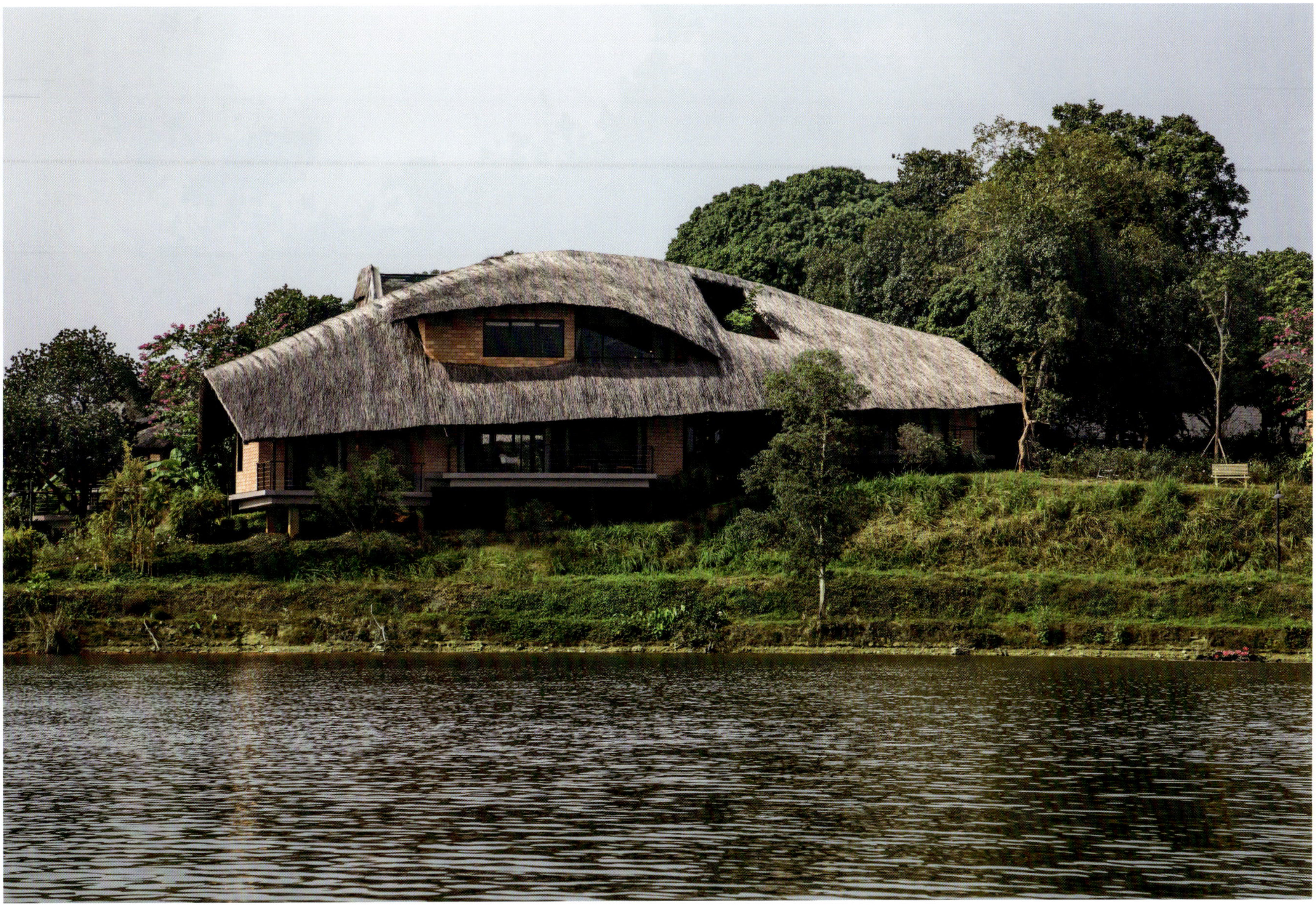

STRAW HOUSE

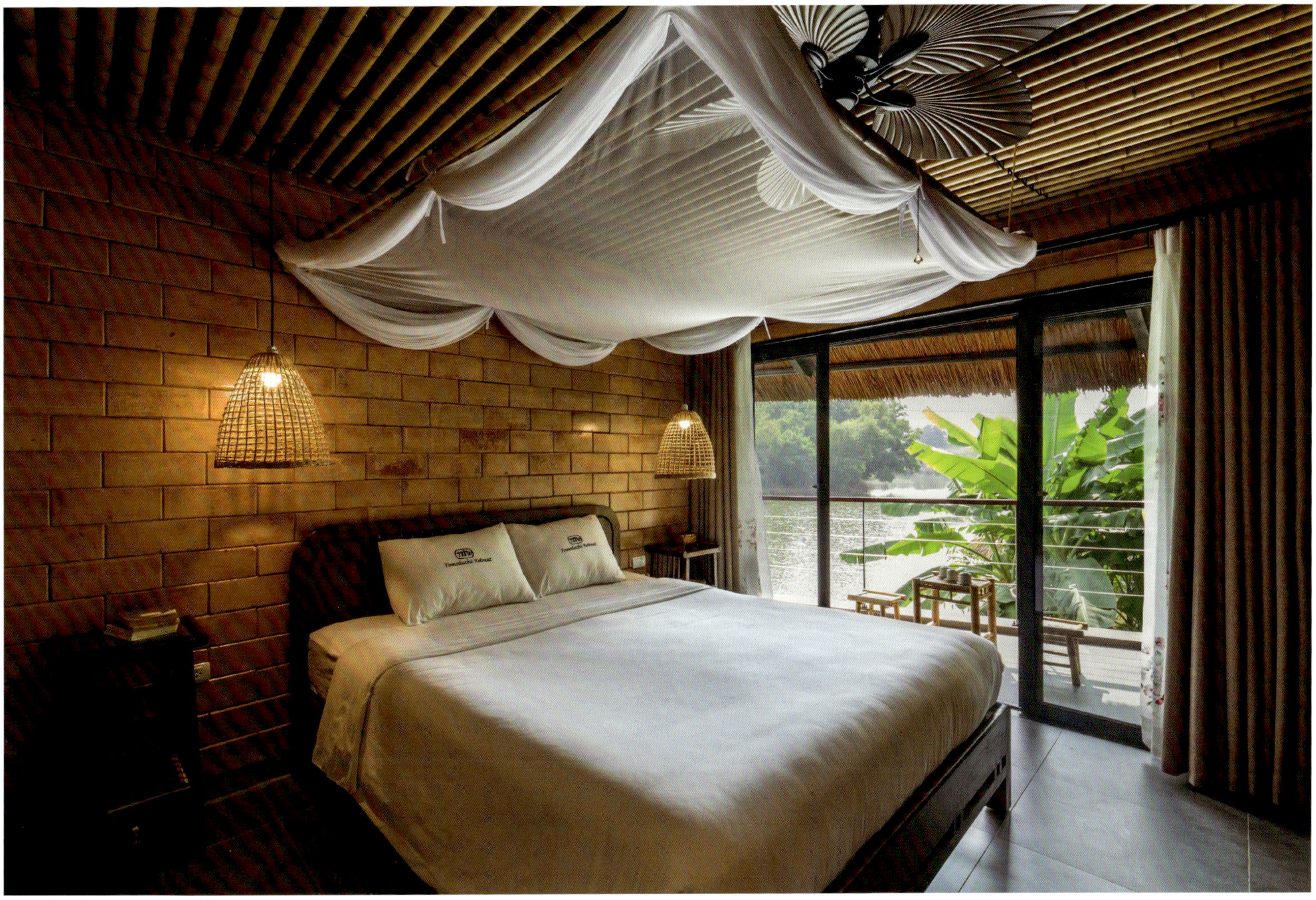

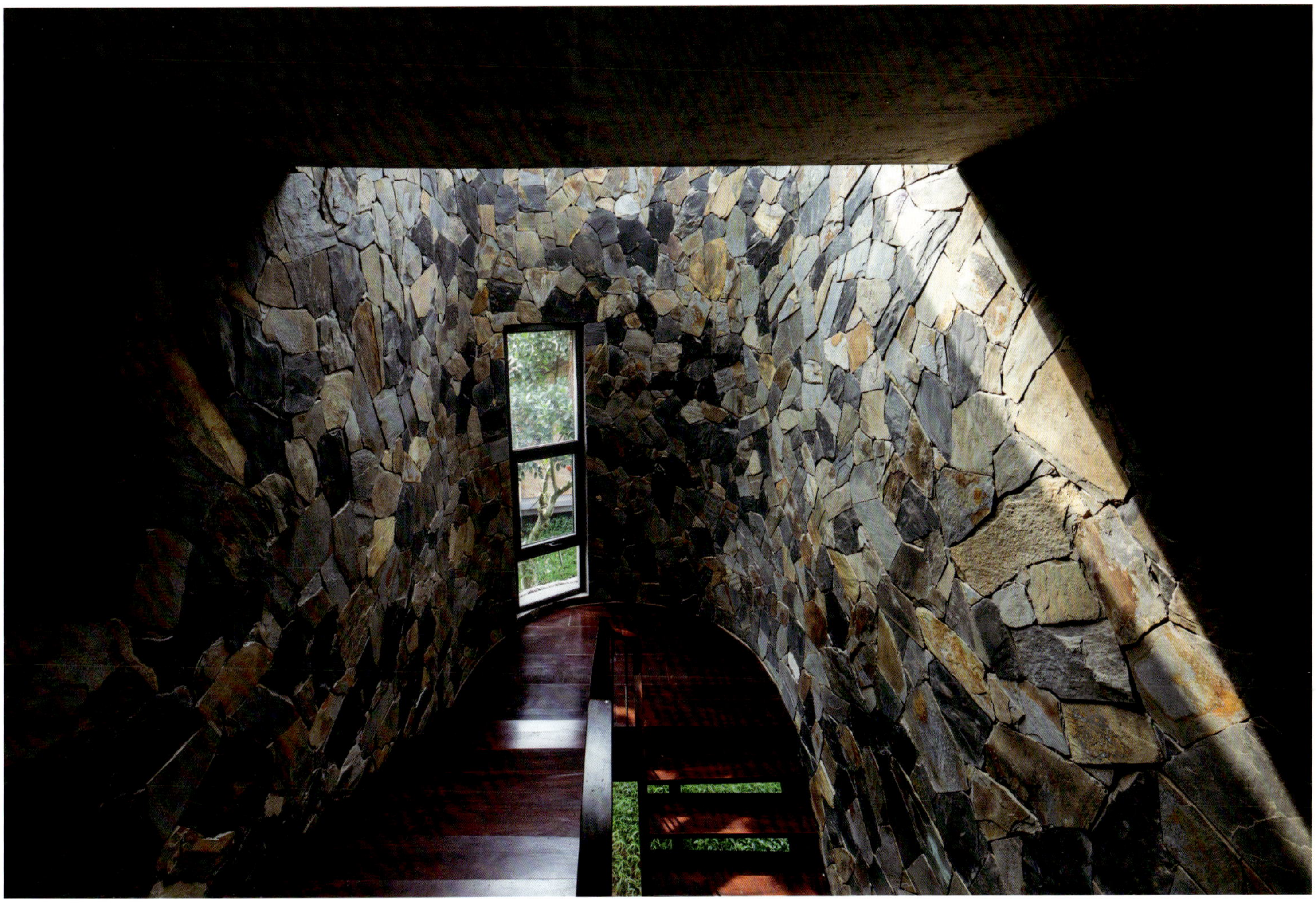

Kazunori Fujimoto Architect & Associates
HOUSE IN AJINA
2019 | Hiroshima, Japan

This dignified, towerlike residence in Hiroshima is built into a steep slope overlooking the Inland Sea. The house has views of the island Miyajima and the torii gate of its shrine, which appears to be floating in the water. The intention was to create a dwelling that could spread freely in both directions, while framing views of the shrine in the most respectful way possible. The starting point for the design was a deconstruction of the box form. The south facade was given De Stijl-type treatment in which cubic planes are layered over one another, imbuing it with a sense of rhythm and dynamism. On the north facade, at road level, the main entrance is concealed by a slim concrete panel that creates a porch. Entering, one descends a dark staircase and emerges into a light-flooded kitchen and living space with a ceiling one-and-a-half floors-high; this transforms a normally functional space into something lofty and templelike. Three stacked horizontal openings in one corner admit light and frame abstract views of the sky, clouds, and treetops. A large rectangular window visible from the street gives a glimpse of the staircase and an opening beyond, creating transparency and a sense of intrigue. The deliberately austere interior, whose walls are made of minimalist concrete slabs, allows the focus to remain on the sea and its shrine. The whole house has a sense of mystery and serenity.

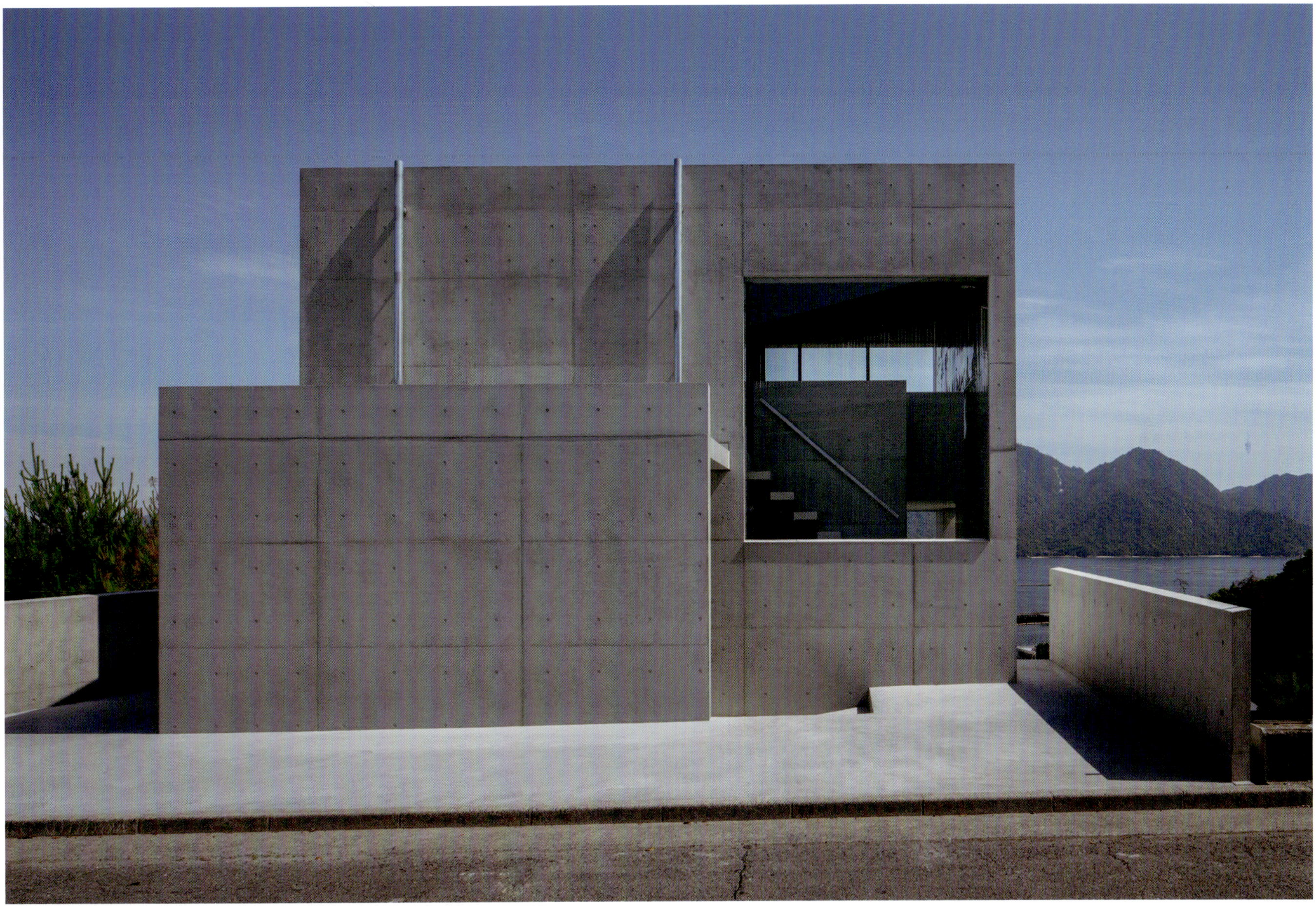

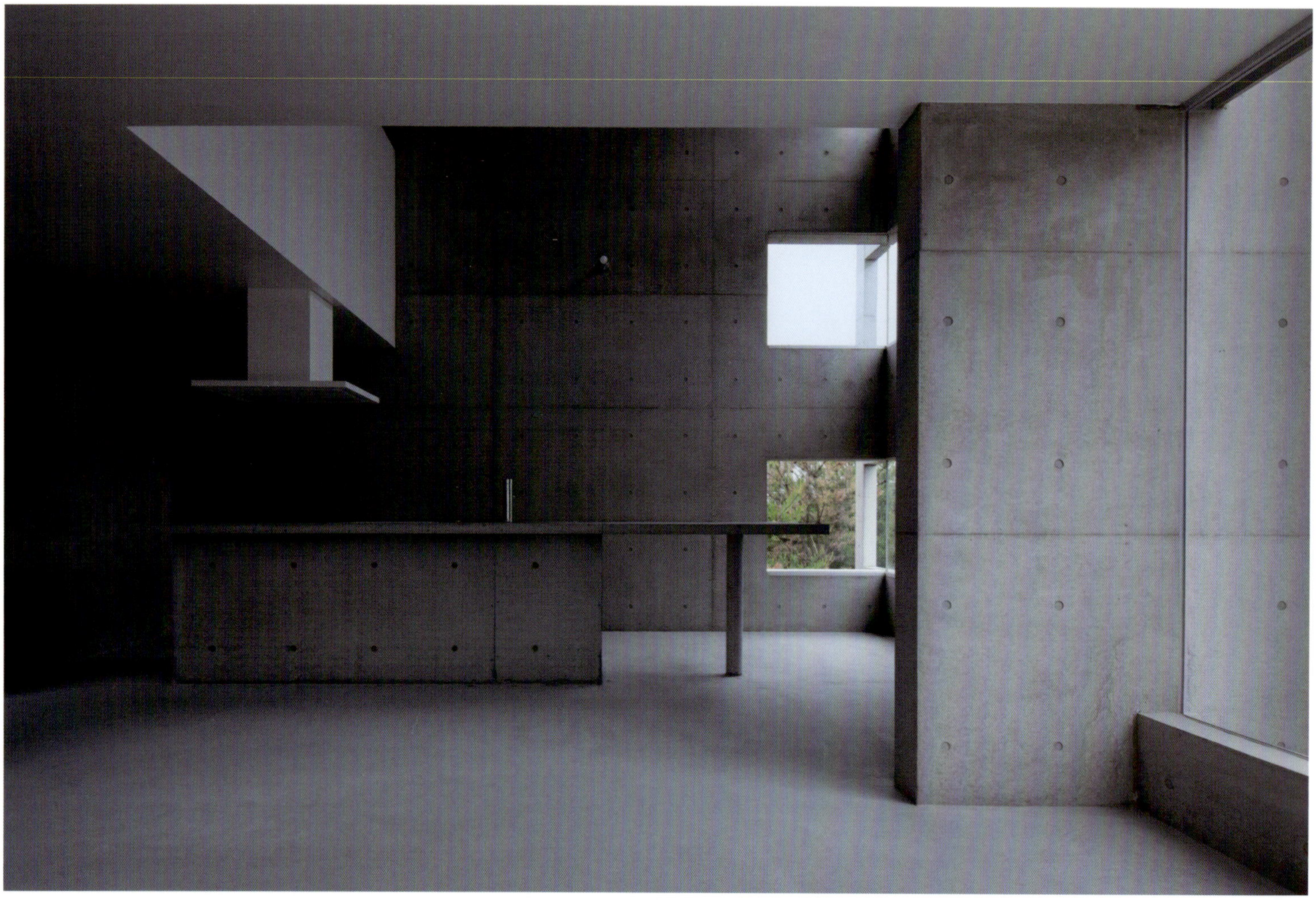

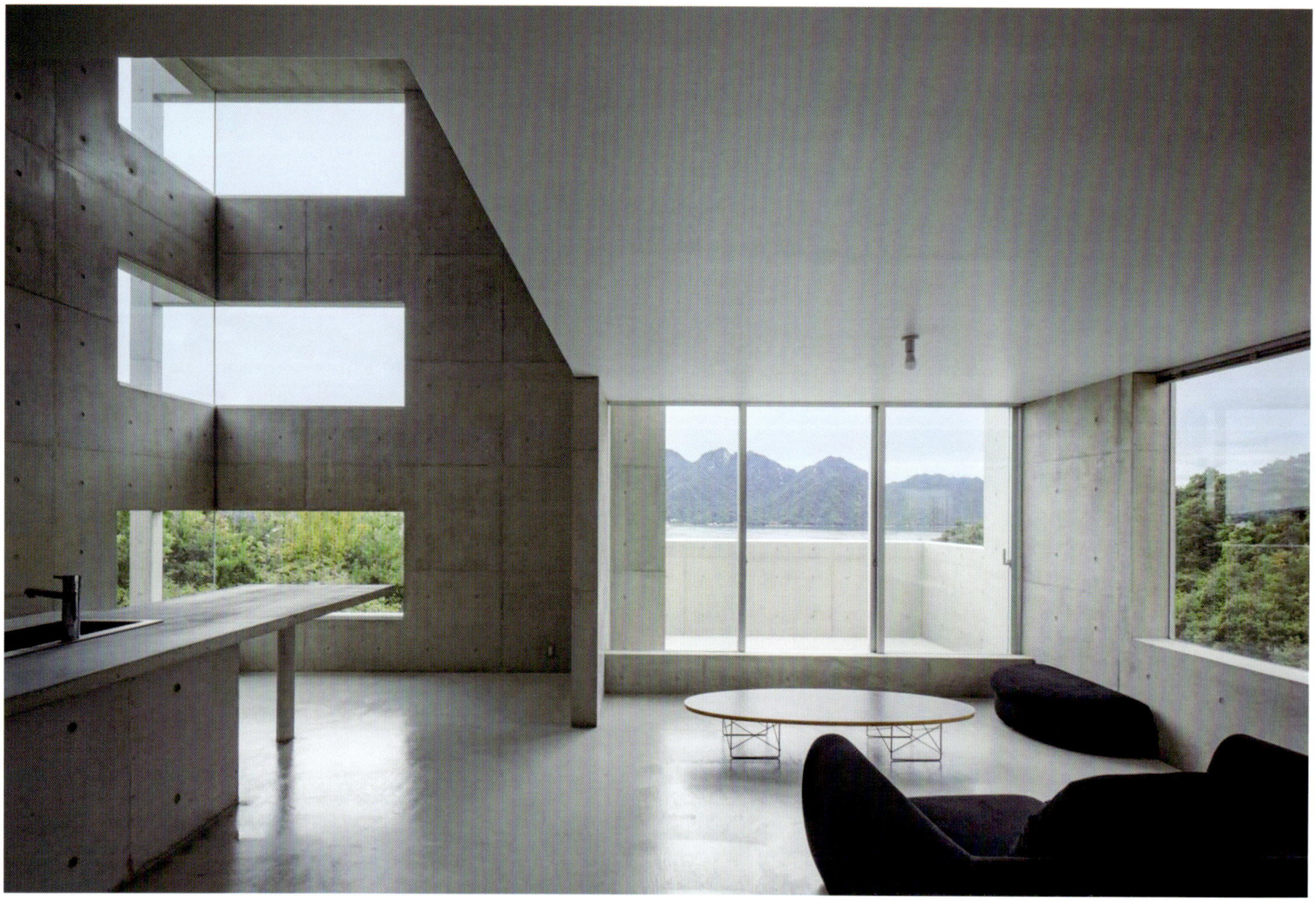

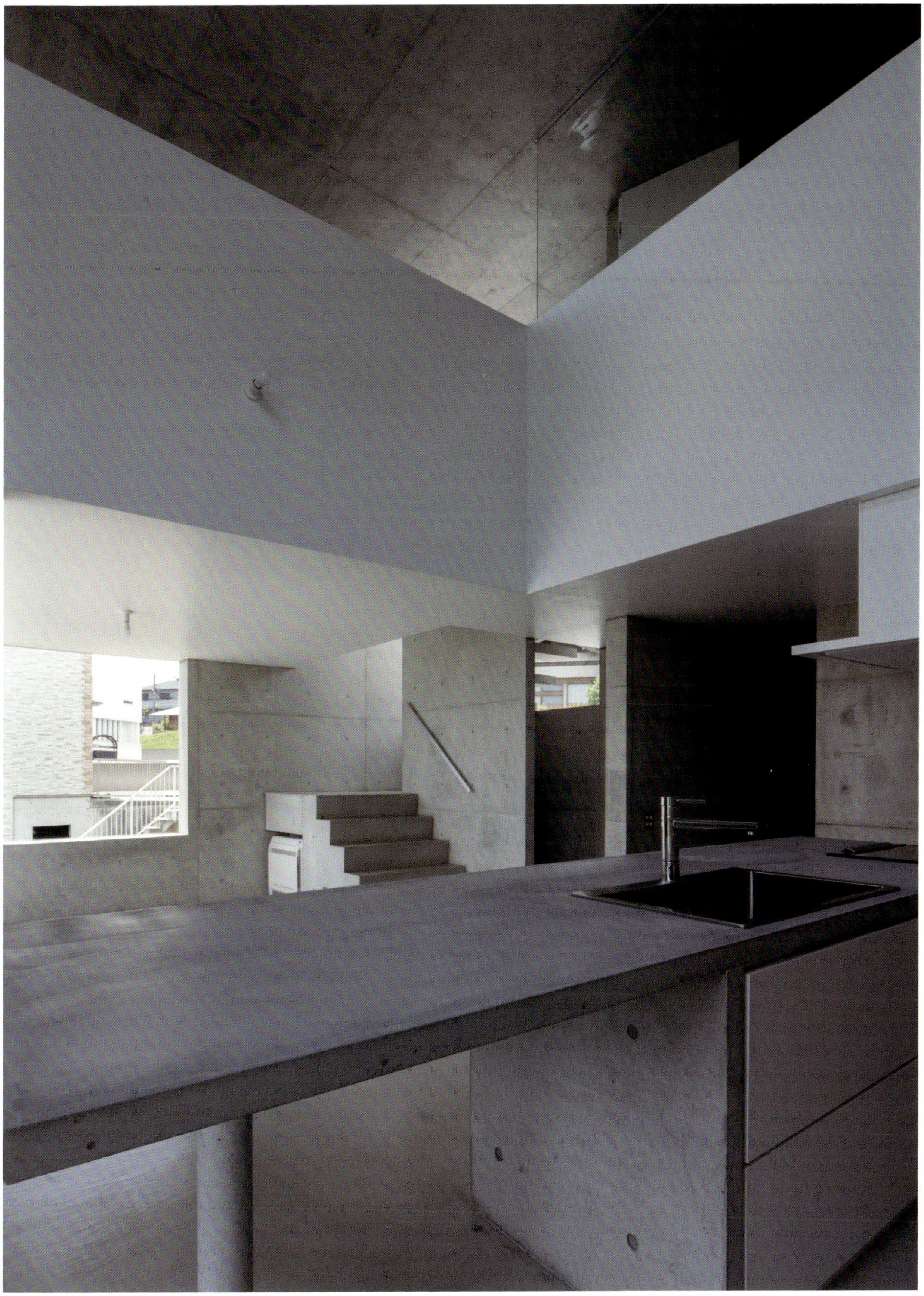

Aleksi Hautamäki and Milla Selkimäki
PROJECT Ö CABIN
2019 | Kimito Island Municipality, Finland

After searching for five years, two designers found the perfect place to build a retreat: Kimito, a tiny, triangular, and previously uninhabited island in the Turku Archipelago. The architectural style was an easy choice—a gabled-roof house, an archetype used throughout the region—but it was designed to be low and narrow enough to enable long expanses of glazing and constant views of the sea. Surrounded by pines, perched on a stony escarpment, the dwelling actually consists of two separate volumes set at a slight angle to one another. The guesthouse has a living room, kitchen, and bedroom at one end, and a sauna and bathroom at the other; the two zones connect via a decked courtyard, meaning the outdoors is always an integral part of being there. Reflecting the couple's passion for design and hand-building, the second volume includes a workshop with large folding doors opening on to a patio. Totally off-grid, the house is equipped to convert brine from the Baltic Sea into purified water for drinking and washing using solar-powered reverse osmosis, with the capacity to store up to 317 quarts (300 liters). The living space is glazed on three sides, flooded by views of the pearlescent sea, and there are calming ocean views from the sauna.

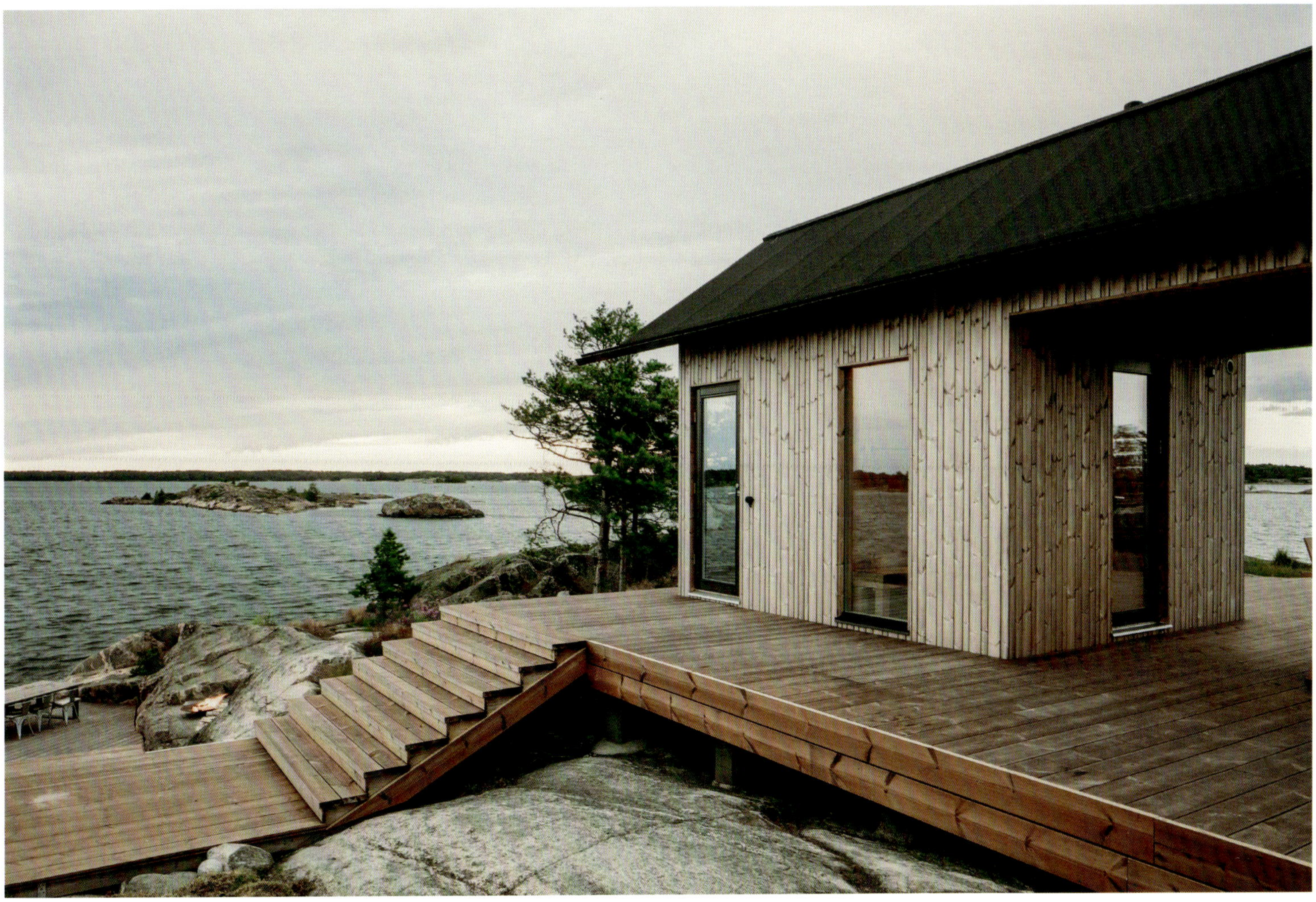

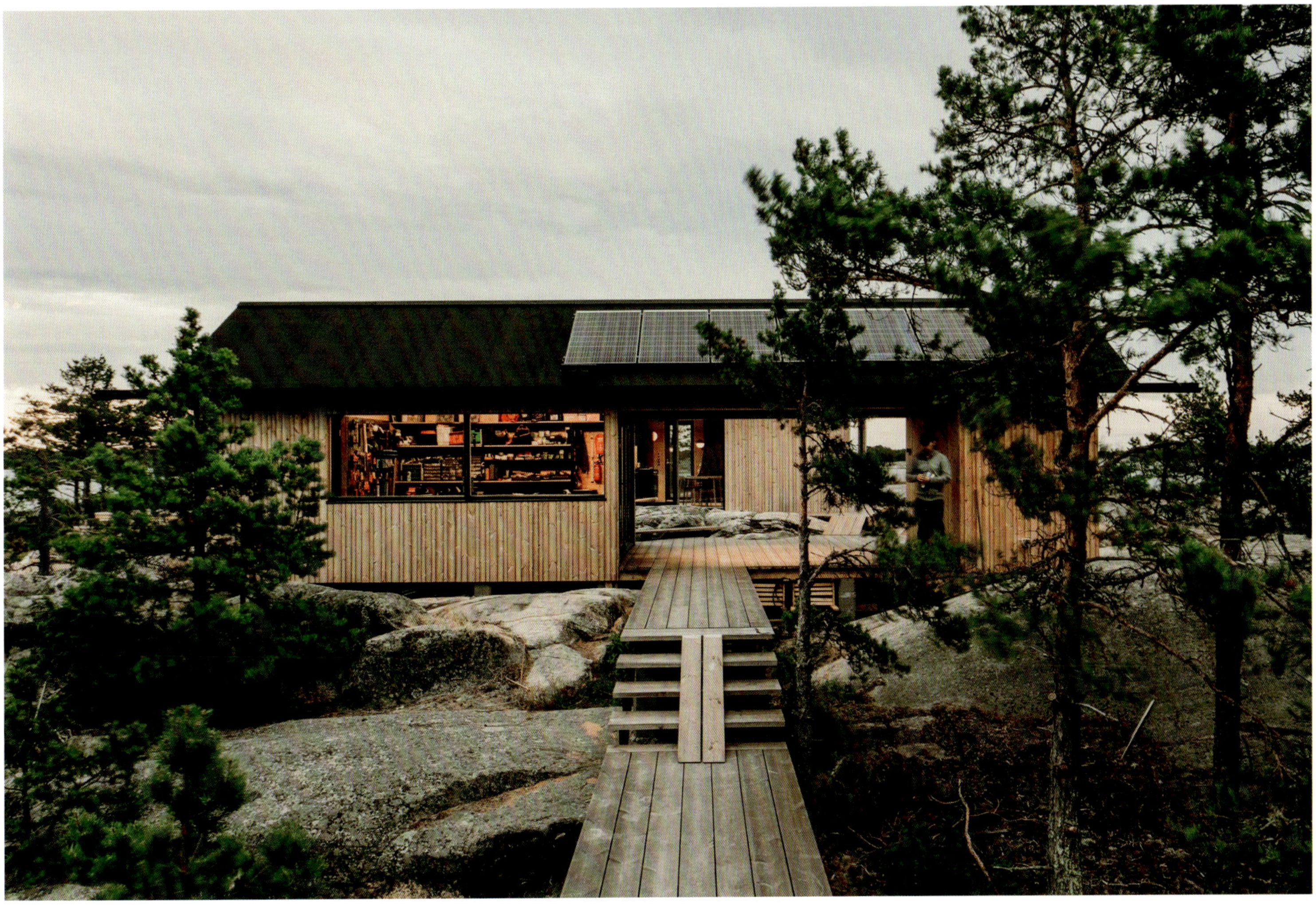

PROJECT Ö CABIN

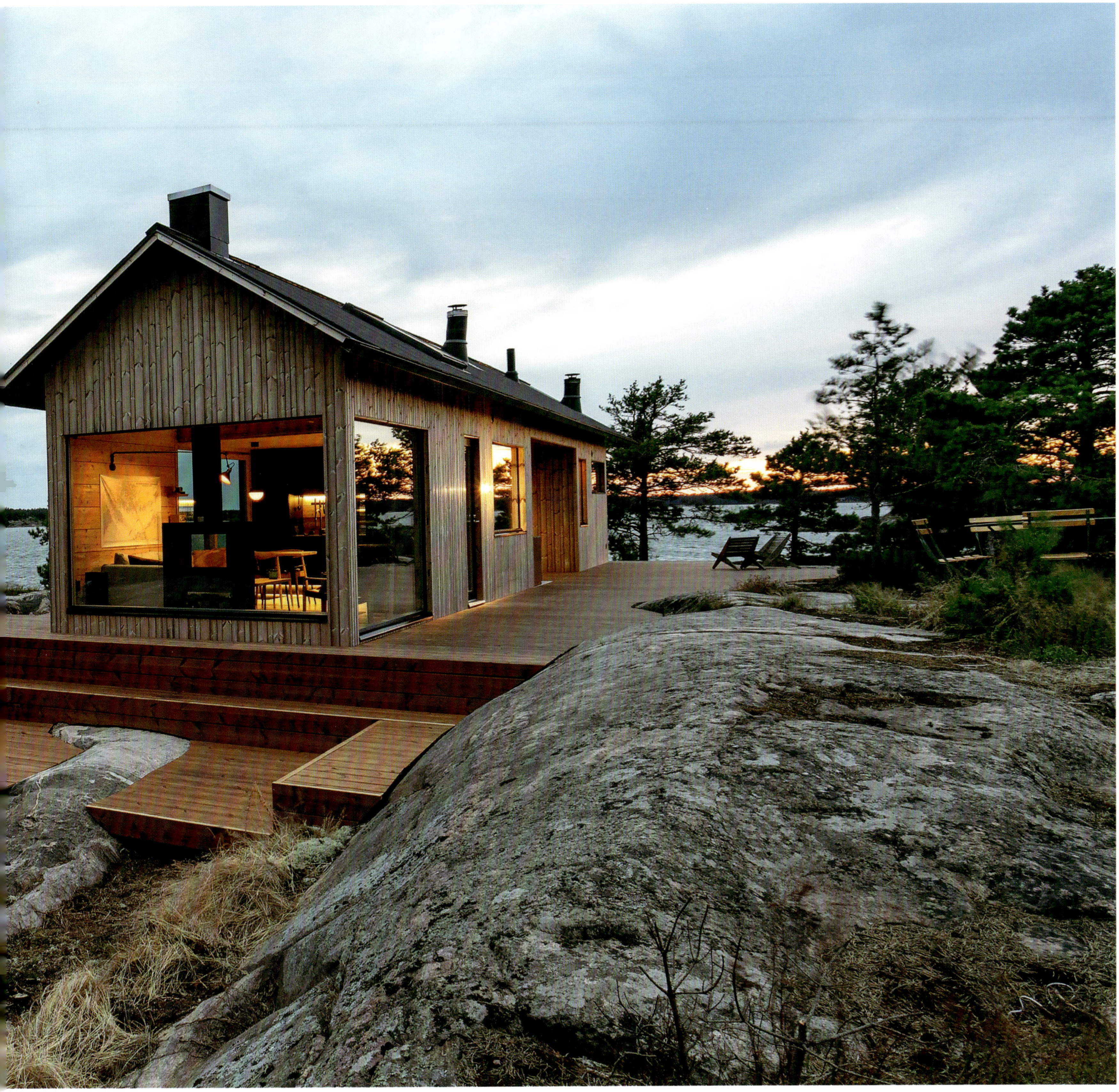

PROJECT Ö CABIN

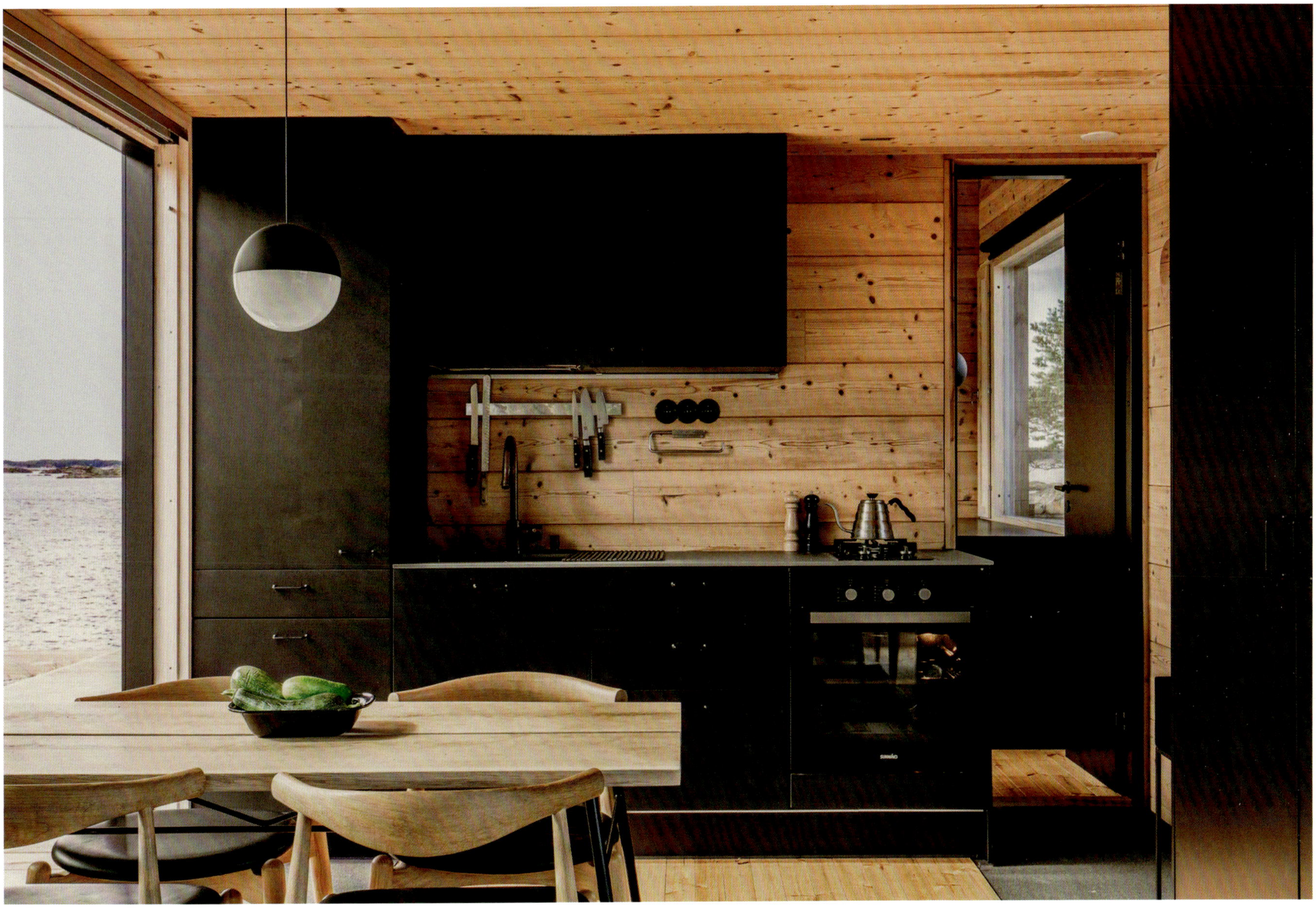

Grove Architects
BUNDEENA BEACH HOUSE
2018 | Bundeena, NSW, Australia

This unostentatious weekend home achieves a great deal through its abstract forms, clever use of materials, and imaginatively configured internal space. Bundeena Beach House replaces an older, rundown shack on a rocky outcrop overlooking Royal National Park beach, just south of Sydney, Australia. The design prioritizes sea views and includes three bedrooms, music and media rooms, and both indoor and outdoor social areas. The house comprises two rectangular volumes connected by a flat roof. Its public, road-facing side is low-key: a single story with the garage screened by sliding wooden doors and a green roof that softens the building's outline. At the rear—the private side—forms become more dramatic, rising to two stories, with the upper floor cantilevering outward to create a shady overhang. Corten steel external cladding is sleek but not overly obtrusive, while the cedar battens elsewhere on the facade form a softer natural counterpoint to metal. Timber, steel, and concrete create a cool, neutral interior in which to recharge. A galleried, double-height living room is an impressive space, and above this is the central focus of the house: a dramatic, butterflied skylight that gives the building an unusually dynamic profile and casts shifting geometric patterns of light and shadow on the white walls.

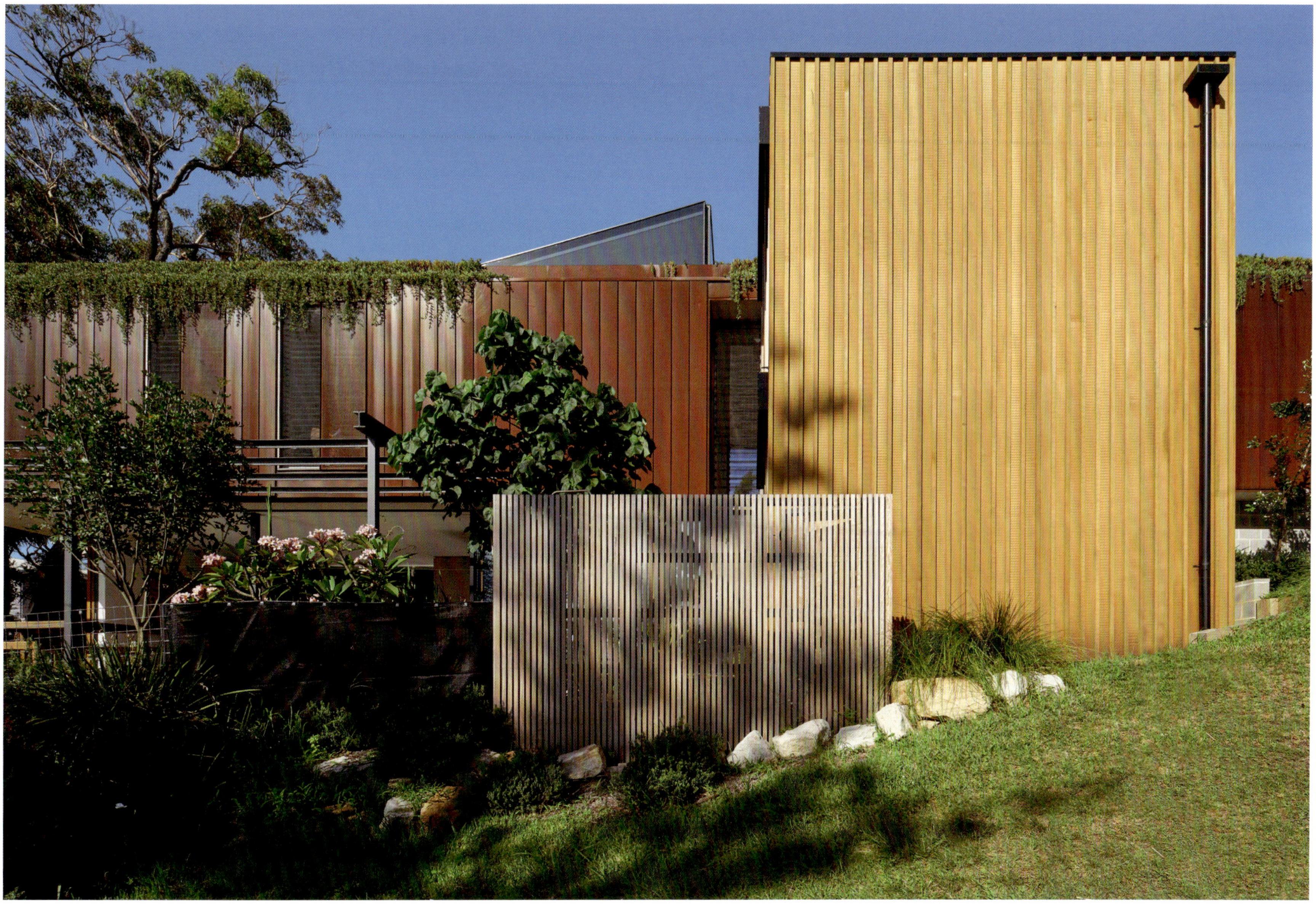

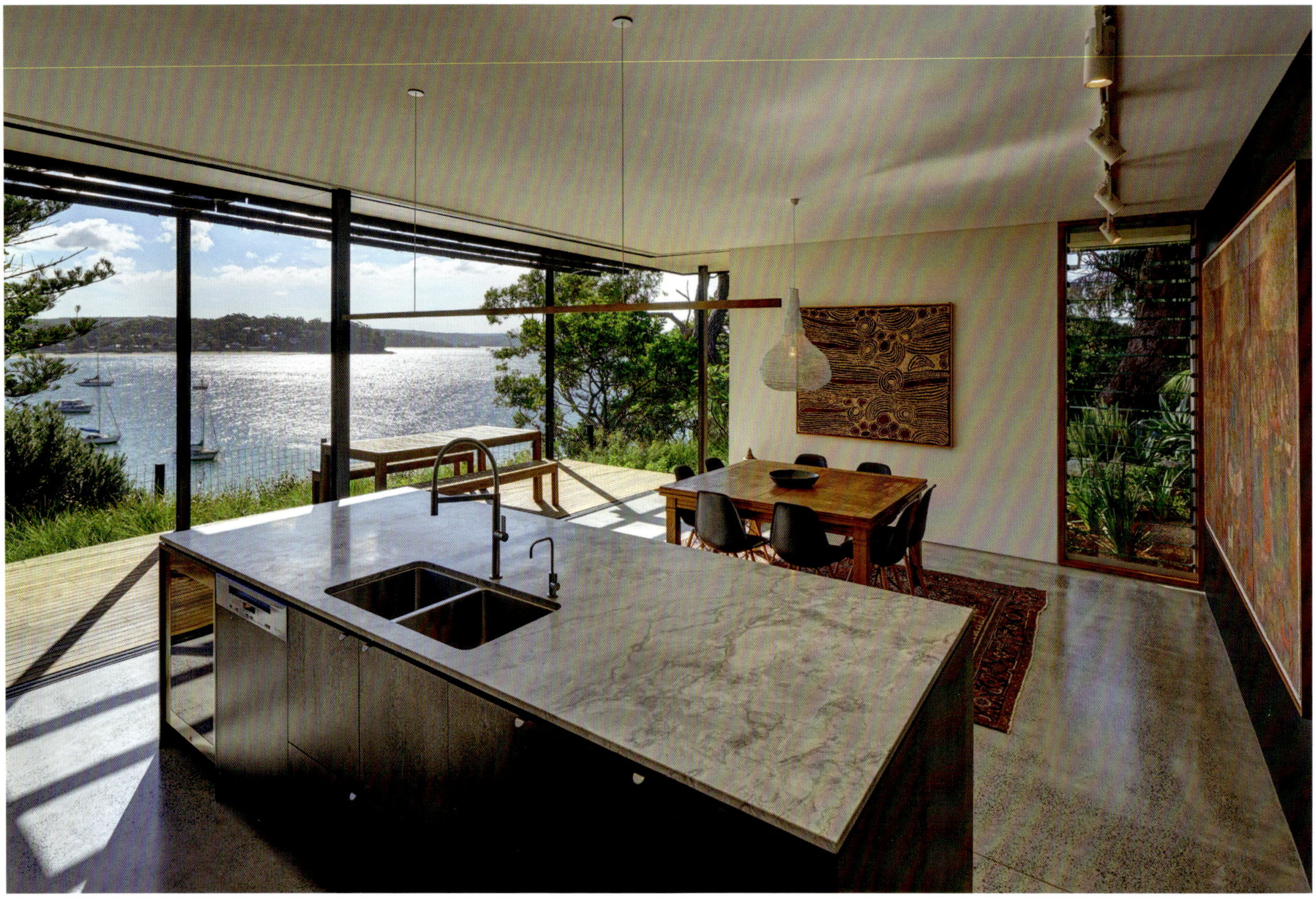

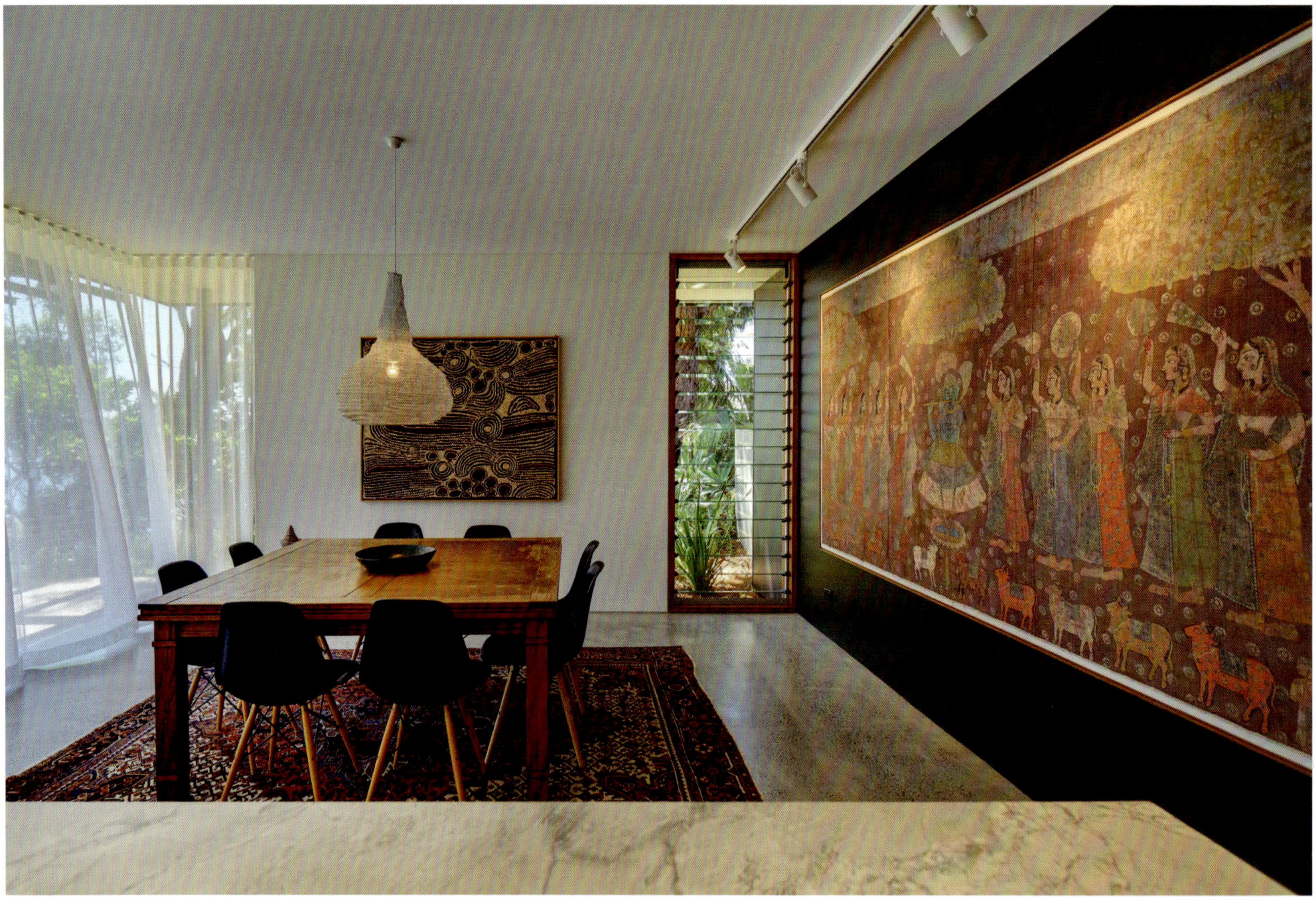

BUNDEENA BEACH HOUSE

TAOA Design
LANDSCAPE HOUSE
2019 | Beijing, China

Resembling a series of interlocking crystal-and-metal boxes, this lakeside house in Beijing pays homage to the qualities of water with its transparency and clever facade treatment. It was built on the site of a large existing house in a built-up area. However, the new house extends the original footprint, making a stronger connection with the outdoors and the lake, and creating a more natural flow between its various elements. The residence extends over three levels, including a basement. Most living spaces are at ground level so that they can spill out onto terraces shaded by elegantly cantilevering overhangs. Two internal courtyards form a focus—one is on the first floor, while another is sunken, like a subterranean field, so that it can bring as much light as possible into the dwelling. The copious glazing provides plenty of daylighting and vistas of the lake, but could also potentially compromise privacy. Therefore, the facade is made of overlapping permeable surfaces. White perforated metal shutters, both inside and outside the house, cast shadows on the massive sheets of glass that resemble droplets of water or air bubbles. This complex layering creates shade and keeps the household screened, while paradoxically suggesting fluidity, transparency, and openness.

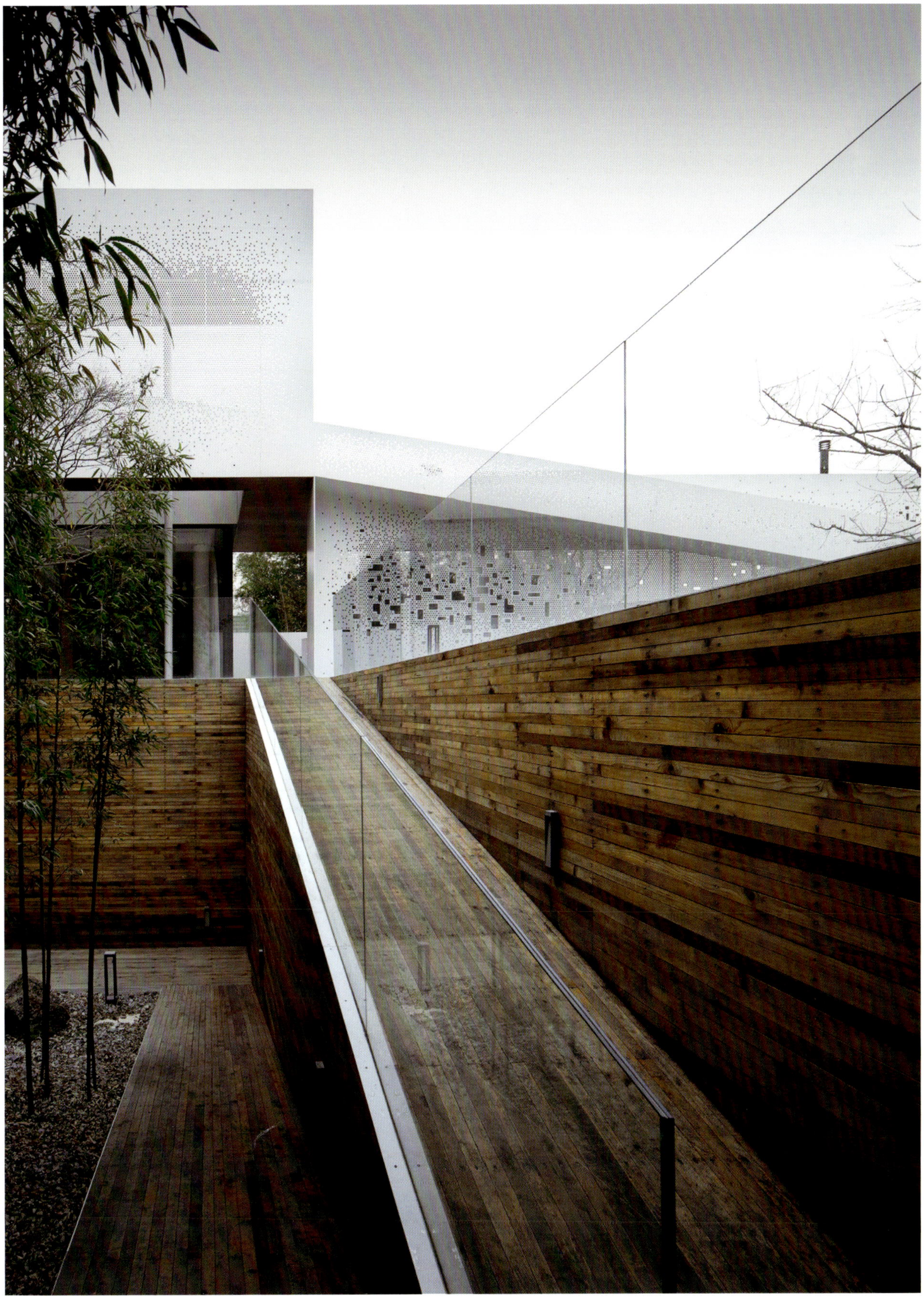

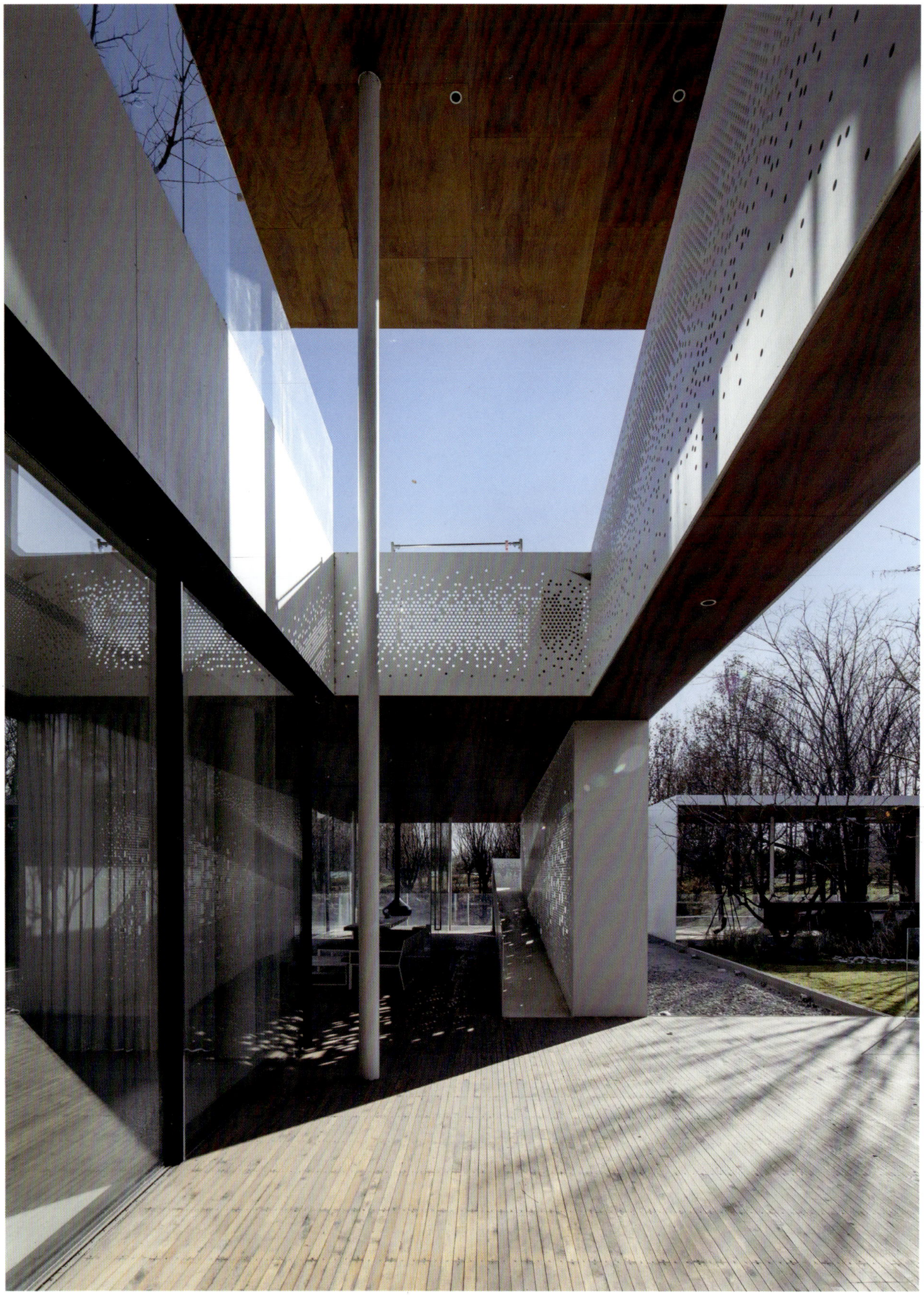

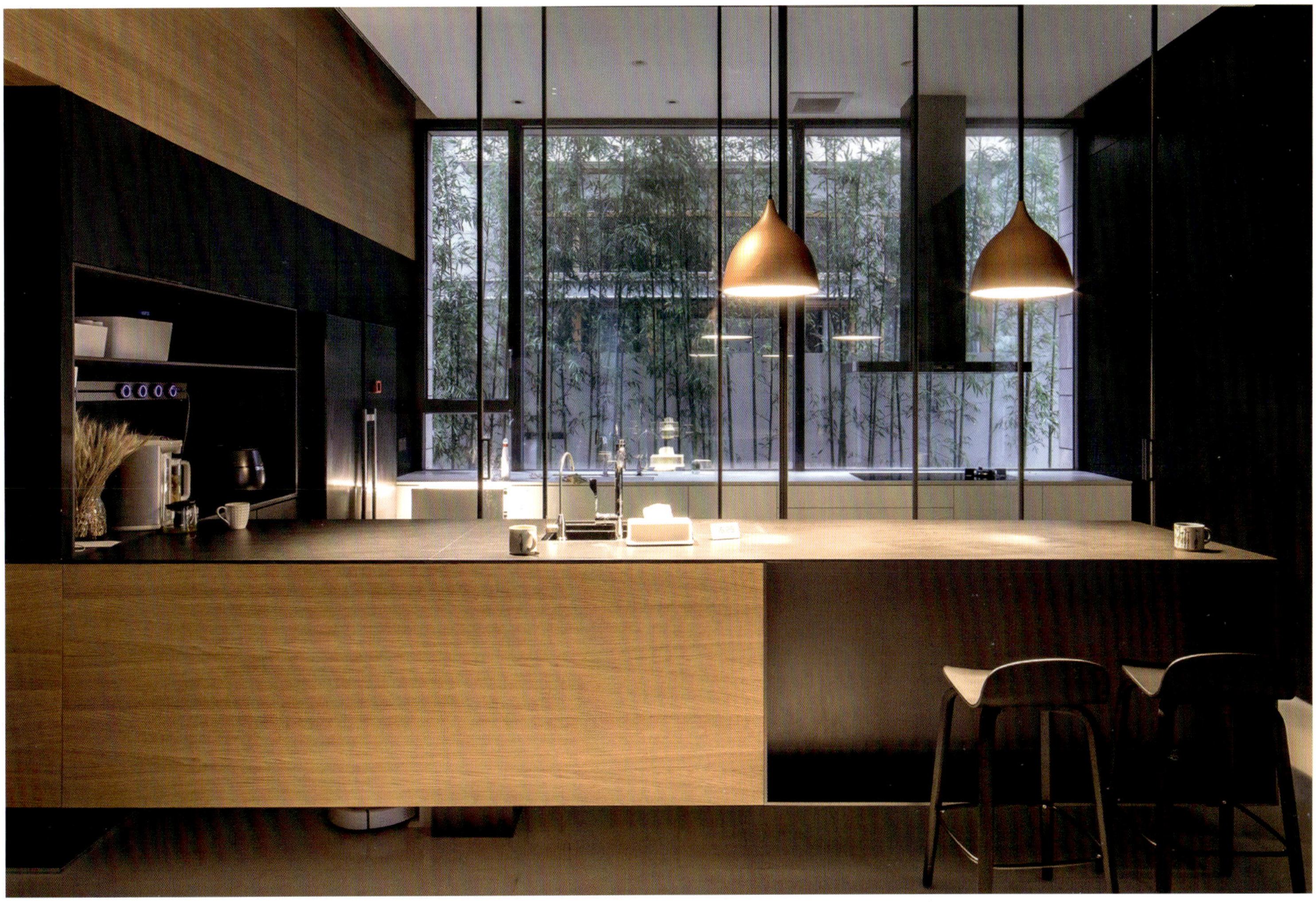

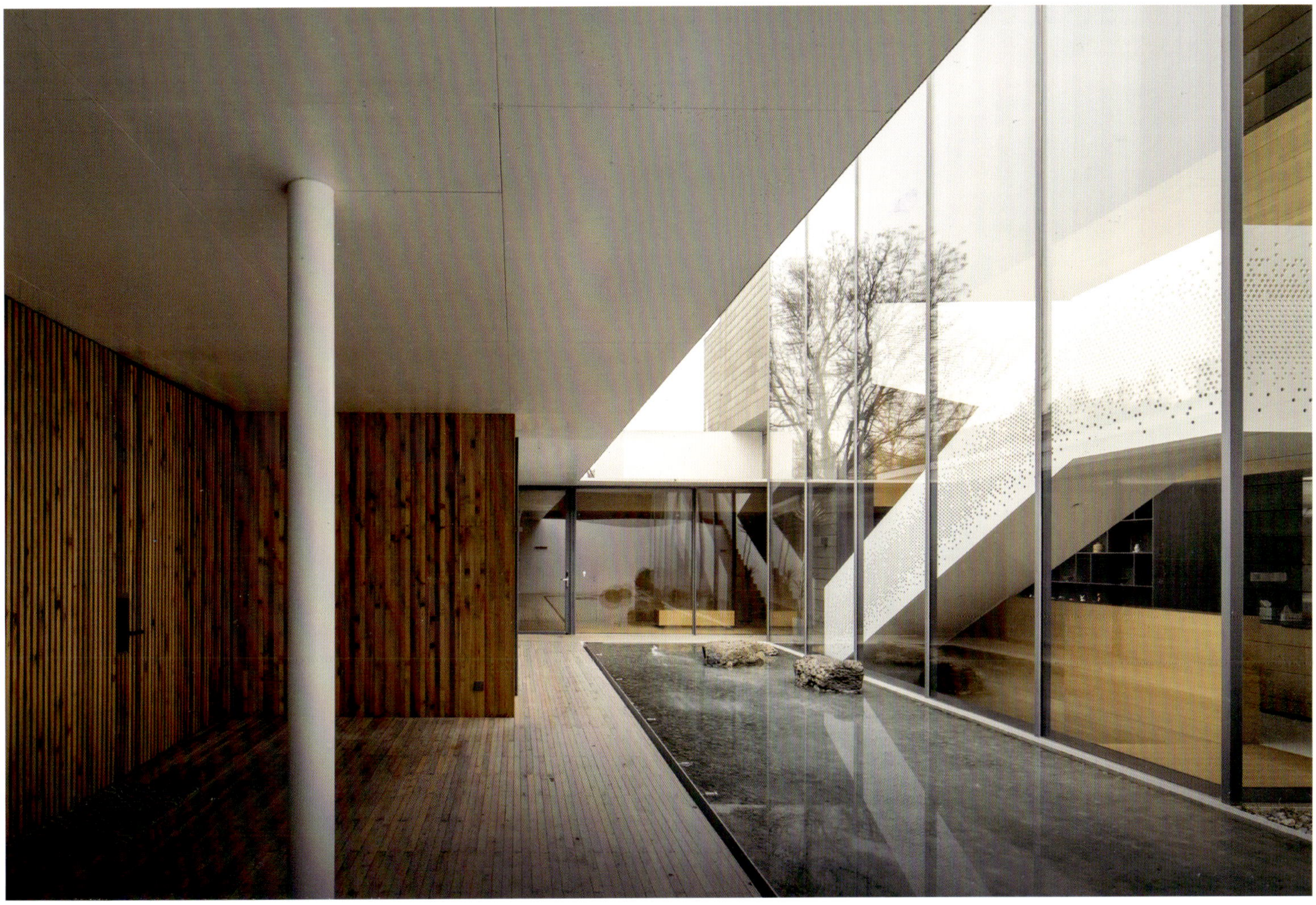

Vandkunsten Architects
MODERN SEAWEED HOUSE
2013 | Læsø, Denmark

Læsø, in the North Sea bay of Kattegat, is famous for its houses with eelgrass-thatched roofs. Unlike wood, seaweed has always been abundant on the Danish island, and the material has numerous advantages. It needs no farming, simply washing ashore. Seaweed is also naturally waterproof, a great insulator, and durable, lasting about 150 years. But by the 2000s, the number of houses using seaweed on Læsø had dwindled to around twenty, and so Realdania, a philanthropic housing association, commissioned Vandkunsten Architects to design a contemporary take on the vernacular seaweed house. The architects proposed a simple, single-story timber-frame dwelling with a pitched roof. Rather than simply thatching it, they realized seaweed's qualities could be more widely exploited. It was stuffed into string-netting bags to create bolsters and attached in lengths to the facades and roof. The eelgrass was also packed into timber crates placed behind walls and under floors for insulation, and matresslike panels filled with it cover the entire ceiling. Since the house accommodates two families, seaweed's soundproofing properties were an added bonus. A double-height living room and kitchen is at the home's center, while bedrooms are tucked at both ends and in the loft. Thanks to the eelgrass, the house has a negative carbon footprint. The softly quilted facades and roof give it a welcoming, cosseting aesthetic, and the organic materials create an ongoing bond with the sea.

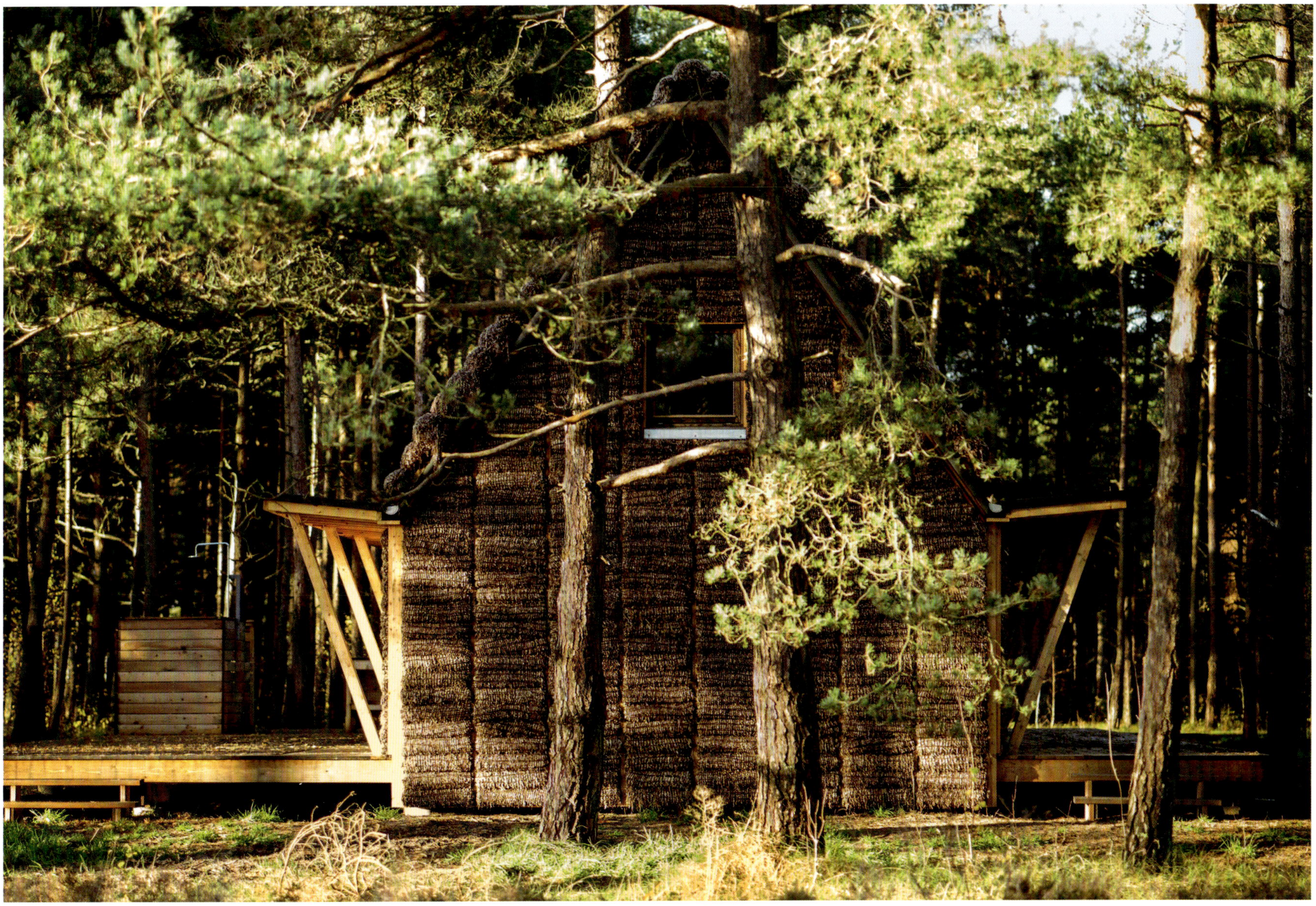

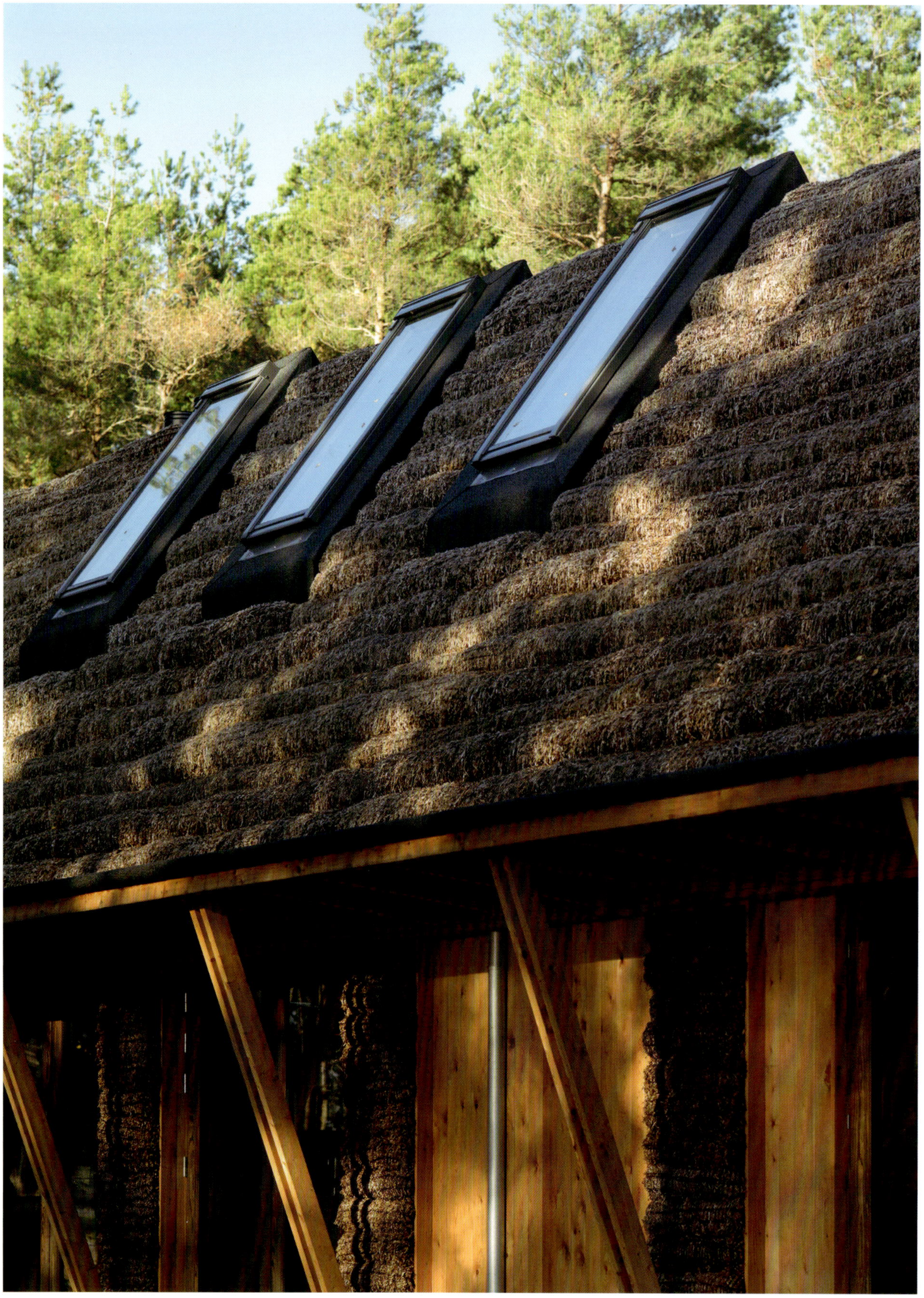

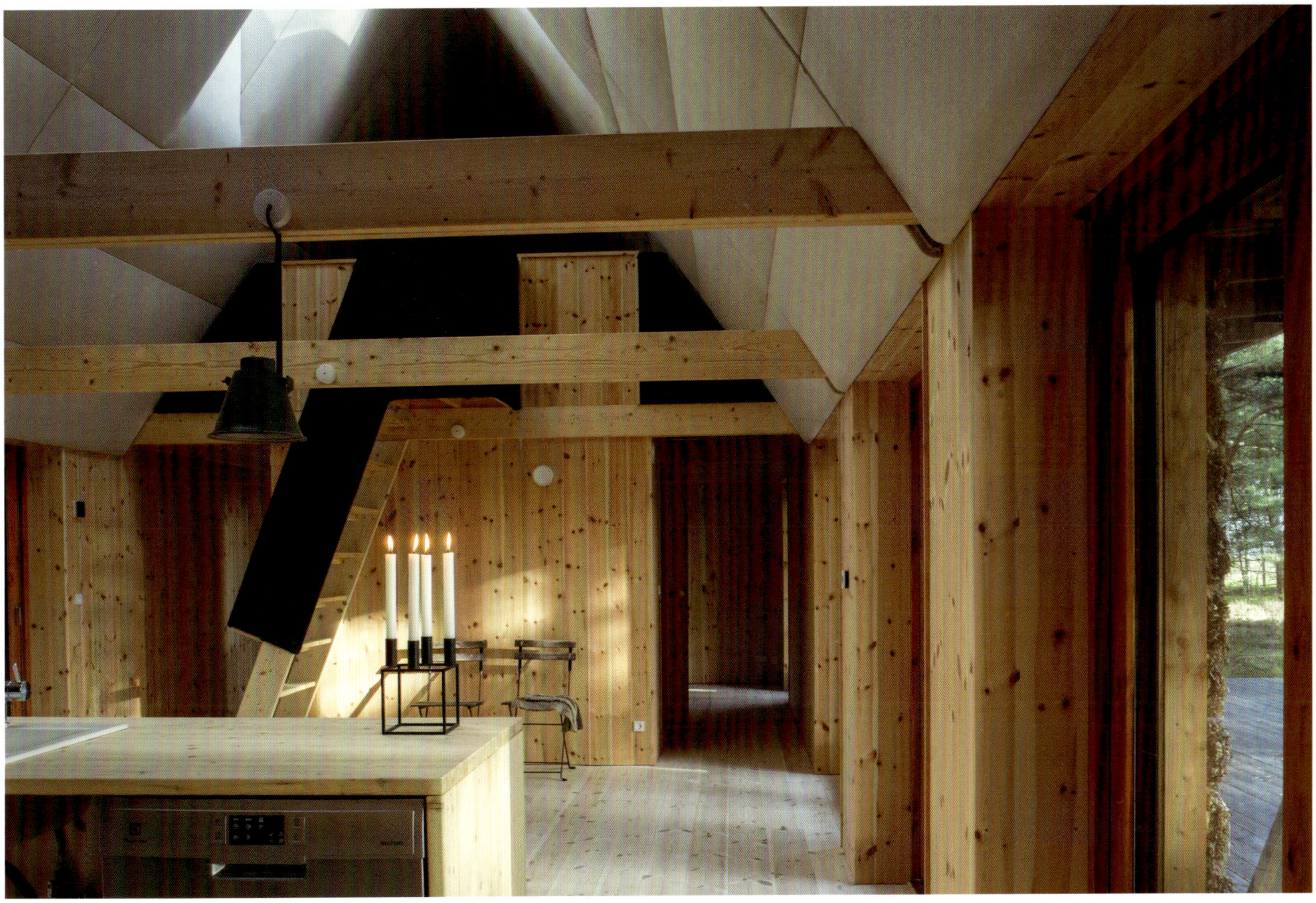

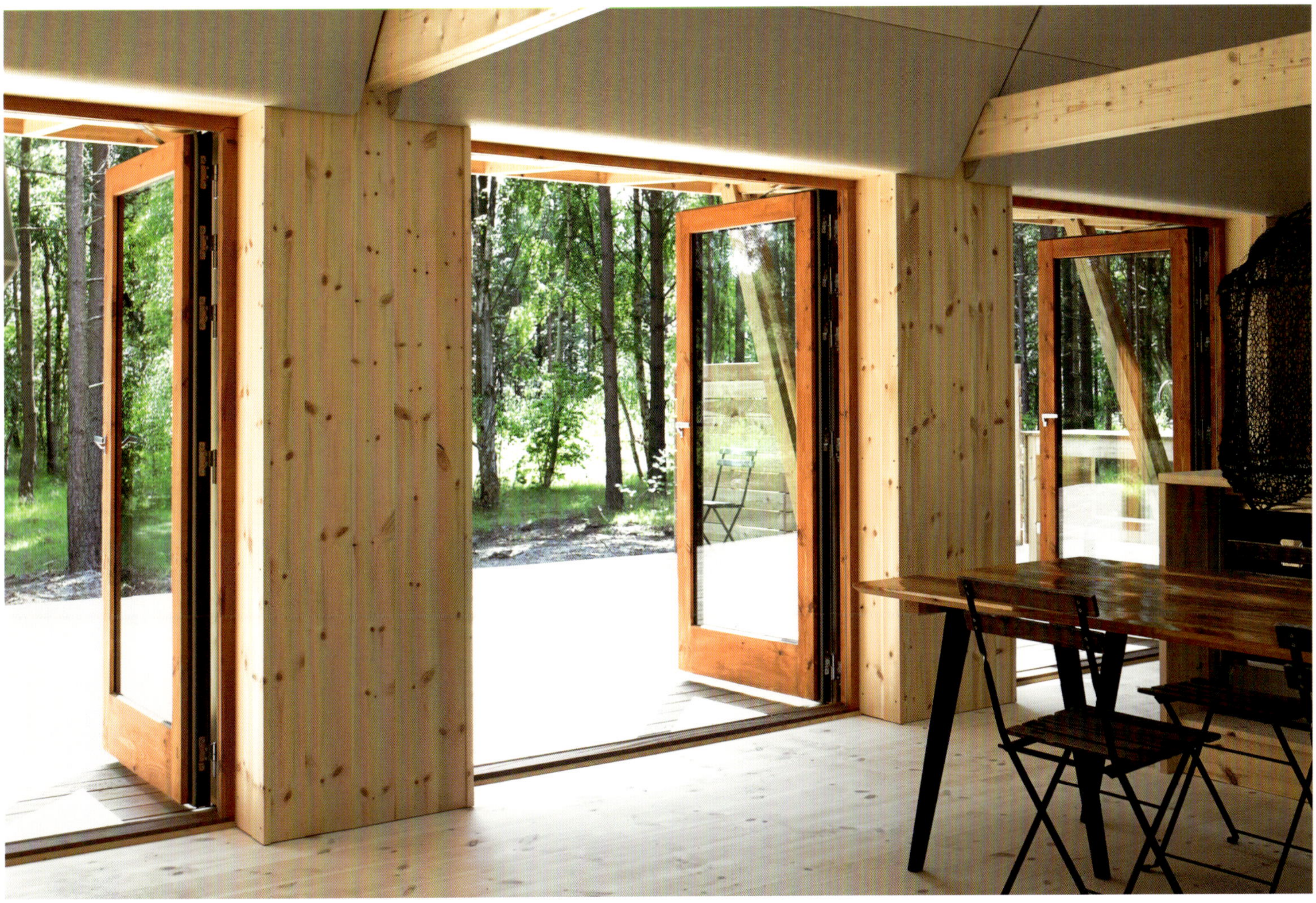

John Pardey Architects
NARULA HOUSE
2020 | Wargrave, England, UK

It might seem counterintuitive to build a residence in the middle of a flood plain, but water has been made an integral part of Narula House, transforming it into a building of striking abstraction. Its location on the banks of the River Loddon, a tributary of the Thames, makes regular deluges likely. The architects made a virtue of this by raising the house on steel stilts to take it well above the usual water level: when the river does swell, living there is like being on board a modernist cruise liner. Set back at an angle the house has a linear form that serves as a counterpoint to the curving waterway. This alignment also frees space for a large lawn between the house and the river.

Access is gained via a staircase at the rear leading to a courtyard and a separate guest pavilion. On the east side of the courtyard, there is an open-plan living-dining area, and to the west, bedrooms, which all have views of the river. Elements of the design suggest water's cool lucidity—the building is clad in larch with a translucent coating that creates a bright white finish, while the interior is inundated with light reflected off pale timber flooring and white walls. Narula House is not only sleek and stylish—it also makes a bold statement about working with rather than against nature.

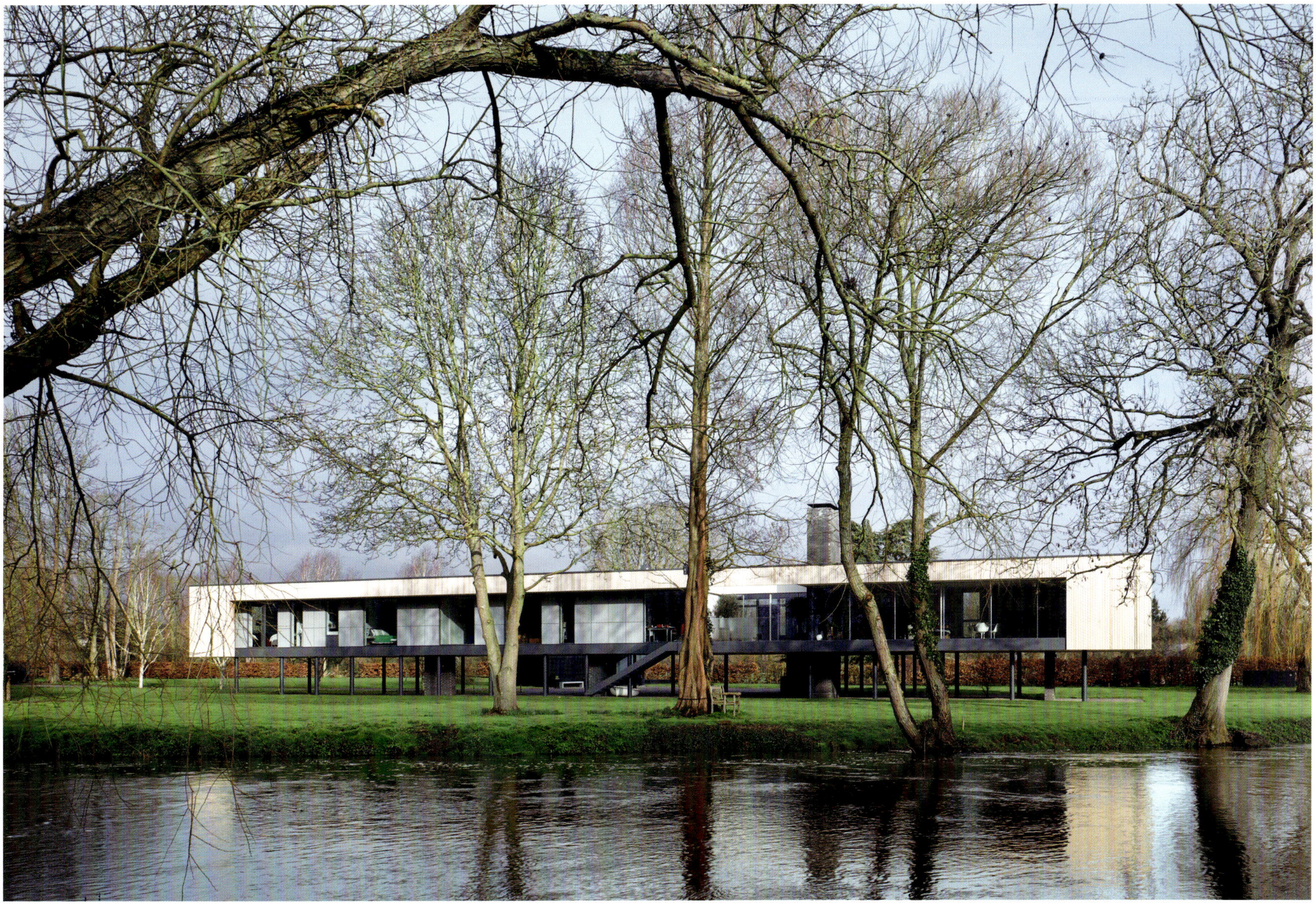

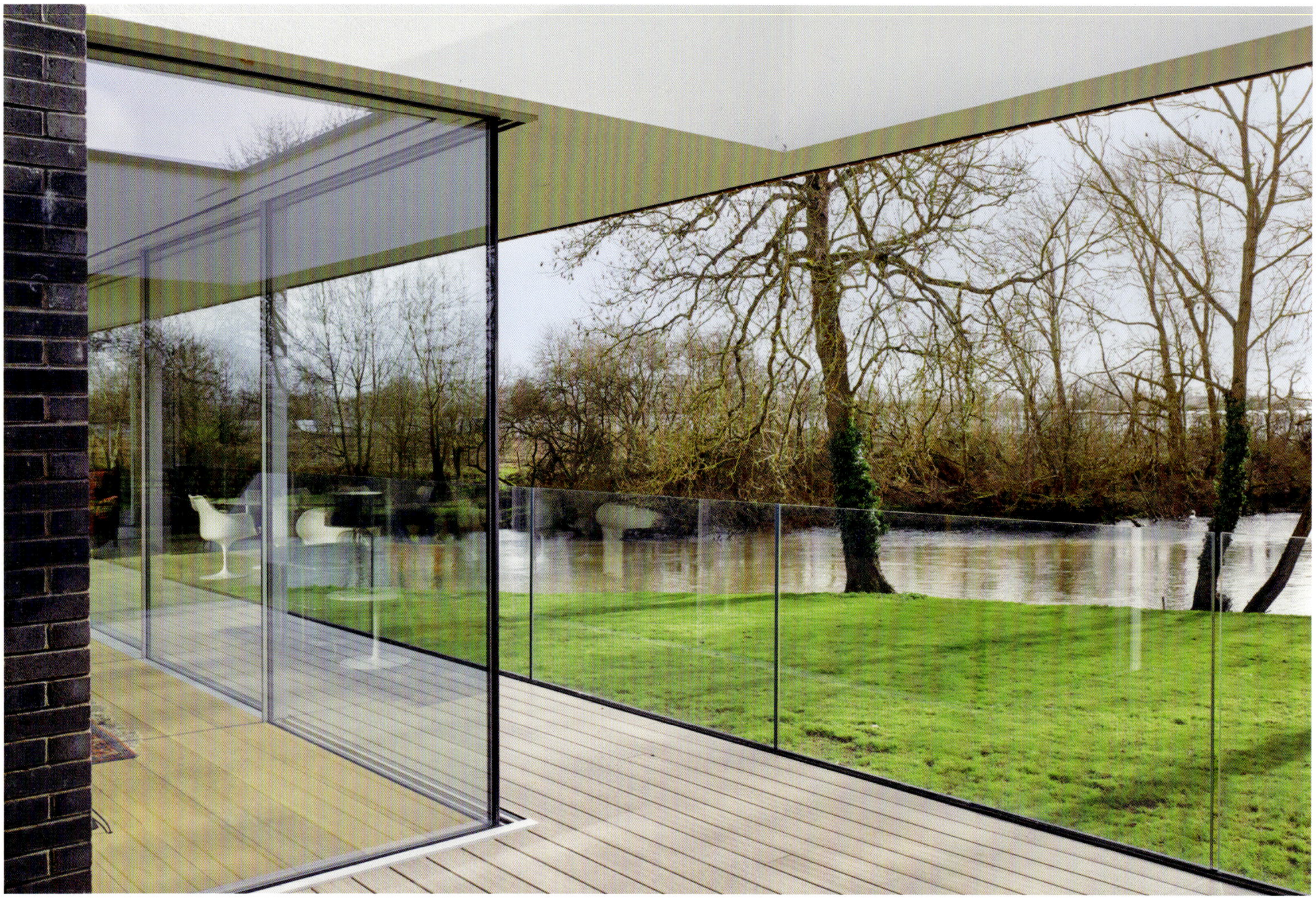

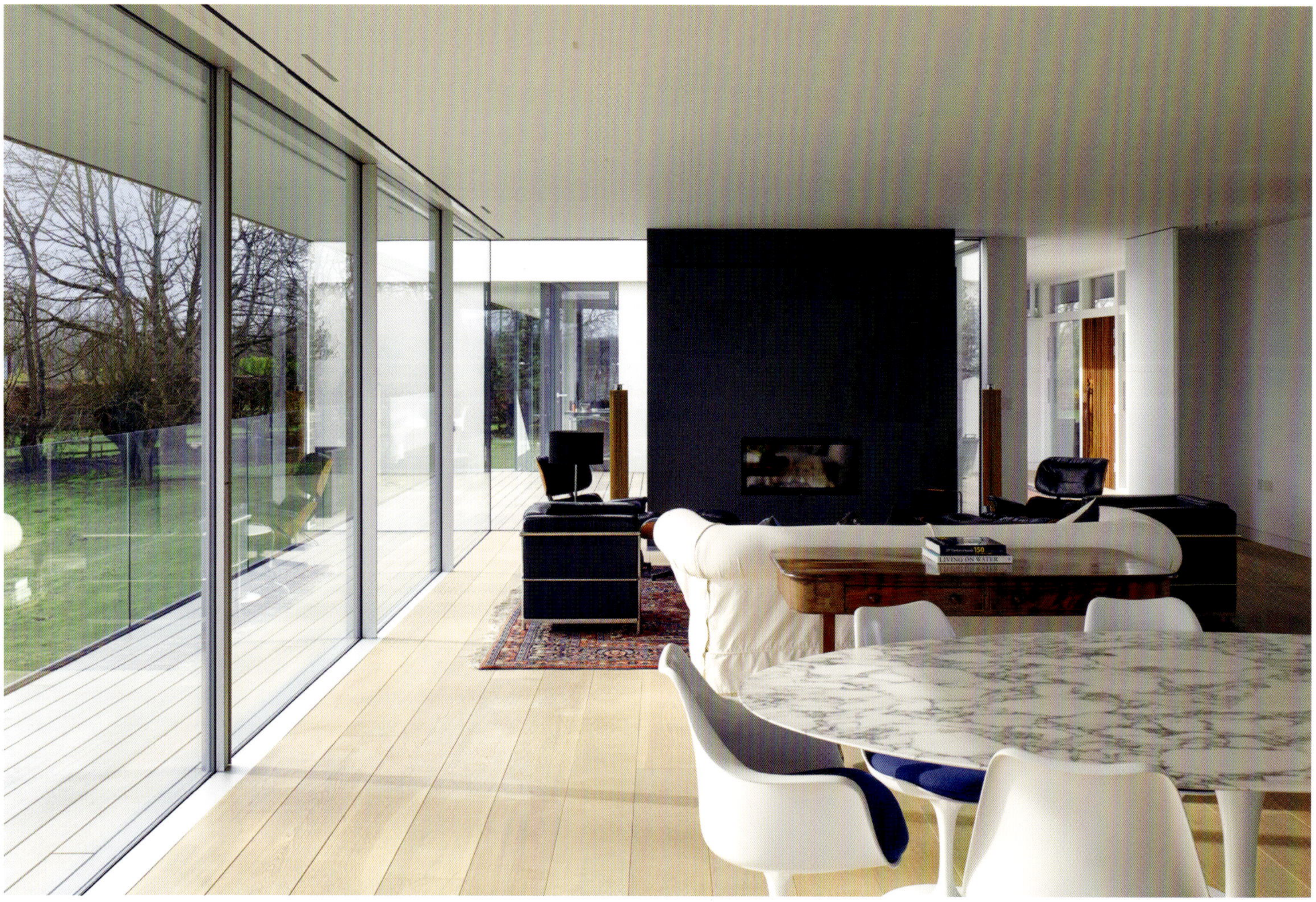

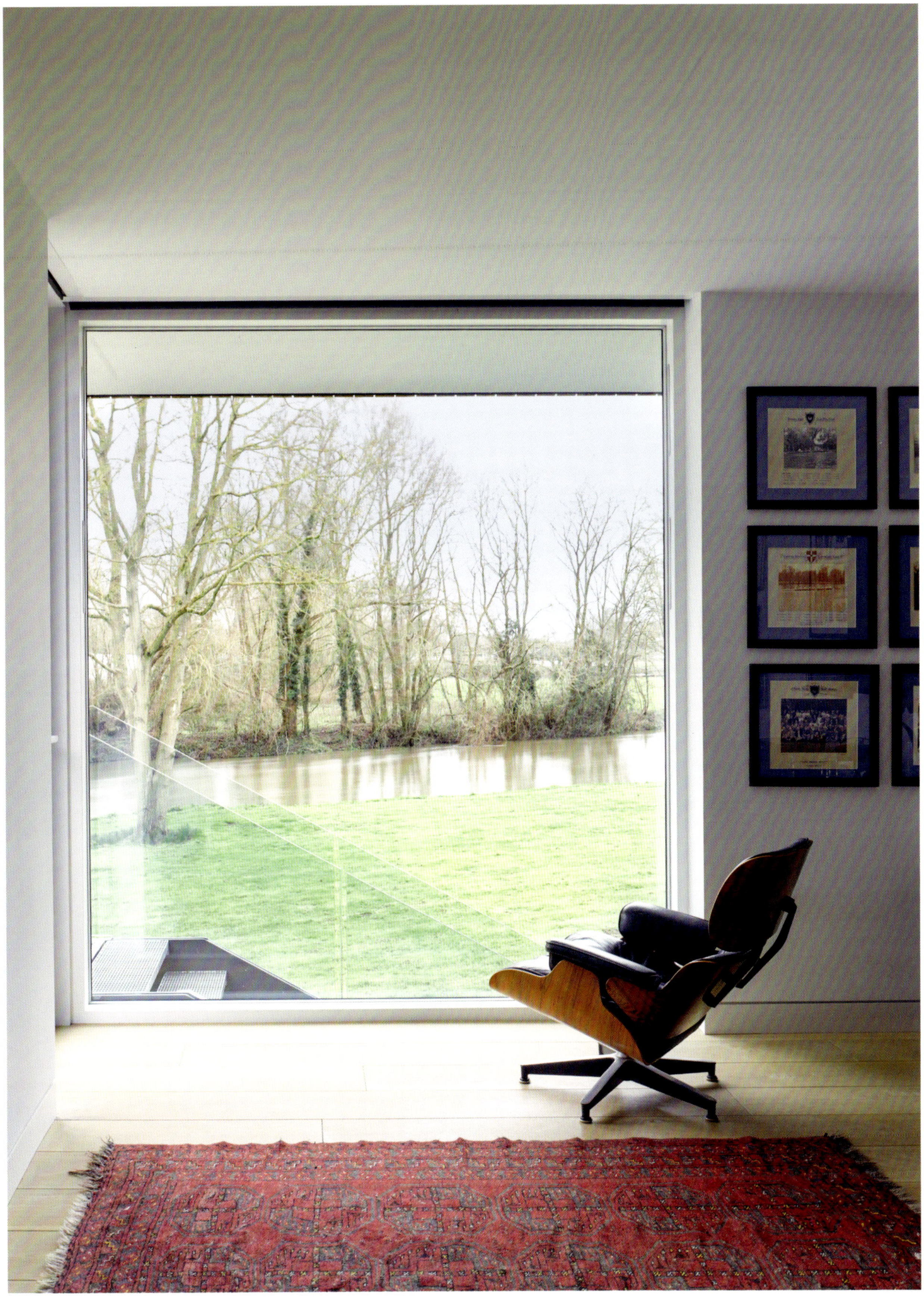

INDEX

Page numbers in **bold** refer to illustrations.

1+1>2 Architects
  Straw House 222, **222–25**

Aculco, Mexico 122, **122–27**
Aculco Residence (Pérez Palacios Arquitectos) 122, **122–27**
Alpine Vistas (Intuitive Architects) 24, **24–27**
Alqadi, Malek 168
Ampuero Yutronic
  Casa Hualle 154, **154–57**
An Cala (Mary Arnold-Forster Architects) 114, **114–17**
Anne Carrier Architecture
  Résidence Le Nid 198, **198–201**
Architectural Affairs
  Pavilion House 90, **90–93**
Artistree
  Yoki Treehouse 52, **52–55**
Atelier Villa (Formafatal) 172, **172–77**
Austin, TX, USA 52, **52–55**
Austin Maynard Architects
  St Andrews Beach House 210, **210–13**

Baie-Saint-Paul, QC, Canada 198, **198–201**
Bali, Indonesia 108, **108–13**
Bear Lake, ID, USA 86, **86–89**
Beijing, China 240, **240–43**
Beltrame, Claudio
  Pigna 66, **66–69**
Bend, OR, USA 144, **144–47**
Bivouac Luca Pasqualetti (Roberto Dini and Stefano Girodo) 34, **34–37**
Boar Shoat (Imbue Design) 86, **86–89**
Boreraig (Dualchas Architects) 202, **202–205**
A Brutalist Tropical Home (Patisandhika and Dan Mitchell) 108, **108–13**
Building Arts Architects
  Kawagama Boathouse 214, **214–17**
Bundeena, NSW, Australia 236, **236–39**
Bundeena Beach House (Grove Architects) 236, **236–39**
Buxton, VIC, Australia 128, **128–31**
Buxton Rise (Buxton Rise) 128, **128–31**

Canales, Fernanda
  Casa Bruma 94, **94–99**
Cape Town, South Africa 38, **38–41**
Casa Bruma (Fernanda Canales and Claudia Rodriguez) 94, **94–99**
Casa Caldera (DUST) 182, **182–87**
Casa Falk (Luciano Giorgi) 140, **140–43**
Casa Hualle (Ampuero Yutronic) 154, **154–57**
Casa La Roja (Felipe Assadi Arquitectos) 48, **48–51**
Casa Patios (Rama Estudio) 100, **100–103**
Catuçaba, Brazil 80, **80–85**
Catuçaba House (Studio MK27) 80, **80–85**
CO-LAB Design Office
  Tulum Treehouse 70, **70–75**
Cohesion
  Folly Cabin 168, **168–71**
Costa Rica Treehouse (Olson Kundig) 20, **20–23**

Dans L'Escarpement (YH2) 10, **10–13**
D'Arcy Jones Architects
  Deep Cove House 218, **218–21**
Dini, Roberto
  Bivouac Luca Pasqualetti 34, **34–37**
Diogo Aguiar Studio
  Pavilion House 90, **90–93**
Dock House (SAA Arquitectura + Territorio) 42, **42–47**
Dornier, Alexis
  House Aperture 118, **118–21**
Dorset, ON, Canada 214, **214–17**
Dualchas Architects
  Boreraig 202, **202–205**
DUST
  Casa Caldera 182, **182–87**

Falk, Hans 140
Faulkner Architects
  Lookout House 178, **178–81**
Felipe Assadi Arquitectos
  Casa La Roja 48, **48–51**
Fira, Santorini, Greece 206, **206–209**
Folly Cabin (Cohesion) 168, **168–71**
Formafatal
  Atelier Villa 172, **172–77**

Format Architects
  Buxton Rise 128, **128–31**
Format Engineers
  Varden 132, **132–35**

Giorgi, Luciano
  Casa Falk 140, **140–43**
Girodo, Stefano
  Bivouac Luca Pasqualetti 34, **34–37**
Gjesåsen, Norway 60, **60–65**
Grove Architects
  Bundeena Beach House 236, **236–39**
Guimarães, Portugal 90, **90–93**

Hacker Architects
  High Desert Residence 144, **144–47**
Hale Lana (Olson Kundig) 148, **148–53**
Hautamäki, Aleksi
  Project Ö Cabin 230, **230–35**
High Desert Residence (Hacker Architects) 144, **144–47**
Highland Park, IL, USA 104, **104–107**
Hiroshima, Japan 226, **226–29**
House in Ajina (Kazunori Fujimoto Architect & Associates) 226, **226–29**
House Aperture (Alexis Dornier) 118, **118–21**

IA Arquitectos
  Mountaineer's Refuge 14, **14–19**
Imbue Design
  Boar Shoat 86, **86–89**
Intuitive Architects
  Alpine Vistas 24, **24–27**
Isle of Skye, Scotland, UK 202, **202–205**

Jansson, Tove 60
Johan Sundberg Arkitektur
  Summerhouse Solviken 56, **56–59**
John Pardey Architects
  Narula House 248, **248–51**
Joshua Tree, CA, USA 168, **168–71**

K-Studio
  Villa Mandra 158, **158–63**

INDEX

Kapsimalis Architects
  Villa Drop 206, **206–209**
Kawagama Boathouse (Building Arts Architects) 214, **214–17**
Kazunori Fujimoto Architect & Associates
  House in Ajina 226, **226–29**
Kona, HI, USA 148, **148–53**

Læsø, Denmark 244, **244–47**
Landscape House (TAOA Design) 240, **240–43**
Lasso, Ecuador 100, **100–103**
Lookout House (Faulkner Architects) 178, **178–81**
Lorne, VIC, Australia 192, **192–97**

Malan Vorster Architecture
  Tree House Constantia 38, **38–41**
Malborghetto Valbruna, Italy 66, **66–69**
Mary Arnold-Forster Architects
  An Cala 114, **114–17**
Mills, Rob 192
Mitchell, Dan
  A Brutalist Tropical Home 108, **108–13**
Modern Seaweed House (Vandkunsten Architects) 244, **244–47**
Mölle, Sweden 56, **56–59**
Morion Ridge, Aosta Valley, Italy 34, **34–37**
Mountaineer's Refuge (IA Arquitectos) 14, **14–19**
Mykonos, Greece 158, **158–63**

Narula House (John Pardey Architects) 248, **248–51**
Nedd, Scotland, UK 114, **114–17**
Norwegian Trekking Association 132

Ocean House (Rob Mills Architecture & Interiors) 192, **192–97**
Olson Kundig
  Costa Rica Treehouse 20, **20–23**
  Hale Lana 148, **148–53**
  Rio House 28, **28–33**

Pan Treetop Cabins (Espen Surnevik) 60, **60–65**

Pasqualetti, Luca 34
Patisandhika
  A Brutalist Tropical Home 108, **108–13**
Pavilion House (Architectural Affairs and Diogo Aguiar Studio) 90, **90–93**
Pérez Palacios Arquitectos
  Aculco Residence 122, **122–27**
Pichicuy, Chile 42, **42–47**
Pigna (Claudio Beltrame) 66, **66–69**
Project Ö Cabin (Aleksi Hautamäki and Milla Selkimäki) 230, **230–35**
Pucón, Chile 154, **154–57**
Puntarenas, Costa Rica 172, **172–77**

Rama Estudio
  Casa Patios 100, **100–103**
Ravine House (Wheeler Kearns Architects) 104, **104–107**
Résidence Le Nid (Anne Carrier Architecture) 198, **198–201**
Rio de Janeiro, Brazil 28, **28–33**
Rio House (Olson Kundig) 28, **28–33**
Rob Mills Architecture & Interiors
  Ocean House 192, **192–97**
Rodriguez, Claudia
  Casa Bruma 94, **94–99**

SAA Arquitectura + Territorio
  Dock House 42, **42–47**
St Andrews Beach, VIC, Australia 210, **210–13**
St Andrews Beach House (Austin Maynard Architects) 210, **210–13**
Saint-Faustin-Lac-Carré, QC, Canada 10, **10–13**
San Esteban, Chile 14, **14–19**
San José de Maipo, Chile 48, **48–51**
San Rafael Valley, AZ, USA 182, **182–87**
San Simón Cabins (Weber Arquitectos) 164, **164–67**
Santa Teresa, Costa Rica 20, **20–23**
Selkimäki, Milla
  Project Ö Cabin 230, **230–35**
Son Tay, Vietnam 222, **222–25**
SPINN Arkitekter
  Varden 132, **132–35**

Storfjellet Mountain, Norway 132, **132–35**
Straw House (1+1>2 Architects) 222, **222–25**
Stromboli, Aeolian Islands, Italy 140, **140–43**
Studio MK27
  Catuçaba House 80, **80–85**
Summerhouse Solviken (Johan Sundberg Arkitektur) 56, **56–59**
Surnevik, Espen
  Pan Treetop Cabins 60, **60–65**

TAOA Design
  Landscape House 240, **240–43**
Tree House Constantia (Malan Vorster Architecture) 38, **38–41**
Truckee, CA, USA 178, **178–81**
Tulum, Mexico 70, **70–75**
Tulum Treehouse (CO-LAB Design Office) 70, **70–75**

Uluwatu, Bali, Indonesia 118, **118–21**

Valle de Bravo, Mexico 94, **94–99**, 164, **164–67**
Vancouver, BC, Canada 218, **218–21**
Vandkunsten Architects
  Modern Seaweed House 244, **244–47**
Varden (SPINN Arkitekter and Format Engineers) 132, **132–35**
Villa Drop (Kapsimalis Architects) 206, **206–209**
Villa Mandra (K-Studio) 158, **158–63**

Wanaka, New Zealand 24, **24–27**
Wargrave, England, UK 248, **248–51**
Weber Arquitectos
  San Simón Cabins 164, **164–67**
Wheeler Kearns Architects
  Ravine House 104, **104–107**

YH2
  Dans L'Escarpement 10, **10–13**
Yoki Treehouse (Artistree) 52, **52–55**

[1] AIR
Fernando Alda: 48, 49, 50, 51; Anne Bråtveit/House of Pictures: 63, 64, 65; Brechenmacher-Baumann: 70, 71, 72, 73, 74, 75; Maxime Brouillet: 10, 11, 12, 13; Federico Cairoli: 14, 15, 16, 18, 19; Massimo Crivellari: 66, 67; Simon Devitt: 24, 25, 26, 27; Stefano Girodo: 37; Nic Lehoux: 20, 21, 22, 23, 28, 29, 30, 32, 33; Adam Letch: 38, 39, 40, 41; Adele Muscolino: 34, 35, 36; Rasmus Norlander: 60, 61, 62; Peo Olsson: 56, 57, 58, 59; Nico Saieh: 42, 43, 45, 46, 47; Smiling Forest Photography: 52, 53, 54, 55; Laura Tessaro: 68, 69.

[2] EARTH
Ernesto Arriagada: 128, 129, 130, 131; David Barbour Photography: 114, 115, 116, 117; Rafael Gamo: 94, 95, 97, 98, 99, 122, 123, 125, 126, 127; Fernando Guerra: 80, 81, 82, 83, 84, 85, 90, 91, 92, 93; Imbue Design: 86, 87, 88, 89; JAG Studio: 100, 101, 102, 103; kie/@kiearch: 118, 119, 120, 121; Tommaso Riva: 108, 109, 110, 111, 112, 113; Tom Rossiter: 104, 105, 106, 107.

[3] FIRE
BoysPlayNice: 172, 173, 174, 175, 176, 177; Jeremy Bittermann / JBSA: 144, 145, 146, 147; Claus Brechenmacher: 158, 159, 161, 162, 163; Joe Fletcher: 178, 179, 180, 181; Felipe Fontecilla: 154, 155, 156, 157; Sam Frost: 168, 169, 170, 171; Cade Hayes/DUST: 182, 183, 184, 185, 186, 187; Nic Lehoux: 148, 149, 150, 152, 153; Sergio López: 164, 165, 166, 167; Tor Even Mathisen: 132, 133, 134, 135; Tommaso Sartori: 140, 141, 142, 143.

[4] WATER
Maxime Brouillet: 198, 199, 200, 201; James Benedict Brown: 203; Kazunori Fujimoto: 226, 227, 228, 229; Marc Goodwin/Archmospheres: 230, 231, 233, 234, 235; Huntley Hedworth: 202; Helene Høyer Mikkelsen/Realdania By & Byg: 244, 245, 246, 247; Yiorgos Kordakis: 206, 207, 208, 209; Andrew Lee: 204, 205; Mr Tao Lei: 240, 241, 242, 243; Caitlin Mills Photography: 192, 193, 194, 195, 196, 197; © James Morris: 248, 249, 250, 251; Michael Nicholson: 236, 237, 238, 239; Hiroyuki Oki / 1+1>2 Architects: 222, 223, 224, 225; Ema Peter: 218, 219, 220, 221; Derek Swalwell: 210, 211, 212, 213; David Whittaker: 214, 215, 216, 217.

Cover image: Peo Olsson

Phaidon Press Limited
2 Cooperage Yard
London E15 2QR

Phaidon Press Inc.
65 Bleecker Street
New York, NY 10012

phaidon.com

First published 2021
© 2021 Phaidon Press Limited

ISBN 978 1 83866 250 9

A CIP catalogue record for this book is available from the British Library and the Library of Congress.

All rights reserved. No part of this publication may be reproduced, stored in a retrieval system or transmitted, in any form or by any means, electronic, mechanical, photocopying, recording or otherwise, without the written permission of Phaidon Press Limited.

Commissioning Editor: Emilia Terragni
Project Editor: Emma Barton
Production Controller: Lily Rodgers
Design: SJG/Joost Grootens, Dimitri Jeannottat, Julie da Silva, Megan Adé
Text: Rachel Giles

Printed in China

The publisher would like to thank Jamie Ambrose, Sarah Bell, Vanessa Bird, and Lisa Delgado for their contributions to the book.